The Cassandra Conference

The Cassandra Conference

Resources and the Human Predicament

EDITED BY
PAUL R. EHRLICH AND JOHN P. HOLDREN

Texas A&M University Press
College Station

Library of Congress Cataloging-in-Publication Data
Cassandra Conference (1985 : Texas A&M University)
    The Cassandra Conference.

    Sponsored by and held at Texas A&M University,
May 6–7, 1985.
    Includes bibliographies and index.
    1. Human ecology—Congresses. I. Ehrlich, Paul R.
II. Holdren, John P. III. Texas A&M University.
IV. Title.
GF3.C37 1985   304.2   86-23070
ISBN 0-89096-295-2

Contents

About Earl Cook

EARL COOK received his B.S., M.S., and Ph.D. degrees from the University of Washington, Seattle. He also studied at the Universities of Paris and Geneva. He worked as a hard-rock miner, field geologist, and photo-geologist; taught field geology at Stanford University; served as Dean of the University of Idaho College of Mines and Director of the Idaho Bureau of Mines and Geology; and was Executive Secretary of the Division of Earth Sciences in the National Academy of Sciences.

He came to Texas A&M University in 1965 as professor of geology and associate dean of the new College of Geosciences. In 1968 he accepted a joint appointment as professor of geology and geography, and from 1969 to 1971 he directed the university's Environmental Quality Program. From 1971 to 1981 he served as the dean of the College of Geosciences, and in 1981 he was named Harris Professor of Geology and Geography. In the same year he was awarded the gold medal for distinguished achievement by the Geosciences and Earth Resources Advisory Council of Texas A&M.

Dr. Cook's articles on resource and environmental problems appeared in the most widely circulated general scientific publications, such as *Science, Scientific American,* and *Technology Review,* as well as in more specialized professional journals. His book *Man, Energy, Society,* published in 1976, was and is a masterful interdisciplinary synthesis of the geological, technological, economic, political, and cultural dimensions of the energy issue.

He was known to his friends and colleagues not only for his formidable breadth and depth of intellect but also for an inventive, wry sense of humor that permeated both his writing and his presence. Earl died in October, 1983. He is survived by his wife, Violetta Burke Cook, and his children and stepchildren, Jeanette, Randall, and Cynthia Cook and Jennifer and Jonathan Burke.

Editors' Preface

Paul R. Ehrlich and John P. Holdren

THE NAME "Cassandra," often used interchangeably with "prophet of doom," is interpreted by many people in a pejorative way: they think that the term refers to someone whose warnings about the future will turn out to be wrong. But the Cassandra of Greek mythology was right in her warnings. The tragedy was that she was not believed; if her warnings had been heeded, the disasters she foresaw could have been averted.

Cassandra, the daughter of King Priam of Troy, was given the gift of prophecy by the god Apollo in return for her promise to sleep with him. When Cassandra decided to remain a virgin and reneged on her promise, Apollo punished her with a curse: her prophecies, though accurate, would not be believed. When the Greeks seemingly abandoned their siege of Troy and left behind a large wooden horse outside the gates of that walled city, Cassandra predicted disaster if the horse was brought in. The Trojans ignored her warning and dragged the wooden horse, containing concealed Greek soldiers, into their previously impregnable city. The result was the destruction of Troy.

The late Earl Cook was a distinguished earth scientist, an outstanding educator and administrator, and a Cassandra in the most positive sense of that name. A believer in the potential of human beings to better their condition through wise use of technology, Earl recognized—sooner and more clearly than most—that misuse of technology and the physical resources of the planet could derail the engine of progress and lead to disaster. In countless articles and speeches he warned, with uncommon eloquence, against the dangers of overconfidence in our technology and of insensitivity to the finitude of physical resources. He did so not through love of bad news but in the hope that clarifying the dangers would lead to effective evasive action.

The Cassandra Conference was organized to honor Earl Cook's memory and to celebrate the importance of "early warning." It brought together from around the United States outstanding analysts of the human predicament—of overpopulation and poverty, of declining resource availability, of an imperiled environment, of the increasing probability of nuclear war. Their work has been sound, and, as is evident in the contributions assembled in these proceedings of the conference, both their warnings and their prescriptions for avoiding calamity are persuasive.

To a large degree, however, conclusions such as these remain unheard or unheeded by those whose decisions are charting the course of the United States and the rest of the world. As a result, whether society will take the needed evasive action remains in doubt. We hope, however, that bringing together these contemporary Cassandras to update their findings and to communicate them jointly in this volume will help improve the odds.

PAUL R. EHRLICH
JOHN P. HOLDREN

Acknowledgments

We are grateful to the Colleges of Geosciences, Liberal Arts, and Agriculture of Texas A&M University, whose sponsorship made the Cassandra Conference possible; to Frank E. Vandiver, President of Texas A&M, for his hospitality; and to Earl Cook's widow, Violetta Burke Cook, whose energy, organization, intelligence, and warmth held it all together.

PAUL R. EHRLICH
JOHN P. HOLDREN

The Cassandra Conference

1.
Cassandra's Role in the Population Wrangle

POPULATION THEORY is a strange specialty. Ask a well-informed man what specialist he should consult about population questions, and he is likely to say, "A demographer, I suppose." Then ask him to name the authors whose works have contributed most to our understanding of population. If he is especially well informed, he will cite some of the following: Joseph Townsend (1786), Robert Malthus (1798), William Vogt (1948), Fairfield Osborn (1948), Robert Cook (1951), Harrison Brown (1954), King Hubbert (1956, 1981), William and Paul Paddock (1967), Paul Ehrlich (1968), Jack Parsons (1971), Herman Daly (1973, 1977), Earl Cook (1976), and William Catton (1980).

It should be noted that not one of the authors on this list was trained as a demographer. For contrast, put together a list of the trained demographers who now occupy the most prestigious academic positions. Then ask, "What deep insights into population problems have these men contributed?" I'm afraid one would have to answer, "None."

When we want to know something significant about population, we do not canvass the writings of demographers, the supposed specialists in the subject. A strange situation. It is as though, when faced with a medical problem, we would avoid consulting medically trained people. Some critics say that the public's choice of population experts is perverse, that people really should listen only to licensed demographers. I disagree.

I think that the average person's instincts are right: population insights come not out of demography (as presently practiced) but out of the larger view taken by exceptional people who have come to the subject of population from various directions. Either demographers say nothing about the human significance of the figures they play with, or they tell us "not to worry." There are honorable exceptions, of course; Joseph Spengler (1978) is one. But the vast majority of demographers imply that things will just naturally turn out all right in the end. Providence plays a large role in the thinking of demographers (Hardin, 1982, p. 148). The other group, by contrast, has made its mark by arguing that humanity has grounds for worrying about the consequences of continued population growth. Civilizations *have* perished in the past (Toynbee, 1948; Culbert, 1973). What justification have we for believing that Providence will take care of ours?

So the argument goes on, between Pollyannas on the one hand and Cassandras on the other. I am not willing to label it a conflict between professionals and amateurs. I think the conventional identification of the professionals would, in this case, be wrong. I call your attention to the engineer Samuel Florman's definition of a professional as "a person who stays alert while others doze, whose sense of responsibility does not require the stimulation of catastrophe" (Florman, 1984). The Cassandras of population are "amateurs" only in the strict etymological sense that they are persons who love their subject; the licensed specialists come closer to being "amateurs" in Florman's sense.

What Is Truth?

But enough of name-calling. We want to know what the truth is, regardless of who says it. The word "truth" is seldom invoked in public discussion, but the high emotion apparent in participants on both sides of the population controversy is consistent with the hypothesis that each antagonistic group perceives truth as being raped by the opponents. An explicit discussion of "truth" is in order.

The first point to be made is that the connection of truth with statements about the future is no simple one. Surprising as it may be to those who confine their activities to the natural sciences, human beings sometimes find themselves in situations in which it is impossible to speak the truth. Consider the following example. On Monday a newspaper reporter asks the secretary of the treasury, "Is it true that you are going to devalue the dollar this coming Friday?" Let us suppose that a Friday devaluation is, in fact, the secretary's firm intention. How should he respond to the question?

If the secretary says, "Yes," he makes a false statement, because the moment his statement becomes publicly known he has, in fact, devalued the dollar on Monday, not Friday. If, on the contrary, he convincingly says, "No," he lies in a different way (as will become apparent on Friday). There is no way an individual in his position, challenged with such a question, can speak the truth.

We can make sense of this awkward situation if, when dealing with the future, we abandon the idea of a unitary truth. Let us replace unitary truth with a taxonomy that distinguishes three classes of truth (Hardin, 1961):

Class I: Those truths that are unaltered by the saying of them.
Class II: Those truths that are made true by being said.
Class III: Those truths that are destroyed in the act of being said.

Investigators in the natural sciences live in a world of class I truths. With great precision astronomers predict the solar eclipses of the year 2000, confident that neither suppressing nor publicizing their predictions will have the slightest effect on what happens in the heavens. Such is the world of physicists, chemists, and geologists. It is also the world of biologists, provided they are careful not to get their studies entangled with the human mind.

More striking is the situation of the behavioral scientists, who live in a world in which what happens is influenced by human expectations. Under certain circumstances publicized expectations about human behavior may actually cause — or contribute to the causing of — behavior that otherwise would not occur. Such class II truths have been called "self-fulfilling postulates" (MacIver, 1948) and "self-fulfilling prophecies" (Merton, 1949). Even before sociologists explicitly labeled this kind of truth, medical scientists had taken cognizance of class II effects in their design of clinical tests, inventing a method that was later christened the "double-blind test" (Gold, Kwit, and Otto, 1937).

As for class III truths, we have already seen an example in the story about the secretary of the treasury. Mark Antony's famous speech beginning with the words, "I come to bury Caesar, not to praise him," is another example (Shakespeare, 1599). At the beginning of Antony's harangue it is not obvious what his intentions are; clarity comes only when he switches to the mode of class II:

> You are not wood, you are not stones, but men;
> And, being men, hearing the will of Caesar,
> It will inflame you, it will make you mad.
>
> *Julius Caesar,* act 3, scene 2

And, as Shakespeare tells it, Antony's prediction becomes fact. Why did Antony not begin in the class II mode? Why was it more effective to begin with a class III statement, a "falsehood," if you want to call it that?

This is all very awkward. Once we leave the world of class I truths, it is not a wholly determinate matter which mode we are operating in. Language becomes a form of action, and what happens in the future becomes the resultant of all the vectors involved, many of which may be un-known to the speaker. Natural scientists, immersed in the warm security of class I truths, do not always fully appreciate the peculiar position of behavioral scientists, who cannot evade tripartite truth. One wonders whether Alfred Kinsey, trained in the natural sciences, fully realized that he was moving from a one-truth world to a three-truth world when he shifted his attention from wasps and oak galls to human sexuality (Kinsey, 1948).

Cassandra versus Pollyanna

We are now in a position to understand the durability of the quarrel between the Cassandras and the Pollyannas of population. Dan Luten (1980) put his finger on a central point when he remarked that "the optimists hope their forecasts are self-fulfilling. The pessimists hope their forecasts are self-defeating." In the terms used here, optimists advance class II truths, while pessimists employ those of class III.

Optimists seem to be unaware of the contrast in modes. Pollyannas both believe in their forecasts and want them to come true. Cassandras, by contrast, believe that their forecasts are correct projections of present trends, but they certainly do not want them to come true. They hope that publicity will result in their falsification. George Orwell undoubtedly hoped that his novel *Nineteen Eighty-four* would help prevent the world he de-scribed from becoming a reality. (Perhaps his scenario *did* cause its own falsification. History is unique, unrepeatable, and cannot be constricted into a controlled experiment; hence we can never *prove* the effects of Cas-sandran statements.)

The public must learn to recognize the difference in the motives of Cassandras and Pollyannas. The statements of Cassandras are would-be class III truths; those of Pollyannas are would-be class II truths. Under Florman's definition the Cassandras have a better claim to be called pro-fessionals than do the Pollyannas.

Demography as Pathological Numeracy

Since World War II, particularly since *Sputnik,* scientists approaching problems of education have recommended, in the strongest terms, that lit-eracy be augmented with numeracy (Hardin, 1985). I am thoroughly in agreement with this recommendation. But every virtue can be a vice, and it is quite possible to use numbers to escape thinking. Nowhere is this more apparent than in the field of population. It is my contention that most of the numerical data generated by demographers not only fails to give us the answers we want but also, by distracting us, prevents us from looking for the most general principles of population theory. Let me make my case by displaying the pathological numeracy of contemporary population literature.

To begin with, the precision of demographic data is generally misleading. Most printed estimates of national populations are derived from the United Nations, so let us look at the UN data for mid-1984. The population of Burma is given as 38.513 million. How accurate is that estimate? No one knows. By its own rules the UN must accept whatever figures a country's government supplies, and the less-developed countries generally do not have agencies capable of taking good censuses. Moreover, national policy often favors exaggerating or minimizing the total. It is generally believed that figures for less-developed countries (which make up the majority of the world's population) may be off as much as 10 percent. That being so, we are justified in believing that Burma's 1984 population lay between 34.7 million and 42.4 million. Obviously the last three figures of the UN estimate of Burma's population are fictitious. Either the number should have been rounded off to 39 million, or the range should have been given as 35 million to 42 million. Even the census figures for an advanced nation like the United States are thought, on much better evidence, to be in error by a percentage point or two. You can read many thousands of pages of UN literature without encountering even a hint of the truth.

More important than absolute numbers are rates—birthrates, death rates, population-growth rates. These are derived by dividing the reported numbers (of births and deaths, for instance) by the estimated population, so the relative uncertainty of the rates is at least as great as the uncertainty of the population totals. Some of the figures published by the UN are even more dubious—for instance, literacy rates ("Write your name on this piece of paper. . . . Good! You're literate!"). When we realize that a nation reported to be 30 percent literate is being given the benefit of the doubt, we despair of the advance of democracy in the poor countries of the world.

Obsession with figures has led demographers to generate a literature that is singularly useless. Take, for instance, what are called "KAP studies," studies of Knowledge, Attitudes, and Practices in the area of birth control. The typical KAP study begins with a year or two of careful planning, followed by two years of detailed questionnaire filling in a foreign country, and then two more years of statistical analysis back home—say five years of work. And what have you got? An estimate of what people, in the recent past, *told* some busybody about their personal lives, in response to questions that may not have been too well worded to begin with. By the time the results are published, the target population will probably have changed. Such change may be partly attributable to the questionnaire itself, for interrogators operate in a world of tripartite truth.

How is one to interpret reported differences between countries and cultures? If a given practice "is approved of" by 27 percent of one country but 38 percent of another, what follows? Are the figures obtained by different interrogators comparable? Are the people of different cultures equally candid and honest in their answers? What predictions can we make of the future on the basis of KAP findings?

In the early 1980s a modification of KAP studies was carried out under the title "World Fertility Survey." Despite the title the study told us more about women's expressed intentions than about their actual performance. This massive survey cost tens of millions of dollars. What do we have to show for the vast sums spent on the "World Fertility Survey" and the hundreds of KAPs? Only two things for certain: employment for demographers and Ph.D. degrees for graduate students. In a world in which unemployment is so serious a problem, perhaps we should not denigrate such employment, but one cannot but wonder whether the subsidizers of the studies would be happy with the expenditure of their funds if they fully understood the nonproductivity of the work.

Demography and Natural Sciences Contrasted

If the figures cranked out by demographers were data in the natural sciences, one could confidently hope that further work would remove major criticisms by refining the figures, thus making them useful. In demography it is unrealistic to entertain such a hope, for a number of reasons.

In the first place, we need to understand the difference between *precision* and *accuracy*. The distinction described below has, to my certain knowledge, been observed in the natural sciences for fifty years; I suspect it has been followed for more than a century. Yet a survey of nine well-known dictionaries (including the unabridged *Oxford* of 1933) failed to find one that made the distinction commonly adhered to in the natural sciences. This distinction can best be exhibited by quoting the words of the *O–SCZ Supplement* to the *Oxford English Dictionary* (Burchfield, 1982), where *precision* is defined as follows: "In numerical work, the fineness of specification, as represented by the number of digits given and distinguished from *accuracy* (the nearness to the true value)."

Why should it take something like a century for this important distinction to be recognized in dictionaries? The long delay in the diffusion of knowledge and ideas is understandable under the rubric of C. P. Snow's "two cultures"—the scientific culture and the humanistic culture—between which there is little communication (Snow, 1964). Dictionaries are put together by members of the humanistic culture, most of whom understand very little of the techniques of dealing with numbers.

The importance of the distinction is shown by a discussion of the 1980 census, which gives the population of the United States as 226,545,805. That is precision to nine places. What is the accuracy? Obviously that is harder to determine, but few demographers believe the error can be less than 1 percent. So the official figure is accurate only to the first two places; the third may be in error by two or more digits—that is, by 2 or more *million* people. Since an undercount is far more likely than an overcount, the true figure probably lies between 228 million and 231 million. The last six digits of the published figure, 545,805, though honestly produced by the machinery of the census, are pure fiction as far as accuracy is concerned. Demography will become more credible when the low accuracy of its data is routinely acknowledged. Published figures should be restricted to the number of "significant places," i.e., the number of digits that include no more than the first one that is in error. Those who do not understand the difference between precision and accuracy easily assume that a precise figure is an accurate one.

The natural sciences and demography differ in another regard: substantive significance of "statistically significant" data. The atomic weight of hydrogen is 1.00797, and it would matter a great deal if the true weight were 1.00800. Atomic weights are woven into an intricate web of interdependent facts and theories; the interdependency is a good reason for laboring hard to increase the precision of their measurement. It would be difficult to cite a demographic statistic for which precision (or accuracy) matters much. What difference would it make if the true population of the United States in 1980 was either 220 million or 240 million?

When the measurement of an entity is accurate, different methods of measurement result in nearly identical figures. In physical chemistry the "universal gas constant," called R, has been determined by many different methods, some of them quite surprising. The results have been gratifyingly consistent. In social sciences, particularly in attitude surveys, even the slightest alteration of the methods of measuring is likely to yield discrepant results. Even when the methods do not seem to be intuitively different, they are likely to produce inconsistent figures. It is hard to have confidence in such data.

Given these realities, it is no wonder that demography (as well as other social sciences) is "data-rich and theory-poor." It is a risky thing for a demographer to generate theory from data of low accuracy. The assumption that theory should be firmly tied to a "data base"—a productive assumption in the natural sciences — ensures that demographers will have little to say to a public that craves enlightenment on population matters.

Quite often rates are more important than absolute measures of state. Nowhere is this more true than in population studies. The relative magnitude of fertility and death rates generally has more meaning for the future than does absolute population size.

Even when we can determine these rates with sufficient accuracy, we still may not be able to plan well for the future. Which way is the population trending? If we could reliably identify trends, perhaps we could control the future. Unfortunately, as René Dubos has said, "Trend is not destiny." The trend toward lower fertility in the United States during the 1930s was reversed in the 1940s; in 1957 the trend was reversed again, falling slowly until the mid-1970s, when another reversal took place. If the experience of the century to date is a reliable guide, we might be led to predict that whatever trend is evident at the moment will be reversed in twenty or thirty years. But even that prediction is not trustworthy, for it assumes a trend of another sort. Demographic theory is simply not adequate to the demands the public would like to impose on it.

Folk Wisdom as the Foundation of Population Theory

My major thesis is the following: As concerns population problems the Pollyannas build their theories on data that are high in precision and low in accuracy, often expressed in statements not recognized as being class II truths. Cassandras, in contrast, rely almost entirely (though perhaps unconsciously) on nonnumerate folk wisdom, sometimes expressed as class I truths, sometimes as class III truths. In contemporary society precise but inaccurate statements are a la mode; folk wisdom is not. This reason alone is enough to account for the greater popularity of our Pollyannas. In addition there is the very human factor epitomized in a statement attibuted to Bertrand Russell: "Most men would rather die than think. Many do."

Being a Cassandra, I favor folk wisdom as the foundation for population theory. In what follows I cite what seem to me to be the major elements of folk wisdom utilized by population Cassandras in the construction of their world view. Some of them will no doubt seem very simpleminded, but in their simplicity lies their strength.

1. *Not all things are possible.* This surely does not need saying? Ah, but it does! The idea of Progress (Bury, 1932) has become a religion for many in our time. As evidence consider a statement made by the astronaut Scott Carpenter, when he shifted his attention from "space" to the oceans:

"I know—I am absolutely positive—that anything a man can imagine, he can accomplish" (Perlman, 1969). This is of a piece with the title of a once-popular song, "Wishing Will Make It So." This attitude cannot be reconciled with science. Since the discovery of the laws of thermodynamics in the middle of the nineteenth century it has been clear that science is built on what have been called "impotence principles," those statements that tell us what we *cannot* do (Whittaker, 1942).

2. *We live in a limited world.* The universe may or may not be limitless, but for all practical purposes the world that is exploitable by mankind *is* limited. It is just barely possible that spaceships might someday move a few human beings to the planets of a distant star, but the exorbitant energy cost of "solving" the population problem in that way rules out this "solution." As of this writing, it would mean shipping off 226,000 persons a day just to keep the earth's population from increasing (based on Hardin, 1959).

The two books most effective in reopening people's minds to the idea of limits were published almost simultaneously: *The Limits to Growth* (Meadows et al., 1972) and *Small Is Beautiful* (Schumacher, 1973). Predictably these works evoked a storm of refutations from the Pollyanna camp. Such titles as *Models of Doom* (Cole et al., 1973) clearly show that most of the critics made the standard error of assuming that the Cassandras were voicing class II truths, when in fact they were publicizing class III statements: "We must mend our ways, or else." Subsequent attempts to spell out the practical consequences of living in a limited world (Hardin, 1982, p. 205) have met with no interest whatever, perhaps because the recommendations are too frightening. Advance planning for truly revolutionary change may be impossible; *Muddling toward Frugality* (the title of a book by Warren Johnson, 1978) seems to capture the spirit of our age.

3. *There can be too much of a good thing.* The idea of the mean, of temperance in desires, is at least as old as classical Greek civilization; but it is not a dominant idea in our time. On the contrary, hundreds of books have titles that imply the more the better; very few have a title anything like John Sparrow's *Too Much of a Good Thing* (Sparrow, 1977). There is not much commercial profit to be made in promoting temperance.

Another way to put this principle is the following: *The maximum is not the optimum.* Determining the maximum demands only precision in the use of the differential calculus; determining the optimum is much more difficult because it calls for accuracy. Defining the optimum requires clear thinking about values. Approaching the problem of the optimum population, we should first ask, "Does God give a prize for the maximum number of human beings?" (Hardin, 1982, p. 190). This is conservation's secret question. It is almost never asked. Pollyannas pretend that they do not hear the question.

4. *A chain is only as strong as its weakest link.* This statement gives the idea in its most ancient, most general form. Coming closer to population problems, we have what the nineteenth-century chemist Justus von Liebig called the "Law of the Minimum." In 1934 the botanist W. P. Taylor worded Liebig's principle as follows (Allee et al., 1949, p. 635): "The growth and functioning of an organism is dependent on the amount of the essential environmental factor presented to it in minimal quantities during the most critical season of the year, or during the most critical year or years of a climatic cycle."

This is one of those profound and simple ideas that are often neglected because they are difficult to express in simple language. But we cannot make much progress on the problem of the optimum without at least implicitly invoking Liebig's principle. Malthus, in speaking of the "subsistence" of a population, apparently had food in mind (and possibly shelter and clothing, too). He did not foresee the time when technical ability to convert various material goods one into another would replace his "subsistence" with energy, or, more exactly, with negentropy. No sooner was that variable accepted as the "weakest link" or "limiting factor" in the human equation than the transmutation of elements and Einstein's $E = mc^2$ entered the scene. The limit of population growth once more became unclear. The importance of energy as a limiting factor is still controversial, but this controversy need not delay us, for there is another factor in population growth that is clearly limiting. It is neither matter nor energy but communication.

Communication: The Ultimate Diseconomy of Scale

As population increases, some aspects of human life become better, others worse. Improvements are often attributable to economies of scale. The cost of manufacturing an automobile is strikingly less when millions are made a year instead of thousands. For each production process the unit-cost curve finally levels off, but we can seldom be sure that there is not some other method of production that will optimize unit cost at a higher production level. As far as material production is concerned, we cannot confidently identify the level at which the advantages of a large population have reached their limit.

There is, however, one supremely important function that suffers from *dis*economies of scale *throughout its entire range:* communication. Democracy, however defined, depends on efficient communication among its members. Ideally, everyone should know what all his fellow citizens think. Ideally, every citizen should communicate with every other citizen. The classical New England town meeting is the epitome of participatory democracy. Unfortunately, it malfunctions once the number of members rises much above two hundred.

The essence of the democracy-communication problem can be seen in a simple mathematical model. Let the number of citizens be n. If every citizen can communicate with every other, there must be $n(n-1)/2$ lines of communication. This may also be written as $n^2/2 - n/2$. As n increases, the relative importance of the squared factor becomes ever greater; so, as a useful approximation, we may say that n units require n^2 lines of communication. Since it takes time to establish and use lines of communication, we may say that the *communication load of a democracy goes up as the square of its population size.*

Another way to put the problem is this: Since skimping on communication makes misunderstanding more probable, we can say that the probability of misunderstandings in a democracy goes up as the square of population. Since misunderstandings generate disorder, we can say that the probability of social disorder is proportional to the square of the population.

The severe limitation on the size of a town-meeting form of democracy becomes immediately understandable. The common people, despite all the democratic rhetoric to which they have been exposed, understand "in their bones" the irreconcilability of large numbers and democracy. One adaptive response to large numbers is to replace simple democracy with representative democracy. The people then express their will (as best they can) through their representatives. Let us see what that means for the United States (Abelson, 1976). We have 100 senators and 435 representatives. As of 1976, when the population was about 230 million, this meant that there was 1 legislator for about every 430,000 people. That is quite a bottleneck for "the voice of the people."

Over the past fifty years an adaptation to this heavy communication load has been developed: large congressional staffs. As of 1976 about 17,000 office workers were helping the legislators, about 32 per legislator. No legislator could possibly deal personally with all the communications of his constituents, but the staff organization permits him to deal indirectly with them. Legislators with the biggest staffs must create a hierarchy among staff members to further subdivide the communication load. Adding 17,000 to 100 plus 435 yields 17,535 Congress-related people dealing with the communications of 230 million citizens. This is a ratio of about 13,000 citizens per communication receiver in Washington, D.C. Just 3 percent of the receivers are principals. Each additional hierarchical level, necessary though it is, weakens "the voice of the people" that much more.

Investigation shows that each kind of hierarchy suffers from the same diseconomy of scale: the communication load goes up as the square of the population. Increasing the number of levels in the hierarchy makes it possible to deal with a greater load per unit time, but the possibility of misunderstandings surely increases as the number of levels increases. In a world of limited time (the only world human beings know), there is no way to beat the system.

The matter can be put another way: Instead of thinking of democracy as an all-or-none phenomenon, we should think in terms of the *quantity of democracy*. It then becomes apparent that *the greater the population, the less the democracy*. One of the few people to develop this idea clearly and in detail is the English engineer Jack Parsons (1971), in his *Population versus Liberty*. Since population growth causes the decay of democracy, it follows that lovers of democracy should hold that their most important task is to control the growth of population.

Pollyannas who think that God gives a prize for the maximum number of people generally express the utmost abhorrence of proposals to limit the freedom to breed, not recognizing that only by giving up the freedom to breed can we retain other freedoms. To put the matter bluntly, if God gives a prize for the maximum number of people, then God is a sadist with totalitarian leanings.

What we call *the* population problem is, then, the problem of finding an acceptable way of giving up what has been a widespread, though not universal, freedom in the past, namely, the freedom to breed. In the past we could cling to this freedom because of the providential presence of crowd diseases, which acted as a deus ex machina to keep human populations from breeding themselves into misery (not that disease and death are all that pleasant). This god, this deus, is dead now, and we must learn to live without it. Exactly *how* we will control breeding is open to debate. Controls need not be brutally direct; many indirect incentives and disincentives are available. The problem is one of social engineering. This is a problem for the future—the *near* future.

As concerns the material resources of the earth, one Pollyanna has assured us that "the future quantities of a natural resource such as copper cannot be calculated because . . . copper can be made from other metals; and . . . only the total weight of the universe . . . would be . . . a theoretical limit" (Simon, 1980, p. 1435). The same Pollyanna has also said flatly that "there's no such thing as a law of diminishing returns" (Simon, 1982). If that is true, then there is no such thing as diseconomies of scale—only lovely direct economies that Providence has so kindly blessed us with.

As for energy, another Pollyanna told us, way back in 1954, that electrical energy will someday be "too cheap to meter" (Lewis Strauss, p. 50, in Ford, 1982). Almost without exception natural scientists think that both of these Pollyannas are mistaken, but intelligent planning need not wait on settling the argument. The burden of communication presents us with an inescapable diseconomy of scale. If the Pollyannas are right about matter and energy, a society committed to freedom to breed can increase its numbers to the point where all other freedoms are lost, following which even the freedom to breed will finally disappear in the most brutal manner. Such is the end of Pollyanna's dream.

By failing to understand the inverse relation between population size and the quantity of democracy, some societies may be pushed into totalitarianism. Other societies may become intelligent enough to ignore the Pollyannas of population. I hope that ours is one of the second group. Survival depends on taking Cassandra seriously.

References

Abelson, P. H. 1976. More laws, more complexity. *Science* 192:1291.

Allee, W. C., et al. 1949. *Principles of animal ecology.* Philadelphia: Saunders.

Brown, H. 1954. *The challenge of man's future.* New York: Viking.

Burchfield, R. W., ed. 1982. *A supplement to the Oxford English dictionary.* Vol. 3, O-Scz. Oxford: Clarendon Press.

Bury, J. B. 1932. *The idea of progress.* London: Macmillan.

Catton, W. R., Jr. 1980. *Overshoot.* Urbana: University of Illinois Press.

Cole, H. S. D., et al. 1973. *Models of doom.* New York: Universe Books.

Cook, E. 1976. *Man, energy, society.* San Francisco: Freeman.

Cook, R. C. 1951. *Human fertility: The modern dilemma.* New York: Sloane.

Culbert, T. P., ed. 1973. *The Classic Maya collapse.* Albuquerque: University of New Mexico Press.

Daly, H. E. 1977. *Steady-state economics.* San Francisco: Freeman.

————, ed. 1973. *Economics, ecology, ethics.* San Francisco: Freeman.

Ehrlich, P. 1968. *The population bomb.* New York: Ballantine.

Florman, S. C. 1984. Disasters and decision making. *Technology Review.* 87(1):8–9.

Ford, D. 1982. *The cult of the atom.* New York: Simon and Schuster.

Gold, H., N. T. Kwit, and H. Otto. The xanthines (theobromine and aminophylline) in the treatment of cardiac pain. *Journal of the American Medical Association* 108:2173–79.

Hardin, G. 1959. Interstellar migration and the population problem. *Journal of Heredity* 50:68–70.

————. 1961. Three classes of truth: Their implications for the behavioral sciences. *ETC.* 18:5–20.

————. 1982. *Naked emperors.* Los Altos, Calif.: Kaufmann.

————. 1985. *Filters against folly: How to survive despite economists, ecologists, and the merely eloquent.* New York: Viking.

Hubbert, M. K. 1956. Nuclear energy and the fossil fuels. In *Drilling and production practice*. Dallas: American Petroleum Institute.

————. 1981. The world's evolving energy system. *American Journal of Physics* 49:1007–29.

Johnson, W. 1978. *Muddling toward frugality*. San Francisco: Sierra Club.

Kinsey, A. C. 1948. *Sexual behavior in the human male*. Philadelphia: Saunders.

Luten, D. B. 1980. Ecological optimism in the social sciences. *American Behavioral Scientist* (September–October).

MacIver, R. M. 1948. *The more perfect union*. New York: Macmillan.

Malthus, T. R. 1798. *An essay on the principle of population*. Many editions.

Meadows, D. H., et al. 1972. *The limits to growth*. New York: Universe Books.

Merton, R. K. 1949. *Social theory and social structure*. Glencoe, Ill.: Free Press.

Osborn, F. 1948. *Our plundered planet*. Boston: Little, Brown.

Paddock, W., and P. Paddock. 1967. *Famine—1975!* Boston: Little, Brown.

Parsons, J. 1971. *Population versus liberty*. London: Pemberton Books.

Perlman, D. 1969. An interview with M. Scott Carpenter. *Look Magazine* 33(2):70.

Schumacher, E. F. 1973. *Small is beautiful*. New York: Harper & Row.

Simon, J. L. 1980. Resources, population, environment: An oversupply of false bad news. *Science* 208:1431–37.

————. 1982. Interview by William Buckley on "Firing Line" (TV). *Population and Development Review* 8:216.

Snow, C. P. 1964. *The two cultures and a second look*. Cambridge: University Press.

Sparrow, J. 1977. *Too much of a good thing*. Chicago: University of Chicago Press.

Spengler, J. J. 1978. *Facing zero population growth: Reactions and interpretations, past and present*. Durham, N.C.: Duke University Press.

Townsend, J. 1786. *A dissertation on the poor laws*. Berkeley: University of California Press, 1971.

Toynbee, A. J. 1948. *A study of history*. New York: Oxford University Press.

Vogt, W. 1948. *Road to survival*. New York: Sloane Associates.

Whittaker, E. T. 1942. Some disputed questions in the philosophy of the physical sciences. *Proceedings of the Royal Society of Edinburgh* 61:160–75.

2.
Climate and Food:
Signs of Hope, Despair, and Opportunity

CLIMATE PLAYS a major direct role in global survival through its powerful influence on the long-term geographic patterns and year-to-year productivity of food systems. In some circumstances that influence appears pervasive, as climatic determinists would expect. But a careful examination of case studies involving climatic shocks to food systems shows that society has as much if not more influence. Perhaps what is most disturbing about the food and climate situation is that many Cassandras have warned us of potential dangers, many of which could have been mitigated had we only chosen to do so. Nevertheless, we should, of course, continue to raise the issues—I am sure that is how Earl Cook would have wanted it.

Environmental Stress in Subsistence Cultures

Societies with fairly simple social and economic structures have long had to deal with environmental stress. Anthropologist Elizabeth Colson, of the University of California at Berkeley, has studied several such groups, hoping to find the common responses they have used to adapt to such adversity. One group she studied was the Makah people, hunters of the Pacific Northwest coast.

From ancestral accounts it appears that the Makah knew that the abundance of sea mammals, fish, and birds in the Cape Flattery waters varied. To cushion themselves against changes in their harvest, they exploited a number of different sea and land plants and animals. As a result

Adapted from Stephen H. Schneider and Randi Londer, *The Coevolution of Climate and Life* (San Francisco: Sierra Club Books, 1984).

the disappearance of one or more species "did not leave them vulnerable or force them into sudden experimentation or improvisation" (Colson, 1979). The fifty-year disappearance of the fur seal during the eighteenth century, for instance, was not a catastrophe for the Makah because they had diversified. But later, with the advent of lucrative markets for fur seals, they ignored the lessons of their ancestors and became economically dependent on the animals. When fur seals became scarce again at the end of the nineteenth century, the Makah suffered the consequences of opting for such economic "progress"; they had become less resilient in the face of environmental stresses.

As a result of this and other studies, the anthropologist lists five devices that self-reliant peoples use to decrease their vulnerability to environmental stresses:

1. Diversification of activities, rather than specialization or reliance on a few plants or animals.

2. Storage of foodstuffs.

3. Storage and transmission of information on what we can call famine foods.

4. Conversion of surplus food into durable valuables that can be stored and traded for food in an emergency.

5. Cultivation of social relationships to allow the tapping of food resources of other regions.

According to Colson, the extent to which societies ignore these devices determines how vulnerable they become to damage from climatic causes.

The Irish Potato Famine

The Irish potato famine of 1845–50 has become a classic in the literature of environmental disasters. Cool, damp weather contributed to potato blight in nineteenth-century Ireland. The result was drastically reduced potato harvests, which contributed to millions of deaths by starvation and forced migrations that reduced the Irish population by nearly half. The story has an age-old double moral: If a population grows too large, food demands will outstrip food supplies; if people depend on a monoculture for their food, they risk devastation if that single subsistence crop is adversely affected by climatic stress or disease.

The lessons of this famine do not seem quite as straightforward, however, when the Irish experience is compared with a similar potato blight that occurred at the same time in the Netherlands. Both countries suffered considerably between 1845 and 1850. But, as economic historian Joel Mokyr has shown, during this period in the Netherlands fewer people suffered. That is, excess deaths[1] and decreases in births (compared with those in a precrisis year) were some fifteen times less severe in the Netherlands than in Ireland (Mokyr, 1980). Moreover, forced migration from Holland after 1850 was a trickle compared with the flood from Ireland. Nevertheless, Holland did sustain heavy losses, at least by today's standards. Mokyr estimates that the number of famine-caused casualties in the Netherlands was about 126,000. At the same time Belgium was also enduring harvest failures. Yet the increase in the death rate in Belgium was far below that in the Netherlands.

Why did these three countries differ in their vulnerability to short-term food-production stresses? Mokyr attributes the variations in resilience primarily to the different levels of industrialization and of economic diversification in these countries. According to him, the western countries that modernized their economies during the first half of the nineteenth century, in this case represented by Belgium and (slightly less so) by Holland, were able to withstand much better these environment-induced commodity shortages. Agricultural commercialization accompanied industrialization in these then-developing countries. This meant that more produce was sold in the market and more people were buying their food than growing it. Such development implies that fewer people were living a hand-to-mouth life; more had money to purchase food, especially when local harvests failed because of climatic or other adversities. For this food trade to take place, an economic and political infrastructure for marketing, storage, and transport had to have developed. Such an infrastructure evolved with industrial and economic growth and the political will to encourage it. But in Ireland, burdened with colonial rule, there was much less infrastructure and economic diversity.

Unfortunately, we can only speculate about the comparative yield losses in Ireland, Holland, and Belgium. Thus our evaluation of the relative importance of environmental versus economic and political factors can be only a qualitative one. Nevertheless, it seems reasonable to conclude that economic and social factors contributed significantly to the vastly different levels of damage from the potato blight experienced in the three countries.

---

[1]Excess deaths are those above normal expectations. They occur during a time when certain events (such as a food crisis) are believed to create more than the usual number of deaths.

The Sahelian Drought

A more modern example of a climate-related disaster took place in the Sudano-Sahel region of north-central Africa, just south of the Sahara Desert. Nearly everyone agrees that during the early 1970s two predominant events took place in the sub-Saharan region of Africa: annual rainfall for several years running was generally well below long-term averages, and famine occurred along with considerable losses of livestock and crops. While most analysts of the Sahelian crisis believe that these two events were cause and effect, respectively, this view is increasingly being challenged. A number of conflicting interpretations of the Sahelian drought cloud the general view of what should have been done to offset its effects—and what might currently be done as a matter of policy to prevent people from suffering in the future as a result of climatic variations.

Climatic Trend as Cause

One theory, propounded by Reid Bryson, is that the suffering followed drought caused by a cooling trend in the Northern Hemisphere, creating a "Sahelian effect"—shifts in the monsoon rains in the Sahelian part of Africa and the northern parts of India (Bryson and Murray, 1977). If this theory is correct, and such a Sahelian effect continues to suppress the monsoon rains in inhabited areas, deserts will spread southward, and hundreds of thousands or more will die—or be forced to migrate—in succeeding decades. This is a controversial position, particularly since Bryson attributes part of the cooling trend to atmospheric aerosols generated from activities outside the Sahel. The inherently divisive nature of potentially human-induced climatic modification is obvious from this example, regardless of whether the assumed modifications were perceived, rather than proved, to be true.

Climatic Fluctuations as Cause

Other researchers contend that droughts in the Sahel are a regular hazardous feature of the climate, and not part of an evolving trend. The 1970s event, they say, was much like previous extremes (Hare, 1979). Climatologist Helmut Landsberg, of the University of Maryland, has suggested that the recurrence of drought was "an entirely foreseeable event, if not precisely predictable on a time scale as to when it would strike" (Landsberg, 1979). Both Landsberg's view of climate as a hazard and Bryson's view of climate as a trend suggest that populations of humans and animals were too high to be sustained in bad climate years.

Inappropriate Technology and Foreign Aid as the Culprits

Political scientist Michael Glantz, of the National Center for Atmospheric Research, stresses another aspect of the problem. He says that Western countries intervened with an inappropriate technology that exacerbated the drought's impact. Foreign aid financed the digging of wells, or boreholes, which upset the established nomadic way of life that was well adapted to periodic droughts (Glantz, 1977). While these wells provided a short-term solution to the perennial problem of water shortage in the Sahel, they encouraged nomads to increase their herds' sizes beyond the long-term carrying capacity of the land and to stay in areas close to the wells. As a consequence, the herds overgrazed these areas and depleted and trampled the vegetative cover.

Social Structure as Cause

Still others believe the roots of the Sahelian crisis to be even more deeply imbedded in social factors. In their book *Food First,* Lappe, Collins, and Fowler (1978) argue that the governments that took over after independence in the Sahelian countries forced peasants to grow cotton for French export markets, even though the soil of this region was ill-suited to yearly cotton growing. Over the centuries Sahelians had developed a way of coping with periodic drought. Farmers traditionally rotated millet and legumes to replenish soil nutrients and to nourish themselves. But the continual planting of cotton depleted the soil, forcing further expansion of cotton cropping and locking up of land and other resources that would otherwise have been used for farming and grazing. Thus, in this view, modern technological, social, economic, and political influences actually increased the vulnerability of subsistence farmers and nomads to climate stress. Only by overthrowing "elites" who "put profits ahead of people" will the harm of periodic bad years be alleviated, they believe. In a similar vein Argentinian meteorologist and social critic Rolando Garcia led a major study on the events in the Sahel and published his controversial views in a book entitled *Nature Pleads Not Guilty.* He decries "the official view"—malevolent nature, overpopulation, and indigenous mismanagement—of the Sahelian catastrophe and argues that it was a "structural problem, the unavoidable consequence of a system" that combines the "prevailing international economic order," plus the "international division of labor," the application of "comparative advantages," and the "prevailing ideas on international aid" (Garcia, 1981). He suggests "structural adaptations" to prevent recurrence of catastrophes (based on reduction of the influence of market economics), redefinition of the value of "productivity" (to deemphasize output and encourage resilience), and reformulation of productive organization to aid in agricultural work.

The Technology and Free-Market Incentive View

Another interpretation forwards the opposite view: that the only way to avoid chronic food shortages and to build food-growing capacity is to give farmers a bigger stake in a growing economy through greater cash sales. Producers need an incentive to purchase necessary technologies, such as fertilizers, to increase production, according to food analysts Sterling Wortman and Ralph Cummings (1978).[2] Access to markets and the profit motive, they argue, would encourage farmers to grow more food—whether cash or subsistence crops. More food and production are, of course, the best means of preventing famine.

Summary

The example of the Sahelian disaster shows that climate is only one element of societal vulnerability to climatic stresses. While nearly all analysts would concede this point, the differing emphasis placed on environmental, social, and political factors often stems more from the differing ideological viewpoints of the analysts than from disagreements over the events themselves. Missing, incorrect, or distorted facts have been piled on top of the conceptual differences, providing even further cause for disagreement over interpretation of cause and effect.

To put the climatic factor in meeting world food needs into better perspective, we turn next to the U.S. Great Plains, the principal food-exporting region of the world.

The Weather-Technology Debate: The U.S. Great Plains

The percentage of world oil exports dominated by the Organization of Petroleum Exporting Countries (OPEC) is dwarfed by the portion of

---

[2]These authors argue (p. 7) that "one objective of agricultural development must be

the world grain trade controlled by the United States. It was this fact that led some members of recent administrations to revive the views of the early 1970s of former Secretary of Agriculture Earl Butz that the United States should use its food as a "weapon" to influence potential purchasers. It may be helpful to look beneath the political rhetoric to determine how the United States became the major grain exporter and how stable the high agricultural production of the United States has been — or might continue to be — over time.

From 1958 to 1973 the weather in the Great Plains was exceptionally good for agriculture. High productivity in the United States and growing world food demands after shortfalls in the USSR and India in 1972 led the federal government to encourage the country's farmers to plant all available land. The hope was to achieve bumper crops that could be sold to the burgeoning markets abroad. Secretary Butz was so confident in the continued success of this scheme that the land-bank program (originally established as a soil-conservation and price-stabilizing measure after the Dust Bowl of the 1930s) was curtailed. Under the land-bank program the government had paid farmers not to plow on selected lands. Even though a significant portion of U.S. croplands had been set aside, huge surpluses of North American grain grew in the 1960s and early 1970s; but there were too few paying customers to buy these surpluses, and farmers complained of a glut on the market. Thus the government bought the surplus grain, storing it for food emergencies or using it for food aid under Public Law 480 — the so-called Food for Peace Bill. In the mid-1960s Public Law 480 food had helped India stave off a major famine following poor growing-season weather (see fig. 2.1).

Several agrometeorologists then said that usually benign weather in the United States in the 15 years before 1973 had helped boost crop yields and reduce variability in the yields from year to year. U.S. Department of Agriculture (USDA) experts claimed that technological advances in agriculture, not climatic conditions, were responsible for the bumper harvests. These modern practices, the experts believed, made U.S. food production nearly impervious to weather variations. Thus the USDA declared that food reserves as a hedge against such potentially hazardous fluctuations were largely unnecessary and also held down farm income needed to encourage full production. A heated exchange ensued on the relative roles of weather and technology in determining crop-yield variabilities.

---

to allow individual families to produce a surplus for sale so that the total output of a locality exceeds total local requirements and permits sales to urban centers, other rural regions, or international markets. Imports required for higher productivity must be purchased and markets for products must be established. In short, traditional farmers must be brought into the market economy" (Wortman and Cummings, 1978).

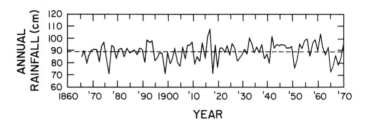

Fig. 2.1. Rainfall over monsoon-dominated India. From Parthasararthy and Mooley, 1978.

James McQuigg, one of the skeptical agrometeorologists, headed a team of scientists in Columbia, Missouri, that studied this question. In 1974 they issued a report claiming that the chance of experiencing another 15 consecutive years of comparably good weather was about "one in 10,000" (McQuigg et al., 1973; Thompson, 1975). During the mid-1970s McQuigg and his colleague Louis Thompson, dean of Agriculture at Iowa State University, became embroiled with the USDA in a major controversy. The debate was over the relative contribution of technological advances and good weather conditions to the high yields and the low-yield variability experienced between 1958 and 1973 (Schneider with Mesirow, 1976). Understanding the debate requires a close look at several interrelated issues. These include how yield variability in one nation is coupled with trade to other nations; how climatic variability is distributed around the world; crop-climate timetables, or phenology; the cultural practices of farmers; soils and their protection; and, of course, data on how crops have performed over the past few decades in the face of technological change and climatic fluctuations.

U.S. Grain Trends in the Technological Period

During the homesteading era of the late 1800s growers were generally successful. Good weather encouraged the settlers, and "Rainfall follows the plow" was a popular line on the railroad posters advertising the lure of the Plains. But drought in the 1890s shattered the illusion and drove out many settlers. This pattern of boom-and-bust farming recurred several times, good weather and high-production years being followed by drought years, economic ruin, and disastrous soil erosion (Bark, 1978). The most severe and intensive drought and soil degradation occurred in the 1930s in an area that became known as the Dust Bowl, where average wheat and corn yields plunged 50 to 75 percent, and millions of tons of valuable topsoil were lost. The economic depression of the 1930s was worsened by this climatic depression.

The country learned painful lessons from this experience. The government established the U.S. Soil Conservation Service to help farmers protect the soil; geneticists later developed new crop strains that were better adapted to regional climates; and irrigation and chemical fertilizer were made available to take advantage of the new strains and to aid production. As a result the productivity of the U.S. Plains has increased 200 to 300 percent since the 1930s.

Productivity—that is, yield per unit area—has expanded, primarily owing to increased energy inputs used to power technologies such as field machines, irrigation pumps, and agrochemicals. Thus more crops have been harvested per acre. There has also been more total production (average yield per harvested area multiplied by total harvested area). Similarly, for most grains the variability of yield from year to year as a percentage of long-term mean yield has decreased—that is, the amount of year-to-year yield variability has decreased over time relative to the average yield. But during the decades of technological advances the absolute or total amount of yield variability has increased for most crops in the United States.[3] In other words, the relative variability (year-to-year variability as a percentage of long-term average yield) has usually decreased for a crop in recent years, whereas its absolute variability (year-to-year yield variability by itself) has on the whole increased (Newman, 1978; Schneider with Mesirow, 1976).

This is the heart of the debate, for the next step is to distinguish the role of climate from the role of technological advances in both average-yield and yield-variability trends during the 1960s and 1970s. Some relevant USDA statistics are represented graphically in figure 2.2 (U.S. Department of Agriculture, 1982, 1985). Figure 2.2 shows that the year-to-year fluctuations in yields of total U.S. grains were fairly low before 1973 (we can draw this conclusion from figure 2.2c because the plotted data before 1974 closely follow the upward-sloping trend line with very little scatter). During 1969 and 1970 total grain production dropped (see fig. 2.2a). Two reasons for the dip in production are a decline in the amount of area harvested (fig. 2.2b) and a corn blight that attacked a large portion of genetically similar hybrid strains, slashing corn yields substantially. Total grain yield (see fig. 2.2c) increased close to the trend line until 1973, and then

[3]Consider an example. Corn yields in the first half of the twentieth century fluctuated by some 0.7 metric tons per hectare from year to year, with average yields of about 2 tons per hectare. The relative variability was thus about 30 percent. In the 1970s, however, average yields were some 6 tons per hectare but year-to-year variability increased about 50 percent in this example (over 1 ton per hectare), while relative variability decreased by 50 percent (from about one-third to one-sixth).

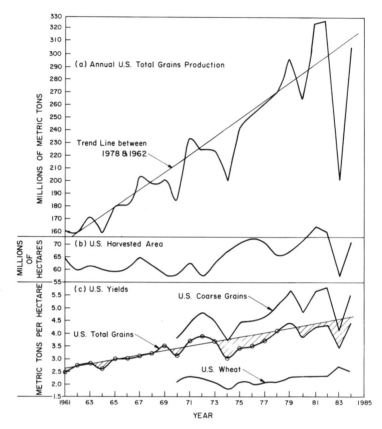

Fig. 2.2. Grain production, harvested area, and yields in the United States, 1961–84. Data from U.S.D.A., 1985.

the yield dropped in 1974, staying well below the trend line until 1978. In 1974 bad weather was a major factor in the corn belt—simultaneously too wet for early planting, too hot and dry for productive flowering, and too cold for anticipated late harvesting. Each weather event occurred at the worst time in the phenological cycles of corn crops in the Midwest. Earl Butz referred to this 1974 anomaly pattern as a "triple whammy."

It is clear from figure 2.2 that after 1973 variability of both grain yield and production increased markedly, just as McQuigg and Thompson had forewarned. Significant increases in the harvested area (fig. 2.2b) were necessary merely to maintain total production close to the trend line, despite the loss of yield below trend between 1974 and 1978 (see the shaded area in fig. 2.2c). The increase in harvested area—which totaled about 25 percent from 1972 to 1976—was largely the result of returning fallowed land to production. These areas typically were fallowed because they had lower production potential or a greater likelihood of suffering erosion than those left under the plow in 1971. Hence at least part of the lower-than-trend yields seen in figure 2.2c resulted from the federal government's encouraging farmers to recultivate relatively inferior land. Another consequence of that government policy was increased soil erosion. In connection with the latter issue, agrometeorologist Norman Rosenberg, of the University of Nebraska, remarked, "Despite the proven beneficial effects of windbreaks planted in the Great Plains during the drought years of the 1930s, many of them are now being removed" because "windbreaks may interfere with the mechanical operation of the large center-pivot sprinkling systems that are revolutionizing irrigation in the Great Plains region" (Rosenberg, 1981).

Without doubt, then, technology has been the prime factor in increasing grain-yield trends. But the debate has continued into the 1980s over whether technology was responsible for the favorable decrease in the United States and Canada during the 1960s and 1970s of relative yield variability— that is, year-to-year variability as a percentage of long-term average yield. As noted earlier, compared to the 1930s, 1940s, and 1950s, when most modern technological aids such as fertilizer, chemical pesticides, herbicides, and new genetic varieties were not widely used (if they were even available), relative yield variability has declined in the last twenty years (Newman, 1978).

Geographer Richard Warrick and some of his colleagues then at Clark University have argued that, although relative yield variability went down in the 1970s compared to the bad years in the 1930s or mid-1950s, agrotechnology is not necessarily responsible (Warrick, 1980). Only if the weather anomalies in the mid-1970s were as bad as those in the 1930s or 1950s, they said, could modern farming practices take credit for the reduced impact of climatic stress on yields. They compiled an index of the severity of summer droughts in the Great Plains from the early 1930s to the late 1970s, shown in figure 2.3. The index reveals that since the era of modern farming methods took hold in the mid-1950s there has not been a set of weather years bad enough to test the hypothesis that technological methods have reduced the fractional variations of grain yield.

Using as a basis yield losses that actually occurred in the mid-1970s, the scientists at Clark attempted to extrapolate the yield losses that might have occurred if the weather in the 1970s had been as severe as that in the 1930s or 1950s. They concluded tentatively that even *relative* yield variability would have been about as bad in the 1970s as in the earlier periods if the weather had been the same as then. Absolute yield variability—already

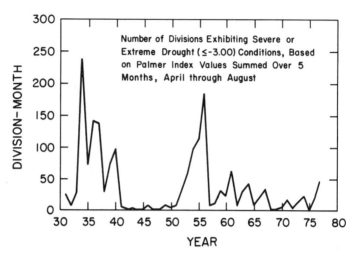

Fig. 2.3. U.S. Great Plains drought area, 1931–77. Based on Warrick, 1980.

larger than before—would have gone up substantially more. Thus the assumption that the North American breadbasket could maintain stable yearly productivity should the climatic dice roll for a few years as they had in the 1930s or mid-1950s is still a dangerous gamble. Now, moreover, the stakes are higher: hundreds of millions of people depend on the stability of the region's harvests. Because of world grain trade, the weather gamble in the Great Plains is no longer the local farmers' alone but the world's.

Who was right in the great weather-technology debate—Agriculture Secretary Butz or his agrometeorological critics? At least regarding the United States, McQuigg and Thompson were justified in their outspoken concerns: farmers in the states of highest grain production had experienced a long lucky streak of good growing weather, and when more nearly average climate finally reappeared, yields tumbled well below trend levels for several years while grain prices spiraled. Really unfavorable weather, like that of the mid-1930s, has yet to recur in the United States; thus we can only speculate about what would happen. However, there was in 1983 a single year of very hot August conditions in the corn belt. Although conditions were not as severe across the Great Plains as the serious drought periods seen in figure 2.3, coarse-grain yields in the United States as a whole were reduced by one-sixth—and by much more in the corn belt. United States production of coarse grains dropped by more than one-third that year because of the heat-induced yield reductions and the simultaneous cut in planted acreage that was caused by a government no-plant program (see fig. 2.2).

World Food Security, Food Trade, and Climate

Through the 1960s world food production outpaced population growth, and many began to believe that the technologies responsible for the so-called Green Revolution had once and for all ended the threat of Malthusian disaster (Brown, 1970; Bickel, 1974). However, the year 1972 badly shook the confidence of the optimists that technology had finally solved the problem of world hunger.

1972: A Bad Year

The year 1972 was not a good year for Bordeaux wines. Indeed, it was characterized by worldwide climatic, economic, and human setbacks: serious droughts in the USSR, India, Southeast Asia, Australia, Latin America, and the Sahelian region of Africa; devastation of the protein-rich Peruvian anchovy fishery; depletions of the grain supplies in many major food-producing areas; soaring food prices everywhere; and resulting famines that eventually killed or debilitated tens of millions of people. In India and Bangladesh alone a million or more excess deaths have been attributed to this bad-weather year (Brown, 1978). Coming on the heels of a number of good harvest years, the bad weather of 1972 made some scientists and a host of writers wonder whether a turning point had been reached that put adverse climatic variations on the rise.[4]

A close look at the collapse of Peru's anchovy fishery in 1972 is now warranted, since it is a good example of climate becoming hazardous to food production and an excellent reminder that the oceans are a significant part of the climatic system. In 1972 the temperature of Peru's coastal waters rose by several degrees. El Niño, a recurring phenomenon associated with the Southern Oscillation, is blamed for disrupting the upwelling process that brings cool deep ocean waters to the surface. Accompanying the increase in water temperature was a weakening of the upwelling of oxygen and nutrient-rich waters from below. The warmer, nutrient-poorer water caused plankton booms to decrease, and the anchovies, higher up the food chain, swam off, failed to spawn, or died. The anchovy was once considered an inexhaustible source of protein; in 1970, Peru's anchovy

---

[4]Among these are Reid Bryson and Hubert Lamb (Bryson and Murray, 1977; Lamb, 1975). An even more alarming report warning of massive climatic disruption to world food security was published by, of all people, the U.S. Central Intelligence Agency. The agency's report became fodder for several climatic pot boilers (Ponte, 1976) and an "instant book" by the "Impact Team" (1977). For a rather negative discussion of these sorts of publications, see Schneider, 1977.

catch had reached a record high of 12.5 million metric tons. But within three years the catch had plummeted to less than 2 million metric tons (Bardach and Santerre, 1981). After a brief recovery to about 4 million metric tons, in 1977 the catch dropped even lower, to less than 1 million metric tons (considerable debate surrounds the question whether climatic hazards or overfishing were principally responsible for this damage [Glantz and Thompson, 1981]).

This major fishery has shown few signs of recovery, and some wonder whether it ever will. Peru's experience echoes the disappearance of California's sardine fishery, related in John Steinbeck's *Cannery Row*. If the Peruvian anchovy follows suit, nearly 20 percent of the yield of fish protein from the ocean will have been lost, a serious nutritional blow.

The combined effects of shortfalls in Soviet, Indian, African, and Peruvian food production led to a 3 percent drop in grain production in 1972, the first such worldwide production setback in many years. Prices spiraled, and death rates climbed. At the same time climatologists became embroiled in public controversy over the role of climate in these events and the likelihood that climate-induced troubles would increase.

The Food Crises of the Mid-1970s

Except in 1974, world grain consumption rose steadily after 1966 (see fig. 2.4d). Total grain yields also dropped about 4.5 percent in 1974 from the 1973 yields (see fig. 2.4c). These yield figures (as well as those shown in fig. 2.2c) are based on harvested rather than planted area. Harvested area is always smaller than planted area, especially in climatic-stress years, when the percentage of land planted but not harvested increases. This is because bad weather or pests make harvesting either fruitless or too expensive to undertake in the damaged crop area. Thus crop yields per planted area are always lower than yields per harvested area, especially in bad years. However, farmers' production costs—as well as the environmental impacts of chemicals and soil erosion from badly managed fields—are usually more closely tied to the number of land units planted than to the number harvested. The yields per harvested areas that are typically quoted by most statistical services (including the USDA and the Food and Agriculture Organization [FAO] of the United Nations) really overestimate actual crop productivity as seen from the perspective of the person planting or investing in agriculture.

Since harvested area increased only about 0.4 percent in 1974 over 1973 (see fig. 2.4b) and yields dropped significantly (see fig. 2.4c), worldwide production in 1974 was set back by about 4 percent—about 51 million metric

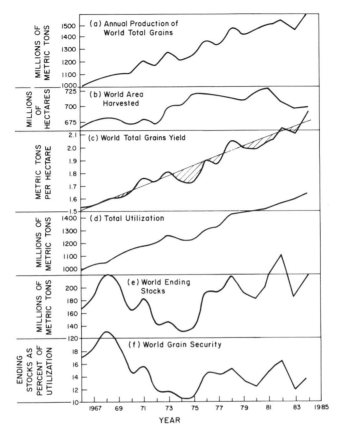

Fig. 2.4. Production, harvested area, grain yields, utilization, ending stocks, and grain security for total world grain production, 1966–84. Data from USDA, 1985.

tons (see fig. 2.4*a*). In addition, the unbroken upward trend for the decade of the 1970s in world grain trade broke in 1974—the only such trade decline over a previous year that decade. These setbacks in production, yield, and trade occurred at a time when food stocks were about the lowest in decades: the USDA estimated that at the end of 1974 stocks had dropped to 134 million metric tons, the lowest in this 18-year record (see fig. 2.4*e*). Because of increasing world population and the affluent countries' demand for feed grains, these reserve stocks represented a significantly smaller percentage of world grain demands than that of 10 years earlier. The worldwide grain shortfall, in conjunction with the U.S. policy (and that of other major grain-exporting countries as well) of liquidating government-held stocks, forced world grain security to a new low (see fig. 2.4*f*).

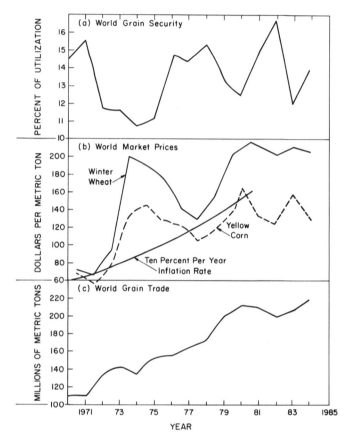

Fig. 2.5. World grain security, world market prices for winter wheat and yellow corn, and world grain trade, 1970–82. Data from USDA, 1985.

It is interesting to compare the world prices of grains (see fig. 2.5*b*) with the index of world food security (see fig. 2.5*a*). An obvious inverse relationship exists, as one would expect from classical market economic theory, since prices go up when supplies dwindle, and vice versa. But a very different picture emerges in figure 2.5*c*, which shows that world grain trade has increased rather steadily regardless of price. The reason for such seeming noneconomic behavior (that is, fairly unresponsive to price) is that the principal purchasers of grains are not the cash-poor, food-needy developing countries but rather the more affluent developed countries (capitalist and socialist alike). The rich, who have considerable elasticity in their purchasing power, are willing to cope with food-price fluctuations while maintaining their dietary standards.

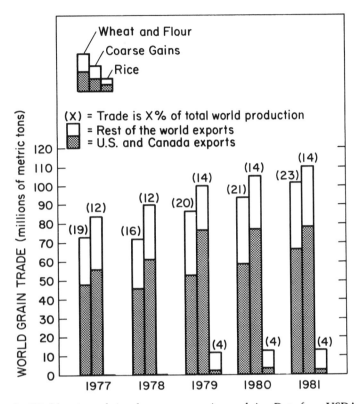

Fig. 2.6. World grain trade in wheat, coarse grains, and rice. Data from USDA, 1982.

Figure 2.6 shows world grain trade for 1977 through 1981 for wheat and flour (usually consumed directly by human beings), coarse grains (usually fed to animals), and (only for 1979 through 1981) rice (also directly consumed by people). The number in parentheses at the top of each bar graph represents trade as a percentage of total world production of that commodity. It is obvious that the rice trade represents a minuscule fraction of total rice production compared to trade in the other commodities, even though total world rice production in 1980 was about 98 percent of wheat and 52 percent of coarse-grain production. This relatively small rice trade simply reflects the fact that most rice is directly consumed near where it is grown, largely as a staple in the diets of Third World countries. Also clear from figure 2.6 is that the United States and Canada control more than half the world's grain exports and that their grip on exportable coarse grains is even greater.

The economic and political significance of the overall trade figures

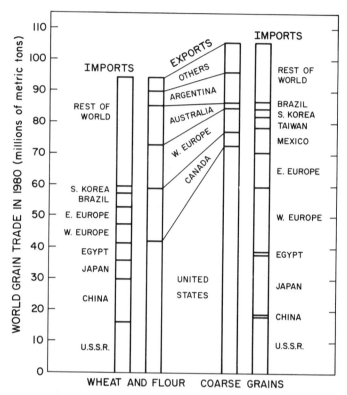

Fig. 2.7. World grain trade in wheat and flour compared with coarse grains, by principal importing and exporting regions. Data from USDA, 1982.

is easier to see in figure 2.7, which expands the wheat and coarse-grain data for 1980 into principal exporting and importing countries. The dominance of the exports by the United States, Canada, and a few other developed countries is once again apparent, but the grain-import story is also quite revealing. Whereas Western Europe is a net exporter of wheat, it is a large net importer of feed grains. This simply reflects the demand in Europe (both East and West—including the USSR) for grain-fed animals, notwithstanding the cost. China, by contrast, is a significant importer of wheat but buys only a negligible quantity of coarse grains. The Chinese have other priorities for their precious foreign-exchange resources than purchases of feed grains. Japan, on the other hand, was the largest single coarse-grain importing nation in 1980, perhaps not surprising in view of Japan's reputedly abundant hard currency and lack of suitable geographic endowment for growing feed grains. Data such as these clearly reveal that the effects of climatic variations on food production are felt well beyond the location of weather anomalies and that the distribution of impacts is hard to predict in advance, given the complex consuming, trading, and producing patterns of various nations.

We have already discussed the consequences of the combination of events that caused food-security problems in the mid-1970s. It might be easy to blame poor weather alone for periods of falling yields, rising food prices, decreasing food supplies, and expanded famine conditions, but it is apparent that other factors are involved: population size, dietary standards, economic well-being, purchasing power, and the political climate controlling access to food supplies. Trading, pricing, agricultural investments, land tenure, food reserves, and food-distribution policies of many countries also figure in. It was the interaction of all these social factors with environmental conditions and farmers' cultural practices that created the food crisis of the mid-1970s.

Although a number of good-weather years returned to most of the world near the end of the decade, 1979 saw bad harvests in India, and in 1980 the weather was hot and dry in the central United States, which led to low yields in summer crops (see fig. 2.2c). The USSR also had disappointing harvests. Thus at the beginning of the 1980s the world had about the same level of grain security that it had had entering the 1970s — about 14 percent. Although this level dropped by an additional percentage point the next year, it had recovered somewhat by 1982. Figure 2.5a shows in quantitative terms how a relatively "safe" margin of food security was quickly eroded in the mid-1970s and again in 1980; in more emotionally tangible terms, the images of old and young victims of food-price rises and famines of the mid-1970s are still vivid and poignant. They remind us of the risks of low food security and high volatility in grain stocks and prices. These memories must not be forgotten.[5]

---

[5] In the summer of 1983 the headlines were again warning of major heat- and drought-related damage to U.S. corn crops. The opening sentence of a page 1 story by William Robbins in the *New York Times,* Sunday, Aug. 21, 1983, reported on the developing situation: "With a swiftness that has shocked both farmers and economists, the nation's burdensome corn surplus has apparently been all but wiped away by a severe drought and a costly government program." One wonders why anyone should be shocked, since this basic scenario is a virtual replay of events less than a decade old. What is shocking is that some farmers and government officials seem never to remember the past. In U.S. Department of Agriculture, *Foreign Agriculture Circular* (FG-23-83), August 15, 1983, the USDA estimated that because of the new government program which pays farmers surplus grains roughly equivalent to acreage they agree to withhold from production (called the Payment in Kind Program — PIK), harvested area in the U.S. for the coarse grains will drop from over 43 million hectares in 1982 to an estimated 33 million hectares in 1983. This 23 percent drop in crop area caused by the government's PIK Program came at the same time the 1983 heat wave struck the corn

Because of the complexity of food-climate interactions, policies for dealing with potential climatic hazards, trends, or resources cannot be formulated in isolation, ignoring other important aspects of the food system. On the other hand, the lesson of the yield and price fluctuations of the 1970s is that climate cannot — as it so often has been in past analyses — be assumed as constant in food policymaking, even if the elements are only one component. To put the climate factor in the perspective of world development, we next touch in some detail on some of the primary factors that affect our ability to meet world food needs. An in-depth treatment of this critical subject for human survival requires volumes.[6] Nevertheless, I hope that the following brief summary will at least point out some of the complexity of food systems.

The Malthusian Situation

Although the percentage increase in total food production for both developing countries (DCs) and less-developed countries (LDCs) is similar over the past few decades, the per capita production is much less in the LDCs. There population growth has almost kept pace with production, whereas in the DCs production has significantly exceeded population growth. Although population and food production have kept up with one another when averaged over all the less-developed nations, figure 2.8 shows considerable differences in this Malthusian statistic among various LDC regions. For example, East Asia has gained in per capita food production, while Africa has faltered. East Asia's success is largely due to rapidly increasing crop yields and a relatively low population growth rate compared with rates of other regions. Africa's plight can be accounted for to a considerable extent by its high rates of population growth — among the highest in the LDCs, as can be noted in table 2.1. Equally troublesome, grain yields have increased but little in Africa since the early 1960s, primarily because the use there of common intensification techniques, particularly

belt. By midsummer the USDA estimated about a 25 percent drop in coarse-grain yields from 1983 relative to 1982. The combined effects of reduced crop area and bad weather ultimately dropped coarse-grain production to a little under 140 million metric tons, a reduction of nearly one-half compared with production in 1982. Stocks of coarse grains had dropped by about two-thirds by the 1984 season. Although, as fig. 2.2 shows, there was some recovery in the following year, this situation has some uncomfortable parallels with the situation just before the food crisis of the early to mid-1970s.

[6] A good example of the volumes required to describe the many aspects of world food systems is U.S. National Academy of Sciences, *World Food and Nutrition Study* (1975). In addition to a 192-page summary volume, five separate volumes of several hundred pages each discuss such subjects as crop productivity, aquatic food sources, weather and climate, nutrition, institutions, policies and social science research, and information systems.

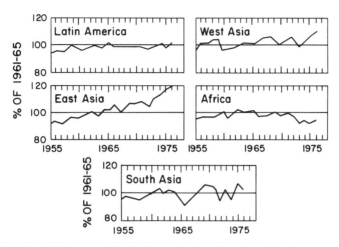

Fig. 2.8. Trends in per-capita food production for selected regions comprising less-developed countries. From Wortman and Cummings, 1978.

chemical fertilizers, to boost production has been relatively meager. Where per capita food production falls over time, people who cannot easily afford to import food are bound to suffer from malnutrition; they are forced to use scarce foreign-exchange reserves — if they have any — to buy food on the world market. Ironically, in some instances LDCs actually export food or other agricultural products — so-called cash crops — to developed nations to garner foreign exchange; this can lead to insufficient production of subsistence crops and starvation in areas where food is shipped out for cash instead of being available to the population (this criticism was brought out earlier in the discussion of the Sahelian drought disaster).[7] Moreover, the foreign exchange so earned is not necessarily spent on improving long-term agricultural development or for emergency food imports to minimize malnutrition in a bad-weather year. Rather, precious foreign currencies are all too often used to buy high-technology gadgets, particularly military hardware.

Food Aid, Food Trade, and Food Consumption

Who are the chief food buyers and sellers? Earlier we noted that Canada, the United States, and Australia accounted for about three-fourths

[7]One example is called the "Hamburger Connection" by Norman Myers, referring to the beef exports from Latin America to the United States to support fast-food hamburger chains (Myers, 1981). Myers, however, was more concerned with the destruction of Central American forests for the purpose of creating pastures to graze animals that would be exported to the United States.

Table 2.1. World Population Data by Region, Mid-1982 Estimates, and with Projections to the Year 2000

Region	No. of Countries	Population (Millions) 1982	Population (Millions) 2000*	Annual Growth Rate (%)†	Doubling Time (Yrs.)‡
Africa					
Northern	6	117	190	3.1	22
Western	16	150	265	3.0	23
Eastern	17	141	246	3.0	23
Middle	9	56	90	2.6	27
Southern	5	34	55	2.5	28
Total	53	498	846	2.9	24
Asia					
Southwest	16	106	171	2.7	26
Middle south	9	988	1,396	2.2	32
Southeast	11	374	519	2.2	32
East	8	1,204	1,441	1.4	50
Total	44	2,672	3,527	1.9	37
Americas					
North	2	256	286	0.7	95
Middle	8	95	142	2.6	26
Caribbean	16	30	41	1.8	38
South					
Tropical	9	209	313	2.4	28
Temperate	3	43	53	1.5	45
Total	38	633	835	1.7	41
Europe	27	488	511	0.4	187
USSR	1	270	302	0.8	88
Oceania	8	24	30	1.3	55
World					
More developed		1,152	1,248	0.6	116
Less developed		3,434	4,835	2.1	33
Total		4,586	6,083	1.7	40

SOURCE: Population Reference Bureau, 1982 World Population Data Sheet, Washington, D.C., 1982.

*Projection to year 2000 based on assumed projections in population growth rates "actually anticipated under a reasonable set of assumptions regarding future birth and death rates," made by Population Reference Bureau.

†Based on population changes during the late 1970s.

‡Assuming that present growth rate continues over the doubling period.

of the wheat exports in 1980 (see fig. 2.7). Europe (East and West), the USSR, Japan, China, and Brazil imported about 60 percent of the wheat sold on the world market. Of the total amount of coarse grains—primarily used for animal feed—the United States exported about three-fourths in 1980 (see fig. 2.7); about 95 percent of this amount went to Japan, the USSR, and Europe (East and West). All told, in 1980 coarse grains (which have become the largest grain trade commodity because of imports by wealthy countries for livestock feed) comprised about half of total world grain production and half of total world grain trade. Rice, on the other hand, as seen in figure 2.6, is one of the smaller food trade commodities. In 1980 rice production was about 20 times larger than rice trade, according to USDA statistics; it is a staple crop in LDCs, where most grains are produced and consumed locally. Twenty percent of coarse grains, on the other hand, are traded.

There was a dramatic drop in U.S. shipments in the form of food aid and concessional sales after the world food crisis in 1972 (from more than 15,000 million tons in the early 1960s to less than 3,500 million tons in 1973) (Wortman and Cummings, 1978; Trager, 1975). But food trade has skyrocketed (see fig. 2.5c), particularly in the form of coarse-grain shipments. In other words, while food sold on concessionary terms or given as aid for direct consumption by human beings has dropped or remained reasonably stable, sales of feed grain—exports of grain for indirect consumption by people—have risen dramatically. The indirect consumption of grain—after it is converted to food energy through livestock—is extremely inefficient. That is, only about one-tenth of the energy content of grains fed to animals is retained by their bodies and thereby available to human consumers. Most of the rest is belched, excreted, or used to maintain the animals' metabolic needs (Pimentel, 1979). Protein intake per capita in DCs is typically two to three times greater than that in LCDs. Animal proteins in the developed countries' diets largely account for this difference (Borgstrom, 1981; Gilland, 1979).

We do not mean to oppose any role for livestock in meeting world food needs. On the contrary, in some climates or geographic conditions livestock that forage are the principal economically viable agricultural product. Moreover, livestock constitute a huge hidden grain reserve in the sense that if there were a global food emergency both the livestock and their intended feed grains could be consumed directly by people. However, economics and politics make this option unlikely, since food emergencies typically occur in countries with few grain or livestock reserves.

Many poorer countries cannot afford—or do not choose—to buy enough grains in the world marketplace to prevent malnutrition by direct consumption, even in times of domestic shortfalls, which are often climatically induced. Balance-of-payments deficits, debts, credit policies, and other economic factors affect their ability or desire to purchase food grains, let alone develop a taste for grain-fed animals.

If a country is not self-sufficient in food production, then, of course, imports must be obtained to prevent famine. Such food transfers can be in the form of hard-currency purchases by nations like Japan or the USSR, concessional sales, or outright donations from private or government donors, as occurred often in the Sahel in the 1970s or Ethiopia in the mid-1980s. However, a number of analysts have opposed such food transfers in principle, often for very different reasons. One rationale is that food transfers for recipient nations create a dangerous dependence that allows suppliers to gain undue political control over the recipients. This view was active policy in China during the years of the Cultural Revolution, when contacts with outside nations were strongly discouraged on ideological grounds of self-reliance. A radically different reason to oppose food transfers has been expressed by those who believe that any nation not self-sufficient in food production is overpopulated and that food transfers merely prop up an unsustainable situation. Examples of such views of food trade are taken up next.

Food Triage

There are some who even question whether food aid is ethical. In a classic and controversial book entitled *Famine—1975!* (1967), William and Paul Paddock suggested somewhat prophetically that by the mid-1970s chronic food shortages in some LDCs would overwhelm the capacities of even the grain-rich countries to provide sufficient aid.[8] Those developing nations whose population growth rates exceeded their capacity for food production were singled out. The Paddocks recommended the adoption of a food policy analogous to the medical use of triage, the World War I battlefield policy. Here is the way it worked in wartime. The wounded were divided into three groups: the hopelessly injured, for whom treatment was unlikely to do any good; the superficially wounded, who despite pain could wait to receive treatment; and the seriously wounded for whom treatment was most likely to be effective. This system was designed to save the largest number of people, given too few doctors and too many patients. The Paddocks believe that world food shortages will reach such propor-

---

[8] Although famine certainly increased in the food crises of the mid-1970s, it was the unwillingness rather than the inability of grain-rich countries that helped sustain the food crisis in some LDCs.

tions that those requesting food aid will have to be either helped or turned away, depending on how desperate they are or how much it is deemed they could — or should — be helped.

For example, the Paddocks suggested that countries like India, with cumbersome bureaucracies and high population-growth rates, cannot be saved and that therefore food should not be "wasted" on them.[9] An oil-rich but food-poor country like Libya probably has enough resources to buy its food in emergencies, so aid need not be sent to it. On the other hand, a country like Pakistan, which the Paddocks believed showed promise of self-sufficiency in the long run, should be given food aid in crises.

Is such a policy unethical? It was condemned as such by many people. But the Paddocks believed that it was a moral alternative, since the triage is designed to save the maximum number of people with limited food aid available (Paddock and Paddock, 1967).

However, their battlefield analogy for the world food situation breaks down when we realize that there is no worldwide shortage of grain (especially if we include feed grains as potentially consumable by people); there are only regional and local shortages. The food-rich are the "triage officers" with their surpluses. Changes in dietary standards or more uniform per capita distribution of existing food could prevent chronic malnutrition or periodic famines — at least for a decade or two more — after which unconstrained population growth would probably outstrip food production, even on a worldwide average basis. Thus, unlike battlefield triage, a policy of food triage today would not save the maximum number of lives possible, unless one accepts the present systems of food ownership and distribution as givens that are beyond negotiation. But the latter is a political caveat, not a moral imperative.

Lifeboat Ethics

While the triage concept may seem a harsh or even immoral view of reality, ecologist Garrett Hardin's well-known doctrine of "lifeboat ethics" is even harsher (Hardin, 1974). Like the Paddocks, Hardin believes that food aid merely tends to discourage the efforts of many less-developed countries to increase their own production and to lower their birthrates. Hence he agrees that offering food aid today will create a less supportable, larger

[9]Although India's population-growth rate remains high in a number of states and its increasing food production is not yet safely ahead of the population growth, its emergency planning helped greatly in 1980, when poor monsoon rains caused production shortfalls. India's grain-reserve policies set up after the painful food crises of 1972 and 1974 were successful in staving off comparable famine conditions in 1980.

population in the future. The crises that have only been delayed would then cause even more people to suffer famine. If food aid were withdrawn today, Hardin suggests, food-deficient nations would have more incentive to solve their problems — and future populations would be relatively smaller and better off in the end. Hardin likens the world and its food problem to a sinking ship: richer nations have managed to get safely into the lifeboats, filling nearly all the seats. The people from poorer nations are splashing about in the sea, desperately trying to climb aboard. In this metaphor there are more people in the sea than empty seats in the boat, so that any attempt to allow all of them on board would only cause the lifeboat to sink, drowning everybody (the metaphor has also been applied to the problem of Latin American immigration to the United States).

Hardin also opposes the idea of an international "food bank," even to help nations through periods of climate-caused food shortages. He argues that those who tend to make the "withdrawals" are often beset by chronic shortages anyway, rendering them unable to make deposits back into the bank. Like the Paddocks' triage analogy Hardin's lifeboat metaphor generated a storm of protests that it was both unethical and likely to create international conflicts.

Global Survival Compromise

Has the world food situation become so critical that either the Paddocks' or Hardin's analogy applies? In 1976, Schneider stated in *The Genesis Strategy* that "the implicit and crucial assumption invoked by these metaphors is that the Earth has already reached or surpassed its carrying capacity" (Schneider with Mesirow, 1976). But the latter has not been established as accepted scientific fact, despite strong pronouncements both pro and con from well-qualified experts. Nobody really knows scientifically just how large the carrying capacity of the earth is now or could be in the twenty-first century. When arguing the ethical issue of food aid, we need to scrutinize the earth's limits and recognize that, although limits do exist, they are not fixed but are dependent on a variety of social, economic, industrial, and agricultural practices. Given the uncertainty about what these practices will be, the triage and lifeboat metaphors do not necessarily apply to the real world. I proposed a "global survival compromise," an alternative policy that would offer short-term emergency aid and longer-term technological assistance and capital investment from the wealthier nations. This assistance would be "coupled to and contingent on mutually agreeable plans betwen the donor and recipient nations to bring about self-sufficiency for the recipients as rapidly as possible but within a fixed time, after which aid would be unnecessary and not forthcoming" (Schneider with Mesirow, 1976). I acknowledged that this could be most costly for developed countries and that developing countries will have to make many painful changes—some of which may not work—to find the best routes toward self-sufficiency. Eventually, I conceded, the alternatives might boil down to triage or lifeboat ethics unless there are "spectacular and unforeseen technological or demographic breakthroughs that would place food supplies comfortably ahead of food needs." But it seems preferable to work to prevent both present and future carrying-capacity catastrophes, even at some risk of enhancing potential long-term problems. This is preferable to accepting such catastrophes as inevitable, thereby practicing triage or lifeboat ethics before it is certain that these analogies do—or will—apply.

This principle of compromise seems to me a more ethical course to steer between an indefinite commitment to outright blanket food or food-technology transfers to nations not yet self-sufficient and an immediate, total abandonment of the undernourished, especially in bad-weather years. In any case, a diversity of national and international efforts to increase sustainable food production and to lower population-growth rates as fast as possible is urgently needed—elements of a similar food and development strategy that scientist and humanist Walter Orr Roberts labeled "pragmatic humanism" (Roberts and Lansford, 1979).

Food-Climate Policy Actions

There is little doubt that making policy related to food-climate interactions will involve technical uncertainty and ethical controversy. Nevertheless, certain obvious actions suggest themselves. We continue with an exploration of these necessary, if minimal, precautions against climatic hazards.

Food Reserves

Short-term, climate-induced fluctuations in food production typically average several percent from year to year worldwide and many tens of percent regionally. To compensate for the hazard implicit in these fluctuations, regional food stocks and food-distribution systems are needed as a hedge against shortfalls. Thus a high priority on a world food-policy agenda should be to identify regional food needs and work out the mechanisms for establishing and distributing the reserves should food emergencies arise. Such mechanisms might include the slaughter of some livestock and transfer of feed grains to direct human consumption. Deciding the terms of access to reserves is a major political component of maintaining food security. It is complicated by the fact that most reserves and surpluses are held by those who are not likely to face food crises and who are disinclined to turn over their bounty to the truly needy, who have least control over food resources.

As another step toward minimizing climatic hazards, nations need to disseminate weather and climate information in a comprehensible form to food producers, consumers, and the government and nongovernment bodies concerned with fluctuations in food production. The World Climate Programme, an international collaboration administered by the World Meteorological Organization and other UN agencies, already lists this step on its international agenda (World Meteorological Organization, 1979).

However, many hundreds of millions of people, particularly peasant farmers in LDCs, do not look toward elaborate international or even national mechanisms to provide them and their families with credible advice or food security. Rather, they rely principally on themselves. Storing part of this year's production to tide one over until next year's harvest is an age-old practice. Adding extra provisions against the precedented possibility that next year might also be bad is similarly venerable. United Nations food-policy analyst Pierre Spitz has studied the pressures that influence peasant farmers in India in their decision on how much food to put aside in the process called self-provisioning (Spitz, 1981). Spitz describes two sets of forces tugging these self-provisioning farmers in opposite directions: one, to keep as much of the food they had grown as possible (the forces of retention), and the other, to release it (the forces of extraction). Many factors combine to favor retention: the fear of lower production and consequent food shortages from future bad weather, concern over future price increases for necessary inputs such as fertilizer, low prevailing prices for farm products, the hope of future price increases, and the possibility of higher rent and taxes. On the other hand, there are considerations that tend to pressure farm families either to seek outside jobs or to sell a larger fraction of each year's harvest to raise cash: the prospect of a future drop in market prices for food (for example, through unusually good weather and oversupply), an immediate increase in rent requiring quick cash, and a rise in the costs of nonfood necessities. Weather fluctuations combine with nonweather-related price fluctuations to compound the difficulty of deciding how to self-provision for each year.

Spitz points out that not all producers in LDCs face the same kinds of dilemmas when weather causes production fluctuations. Large landholders (so-called category *a* producers) who typically produce a big surplus are usually able to survive most production anomalies without catastrophe. But the same is certainly not the case, Spitz asserts, for the "vast majority of poor peasants" in LDCs (so-called category *b* producers). These people are unable to produce enough food to feed their families over an average year and must somehow supplement their insufficient production either by purchasing food with cash earned from other labors or by using food from their remaining stocks, if any (Chambers, 1982).

The impact of a bad year on these different categories of producers is quite the opposite, Spitz writes:

A decline in output, following a drought, for example, forces them into debt to category (*a*) producers, to whom they sell their labour power at a lower wage rate, and to whom they sell what they still possess, including their means of production, at knock down prices; it also obliges them to mortgage their land and, eventually, to sell it. The shocks repeatedly inflicted by climatic variability thus accentuate the long-term tendency for the polarization of these two groups of producers and for elimination of the weakest, who are driven into the cities. [Spitz, 1981]

In this scenario a bad year for the peasant farmers is a windfall for large producers, who can increase their own landholdings at rock-bottom prices.

To minimize this polarization, Spitz suggests, the government must intervene with aid immediately after the harvest, since "it is too late when land has been mortgaged and tools sold in the period preceding the next harvest: the situation cannot be rectified by soup kitchens, the distribution of food, relief works, nor even by loans." Thus Spitz suggests that the solution to this food-climate problem is primarily social and political: "agrarian reform aimed at a more equitable distribution of land" and a "redistribution of economic and political power" (Spitz, 1981). Of course, his solutions, like those mentioned earlier in connection with the Sahel region in Africa, stem from a particular conceptual view of the underlying causes of the problem. But ideological viewpoints aside, the Spitz scenario strongly suggests that reserve stocks and distribution systems as a means of food security need to be examined at both local and more centralized levels to determine just how much security they really provide—and for whom.

Let us step back from the issue of local-scale self-provisioning for a moment and take a broader view of world food security in the face of year-to-year climatic variability. Figure 2.5 suggests that, when grain stocks dip below about 12 to 15 percent of utilization, local scarcities, worldwide price jumps, and sporadic famines are more likely to occur. This suggests that a minimum world level of *accessible* grain stocks near 15 percent of global utilization needs to be maintained as a hedge against year-to-year production fluctuations. Of course, as we have already seen, access to this buffer for those who need it in emergencies is limited by social and economic factors. For such people the inability to use reserves as a hedge is the chief obstacle to achieving a workable world food-security system, whatever the global level of stocks may be, since such stocks in the hands of private owners are often of little use to the needy.

Minimizing Climatic Risks for Producers

While food reserves and distribution systems are primarily security measures for consumers, the financial risks to producers must also be minimized. Farmers in both DCs and LDCs need fertilizers, seeds, labor, and other appropriate technologies, all of which cost money. Often farmers borrow money and then must pay it back from the money they earn by selling crops. Typically debts must be repaid on a fixed credit cycle regardless of how the annual crop turns out. A few bad-weather years can create such severe financial risks to producers (including the ultimate risk of losing the land) that as a "climate defensive" strategy they restrict their investments to production materials such as parts for irrigation systems or fertilizer. This strategy not only tends to lower overall production in the short run but also limits the development of the infrastructure necessary to encourage long-term productivity increases. Thus it is important to ensure that the short-term financial risks of potentially bad weather do not unduly inhibit the producer investments needed to maintain or increase production (Swindale et al., 1981).[10] Crop insurance is one way to accomplish this. But more creative solutions are necessary as well, such as farm loans with flexible repayment terms, analogous perhaps to floating-interest-rate mortgages. Thus in a good production and marketing year producers might pay creditors larger-than-average payments, whereas in lean years payments would be reduced. In this way the burden of adverse climate anomalies on food production and prices would be shared in the general economy, rather than being concentrated wholly on the producer. The concept is akin to the pooling of risk practiced in the insurance industry.

Clearly, specific solutions as well as the relative roles of private and public institutions will have to be tailored to local environmental and po-

---

[10] These authors, from the International Crops Research Institute for the Semi-Arid Tropics, in Hyderabad, India, commenting on the high degree of year-to-year climatic variability faced by Third World farmers in this area, noted that "rain-fed farming is risky in such conditions and farmers are reluctant to invest in crop production," which often contributes to the fact that "traditional agriculture means low but stable yields, low inputs, mixed cropping, large families, low incomes and living standards and outmigration of family members, both seasonal and permanent" (Swindale et al., 1981, p. 139).

litical conditions. Nevertheless, there is a general worldwide need to combine public and private investments at all levels to maintain food security and to protect producers. Developing such measures is an urgent matter for local, national, and international policymakers. It is my hope that along with food reserve policies for the benefit of consumers, producers too will be protected by policymakers against climatic hazards.[11]

Diversity and Security

As we have already hinted, another important strategy for combating food shortages is maintaining diversity—for example, planting a variety of different crops in different places and at different times. Particularly in warmer climates where more than one crop can be planted each year, multiple cropping can both raise yields and offer some measure of natural pest resistance. Diversification also minimizes the vulnerability of a whole cropping system to an adverse climatic anomaly. Moreover, this approach usually requires labor-intensive management, important for employment in many poor nations. As mentioned earlier, in the south-central states of the United States in the summer of 1980 the impact of heat and drought was somewhat mitigated by the diversity of planted crops, since winter wheat benefited, though corn and soybean yields were reduced.

Weatherproofing Crops

Building food-security systems, providing crop insurance, and developing flexible credit schemes for producers are examples of social-protection measures designed to minimize the negative impacts of bad weather. Planting a diverse mix of crop strains to minimize weather- or pest-induced crop failure is an example of a biological protection measure. Technical protection measures make up a third category. Technical measures include installing irrigation systems to overcome drought, blowers or heaters to com-

---

[11]Despite my various writings over the past decade on food reserves and food security issues, I now realize that I did not properly appreciate the importance of this point until a conference on food-climate issues held in Berlin in 1980. Maintaining both consumer and producer protection against year-to-year climate anomalies was one of the very few points upon which both developed and developing country representatives—comprising market and nonmarket advocates—could agree. "The Report of Working Group A: Climate as a Hazard" (pp. xvi–xx) strongly makes the point that producers as well as consumers need protection against climatic variability (Schneider, Bach, et al., 1981).

bat frost, windbreaks to minimize evaporation or wind erosion, and even enclosures to isolate plants or fish from natural elements.[12]

Norman Rosenberg noted that the most efficient weatherproofing technique is simply "proper selection of the land and climate in which the crop can be grown with minimal weather risk" (Rosenberg, 1981). There are, of course, other, more modern techniques of weatherproofing that can be effective protections against bad-weather effects. (Rosenberg details a number of these, including increased capture of precipitation, runoff, or snowmelt; minimum tillage to reduce evaporation from soil and its erosion; various mulching practices; windbreaks; irrigation scheduling optimized to crop-growth stages; reflectants applied to soil or plants to minimize leaf overheating; antitranspirant materials to reduce leaf-evaporation rates; and even modification to plant architecture by a number of means, including breeding of strains designed to take advantage of a particular set of climatic resources.) Despite the growing arsenal of technical weatherproofing fixes, including new kinds of crops, such as salt-tolerant halophytes, which are potentially growable in desertlike areas near seawater, or even synthetic foods, the major stumbling blocks to the success of the more innovative measures are more social than technical (Hodges, 1981; Slater, 1981). As Rosenberg cautioned, "Adaptive research is needed and markets for such crops must be developed before a major conversion can be expected" (Rosenberg, 1981). Although new ideas and products could well have unforeseen promise in the distant future, it seems obvious that the better-known means and meeting world food needs that we have reviewed here could work—if only there were sufficient will to implement them.

"Render unto Weather . . ."

It is obvious that actions for meeting world food needs are both immensely complex and controversial. We have barely outlined the basics. Climate, we have seen, plays a major role both as a resource and as a hazard. While climate is an important component of food production and security, we have also seen that it cannot be viewed (or blamed for disaster) in isolation. The case studies of the Irish and Dutch potato blights have shown that social, political, and economic factors combined with environmental stresses to produce negative fluctuations in yields and create significantly different societal impacts. In an editorial "Render unto Weather . . . ,"

[12]The potential for high yields in controlled environments is good, but indoor climate control systems are problematic, and economic constraints on such "exotic" food production methods remain to be worked out (Hodges, 1981).

printed in the journal *Climatic Change,* political scientist Michael Glantz summarized the situation this way:

It is extremely important to distiguish between direct adverse effects of weather events which could not have been prevented, and other adverse weather-related effects which, in fact, have their origins in political, economic, and social policies. This distinction will make it possible for society to place the blame for the severity of an impact of a particular weather phenomenon where it actually belongs—on the weather event or on society. This distinction also makes it possible to minimize such adverse effects by more adequately matching solutions to the correctly identified problems [Glantz, 1978].

To approach the food-climate problem from any single perspective is almost guaranteed to fail to produce workable solutions. Only an integrated, interdisciplinary attack on the many facets of each region's short- and long-term food needs—combined with mechanisms that give people access to the food—has any hope of success. Some approaches may succeed and others fail. But what is certain is that we must not allow a recurrence of the food-climate crises of the 1970s simply because we failed to do what we already know could help prevent them. I am sure that Earl Cook—and Cassandra—would agree.

References

Bardach, J. E., and Santerre, R. M., 1981, Climate and aquatic food production. In W. Bach, J. Pankrath, and S. H. Schneider, eds. *Food-climate interactions,* pp. 187–233. Dordrecht: Reidel.

Bark, L. D. 1978. History of American droughts. In N. J. Rosenberg, ed. *North American droughts,* pp. 9–23. Boulder, Colo.: Westview Press.

Bickel, L. 1974. *Facing starvation: Norman Borlaug and the fight against hunger.* New York: Readers Digest Press.

Borgstrom, G. 1981. Population growth, nutrition and food supply. In W. Bach, J. Pankrath, and S. H. Schneider, eds. *Food-climate interactions,* pp. 69–79. Dordrecht: Reidel.

Brown, L. R. 1970. *Seeds of change.* New York: Praeger.

———. 1978. *The Twenty-ninth day.* New York: Norton.

Bryson, R. A., and T. J. Murray. 1977. *Climates of hunger.* Madison: University of Wisconsin Press.

Chambers, R. 1982. Health, agriculture, and rural poverty: Why seasons matter. *Journal of Development Studies* 18:217–38.

Colson, E. 1979. In good years and in bad: Food strategies of self-reliant societies. *Journal of Anthropological Research* 35:18–29.

Garcia, R. V. 1981. *Nature pleads not guilty.* Oxford: Pergamon Press.

Gilland, B. 1979. *The next seventy years: Population, food and resources.* Tunbridge Wells: Abacus.

Glantz, M. H. 1977. Nine fallacies of a natural disaster: The case of the Sahel. *Climatic Change* 1:69–84.

———. 1978. Render unto weather . . . , an editorial. *Climatic Change* 1:305–306.

———, and J. D. Thompson, eds. 1981. *Resource management and environmental uncertainty: Lessons from coastal upwelling fisheries.* New York: Wiley Inter-science.

Hardin, G. 1974. Living on a lifeboat. *Bioscience* 24:561–68.

Hare, F. K. 1979. Food, climate, and man. In A. K. Biswas and M. R. Biswas, eds. *Food, climate, and man.* New York: Wiley.

Hodges, C. N. 1981. New options for climate-defensive food production. In L. E. Slater, and S. K. Levin, eds. *Climate's impact on food supplies: Strategies and technologies for climate-defensive food production,* pp. 181–206. Boulder, Colo.: Westview.

"Impact team," 1977. *The weather conspiracy: The coming of the new Ice Age.* New York: Ballantine.

Lamb, H. H. 1975. *The current trend of world climate—a report on the early 1970s and a perspective.* CRU RP3. Norwich: Climatic Research Unit, University of East Anglia.

Landsberg, H. E. 1979. The effect of man's activities on climate. In A. K. Biswas and M. R. Biswas, eds. *Food, climate, and man.* New York: Wiley.

Lappe, F. M., J. Collins, and C. Fowler. 1978. *Food first: Beyond the myth of scarcity.* New York: Ballantine.

McQuigg, J., et al. 1973. *The influence of weather and climate on United States grain yield: Bumper crops or drought.* Report to the National Oceanic and Atmospheric Administration (NOAA), U.S. Department of Commerce. Washington, D.C.: U.S. Government Printing Office.

Mokyr, J. 1980. Industrialization and poverty in Ireland and the Netherlands. *Journal of Interdisciplinary History* 10 (3): 429–58.

Myers, N. 1981. The hamburger connection: How Central America's forests become North America's hamburgers. *Ambio* 10:3–8.

Newman, J. E. 1978. Drought impacts on American agricultural productivity. In N. J. Rosenberg, ed. *North American droughts,* pp. 43–62. Boulder, Colo.: Westview Press.

Paddock, W., and P. Paddock. 1967. *Famine—1975!* Boston: Little, Brown, pp. 206–207.

Parthasararthy, B., and D. A. Mooley. 1978. Some features of a long homogeneous series of Indian summer rainfall. *Monthly Weather Review* 106:771–81.

Pimentel, D. 1979. Energy and agriculture. In A. K. Biswas and M. R. Biswas, eds. *Food, climate, and man,* pp. 98–99. New York: Wiley.

Ponte, L. 1976. *The cooling.* Englewood Cliffs, N.J.: Prentice-Hall.

Roberts, W. O., and H. Lansford. 1979. *The climate mandate.* San Francisco: Freeman.

Rosenberg, N. J. 1981. Technologies and strategies in weather-proofing crop production. In L. E. Slater, and S. K. Levin, eds. *Climate's impact on food supplies: Strategies and technologies for climate-defensive food production,* pp. 157–80. Boulder, Colo.: Westview Press.

Schneider, S. H. 1977. Against instant books. *Nature* 270:650.

———, with L. E. Mesirow. 1976, *The genesis strategy: Climate and global survival,* Chap. 4. New York: Plenum.

———, W. Bach, et al. 1981, Meeting world food needs: Climate as a hazard. In W. Bach, J. Pankrath, and S. H. Schneider, eds. *Food-climate interactions,* pp. xvi–xx. Dordrecht: Reidel.

Slater, L. E. 1981. Synthetic foods: Eliminating the climate factor. In L. E. Slater and S. K. Levin, eds. *Climate's impact on food supplies,* pp. 207–43. Boulder, Colo.: Westview Press.

Spitz, P. 1981. Economic consequences of food/climate variability. In W. Bach, J. Pankrath, and S. H. Schneider, eds. *Food-climate interactions,* pp. 447–463. Dordrecht: Reidel.

Swindale, L. D., S. S. Virmani, and M. C. K. Sivakumar. 1981. Climatic variability and crop yields in the semi-arid tropics. In W. Bach, J. Pankrath and S. H. Schneider, eds. *Food-climate interactions,* pp. 139–66. Dordrecht: Reidel.

Thompson, L. M. 1975. Weather variability, climatic change, and grain production. *Science* 188:535–49.

Trager, J. 1975. *The great grain robbery.* New York: Ballantine.

U. S. Department of Agriculture. 1982. *World grain situation and outlook: Foreign agriculture circular.* Washington, D.C.: U.S. Government Printing Office (August).

———. 1985. *World grain situation and outlook: Foreign agriculture circular FG-4-85.* Washington, D.C.: U.S. Government Printing Office (March).

U.S. National Academy of Sciences. 1975. *World food and nutrition study.* Washington, D.C.: National Academy Press.

Warrick, R. A. 1980. Drought in the Great Plains: A case study of research on climate and society in the U.S.A. In J. Ausubel, and A. K. Biswas, eds. *Climatic constraints and human activities.* Oxford: Pergamon Press.

World Meteorological Organization. 1979. *Proceedings of the World Climate Conference* no. 537. Geneva: WMO.

Wortman, S., and R. W. Cummings, Jr. 1978. *To feed this world: The challenge and the strategy.* Baltimore, Md.: Johns Hopkins Press.

3.
Industrialized Agriculture and Natural Resources

AGRICULTURE DEPENDS on biota, land, water, air, and diverse energy resources. Industrialized agriculture, in particular, depends on fossil energy.
In this chapter an analysis is made of the interdependency of energy, biological, land, air, and water resources in industrialized food-production
systems. Special focus is given to the degradation of land, water, and biological resources and how this affects the use of energy resources.

A sustainable productive environment is essential if we are to continue
to supply food for human society in future decades. This is true now as
never before, as human populations rapidly grow from the current 4.7 billion to the projected 11 billion in the twenty-second century (World Bank,
1984). Population growth plus poor agricultural-management practices are
placing severe pressures on the world's environmental resources.

The environment or ecological system on which productive agriculture depends is comprised of biota, land, water, air, and energy resources.
These resources interact in a dynamic manner to maintain a functional
and renewable system. Energy flows, biogeochemical cycles, and trophic
and genetic feedback mechanisms are but a few of the important interactions that affect the quality of the environment and ultimately its productivity. Changes in one sector of the agroecosystem—for instance, removing vegetation—can cause a reaction in some other segment, such as
soil and water resources in this interrelated system. Such changes often
occur when energy, land, and water are substituted for another in an attempt to keep a degraded environment productive. This chapter examines
the interrelationships of environmental degradation on the use of natural
resources, especially fossil energy, in agricultural production.

Table 3.1. Quantities of Various Inputs to Produce Corn Using Only Labor, Draft Animals, and Mechanization from 1910 to 1983 (All Units per Hectare)

Years	Hand-produced	1910	1920	1945	1950	1954
Labor (hr)	1,200[a]	120[b]	120[b]	57[c]	44[c]	42[c]
Machinery (kg)	1[g]	15[b]	15[b]	22[d]	30[d]	35[d]
Draft animals	0	120[b]	120[b]	*	*	*
Fuel (L)						
Gasoline	*	*	*	120[h]	135[h]	150[h]
Diesel	*	*	*	20[h]	25[h]	30[h]
Manure	*	4,000[i]	4,000[i]	3,000[i]	2,000[i]	1,000[i]
N (kg)	0	0	0	8[d]	17[d]	30[d]
P (kg)	0	0	0	8[d]	11[d]	13[d]
K (kg)	0	0	0	6[d]	11[d]	20[d]
Lime (kg)	0	10[f]	10[f]	145[k]	195[k]	124[k]
Seeds (kg)	11[f]	11[f]	11[f]	11[d]	13[d]	17[d]
Insecticides (kg)	0	0	0	0[d]	0.1[d]	0.3[d]
Herbicides (kg)	0	0	0	0[d]	0.05[d]	0.1[d]
Irrigation (%)	0	*	*	1[m]	1[m]	2[n]
Drying (kg)	0	0	0	43[f]	48[f]	77[f]
Electricity (10³ kcal)	0	*	1[f]	8[f]	16[j]	24[f]
Transport (kg)	*	25[s]	25[s]	170[s]	210[s]	262[s]
Yield (kg)	1,880[k]	1,800[k]	1,880[k]	2,132[d]	2,383[d]	2,572[d]

SOURCES: [a]Estimated from Lewis, 1951; [b]estimated from Pimentel, 1984c; [c]USDA, 1954; [d]Pimentel et al., 1973; [e]Pimentel and Burgess, 1980; [f]estimated; [g]Pimentel and Pimentel, 1979; [h]quantities from Pimentel et al., 1973, and proportions estimated; [i]estimated amount of livestock manure containing 80 percent moisture; [j]USDA, 1979, 1982b; [k]USDA, 1970; [l]USDA, 1981; [m]percentage of corn acreage irrigated, USBC, 1952; [n]percentage of corn acre-

Energy Resources

As recently as 1850 the prime energy resources for society were fuel wood and human labor (EOP, 1977). As shown in table 3.1, the use of fossil fuels by U.S. agriculture and society as a whole did not begin to grow rapidly until after 1900 (Cook, 1976). Today the United States consumes 19×10^{15} kcal (71 quads) per year (DOE, 1983). On a per capita basis this is the equivalent of 9,480 L (2,500 gal) of oil per person per year.

About 17 percent of the total energy used in the U.S. economy is expended in the food system (Pimentel, 1984a). Of this about 6 percent is for production, 6 percent for processing and packaging, and the remaining 5 percent is for distribution and preparation.

The 17 percent represents about 1,500 L (400 gal) of fossil-fuel equivalents expended per person annually just for food. In developing countries

Table 3.1. (continued)

Years	1959	1964	1970	1975	1980	1983
Labor (hr)	35[d]	27[d]	22[d]	17[e]	12[e]	10[f]
Machinery (kg)	42[d]	49[d]	49[d]	50[e]	55[e]	55[f]
Draft animals	*	*	*	*	*	*
Fuel (L)						
Gasoline	155[h]	125[h]	120[h]	60[e]	50[b]	40[f]
Diesel	35[h]	65[h]	80[h]	70[e]	75[b]	75[f]
Manure	1,000[i]	1,000[i]	1,000[i]	1,000[i]	1,000[i]	1,000[i]
N (kg)	46[d]	65[d]	125[d]	118[j]	146[j]	152[j]
P (kg)	18[d]	20[d]	35[d]	65[j]	74[j]	75[j]
K (kg)	34[d]	32[d]	67[d]	75[j]	96[j]	96[j]
Lime (kg)	158[k]	203[k]	220[k]	220[e]	426[l]	426[f]
Seeds (kg)	19[d]	21[d]	21[d]	21[e]	21[e]	21[f]
Insecticides (kg)	0.8[d]	1.1[d]	1.1[d]	2[e]	2[b]	2[f]
Herbicides (kg)	0.3[d]	0.4[d]	1[d]	4[e]	4[b]	4[f]
Irrigation (%)	3[n]	5[o]	9[p]	16[q]	17[r]	18[r]
Drying (kg)	271[f]	725[f]	1,880[k]	2,290[f]	3,200[f]	3,300[f]
Electricity (10³ kcal)	36[f]	60[f]	80[f]	90[f]	100[f]	100[f]
Transport (kg)	287[s]	325[s]	305[s]	298[s]	326[s]	322[s]
Yield (kg)	3,387[d]	4,265[d]	5,080[d]	5,143[t]	6,500[t]	6,500[u]

age irrigated, USBC, 1962; [o]percentage of corn acreage irrigated, USBC, 1967; [p]percentage of corn acreage irrigated, USBC, 1973; [q]percentage of corn acreage irrigated, FEA, 1976; [r]estimated percentage of corn acreage irrigated; [s]transport of machinery, fuel, and nitrogen fertilizer; [t]three-year running average yield, USDA, 1976, 1982a; [u]estimated.

*Greater than 0.

only 10 to 200 L of fossil-fuel equivalents are expended per person per year (Pimentel and Pimentel, 1979; Wen Dazhong and Pimentel, 1984). Further calculations confirm that if the world population of 4.7 billion human beings ate a typical American diet produced with our agricultural technology the total known reserves of oil on earth would last a mere 12 years (Pimentel, 1984b). This is using all known oil reserves only for food production, none for other purposes. Even though not all populations would favor a high kilocalorie and high animal-protein diet, this example clearly emphasizes the limitations of fossil-fuel resources relative to the food needs of a rapidly growing world population.

Ever since the oil crisis of 1973 the quantity of energy expended in U.S. crop production has continued to rise (tables 3.1 and 3.2). Concurrently, the on-farm work force has continued to decline (USDA, 1982a). Some in agriculture proudly point to the fact that only about 3 percent

Table 3.2. The Energy Input for Various Items Used in Corn Production
from 1700 to 1983
(1,000 Kcal per Hectare)

Years	1700	1910	1920	1945	1950	1954
Labor[a]	653	65	65	31	24	23
Machinery[b]	19	278	278	407	555	648
Draft animal[c]	0	886	886	0	0	0
Fuel[d]						
Gasoline	0	0	0	1,200	1,350	1,500
Diesel	0	0	0	228	275	342
Manure[e]	0	0	0			
Nitrogen				118[f]	250[f]	440[f]
Phosphorus	0	0	0	24[g]	33[g]	39[g]
Potassium	0	0	0	13[h]	18[h]	32[h]
Lime[e]	0	3	3	46	61	39
Seeds[m]	44	44	44	161	322	421
Insecticides[n]	0	0	0	0	7	20
Herbicides[o]	0	0	0	0	3	7
Irrigation[p]	0	*	*	125	125	250
Drying[q]	0	0	0	9	10	15
Electricity[r]	0	*	1	8	16	24
Transport[s]	*	25	25	44	58	67
Total	716	1,301	1,302	2,414	3,107	3,867
Ratio[t]	10.5	5.8	5.8	3.5	3.1	2.7
Yield[u]	7,520	7,520	7,520	8,528	9,532	10,288

SOURCES: [a]Food energy consumed per laborer per day was assumed to be 3,110 kcal from
1700 to 1970, 3,300 kcal for 1975, and 3,500 kcal for 1980–83. [b]The energy input per kilogram of steel in tools and other machinery was 18,500 kcal (Doering, 1980). [c]The food energy
per hour of draft-animal use was calculated to be 7,380 kcal (Pimentel, 1984c). [d]One L of
gasoline and diesel fuel was calculated to contain 10,000 and 11,400 kcal (Cervinka, 1980).
These values include the energy input for mining and refining. [e]No charge was made for
the manure input. This input was assumed to be included in either the draft-animal input
or the machinery and fuel inputs. [f]N = 14,700 kcal/kg (Lockeretz, 1980). [g]P = 3,000 kcal/kg
(Lockeretz, 1980). [h]K = 1600 kcal/kg (Lockeretz, 1980). [i]N = 21,000 kcal/kg (Dovring and
McDowell, 1980). [j]P = 6,300 kcal/kg (Dovring and McDowell, 1980). [k]K = 2,500 kcal/kg
(Dovring and McDowell, 1980). [l]Limestone = 315 kcal/kg (Terhune, 1980). [m]It was assumed
that from 1700 to 1920 each kilogram of corn equaled 4,000 kcal, whereas when hybrid seed
was used from 1945 to 1983, the cost was 24,750 kcal/kg (Heichel, 1980). [n]Chlorinated insecticides dominated use from 1945 to 1964, and the energy input was calculated to be 67,000

of the work force is involved in direct farming and thus is feeding the rest
of the U.S. population (USDA, 1982a). This is a misleading statistic, however, because the farmer hardly feeds himself, and he goes to the same su-
permarket that you and I do to purchase food. He depends on Detroit for
his tractors and other farm machinery and equipment; he depends on the
oil industry to fuel his tractors and other implements; and he depends on
the petrochemical industry for thousands of different chemicals that he

Table 3.2. (continued)

Years	1959	1964	1970	1975	1980	1983
Labor[a]	19	15	12	10	7	6
Machinery[b]	777	907	907	925	1,018	1,018
Draft animal[c]	0	0	0	0	0	0
Fuel[d]						
Gasoline	1,550	1,250	1,200	600	500	400
Diesel	399	741	912	912	878	855
Manure[e]						
Nitrogen	676[f]	955[f]	1,837[f]	1,734[f]	3,066[i]	3,192[i]
Phosphorus	54[g]	60[g]	105[g]	195[g]	466[j]	473[j]
Potassium	54[h]	51[h]	107[h]	120[h]	240[k]	240[k]
Lime[e]	50	64	69	69	134	134
Seeds[m]	470	520	520	520	520	520
Insecticides[n]	54	74	110	200	200	200
Herbicides[o]	20	40	100	400	400	400
Irrigation[p]	375	625	1,125	2,000	2,125	2,250
Drying[q]	54	145	376	458	640	660
Electricity[r]	36	60	80	90	100	100
Transport[s]	79	89	84	82	90	89
Total	4,667	5,596	7,544	8,315	10,384	10,537
Ratio[t]	2.9	3.0	2.7	2.5	2.5	2.5
Yield[u]	13,548	17,060	20,320	20,575	26,000	26,000

kcal, whereas from 1970 to 1983 carbamate and phosphate dominated use, and the energy input for these was calculated to be 100,000 kcal/kg (Pimentel, 1980). [o]Phenoxy herbicides dominated use from 1945 to 1959, and the energy input was calculated to be 67,000 kcal/kg, whereas from 1964 to 1983 other types of herbicides dominated use, and the energy input for these are calculated to be 100,000 kcal/kg (Pimentel, 1980). [p]Water used per irrigated hectare was assumed to be 37.5 cm from 1945 to 1970 and 45 cm from 1974 to 1983. The percentages of corn acreage receiving irrigation are shown in table 3.1. The energy required per kilogram of irrigation water pumped from a depth of 100 m was calculated to be 300,000 kcal/cm. [q]The quantity of corn per hectare that required drying is shown in table 3.1. The energy required per kilogram dried was 200 kcal (Peart et al., 1980). [r]Includes energy input required to produce the electricity. [s]For the goods transported to the farm, an input of 275 kcal/kg was included (Pimentel, 1980). [t]Ratio is output/input. [u]An input of 4,000 kcal/kg of corn.
    *Greater than 0.

uses. After the crops and livestock are harvested on the farm, the farmer depends on the transport and food-processing sectors to move and process these foods. Eventually the foods are shipped to wholesalers and are handled by food retailers. Thus for every farm worker it is estimated there are at least two to three farm support workers. If the total work force in the food system is considered, then about 20 percent of the U.S. work force is involved in supplying food (Pimentel et al., 1973). Interestingly, about

20 percent of the work force was also involved in the food system in the United States in the 1920s. The prime difference today is that only a small portion of the work force is situated on the farm.

To clarify the changes in energy use occurring in U.S. agriculture from 1700 to 1983, an analysis was made of the nation's corn production. Corn was selected as the model crop because it is one of the top 10 food crops in the world.

Corn Yields

From 1909 to 1940, U.S. corn yields remained relatively static at about 1,880 kg/ha (about 30 bu/A) (fig. 3.1). But after 1945 corn yields began increasing rapidly. This was about the time that hybrid-corn varieties became available and commercial fertilizers and pesticides and other new energy-intensive technologies were being used (Pimentel et al., 1973).

From 1945 to 1983 corn yields increased about threefold (fig. 3.1), while total energy input into corn production increased about fourfold (tables 3.1 and 3.2). The specific technological changes that have taken place in corn culture, representing U.S. agriculture as a whole during the past 73 years, are examined below.

Labor

As shown in table 3.1, raising corn by manpower alone requires about 1,200 h of labor per hectare per season (Pimentel and Pimentel, 1979). Early native Americans and perhaps a few early European settlers raised corn by hand, but by 1775 most corn culture involved the use of draft-animal power provided by both oxen and horses.

The use of 200 h of ox power to produce 1 ha of corn reduces the manpower input from 1,200 h for hand-produced corn to about 400 h/ha (Pimentel and Pimentel, 1979). Thus each hour of ox input replaced 4 h of manpower input. Estimates are that the effective use of about 120 h of horsepower reduces the labor input for corn production to about 120 h/ha (1 h of horsepower replaces about 10 h of manpower) (Pimentel, 1984c). In the 1910–20 era horsepower dominated U.S. corn production (tables 3.1 and 3.2).

Since the increased reliance on heavy mechanization, labor input in corn production has been reduced to about 10 h/ha (tables 3.1 and 3.2). This is about 1/120 the input required to produce corn by hand; however, this does not take into account, as mentioned, all the indirect labor inputs

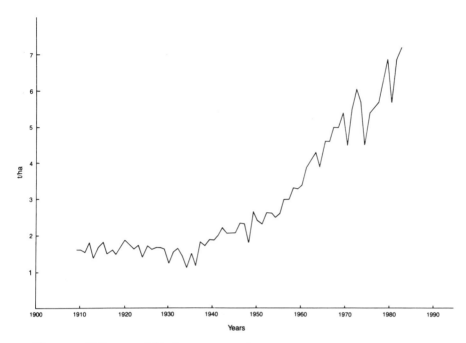

Fig. 3.1. U.S. corn yields from 1909 to the present.

that are associated with agricultural production. If the indirect labor input is taken into consideration, then current U.S. corn production uses about 1/40 to 1/50 the labor input for hand-grown corn. This is still a dramatic reduction in total amount of labor required to produce corn over the past few decades.

Machinery and Power

The development and use of gas-powered engines has had a tremendous impact on U.S. society as a whole and on agricultural production as well. Consider the manpower equivalent present in a gallon of fuel. One gallon (3.79 l) of fuel in a small gasoline engine provides 20 percent of the heat energy produced in the form of power. One gallon of fuel provides the energy equivalent of about 10 hp/h or 100 manpower-h of power, translating into about 2½ weeks of human work equivalents (Pimentel and Pimentel, 1979). This is one reason for the dramatic reductions in labor inputs from 57 h/ha to only 10 h/ha that occurred in U.S. corn production from 1945 to the present (table 3.1).

Interestingly, the total amount of fuel expended per hectare has declined from about 140 L to about 115 L since 1945 (table 3.1). Improved engines, changes from gasoline to diesel fuel, and larger farm machinery are responsible for the decrease. The weight of the machinery per labor-hour, for example, has grown from about 0.4 kg in 1945 to about 5.5 kg/ha in 1983, about a 14-fold increase (table 3.1). Although liquid fuel inputs have declined, the fossil-energy inputs expended to make the larger machinery have risen dramatically.

Initially, the prime fuel used in tractors was 85 percent gasoline and 15 percent diesel fuel (table 3.1). With time a shift toward diesel fuel was made, and today at least 65 percent is diesel fuel (table 3.1). Certainly diesel fuel has advantages over gasoline, providing 20 to 25 percent more power or greater efficiency per unit of fossil energy (CAST, 1975).

This is part of the reason for the decline in total fuel used in 1945 (140 L) to a low of 115 L in 1983 (table 3.1). Another reason for the reduced fuel consumed per hectare has been the use of large farm equipment, which lessens production time so that less fuel is expended per hectare.

Fertilizers

Early agricultural systems, in which crops were cultured by hand, depended on the nutrients that accumulated in the soil and wild vegetation growing on the uncultivated land. For example, in early slash-and-burn agriculture the vegetation was cut and burned to release the nutrients to the soil. The land could then be tilled and planted to crops for 2 years, but usually the land had to lie fallow for about 20 years before sufficient nutrients again accumulated in the soil and vegetation.

Early U.S. agriculture was primarily organically based; that is, nutrients for crop production were provided primarily by livestock manure and green manures (legumes). Usually the farming system required 2 ha of land to produce 1 ha of a crop. For example, 1 hectare was planted to a legume such as clover or vetch, and the following year this legume was plowed under and planted to corn. This two-year rotation system provided an adequate amount of nitrogen for the corn crop each year; however, the soils were slowly depleted of phosphorus, potassium, and calcium because none was added to replace that used by the crops. Eventually fertilizers became available for use on cropland. By 1945 applications of fertilizers averaged 8 kg of nitrogen and phosphorus and 6 kg of potassium per hectare (fig. 3.2). Of these three soil nutrients, nitrogen application rates increased most

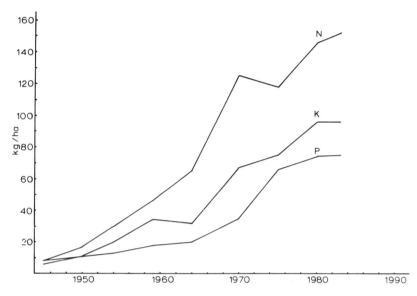

Fig. 3.2. Fertilizer—nitrogen (N), phosphorus (P), and potassium (K)—applied per acre in corn production.

dramatically, reaching a high of 152 kg/ha, or about a 20-fold increase from 1945 to 1983.

Note that the energy inputs for nitrogen alone in 1983 were greater than the total energy inputs for all inputs used in corn production in 1945 (table 3.2). Changes in nitrogen use are a striking example of how U.S. agricultural technologies have changed from 1945 to 1983.

During this 38-year period nitrogen production became 30 percent more efficient, but this did not compensate for the great increase in application rate (Smil et al., 1983), nor did this offset the use of larger, more complicated equipment (Dovring and McDowell, 1980).

Although the amounts of phosphorus and potassium applied per hectare rose significantly from 1945 to 1983, the increases were much less than those of nitrogen. Further, both potassium and phosphorus require significantly less energy per kilogram to produce (table 3.2) than does nitrogen, making their increased use less energy-intensive.

The quantities of lime applied to agricultural land also rose about threefold from 1945 to 1983. Because lime is the least energy-costly of the fertilizers used in corn production, its increased use is not a major consideration (table 3.2).

Pesticides

Little or no pesticide was used in corn production in 1945 (table 3.1). But with the development of the chlorinated insecticides, the quantity of insecticide applied to corn rose from 0.1 kg/ha in 1950 to 2 kg/ha by 1983. With the ban of some chlorinated insecticides in the early 1970s a gradual shift was made from the chlorinated insecticides to carbamate and phosphate insecticides. Along with the change in the chemical formulations of insecticides, the energy inputs per kilogram of pesticide produced rose about 50 percent. Production costs and increased application rate combined to increase nearly 30-fold the total inputs for chemical insect control from 1945 to 1983 (table 3.2).

Dramatic changes in herbicide use also occurred in corn production starting in 1950. The first herbicide used in corn production was 2,4-D, a phenoxy herbicide that was relatively efficient to produce in terms of energy input per kilogram. The newer triazines and other herbicides that were added during the 1960s and later were 50 percent more energy-costly to produce than 2,4-D (table 3.2). As a result of this and higher application rates, the total input for chemical weed control has increased 133-fold from 1950 to date. As with insecticides, not only did quantities of herbicides applied increase, but the newer herbicides required more energy for this production.

Irrigation

Over the decades the use of irrigation for corn production has steadily increased. In 1945 less than 1 percent of the corn acreage was irrigated at an average rate of 1.8 million L of water/ha (tables 3.1 and 3.2). This escalated rapidly until at present about 18 percent is irrigated at an increased rate of 2.2 million L of water/ha. Combined, this has led to nearly a 20-fold increase in energy expended for irrigation during the short 1945–83 period (table 3.2).

Harvesting and Drying

Newer methods of harvesting corn have increased energy expenditures. From early days corn was harvested on the cob and then put in corncribs to be dried by solar energy (sunlight and wind). New machinery has been designed to harvest corn grain directly in the field, and this technology is widely used today. Of course, when corn is harvested directly as grain, it contains 25 to 30 percent moisture and must be dried to a level of 13 to 15 percent moisture before being placed in storage. This process is energy-intensive, about 200 kcal of energy being required to dry 1 kg of corn (tables 3.1 and 3.2). Harvesting corn on the cob and allowing it to dry in corncribs uses about 33 percent less fossil energy than harvesting the corn as grain and then drying it using fossil energy (Hudson, 1984).

Electricity

Electricity is utilized for a variety of tasks on farms, including lighting buildings, moving goods in and out of storage, and running fans and other pieces of equipment. The energy input for electricity given in the calculations in table 3.2 includes the total energy required to produce the electricity. About 3 kcal of coal, for example, are required to produce 1 kcal of electricity (Pimentel et al., 1984).

Transport

Transportation costs have been relatively low in early days because only machinery, fuel, and nitrogen fertilizer transport costs were calculated; the transport costs for the other items were included in the products themselves. Even so, overall energy inputs for transportation more than doubled from 1945 to 1983, confirming the intensiveness of agricultural management over this short period (table 3.2).

Trends in Energy Use in U.S. Agriculture

Energy inputs in corn production have continued to increase from hand and draft-animal power systems to the highly mechanized systems of today (table 3.2). In 1700 only an estimated 716,000 kcal were used to produce 1 ha of corn by hand, whereas today in U.S. corn production 11 million kcal are employed for producing corn, a 15-fold increase in energy inputs. Yields during this period have grown 3.5-fold (tables 3.1 and 3.2).

The energy crisis of 1973 apparently has not slowed the growth of energy use in corn production (table 3.2). These data suggest that an estimated 33 percent rise in fossil-energy inputs in U.S. corn production occurred from 1975 to 1983. Grain yields during the same period also rose 26 percent (tables 3.1 and 3.2).

The 26 percent increase in yield associated with a 33 percent rise in energy use reflects a decreasing return per input kcal during the last 8 years. One improvement in energy use has been a reduction in the total liquid fuel used in farm machinery (tables 3.1 and 3.2). This reduction, as mentioned, was due in part to a change from gasoline to diesel fuel and to use of larger farm equipment. At the same time farmers may be taking better care of their expensive machinery.

Overall, fertilizers have been utilized more effectively. For example, more nitrogen fertilizer is being applied today during the growing season when the crops can use the nitrogen. During the early 1970s some nitrogen was applied to cornfields during the winter months, when farm labor and machinery were less busy. As a result, some nitrogen was wasted as it leached into the groundwater and streams. Nitrogen is a serious pollutant of both groundwater and streams in some parts of the nation today (CEQ, 1978; CF, 1984).

Energy output in the form of grain per kilocalorie of energy input has generally declined with time (table 3.2). For example, producing corn by hand provided 11 kcal of corn per kcal of input. For draft-animal power the ratio was 6:1, and for the highly mechanized system of 1983 the ratio was 2:4.

These analyses emphasize the efficiency of human power in crop production compared with the highly mechanized system of 1983 (table 3.2). It must be stressed however, that in terms of economic inputs and outputs the highly mechanized system is the most profitable. This is because, at present, 1 labor kcal is significantly more expensive in dollars than 1 kcal of fossil fuel.

Solar Energy

The energy inputs from the sun relate to the use of fossil-energy inputs in corn production. The solar energy reaching 1 hectare during the year averages about 14×10^9 kcal (Reifsnyder and Lull, 1965). During an average four-month summer growing season in the temperate region, nearly 7×10^9 kcal reaches a hectare. With a corn-grain yield of 6,500 kg/ha plus another 6,500 kg in stover biomass, the energy in the corn represents about 0.4 percent of the solar energy captured. For the corn grain the percentage is only 0.2 percent, or an input of about 56 kcal of solar energy per kcal of corn grain produced.

Note that the corn produced by hand labor is less than half as efficient in converting solar energy into corn grain as that produced by mechanization in 1983; about 0.1 percent of the solar energy is converted into corn grain in the hand-produced system listed in tables 3.1 and 3.2. Hence about 93 kcal of solar energy input are required to produce 1 kcal of corn in the hand-produced system.

In summary, the highly mechanized corn-production system was more efficient in collecting solar energy and converting it into corn grain than was the hand-produced system. This is true even when the fossil fuel inputs are included in the energy analysis.

Land Resources

Land containing fertile soils is essential for agriculture. In fertile soils the top 13 cm of soil consists of 1 to 4 percent living matter, and 1 to 6 percent of the soil is often nonliving organic matter, the remainder being minerals. At present agriculture and forestry, which cover nearly 70 percent of the U.S. area, use most of the best soils in the nation. Owing to the rapid spread of urbanization and highway networks, however, an area equivalent to Ohio and Pennsylvania was "blacktopped" over in the 30-year period between 1945 and 1978 (Pimentel et al., 1976). This rate of encroachment is now slowing primarily because of a stagnant economy, not because of sound land-management policies.

Almost half of the land that has been taken for housing and highways was the most productive U.S. agricultural land. Clearly this is a serious loss of natural resources. Prevention of such losses can be accomplished only by the adoption of sound land-use policies established by government.

Although a large segment of agricultural cropland has been lost forever because laws did not govern sound usage, the quality of a larger amount, about 40 million ha, has been degraded and lost because soil erosion has not been curtailed (Pimentel et al., 1976). Indeed, many feel that soil erosion is the most serious environmental problem in the nation (OTA, 1982; GAO, 1983). Specifically, soil erosion in U.S. agriculture averages about 18×10^3 kg/ha per year (Lee, 1984). This intense erosion has removed a large portion of the topsoil in the nation. Iowa, for example, recently reported that one-half of its topsoil has been lost during 100 years of farming (Risser, 1981).

The effect of soil loss on crop production is significant, especially when soil depth is 30 cm or less. For example, evidence suggests that corn yields are reduced on average about 4 percent (220 kg/ha) for each 2.5 cm of topsoil eroded (Pimentel et al., 1981). When the soil is from a soil base 20 to 30 cm deep, the loss can be offset by fertilizers and other energy inputs. In such areas about 1,000 kcal are required per kilogram of corn to maintain yields. Thus for 220 kg of a corn-yield reduction a total of 220,000 kcal (~ 22 L of oil equivalents) is required to maintain corn yield.

In a recent field study to simulate erosion, corn yields were reduced from 3.8×10^3 kg/ha to only 0.6×10^3 kg/ha when 18 cm of topsoil were scraped from shallow Andosol and Caliche soils of Mexico (Sancholuz, 1984). With naturally caused erosion the damage would be intensified because valuable lightweight organic matter accompanies this kind of erosion (Lal, 1984). Unfortunately, when topsoil is shallow (10 to 20 cm deep) and most of it is removed, then no amount of added fossil energy will offset the loss (Pimentel et al., 1986).

As mentioned, on some land where erosion has not been severe, increased use of fossil-based fertilizers has up to now helped maintain expected yields. The larger problem is that topsoil itself cannot be quickly replaced. Indeed, it will take centuries. To replace just 2.5 cm (1 in) of topsoil, 200 to 700 years must elapse (Pimentel et al., 1986). A moderate erosion rate of 17×10^3 kg/ha/yr removes 2.5 cm of soil in 20 years. On balance and for all practical considerations, erosion on our land must be prevented.

Solutions to the problem are complicated because a vast array of factors operate to intensify the soil-erosion problem. These include cost of economics, government land-use policies, machinery design and the use of mechanized equipment, social change in the structure of farms, increased agricultural and forestry specialization, and current cropping and harvesting practices in both agriculture and forestry (Pimentel et al., 1976). For example, during the past two to three decades family farms have occupied more acreage; thus each farmer must manage more acres by himself than ever before (USBC, 1983). These farmers feel forced to rely on larger and larger tractors and other kinds of farm machinery. This change in equipment use by farmers intensifies erosion because larger machinery requires planting larger fields to one crop in large monocultures, which increases soil erosion (OTA, 1982).

Furthermore, large tractors and harvesters make it difficult to employ contour planting for soil-erosion control (OTA, 1982) because they are hard to maneuver to follow the contours of croplands. This is also a problem on terraced land that was constructed two to three decades ago and is now too narrow for large machinery. Hence many terraces have been plowed up and destroyed, and the land they helped save is now exposed to erosion.

There are many ways to slow erosion. One new technology is "no-till" crop culture, which entails leaving crop residues and weeds on the soil surface, thus protecting the soil from rain and wind erosion. The technique is effective and may reduce erosion rates up to 100-fold (USDA, 1975). In addition to controlling erosion, no-till culture slows water runoff, thereby helping rainfall percolate into the soil for use by crops.

Accompanying the several advantages of no-till agriculture to conserve soil and water resources are several disadvantages. These include increased pest problems and the need for more seed than is usually required (CAST, 1984). These problems arise because the crop residues left on the surface harbor both insect and plant pathogen pests.

Soil that is tilled kills pests, including weeds, insects, and plant pathogens. With no-till these remain in the crop residues and weeds and cause problems in subsequent growing seasons. As a result two to four times more pesticides must be applied to control weeds, pest insects, plant pathogens, slugs, and mice (Pimentel et al., 1976). Most of the increased pesticide use is for chemical weed control.

In addition, the cool-wet conditions typical of early spring and covered fields often prevent seeds from germinating. To offset the poor germination and guarantee a good stand of a crop like corn, 10 to 25 percent more seed must be planted. Also, nitrogen fertilizer must be increased in no-till culture. Both pesticides and nitrogen fertilizers are energy-expensive, which means that no-till agriculture uses more energy than does conventional agriculture (CAST, 1984).

Water Resources

Water is the major limiting factor in U.S. agricultural production and, of course, for all living plants and animals everywhere (Pimentel et al., 1982). The total amount of water withdrawn from lakes, streams, and groundwater has increased steadily from 1900 to date and now amounts to about 7,200 L per day per person (Murray and Reeves, 1977). Agriculture alone consumes 83 percent of the fresh water that is withdrawn (fig. 3.3), and this consumption rate is expected to increase 17 percent from 1978 to 2000 (USWRC, 1979). The amount of groundwater being removed greatly exceeds replenishment rates throughout most of the nation, but especially in the West (Pimentel et al., 1982).

Crops require and transpire massive amounts of water each growing season. For example, a corn crop that produces 5,600 kg of grain per hectare will take up and transpire about 2.4 million L of water per hectare during the growing season (Penman, 1970). The source of this water is rainfall. In contrast, irrigated crop production requires large quantities of water to be pumped from depths of 1 to 200 m. For example, the production of 1 kg of certain food and fiber products under irrigation in California requires the following quantities of water: 1,400 L for corn, 1,900 L for

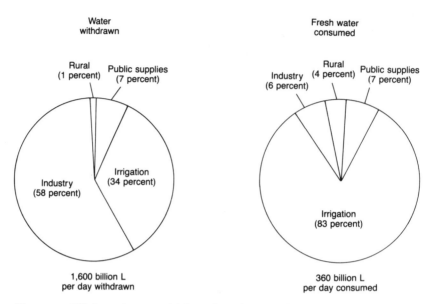

Fig. 3.3. Off-channel water withdrawals in the United States and the proportion of fresh water consumed in 1975. From Pimentel et al., 1982.

sugar (sugar beets), 4,700 L for rice, and 17,000 L for cotton (Ritschard and Tsao, 1978). Water needed to produce 1 kg of grain-fed meat ranges from about 4,200 to 8,300 L when the water input for irrigated grain is included.

When water must be used for irrigation, the fossil-energy inputs for production increase dramatically. For example, applying 60 cm of water for arid corn production increases the energy input about three times that for normal rain-fed corn production (Pimentel et al., 1983). Although fossil energy can be substituted for rainfall, assuming that stream or ground-water is available for pumping, it faces constraints of lower-cost fossil energy and available water resources to be mined.

Atmosphere

Pollution of the atmosphere occurs when fossil fuels are burned and pesticides are applied to crops. Each year billions of tonnes of air pollutants are by-products of fossil-fuel combustion. Four of the air pollutants, SO_2, CO, NO_2, and CO_2, total 4.4×10^{12} kg annually (Wark and Warner, 1976). Fortunately, natural biota act as a sink for some of these air pollutants in the environment. For example, each year microscopic plants remove about 2 percent (more than 700,000,000 kg) of SO_2 from the atmosphere. Although sulfur is an essential element for plant growth and some atmospheric SO_2 is utilized by plants, most vegetation is relatively sensitive even to low concentrations of SO_2 (Howell, 1976). SO_2 not removed by plants is involved in the formation of the air pollutant acid rain.

Annually in the United States an estimated 4.3×10^{12} kg of CO_2 are produced by fuel combustion and released into the atmosphere (Wark and Warner, 1976). Although CO_2 is essential for plant growth and development, vegetation is able to remove only 15 percent of all the CO_2 fuels (Woodwell, 1978). The remaining 85 percent is building up and contributing to the potential "greenhouse effect" of global warming (CEQ, 1980). The global warming is projected to have an overall detrimental effect on U.S. agriculture because the warming is expected to reduce rainfall and increase evaporation (Schneider and Londer, 1984).

A more significant effect today is air pollutants, which are destroying approximately $85.4 million worth of U.S. crops (SRI, 1971). The most severe damage is inflicted on crops grown close to some of the larger cities of the nation. The exact impact of acid rain on crops has yet to be determined.

Little or no data are available on fossil-energy use required to offset the complex effects of air pollution, including reduced rainfall, acid rain, SO_x, and other pollutants. Expanded water and land resources could also be employed for maintaining food supplies.

Biological Resources

Some 200,000 species of plants and animals exist in the nation, and they perform numerous essential functions (Pimentel et al., 1980a). Foremost, some plants and animals are used for human food and the forest products that provide the materials for shelter. In the United States just 10 species of crop plants and 4 species of livestock provide about 80 percent of the food consumed. Many species of natural biota are also essential in maintaining the quality and productivity of agricultural land. These help preserve genetic material for crop and livestock breeding; degrade the immense amounts of wastes produced; clean water and soil of pollutants; recycle vital chemical elements, including biotic nitrogen as fertilizer; and conserve soil and water with vegetation.

In addition, some species of natural biota "fix" nitrogen, thus providing vital nitrogen for crop production. Estimates are that about 14 billion kg of nitrogen are "fixed" biologically in the United States each year

(Delwiche, 1970). Considering that 11 billion kg of nitrogen fertilizer, worth about $4 billion, are also used each year, increased production and use of biological nitrogen would be of immense value. To do this, agronomists, microbiologists, horticulturists, and ecologists must join the investigation to integrate more legumes into the current cropping system and find ways to increase fixation by the microorganisms.

Yet another example of how natural biota perform valuable tasks is the role of insects, especially bees, in cross pollination, which makes possible the production of various fruit and vegetable crops. In this country the yields from some 90 crops, worth about $20 billion, are dependent on insect pollination. Improved pollination of crops would be possible if greater care were practiced in the use of pesticides and some modifications were made in the habitat surrounding crops (Pimentel et al., 1980b).

Improved biological fixation of nitrogen and pollination are only two ways agricultural production can be increased when natural biota are carefully managed. Because of the many vital tasks biota carry out, they are important factors to be considered in planning for an economical and sustainable agriculture.

Conclusion

The resources of land, water, air, biota, and energy are essential to all agricultural-production systems. Industrialized agriculture is now highly dependent on fossil energy, a nonrenewable resource. At present in the United States an estimated 1,100 L of oil equivalents are expended per hectare of agricultural land. About one-third of this energy is being used to reduce manpower inputs from about 1,200 h to only 10 h.

Of major concern is the substitution of fossil energy for the degradation of land, water, and biota resources so that high levels of crop production can be maintained and even augmented. The effect of this has been to mask the basic problem, that of resource degradation, and postpone the implementation of preventive measures. By not recognizing the problem now, the nation is slowly "mining" our valuable nonrenewable resources by substituting a nonrenewable resource, fossil energy. Few agricultural leaders or policymakers appear to be concerned about this degradation of the nation's agricultural resources, or even to be aware that, indeed, the integrity of our land, water, air, and natural biota are in danger.

In trying to assess which problem is the most serious, one is left with the opinion that each in its own way presents a formidable challenge. We can do something about the devastating loss of topsoil. While we cannot manage rainfall, we can be more careful in preventing runoff and conserving moisture. Conserving water and topsoil are complementary. Some slight progress is being made in curtailing air pollutants, but this too touches many sectors of society, and solutions are slow in coming.

What faces us today is the need to focus more research in all areas to support conservation of these vital resources. Combined with this, and just as important, is the task of convincing agriculturists, politicians, and the general public that the ability of agriculture to produce food and fiber in the future depends on their recognition of the problem and willingness to manage resources in a sustainable manner.

References

CAST [Council for Agricultural Science and Technology]. 1975. *Potential for energy conservation in agricultural production.* CAST Report no. 40. Ames, Iowa: CAST.

————. 1984. *Energy use and production in agriculture.* CAST Report no. 99. Ames, Iowa: CAST.

CEQ [Council on Environmental Quality]. 1978. *The ninth annual report of the Council on Environmental Quality.* Washington, D.C.: U.S. Government Printing Office.

————. 1980. *The global 2000 report to the president, Council on Environmental Quality: The Technical Report.* Vol. 2. Washington, D.C.: U.S. Government Printing Office.

Cervinka, V. 1980. Fuel and energy efficiency. In D. Pimentel, ed. *Handbook of energy utilization in agriculture,* pp. 15–21. Boca Raton, Fla.: CRC Press.

CF [Conservation Foundation]. 1984. *State of the environment: An assessment at mid-decade.* Washington, D.C.: Conservation Foundation.

Cook, E. 1976. *Man, energy, society.* San Francisco: Freeman.

Delwiche, C. C. 1970. The nitrogen cycle. *Scientific American* 223(3):137–58.

DOE [Department of Energy]. 1983. *1982 annual energy review.* Energy Information Administration, Office of Energy Markets and End Use. Washington, D.C.: U.S. Department of Energy.

Doering, O. C., III. 1980. Accounting for energy in farm machinery and buildings. In D. Pimentel, ed. *Handbook of energy utilization in agriculture,* pp. 9–14. Boca Raton, Fla.: CRC Press.

Dovring, F., and D. R. McDowell. 1980. *Energy used for fertilizers.* Department of Agricultural Economics Staff Paper 80 E-102. Urbana-Champaign: University of Illinois.

EOP [Executive Office of the President]. 1977. *The national energy plan.* Executive Office of the President, Energy Policy and Planning. Washington, D.C.: U.S. Government Printing Office.

FEA [Federal Energy Administration]. 1976. *Energy and U.S. agriculture: 1974 data base.* Vol. 2. Federal Energy Administration and the U.S. Department of Agriculture. Washington, D.C.: U.S. Government Printing Office.

GAO [General Accounting Office]. 1983. *Agriculture's soil conservation programs miss full potential in the fight against soil erosion.* Report to the Congress of the United States. RCED-84-48. Washington, D.C.: General Accounting Office.

Heichel, G. 1980. Energy attributable to seed. In D. Pimentel, ed. *Handbook of energy utilization in agriculture,* pp. 27–33. Boca Raton, Fla.: CRC Press.

Howell, R. 1976. Effects of air pollution on food production. In *Land use: Food and living,* pp. 61–67. Ankeny, Iowa: Soil Conservation Society.

Hudson, W. J. 1984. Biomass energy and food—conflicts? In D. Pimentel and C. W. Hall, eds. *Food and energy resources,* pp. 207–36. New York: Academic Press.

Lal, R. 1984. Productivity assessment of tropical soils and the effects of erosion. In F. R. Rijsberman and M. G. Wolman, eds. *Quantification of the Effect of Erosion on Soil Productivity in an International Context,* pp. 70–94. Netherlands: Delft Hydraulics Laboratory.

Lee, L. K. 1984. Land use and soil loss: A 1982 update. *Journal of Soil and Water Conservation.* 39:226–28.

Lewis, O. 1951. *Life in a Mexican village: Tepoztlan restudied.* Urbana: University of Illinois Press.

Lockeretz, W. 1980. Energy inputs for nitrogen, phosphorus, and potash fertilizers. In D. Pimentel, ed. *Handbook of energy utilization in agriculture,* pp. 23–24. Boca Raton, Fla.: CRC Press.

Murray, R. C., and E. B. Reeves. 1977. *Estimated use of water in the United States in 1975.* U.S. Geological Survey Circular 765. Washington, D.C.

OTA [Office of Technology Assessment]. 1982. *Impacts of technology on U.S. cropland and rangeland productivity.* Washington, D.C.: U.S. Government Printing Office.

Peart, R. M., R. Brook, and M. R. Okos. 1980. Energy requirements for various methods of crop drying. In D. Pimentel, ed. *Handbook of energy utilization in agriculture,* pp. 49–54. Boca Raton, Fla.: CRC Press.

Penman, H. L. 1970. The water cycle. *Scientific American* 223(3):99–108.

Pimentel, D. 1984a. Energy flow in the food system. In D. Pimentel and C. W. Hall, eds. *Food and energy resources,* pp. 1–24. New York: Academic Press.

———. 1984b. Food for people. In D. Pimentel and C. W. Hall, eds. *Food and energy resources,* pp. 65–90. New York: Academic Press.

———. 1984c. Energy flow in agroecosystems. In R. Lowrance, B. R. Stinner, and G. J. House, eds. *Agricultural ecosystems: Unifying concepts,* pp. 121–32. New York: Wiley.

———, and M. Burgess. 1980. Energy inputs in corn production. In D. Pimentel, eds. *Handbook of energy utilization in agriculture,* pp. 67–84. Boca Raton, Fla.: CRC Press.

———, and M. Pimentel. 1979. *Food, energy and society.* London: Edward Arnold.

———, J. Allen, A. Beers, L. Guinand, R. Linder, P. McLaughlin, B. Meer, D. Musonda, D. Perdue, S. Poisson, S. Siebert, K. Stoner, R. Salazar, and A. Hawkins. 1987. World agriculture and soil erosion. *Bioscience.* 37:277–83.

————, D. Andow, R. Dyson-Hudson, D. Gallahan, S. Jacobson, M. Irish, S. Kroop, A. Moss, I. Schreiner, M. Shepard, T. Thompson, and B. Vinzant. 1980. Environmental and social costs of pesticides: A preliminary assessment. *Oikos* 34:127–40.

————, G. Berardi, and S. Fast. 1983. Energy efficiency of farming systems: Organic and conventional agriculture. *Agricultural Ecosystems and Environment* 9:359–72.

————, S. Fast, W. L. Chao, E. Stuart, J. Dintzis, G. Einbender, W. Schlappi, D. Andow, and K. Broderick. 1982. Water resources in food and energy production. *Bioscience* 32:861–67.

————, E. Garnick, A. Berkowitz, S. Jacobson, S. Napolitano, P. Black, S. Valdes-Cogliano, B. Vinzant, E. Hudes, and S. Littman. 1980. Environmental quality and natural biota. *Bioscience* 30:750–55.

————, L. E. Hurd, A. C. Bellotti, M. J. Forster, I. N. Oka, O. D. Sholes, and R. J. Whitman. 1973. Food production and the energy crisis. *Science* 182:443–49.

————, L. Levitan, J. Heinze, M. Loehr, W. Naegeli, J. Bakker, J. Eder, B. Modelski, and M. Morrow. 1984. Solar energy, land and biota. *Sun World* 8:70–73, 93–95.

————, M. A. Moran, S. Fast, G. Weber, R. Bukantis, L. Balliett, P. Boveng, C. Cleveland, S. Hindman, and M. Young. 1981. Biomass energy from crop and forest residues. *Science* 212:1110–15.

————, E. C. Terhune, R. Dyson-Hudson, S. Rochereau, R. Samis, E. Smith, D. Denman, D. Reifschneider, and M. Shepard. 1976. Land degradation: Effects on food and energy resources. *Science* 194:149–55.

————, ed. 1980. *Handbook of energy utilization in agriculture.* Boca Raton, Fla.: CRC Press.

Reifsnyder, W. E., and H. W. Lull. 1965. *Radiant energy in relation to forests.* Technical Bulletin no. 1344, U.S. Department of Agriculture, Forest Service.

Risser, J. 1981. A renewed threat of soil erosion: It's worse than the dust bowl. *Smithsonian* 11:121–31.

Ritschard, R. L., and K. Tsao. 1978. *Energy and water use in irrigated agriculture during drought conditions.* U.S. DOE LBL-7866. Lawrence Berkeley Laboratory. Berkeley: University of California.

Sancholuz, L. 1984. Land degradation in Mexican maize fields. Ph.D. thesis, University of British Columbia.

Schneider, S. H., and R. Londer. 1984. *The coevolution of climate and life.* San Francisco: Sierra Club Books.

Smil, V., P. Nachman, and T. V. Long II. 1983. *Energy analysis and agriculture.* Boulder, Colo.: Westview Press.

SRI [Stanford Research Institute]. 1971. *Economic impact of air pollutants on plants in the United States.* Project LSD-1056. Menlo Park, Calif.: Stanford Research Institute.

Terhune, E. C. 1980. Energy used in the United States for agricultural liming materials. In D. Pimentel, ed. *Handbook of energy utilization in agriculture,* pp. 25–26. Boca Raton, Fla.: CRC Press.

USBC [U.S. Bureau of the Census]. 1952. *Census of agriculture, 1950.* Vol. 3. Washington, D.C.: U.S. Government Printing Office.

———. 1962. *Census of agriculture, 1959.* Vol. 3. Washington, D.C.: U.S. Government Printing Office.

———. 1967. *Census of agriculture, 1964.* Vol. 2. Washington, D.C.: U.S. Government Printing Office.

———. 1973. *Census of agriculture, 1969.* Vol. 4. Washington, D.C.: U.S. Government Printing Office.

———. 1983. *Statistical abstract of the United States, 1983.* 104th ed. Washington, D.C.: U.S. Government Printing Office.

USDA [U.S. Department of Agriculture]. 1954. *Changes in farm production and efficiency.* Washington, D.C.: Agricultural Research Service.

———. 1970. *Agricultural statistics, 1970.* Washington, D.C.: U.S. Government Printing Office.

———. 1975. *Minimum tillage: A preliminary technology assessment.* Office of Planning and Evaluation. Washington, D.C.: USDA.

———. 1976. *Agricultural statistics, 1976.* Washington, D.C.: U.S. Government Printing Office.

———. 1979. *1980 fertilizer situation.* Economic Statistics Cooperative Service FS-10. Washington, D.C.: USDA.

———. 1981. *Agricultural statistics, 1981.* Washington, D.C.: U.S. Government Printing Office.

———. 1982a. *Agricultural statistics, 1982.* Washington, D.C.: U.S. Government Printing Office.

———. 1982b. *Fertilizer: Outlook and Situation.* Economic Research Service FS-13. Washington, D.C.: USDA.

USWRC [U.S. Water Resources Council]. 1979. *The nation's water resources, 1975–2000.* Vols. 1–4. Second National Water Assessment. Washington, D.C.: U.S. Government Printing Office.

Wark, K., and C. F. Warner. 1976. *Air pollution.* New York: IEP-Dun-Donnelley.

Wen, Dazhong, and D. Pimentel. 1984. Energy inputs in agricultural systems of China. *Agricultural Ecosystems and the Environment* 11:29–35.

Woodwell, G. M. 1978. The carbon dioxide question. *Scientific American* 238(1): 34–43.

World Bank. 1984. *World development report, 1984.* New York: Oxford University Press.

ANNE H. EHRLICH

4.
Development and Agriculture

UNTIL ABOUT a decade ago, the topics development and agriculture were seldom linked in the voluminous literature on the Third World, and that undoubtedly has contributed to the problems now emerging in many poor countries. The industrialized nations never overlooked the importance of agriculture, even after the industrial sectors came to dominate their economies in terms of investment, employment, and income. In many poor countries, governments have established economic policies that favor the urban poor and offer few incentives or support for farmers to produce more food. The lack of communications in rural areas hinders the distribution of seeds, fertilizers, and other materials to farmers and the transport of farm products to markets.

But neglect of the agricultural sector is only one factor that has hastened the appearance of widespread food shortages in developing nations. Attempts to modernize farm practices in poor countries have not always been successful for a variety of reasons. The application of Temperate Zone farming technologies in biologically inappropriate settings such as the humid tropics or fragile arid ecosystems has often been a recipe for failure. In some regions, overcultivation and overgrazing have led to desertification and losses of productivity. And until recently, little effort has been put into improving crops grown in tropical areas. Above all, rapid population growth in developing nations has eaten away any gains in food production and in some regions has even outstripped them.

The enormous tragedy taking place today in Africa is still often at-

I wish to thank Paul Ehrlich, Mary Ellen and John Harte, Cheryl and John Holdren, Richard Holm, and Stephen Schneider for reading and commenting on the manuscript for this chapter. The research for this chapter was supported by a grant from the Koret Foundation.

tributed to an "act of God," although the factors that created it are largely traceable to acts of human beings. While bad luck with the weather evidently has played a part (Kerr, 1985), it is also clear that human actions have gravely intensified the consequences (Walsh, 1984). Why is virtually an entire continent undergoing a catastrophic drought, threatening tens of millions of people with starvation? Why does the outside world persist in viewing this phenomenon as a one-time fluke that can be cured by an infusion of donated food and will never recur? That the crisis began almost two decades ago and never really went away is lost on the public; even mass starvation loses its fascination for the press when it continues year after year.

Much of the agony of Africa that has been displayed on television in the industrialized world could have been prevented, although now it is too late to avert the present disaster and, quite likely, even worse ones in the future. At best, the harshest effects can be mitigated by massive relief efforts, and further damage to the region's life-support systems can be minimized by relocating many of the people and providing substantial assistance to those who stay. But restoration of the land in the most degraded areas to a condition in which it could support a human population even as large as that of 10 years ago could take many decades, if not centuries, of enormous effort (Brown and Wolf, 1984; Walsh, 1984).

A "Cassandra" could point to the lessons to be learned from this tragedy, but would anyone listen? Can potential preventive measures be applied elsewhere, before other regions of the planet are overtaken by a similar fate?

Population and Development

At the heart of the development problem is the population dilemma. Rapid population growth quickly absorbs any gains made in economic development. Resources must be poured into an economy just to maintain the same level of essential services for a rapidly expanding population—to provide more food; more medical and sanitation services; more schools, houses, roads, and hospitals; more fuel; more supplies of every kind for more and more people. Whatever is left over can be used to improve conditions for the people.

But in Africa, where populations have been growing by 2.5 to 4 percent a year, for the past decade and a half little or nothing has been left over. In many countries, the standard of living has slid inexorably downward (World Bank, 1984a, 1984b, 1985; Goliber, 1985). Just one component of living standards, food supplies per person, declined by 10 percent in sub-Saharan Africa between 1972 and 1982; since then they have plummeted by another 10 percent or more (Brown and Wolf, 1984; Brown et al., 1985 and 1986; Goliber, 1985; Sai, 1984). The shortfall has had to be made up — to the extent that it has been made up — by importing food, which those faltering economies can ill afford, or by food donated by the rich countries.

Some African leaders still cling to the illusion that their nations can support many times the populations they now have. Resource experts have assured them that their currently "underexploited lands" can be turned to agricultural production with an abundance rivaling Iowa's (Johnson, 1984), although anything of the sort has yet to be demonstrated even with well-supported local pilot projects. Thus until the current crisis began, African leaders remained complacent about their nations' unprecedented rates of population growth. Most countries have established family-planning programs, but many of those offer birth-control services only for health and welfare reasons and are poorly supported at best by their governments. Often the family-planning services are available only in major cities and thus are inaccessible to more than two-thirds of the people.

Population Momentum

Sub-Saharan Africa's rapid population growth and deepening poverty are only two of the starkest examples of what could become a global phenomenon. Demographers project continued growth of the world population for a century or more because of the momentum built into age compositions (Ehrlich et al., 1977), especially in developing nations. The world population is now increasing by an average of about 1.7 percent a year and is projected to expand from about 5 billion today to over 10 billion before growth can be ended by humane means — that is, through limitation of births (World Bank, 1984a; Frejka, 1981).

In Africa, with rates of natural increase averaging nearly 3 percent a year (Populations Reference Bureau, 1985) and fertility rates in some countries still rising, the outlook is for a tripling or even quadrupling of most populations before growth could be ended through birth control (assuming no rise in death rates). Rates of population growth are nearly as high in the developing nations of Latin America and Asia (averaging 2.4 and 2.1 percent, respectively, excluding China), and their gross national products (GNPs) and food production are not expanding much faster. Significant declines in birthrates have occurred in some countries, but depressingly little change has been seen in most of them.

Family-planning programs can facilitate the reduction of birthrates, but other aspects of development seem to be crucial to their success. The availability of contraceptive services does not ensure their use; people first must want smaller families. The elements of development that experience has shown to foster such desires include improvements in health, nutrition, and sanitation, which lead to lower infant mortalities and longer life expectancies, and education, especially of women (Birdsall, 1980; Cutright, 1983). In general, birthrates have fallen in societies that have fulfilled these conditions and have strong family-planning programs, independent of other measures of development, such as increases in per capita GNP. Where these conditions have not been met, birthrates have remained high.

The Chinese Phenomenon

The most important family-planning success story has been that of the People's Republic of China, which has reduced its rate of natural increase to about 1 percent from a high of over 3 percent in the early 1960s (U.S. Bureau of the Census, 1984; Zheng, Jian, et al., 1981). Besides having an extremely strong family-planning apparatus backed by other policies to encourage small families, China has met the primary social prerequisites for success: the infant mortality rate is approaching those in developed nations, average life expectancy is over 65 years and rising, basic health care is available to the entire population, and children of both sexes are almost universally educated.

But China is an exceptional case in other respects as well. Beyond recognizing that rapid population growth was hindering progress in development, China's leaders took a cold, hard look at their nation's natural resources and concluded that no more than 650 to 700 million people could be supported on a long-term sustainable basis at a desirable standard of living. As the population passed the 1 billion mark, the Chinese government set a goal not only of ending population growth as soon as possible but of *reducing* the population to the sustainable level. To accomplish this goal, the famous "one-child family" policy was launched. Despite some problems of public acceptance and administrative abuses that have attended the program, it seems likely that on the whole it will avert more human suffering than it causes.

No other nation, rich or poor, has made such an assessment of its resource base. Nor has any other set a goal of *reducing* its population size. Indeed, most industrialized nations have yet to formulate any population policies apart from regulating immigration. The populations of nearly all the developed nations are growing relatively slowly—less than 1 percent per year—and a few are very slowly shrinking. Yet, with less than one-fourth of the world's people, they account for the vast bulk of global resource consumption and much more than their share of environmental deterioration (Ehrlich et al., 1977).

The World Food Situation

Among the resources dominated by the rich countries are agricultural resources. The most favorable ratios of people to arable land are found in developed regions (table 4.1), as are most of the surplus grain production, the bulk of fisheries yields and supplies of meat, fertilizers, pesticides, farm machinery, and so forth (U.S. Department of Agriculture, 1984a; World Bank, 1982). While the disparities in the distribution of these resources between rich and poor nations are less extreme than those of mineral resources, they are perhaps more closely connected to the real wealth of nations and certainly to the quality of life.

Hunger and Malnutrition

Chronic hunger, if not starvation, is an accompaniment of life throughout the developing world (and is not unknown in some rich countries). In most low-income and many middle-income nations, food supplies are at or below the minimum required to feed the population as measured in calories available per capita, not allowing for uneven distribution (FAO, 1984). But food is never evenly distributed. In many poor countries, distribution is highly unequal; the wealthiest classes may have access to twice as many calories per person per day as the poorest groups. Among the poor, infants and small children are most vulnerable to inadequate diets and are most likely to have them.

The United Nations Food and Agriculture Organization (FAO) has very conservatively estimated that, worldwide, perhaps a half billion people — mostly children — are seriously undernourished (FAO, 1981); in 1980 the World Bank estimated that nearly 800 million people worldwide were in "absolute poverty," defined simply as being "too poor to buy food" (Birdsall, 1980). UNICEF maintains that 15 million children die each year of malnutrition and other poverty-related causes and that one of every four children in the developing world is suffering from "invisible malnutrition," which can appreciably handicap growth and learning (UNICEF, 1982). The calamity now unfolding in Africa has undoubtedly swelled the numbers of the world's malnourished, and their condition is painfully visible.

In a global context, however, the numbers of African famine victims are small — only a few million. Worldwide, the *proportion* of hungry people in the world has changed little in the last few decades, although their

Table 4.1. Per Capita Cropland, Hectares

Region	1955	1980
Australia and New Zealand	2.105	2.531
Canada	2.548	1.853
USSR	1.138	0.874
United States	1.132	0.837
South America	0.534	0.521
Sub-Saharan Africa	0.578	0.446
Eastern Europe	0.500	0.398
North Africa and Middle East	0.711	0.423
Central America and Caribbean	0.496	0.302
Western Europe	0.316	0.248
South Asia	0.342	0.227
Southeast Asia	0.253	0.196
China	0.164	0.102
Other East Asia	0.085	0.060
World	0.453	0.318

SOURCE: Urban and Volrath, 1984.

absolute *numbers* have steadily risen in tandem with population growth. But does this prevalence of hunger arise from real resource constraints? Or is it, as some claim (Simon and Kahn, 1984), just the result of inhumane and inequitable policies? Could better distribution of resources—including food itself—solve the problem?

Despite the persistence of the poor and hungry underclass, population growth has been accommodated for many decades by steadily rising food production, and the world trade network can ship emergency food supplies to famine areas quickly and efficiently. Cornucopian optimists assume that the historic trend of rising food production will continue into the indefinite future and that adjustments in economic policies will eventually solve the problems of the destitute millions (Johnson, 1984). But the evidence is mounting that, although changes in policies could do much to alleviate present problems and prevent worse to come, real constraints to raising food production and expanding the human resource base do exist and are increasingly asserting themselves.

Trends in Food Production

Since World War II, global population growth has been outpaced by increases in world food production, usually measured by the harvests of cereal grains—wheat, rice, and "coarse grains" (a category including maize, sorghum, millet, and rye). Cereals form the main feeding base of humanity and comprise about two-thirds of the world's food harvest by weight.

Nearly one-third of the global grain harvest, however, is fed to livestock rather than to people. Because energy is lost in each upward step of any biological food chain, several times more grain is needed to deliver an equal number of calories in meat or dairy products than that obtained when the grain is directly consumed by human beings (Ehrlich et al., 1977). In industrialized nations, two-thirds or more of the grain supply is used as feed, while in developing nations the grain fed to livestock is usually a very small fraction of that consumed.

The generally continuous upward trend of global grain production in past decades has concealed a number of significant shifts in the world food situation. One of the most important changes has been a slackening in the rate of increase in food production since the 1950s. The 1970s and early 1980s brought not only drops in some years of production *per capita* but even absolute declines of 2 percent or more in some years, which had not previously been experienced. Meanwhile, the population inexorably climbed by nearly 2 percent every year.

In 1983 global grain production dropped by 6 percent. Most of the loss occurred in the United States corn crop, which sizzled under temperatures over 100° F for several weeks that summer. This rather substantial drop in the grain harvest passed largely unnoticed by the public because (1) it followed a year of bumper harvests, (2) production was high in other regions, (3) corn is used mainly for livestock feed, and (4) demand for feed grains on the world market had been sharply reduced by the recession. Moreover, declines in feed supplies generally result in higher meat prices rather than food shortages.

The overall loss of momentum in food-production increases is even more clearly revealed by the trend in worldwide grain production *per person.* Before 1971 per capita grain production increased steadily each year, but since then it has fluctuated between averages of 304 kg (in 1972) and 348 kg (in 1978) per person each year, only twice exceeding 335 kg (Brown et al., 1984; USDA, 1984b) until 1984 and 1985 (USDA, 1986), when that level was reached again. The slowdown in food-production increases would have been more noticeable if the rate of global population growth had not fallen from 2.2 percent a year to 1.7 percent a year between 1965 and 1984 (assuming that the trend in food production was not significantly affected by the slower population growth).

The Trade Gap

The worldwide averages of grain production conceal great differences among regions in relative food production. Although in the last few decades, many developing countries have increased their harvests more rapidly than have the developed nations, their much faster population growth has meant little or no gain in food production per person. In some regions, especially in sub-Saharan Africa, population growth has outstripped food production. The result has been a remarkable change in world food trade patterns.

Before 1940, Europe was the only significant food-importing region in the world; all others were net exporters. By the late 1970s, only a handful of nations were exporting grains: the United States (the source of over half of all exported grain), Canada, Australia, Argentina, Thailand, and the European Common Market (USDA, 1984b, 1986). More than 100 nations around the world now depend to some degree on grain imports to feed their populations. A dozen or more nations import more than half of their food; several others soon will.

During the 1970s, an increasing fraction of global grain production was traded on the world market, and in some years the fraction approached 20 percent. An even faster-growing share of the grain trade has been going to developing nations, which in earlier decades were at least self-sufficient in cereals. The recession of the early 1980s and the rising debt burdens of developing countries dampened the trend somewhat, possibly increasing the proportion of hungry people in the poorest classes. Even so, by 1986 the developing nations' share of world grain imports had risen to 75 percent (USDA, 1986), and the outlook was for increasing dependency on imports to meet rising food needs (FAO, 1981).

The Yield Gap

A widening discrepancy in average yields (harvest per hectare) of crops between industrialized and less-developed countries has contributed to the growing differences between the two groups of nations in per capita food supplies. In the late 1960s and 1970s average yields rose impressively in many developing countries because of increasing use of higher-yielding varieties of crops—mainly wheat and rice—together with fertilizers and other modern inputs—the so-called Green Revolution. But the adoption in poor countries of high-yield strains and fertilizers has lagged well behind that of developed countries, especially since the price of petroleum (on which high-yield technology is heavily dependent) quadrupled in 1974 and doubled again in 1979.

In the mid-1970s, reflecting differences in the use of modern technology, especially fertilizer use, average yields of wheat in developed nations were 50 percent higher than those in developing countries and those of rice and maize were nearly three times higher (FAO, 1981). Average grain yields in Africa, where fertilizer use is still very limited, are only about a third as high as those in North America. In some of the poorest countries, yields are smaller than those in the United States by factors of five or six (FAO, 1981; World Bank, 1984a; USDA, 1985).

Applying fertilizers to crop varieties that are responsive to them at first produces dramatic increases in yields, but further additions of fertilizer bring diminishing returns. Fertilizing in industrialized nations has now nearly reached saturation; additional applications produce little or no increase in yields. Fertilizer use has also increased enough in developing regions for the diminishing returns to be noticeable in global grain-production figures. Around 1980, for each ton of fertilizer added per hectare, global average grain yields rose less than 6 tons, whereas in the 1950s they had risen by almost 12 tons (Brown et al., 1984).

The diminishing returns from increased rates of fertilizer use have also doubtless been a factor in the slackening rate of growth in global food production. Only in some of the poorest nations are fertilizing levels still so low that dramatic increases in yields may yet be obtained by that means. Between 1950 and 1985, an 8-fold increase in worldwide fertilizer use contributed to a 2.5-fold rise in world grain production. That record is not likely to be duplicated in the next 35 years. Even if another equivalent boost in crop yields were in the cards, the higher costs of fossil fuels—which are essential for manufacturing fertilizers—would preclude another 8-fold increase in fertilizer production. Indeed, even farmers in rich countries have been forced by rising costs to cut back their fertilizer applications and accept slightly lower yields.

Distribution and Cash Crops

The argument has been raised (e.g., Lappé and Collins, 1977) that a major reason for the growing gap between industrial and developing countries in food production is exploitation of the poor countries by the rich ones. Farmers in poor countries are encouraged to produce crops for export to rich nations, to the detriment of food production for the local population. Cash crops, such as coffee, tea, cocoa, hemp, sugar, tropical fruits, and vegetables, are usually more profitable to farmers than are subsistence crops for the local market. Moreover, agricultural policies of developing nations often favor production of cash crops by giving farmers who grow them preferential access to credit, fertilizers, and other inputs (Brown et al., 1984, 1985).

There is considerable truth to this argument, and there undoubtedly have been cases in which investors from rich countries have grossly exploited the land and the people of developing nations. The destruction of forests in Central America to graze cattle to produce cheap hamburgers for fast-food chains is one well-known example (Ehrlich and Ehrlich, 1981). Europeans have attempted similar schemes in Africa. In Mexico and Central America, the production of fruits and vegetables for export to the United States, using dangerous pesticides that are banned or closely regulated in the United States, is another (Lappé and Collins, 1977; Ehrlich et al., 1979). The result of these practices has often been environmental deterioration, degradation of the land, and impoverishment of the local farmers and workers, after which the investors reinvest in other enterprises. People in rich countries thus profit by damaging the resources of poor countries.

But most of the developing nations have little choice but to export farm products; they have no petroleum, copper, or other valuable raw materials to trade for oil, grain, fertilizers, or manufactured goods that they cannot make for themselves. In the last decade, largely because of higher oil prices, their negative trade balances and mounting debts have made the need to export all the more urgent. Growing and exporting cash crops is not necessarily destructive; it does allow importation of needed goods. When traded for other agricultural products, cash crops can make available a more varied choice of foods. Abuses occur when workers and farmers are exploited and land-use decisions are unwise; these problems can be avoided by a vigilant government.

While cash crops undoubtedly displace subsistence crops wherever they are grown, it seems unlikely that they are the main cause of food-production shortfalls in most developing nations. To the extent that cash-crop farmers are the primary recipients of credit and inputs while subsistence farmers are denied them, domestic food production certainly suffers. The same is true when cash crops are allocated the best, most productive land. But these again are matters of national policy which can (and should) be corrected.

The Underpinnings

Even though many developing countries have been encountering difficulty in increasing their food production more rapidly than their populations are expanding, this does not mean that crop yields in poor countries cannot still be considerably raised. Obviously in many countries opportunities remain for modernizing agriculture on suitable croplands. But how much opportunity remains for expanding world food production, especially in less-developed regions, where 90 percent of future population growth is projected to occur?

Answering this question requires an assessment of the natural resources that underlie all agricultural systems: the land base, soils, dependable water sources, and so forth. Unfortunately, there are limits to the availability of these resources, and all are under increasing pressure for competing uses. Even more to the point, in some cases intrinsically renewable resources such as soil and fresh water are being treated as if they were nonrenewable.

Land

As populations continue to increase, so does the number of people that must be supported by the food produced from each hectare of arable land. New land is being added to the global cropland base, but at a far slower rate—roughly 0.2 percent a year—than that of population growth. Since the mid-1950s, the average number of people per hectare of arable land worldwide has risen by about 30 percent (Urban and Volrath, 1984). Meanwhile, the rate of expansion of cropland has steadily diminished for several decades as fewer and fewer suitable areas remained available for conversion. Another reason for the slowing of cropland expansion is that development costs have risen because the remaining new land is less accessible and is generally inferior in quality to that already under cultivation.

Today, about 11 percent of Earth's ice-free land surface is under crops, about 24 percent is pasture, and over 30 percent is forest or woodland (FAO, 1985). All of the cropland and pasture and much of the forest—nearly two-thirds of the planet's land surface—are now exploited in one degree or another by human beings. Table 4.2 shows the patterns of world land use and changes between 1966 and 1980. The category "other" includes urban and other developed land (about 1 to 2 percent), deserts, mountaintops, and other biologically unproductive areas.

Land put into crops must, of course, be removed from some other category—usually pasture or forest. Additions to cropland (about a 5 percent net increase between 1966 and 1980) have been achieved by claiming land from pasture and forest; most of that taken from pasture was compensated by converting forest to pasture. Meanwhile, sizable amounts of land, often of high quality, have been taken out of agricultural production for various kinds of development, such as urban expansion, highways, airports, energy development, and reservoirs. Large tracts of land also have been lost to agriculture as a result of deterioration (see below).

While a quantity of land at least equal to the present cropland base is considered *potentially* arable, in practical terms little new land is likely to be cultivated in the foreseeable future. Most responsible estimates of the probable net increase in the world cropland base in the last two decades of the twentieth century are 5 percent or less (Urban and Volrath,

Table 4.2. World Land-Use Patterns

Land Use	Million Hectares		Percent	
	1966	1980	. 1966	1980
Cropland	1,381	1,452	10.6	11.1
Permanent pasture	3,122	3,117	23.9	23.8
Forests and woodland	4,236	4,093	32.4	31.3
Other land	4,336	4,413	33.1	33.8
Total	13,075	13,075	100.0	100.0

SOURCE: Urban and Volrath in USDA, 1984a.

1984). In recent decades, as the rate of cropland expansion has fallen, a rising proportion of the gains in food production has come from increasing yields on already cultivated land.

The human population is projected to expand by over 1.5 billion— more than one-third—between 1980 and 2000 (U.S. Bureau of the Census, 1984). Because of the difficulties and costs of opening new land and the inferior quality of what remains, the overwhelming bulk of increases in food production needed to feed those additional people must be gained by further increasing yields on the existing cropland base. Yet, while opportunities to open new land are becoming fewer, the quality of much of the land already under cultivation has been declining as well.

Soil

A substantial portion of the agricultural land of the world has undergone deterioration owing to soil erosion, desertification, or to salinization or waterlogging of irrigated tracts. Some land has deteriorated to the point where it is no longer economically productive and has been taken out of production (Dregne, 1982; Brown and Wolf, 1984).

Soil specialist Harold Dregne, of Texas Tech University, estimates (1982) that severe or very severe desertification has occurred on significant portions of agricultural land on all the continents. Dregne broadly defines desertification as "deterioration of terrestrial ecosystems under the impact of man," thus applying the term to degradation of land in humid areas as well as in arid or semiarid ones. Severely desertified land is characterized as in "poor range condition" with heavily eroded soil and/or with crop yields reduced by 50 percent or more. Under very severely desertified conditions, rangeland is essentially denuded of vegetation, and cropland yields are reduced by over 90 percent.

According to Dregne's evaluation, moderate desertification, in which crop yields have been reduced by 10 to 50 percent, is exceedingly widespread. Over half the agricultural land in Australia and 40 percent of that in Africa and Asia has been moderately or severely desertified, as has 30 percent of the agricultural land in North and Central America and slightly more in Europe. Only South America has escaped with less than 30 percent of its agricultural land significantly damaged. Overall, nearly 40 percent of the world's agricultural lands have been moderately desertified or worse.

While desertification has several manifestations, soil erosion is a major one. Soil is a complex material composed of crumbled rock, decomposing organic matter, and myriad tiny organisms — an intricate ecosystem in itself. Fertile soil is built up over centuries by the organisms that live (and die and decompose) on the land. In a natural grass or forest ecosystem, soil is normally lost through erosion at extremely slow rates, which are compensated by the almost equally slow processes of replenishment (Ehrlich et al., 1977; Brown and Wolf, 1984). Cultivated land, on the other hand, can erode much more rapidly, especially on slopes or in areas exposed to high winds. When appropriately treated, with frequent rotation of crops, fertilization with manure, crop residues, and other organic materials, and protection against erosion, soil can even be improved in quality and depth.

Unfortunately, a great deal of today's farmland is not being treated appropriately, and soil erosion has become virtually a worldwide epidemic. The losses of topsoil to wind and water in the United States are the best-documented case. Cropland erosion in the United States above the "tolerance levels" (rates that would eventually result in declines in productivity) amounted to 1.7 billion tons in 1982, according to a detailed survey by the U.S. Soil Conservation Service (Brown and Wolf, 1984). Equally or more horrendous losses are estimated to be occurring in the Soviet Union, China, India, and a host of smaller countries.

Brown and Wolf have estimated the total annual worldwide rate of soil erosion occurring *above the tolerance levels* (which may be overgenerous, in that tolerance levels are generally higher than the actual rates of replenishment). They concluded that some 25 billion tons of soil are lost each year, over half the losses occurring in the four nations named above. Other countries known to have suffered especially severe erosion are Ethiopia, Bolivia, Peru, Nepal, Pakistan, Indonesia, Iran, and South Africa.

Sooner or later, losses of topsoil lead to declines in productivity, although increased fertilizer applications can mask the effects until the damage is fairly far advanced. All things being equal, however, corn and wheat yields fall roughly 6 percent for each inch lost from topsoil of average quality and depth (Brown and Wolf, 1984). Information from tropical areas is scanty, but indications are that productivity may fall even faster as thin, fragile tropical topsoils are depleted.

Once soils have been seriously depleted by erosion, their fertility is, for practical purposes, lost forever. Restoration of damaged soils is possible, but it requires decades, even centuries, of intensive effort. Far less costly in time and resources is protecting the soil in the first place. But too often economic pressures make even the relatively minor costs of protecting soil too high. This is the case in the United States, a nation that can surely "afford" the costs of soil conservation. In developing countries, farmers have little or no support from their governments to take protective measures and no incentive to do it on their own. The daily need to feed their families takes precedence over the long-term need to protect topsoil.

Water

An agricultural resource that has long been taken for granted is fresh water. One effective way to increase crop yields on good land is to increase the availability or the dependability of water, usually through irrigation. Water for irrigation can be provided from surface supplies, such as rivers or reservoirs created by dams; another source is water pumped from underground aquifers (Ehrlich et al., 1977; Ambroggi, 1980; Postel, 1984). By the mid-1980s, some 17 percent of the world's cropland was irrigated. Because the dependability of water is so important, irrigated land is considerably more productive than most other cropland; about a third of the world's crops are grown on irrigated land.

Expanding the amount of cropland under irrigation is an obvious way to increase food production. Unfortunately, irrigation is often a temporary measure. The buildup of salts in irrigated soils is a common cause of desertification. On poorly drained land, moreover, the water table may rise until the crop roots are essentially drowned (waterlogged). Either situation can be prevented or postponed for a long time by relatively sophisticated irrigation methods that apply small amounts of water directly to individual crop plants; but high installation costs are usually an effective barrier to using them.

Furthermore, reservoirs sooner or later silt up, and as deforestation and overgrazing in watersheds continue unabated, the rate of silt-up accelerates. When it was built, the Aswan High Dam of Egypt, completed in the mid-1970s, was expected to operate for at least a century. But accelerating deforestation and desertification in the watershed of the Nile have led to rapid siltation of the reservoir and reduced the expected useful life of the dam to less than 50 years.

Similarly, irrigation by pumping groundwater is a short-term enterprise if the rate of withdrawal exceeds the rate of natural recharge. Aquifers contain vast quantities of water, far more than falls annually on the surface as rain or snow. But the water stored underground has accumulated over geologic ages and is recharged very slowly if at all, and only a small fraction of it is economically accessible. When groundwater withdrawals exceed the rate of recharge, as they do in many areas around the world, from the richest to the poorest nations, the resource in effect is being "mined"—treated as a nonrenewable resource.

Some heavily exploited aquifers have been depleted to the point that pumping is no longer economically feasible, forcing abandonment of irrigation. Several aquifers in the United States, including the vast Ogallala aquifer underlying the Great Plains, are in this situation. Steady expansion of irrigation in the Great Plains from the 1940s was a major factor in the increasing U.S. grain production for three decades. By the early 1980s, however, as much of the aquifer became seriously depleted, the acreage of land under irrigation in the southern Great Plains began to shrink (Postel, 1984). Depletion of aquifers has been noted in many other parts of the world, from China and India to southern Europe and sub-Saharan Africa.

In some instances, aquifers have collapsed, leading to land subsidence. These aquifers may never be recharged. Saltwater intrusions have occurred in some aquifers in coastal areas such as California, Florida, and the East Coast. Recovery of these resources too may be problematic, at least on a time scale of interest to society.

An additional threat to aquifers, mainly in developed nations such as the United States, is the seepage into them of toxic materials of various sorts from improper disposal. Many of these poisons are long-lived in any case, but the organisms that normally break down dangerous substances on the surface are not present underground. Once they reach an aquifer, toxic substances are extremely difficult to remove, and in the absence of chemical breakdown they persist virtually indefinitely. It has been estimated that by the year 2000 as much as one-fourth of the world's accessible freshwater resources, surface and underground, may have been rendered unusable by pollutants (Ambroggi, 1980).

Fresh water is nevertheless a renewable resource, and the supply is not so much short as inopportunely distributed. Few suitable sites remain for damming and diverting surface-water sources for irrigation in developed nations, and indeed further diversion of surface water more and more threatens other values, such as fisheries, wildlife, and recreation. There is also intensifying competition over water for other uses in relatively water-short areas such as the western United States. These problems could be solved by common sense and careful management of the limited supplies, although they are often resolved by political clout or short-term economic considerations.

The situation is different in developing countries, however. Most of them (with the principal exception of China) have only begun to harness their surface-water supplies, even though in some areas depletion of aquifers has become a problem. There is no question that management and control of surface-water resources could help boost agricultural production in many poor countries, and contribute to development in other respects as well by providing flood control and electric power, among other things. But such development must be planned carefully to avoid excessive environmental damage and to maximize the benefits to the local people. Efforts should also be made to prolong the delivery of those benefits by protecting the watershed that feeds the dam against soil erosion and by using irrigation methods that minimize salt accumulation and avoid waterlogging.

Similar care must be taken in tapping aquifers. The lessons of the Sahel, where abundant water from tube wells permitted an overexpansion of herds and the acceleration of desertification, which led to famine, should not be forgotten.

Problems in Agricultural Development

Success with the Green Revolution in some developing regions has induced the belief in many quarters (Simon and Kahn, 1984) that the potential for increased agricultural production in all developing nations is almost limitless. But in the past decade, expansion of the Green Revolution has been disappointing for various reasons, including the rising cost of fossil fuels. It is commonly overlooked that the early successes occurred mainly in temperate regions such as India's Punjab, northern Mexico, and the Middle East (the principal exception being some tropical rice-growing areas of Asia). Attempts to transfer agricultural technologies developed in the North Temperate Zone to tropical and subtropical settings, however, have often failed because the technologies were inappropriate to the soils, climates, and ecological conditions of those regions.

Tropical Agriculture

Such failure has most often followed attempts to convert moist tropical forest areas to farms or pasture. The nutrients in a tropical forest are mostly present in the vegetation, not in the soil. The thin, fragile soils characteristic of many tropical regions can support crops for only a few years; even grazing may be only temporarily profitable. Exposure to the sun and rain and depletion of remaining nutrients by crops or grazers often quickly turn the farms into wastelands (Ehrlich and Ehrlich, 1981). The only form of agriculture that has proved sustainable in many moist tropical regions is shifting cultivation (milpa), which itself is causing widespread degradation of troical forests as the populations dependent on it expand and intensify their operations.

The Temperate Zone practice of growing crops in extensive monocultures, which are vulnerable to attacks by pests and crop diseases, is especially ill-suited to the tropics. Pest and disease problems are exacerbated by the year-round growing conditions. The thin soils are poorly protected by monocultural row crops and are quickly eroded or leached of nutrients by heavy tropical rains (Ehrlich et al., 1977). And soil erosion can be accelerated by extensive use of farm machinery.

Crop Improvement and Genetic Resources

Until lately, research on increasing crop yields focused almost exclusively on crops that thrive in temperate regions but not in the tropics, with the salient exception of rice. Crops traditionally grown in Africa, in particular, have been slighted in this way; rice is not a significant crop there. Only in the last few years has any effort been invested in developing higher-yielding varieties of millet, sorghum, cassava, and other important African crops (Brady, 1985; Cross, 1985). The traditional strains of these crops are not especially responsive to fertilizers; hence increased use of fertilizers and other inputs has little effect on their yields.

Because crop improvement by selective breeding is a time-consuming, tedious process, 10 to 20 years are normally required before a new crop strain can be developed, adequately tested, and adopted over a wide area. The appearance of a green revolution in Africa has thus been seriously delayed by the neglect of tropical crops in agricultural-research programs, in addition to other serious barriers.

Selective breeding also requires the existence of genetic resources — genetically differing domestic or wild strains of each crop — with which to breed new varieties (Ehrlich and Ehrlich, 1981). These resources are equally essential for the success of "gene-splicing" technologies, although this has been concealed to some extent by the hoopla over their potential for creating "new" crop varieties. But the contribution, at least in the foreseeable future, of these techniques seems more likely to be mainly in speeding up the selective breeding process and permitting hybridization between more distantly related crop species than is feasible with traditional methods.

One consequence of the Green Revolution has been the tendency for all the farmers in an area to switch to a single improved crop variety where they previously may have grown dozens of traditional strains. Consequently, the traditional strains, unless deliberately preserved by some farmers or maintained in a seed gene bank, are lost forever—one more renewable resource rendered nonrenewable. The danger in such areas as tropical Africa is the loss not only of valuable varieties of well-known crops but also of little-known, indigenously grown species of crops whose potential value for increasing food supplies or enhancing the quality of local diets may be recognized too late.

Toward Ecological Agriculture

In view of the failure of transposed Temperate Zone agriculture in many tropical and subtropical areas, the need is for the development of new cropping systems, or improvements of traditional ones, that will be much more productive and remain productive over the long term. Research has just begun in developing "ecological" farming techniques, which feature multiple cropping (growing of several different crops intermixed), alternate cropping (planting of different crops in alternate rows and/or overlapping in time), and minimal use of farm chemicals.

Multiple cropping, with appropriate mixes, has the advantages of sharply reducing pest problems, fertilizer needs, and soil erosion. The disadvantages are that such regimes are highly labor-intensive and require considerable knowledge and sophistication to manage them successfully (Gleissman et al., 1981; Gleissman and Amador, 1980). Such systems, moreover, must be carefully adjusted to the local soils and microclimate; what works in one place may fail only a few miles away on a different type of soil.

Establishing successful systems of this sort will almost certainly take even more time than developing and introducing a single new crop variety, as well as much careful research and the knowledgeable cooperation of millions of farmers. The latter might be achieved through a system of farmer education and information resembling the U.S. extension program or farmers' cooperative organizations like those that have been successful in Japan and other East Asian nations. Another useful model is that of China, where experimentation on both crop strains and cropping systems is carried on in individual communes. Successful innovations are quickly adopted by the commune farmers, and networks exist to transfer new seed stocks and information to other communes.

It has begun to be recognized by international-aid agencies that the answers to agricultural development in the tropics—and particularly sub-Saharan Africa's predicament—must come from changes and improvements in farming systems (Cross, 1985; Mellor, 1985; World Bank, 1984a). Accomplishing this, when the systems have yet to be designed, will be a monumental task in the face of the poverty, lack of infrastructure and communications, and severe economic problems already present, plus unprecedentedly rapid population growth. For Africa the question also arises whether the current land degradation caused by the drought and unsustainable agriculture might not preclude the establishment of new systems.

The bottom line for agricultural development is that opportunities for increasing food production in developing nations still exist but that they are not as abundant as some would believe. Also, successful implementation of development efforts will be much more difficult than it was earlier, partly because the easy measures have already been taken, partly because rising population pressures allow less margin for error, and partly because economic and resource constraints are formidable. Time is growing very short for the development and establishment of new crop varieties, let alone entirely new farming systems. Population growth will not wait.

Carrying Capacity

How many human beings can be supported on Earth? This is no easy question to answer — and not just because of large uncertainties regarding the resource base or possible changes in technology that might permit even greater numbers to be supported in the future. The important questions that must be answered first are: For how long must the population be supported? At what average standard of living? Using what technologies? Under what sort of political and economic organization?

Limits to Agricultural Production

The technological and social factors that affect carrying capacity are for the most part beyond the scope of this chapter. Estimating just the potential capacity of agricultural production is difficult and fraught with uncertainties. A number of investigators have tried to assess how many people could be supported by agriculture, sometimes using strange assumptions and with diverse results (summarized in Gilland, 1983). Some calculations have suggested that, *in theory,* sufficient food could be produced to support as many as 40 billion people with strictly vegetarian diets, assuming a two- to threefold expansion of global cropland area and enormously increased average crop yields. Even somewhat more realistic estimates postulate a doubling or tripling of today's agricultural production.

Bernard Gilland (1983) has calculated, with relatively conservative assumptions, especially regarding the potential agricultural productivity of the humid tropics, that the global food harvest could be increased by a factor of about 2.6. Food production at that level would be enough to provide sustenance at a fairly generous level for 7.5 billion human beings or, on largely vegetarian diets, as many as 11 billion. He reckoned that this could be done without significantly expanding the cropland base but with a massive increase in the use of fertilizers and other inputs. He conceded that lack of phosphate supplies might present a serious problem within a few decades and indicated that, at the very least, heavy demand would be put on the world's energy supplies by severalfold increases in production of the two other principal fertilizing elements, nitrogen and potassium.

A more detailed study undertaken by the FAO and the International Institute for Applied Systems Analysis (IIASA) attempted to estimate the carrying capacity of developing regions in terms of their food production capabilities (FAO and IIASA, 1982). The study combined detailed soil and climate data by area and compared these with the growth requirements of major crops. With this information, the potential food-production capacity of each area was assessed according to each of three levels of farming technology, measured by low, intermediate, and high levels of farm inputs (high-yield seeds, fertilizers, etc.).

In most developing countries today, average input levels fall between low and intermediate, with Africa barely above the low level. The high level corresponds to that prevailing in industrialized nations. In the FAO-IIASA study, the assessment of potential food production at appropriate levels was compared with the actual population of each country in 1975 and the projected population for the year 2000.

Of 117 developing countries, about 30 were shown to be on a collision course between their food-producing capacities and their population growth (Harrison, 1984). No fewer than 54 nations (termed "critical countries"), containing over a billion people, would have been unable to support their 1975 populations at the low-input level, even if *all* their potentially arable land were devoted to growing nothing but food crops for local consumption. This assessment assumed that only the particular food crops most ideally suited to the local soils and climate would be grown and made no allowance for animal production, crops for export, or nonfood crops such as cotton, tea, or fuelwood. The 1975 population in excess of the carrying capacity was over a quarter billion. And, of course, the populations of developing nations have increased by an average of more than 30 percent in the last 12 years.

Applying the intermediate level of inputs changes the 1975 picture considerably: only 24 countries would have exceeded their carrying capacities, and the excess population would have been only about 4 percent. But, of course, relatively few developing nations have yet reached, or even closely approached, the intermediate level of inputs—still less in 1975.

The projected outlook for 2000 is not encouraging. Even with substantial increases in irrigated area, the number of critical countries rises to 64, with a combined population of about a billion. Despite a projected population increase of 83 percent in developing nations between 1975 and 2000, the population in the critical countries remains roughly the same, because India is removed from the list, thanks to expanded irrigation. But this time the excess population amounts to nearly half the people in the critical countries.

Again, the picture brightens somewhat, though not enormously, if higher inputs are postulated. With intermediate inputs, only 36 nations, with less than half a billion people, are critical in 2000. Even with high inputs, 19 countries are beyond their carrying capacities.

While the outlook presented in this study is anything but optimistic, many of its underlying assumptions are unrealistically so. One is the highly questionable assumption that all the potentially arable land in tropical regions, including moist tropical forests, could (or should) be converted to permanent agriculture. The study's conclusion, based on that assumption, that the equatorial regions are generally underpopulated is therefore extremely questionable. That all arable land would be used for growing subsistence crops is very doubtful; other important uses for land would surely reduce the area in crops by a significant fraction. It is also unlikely that people would always grow the crops most ideally suited to their areas, regardless of their traditions and preferences. And it surely is unrealistic to expect no production of animals or nonfood crops. The study does, however, give the lie to the argument that people could feed themselves in developing countries if they were not growing cash crops for export.

Even if the assumptions underlying the findings of the study are rather unrealistically optimistic, one can draw from it a number of interesting conclusions. The first and most obvious is that developing countries as a group have outstripped or soon will outstrip their food-producing capacities in relation to the technology now available or likely to become available in the near future. It seems improbable, for instance, that most of these countries will achieve the intermediate level, let alone the high level, of inputs by 2000. And population growth is not expected to be slowed significantly by then. Finally, if the carrying capacities of nations containing a sixth or more of the world's population of 6 billion may be exceeded by 2000, what does that imply for a world population of 10 billion a century later?

A major omission of the study is any assessment of the food-growing capabilities of the developed nations. At present, most surpluses of food are produced in those countries, and they generally are expected to continue to fill the growing gaps in poor nations between population and food production. But the rich countries are closer to reaching their maximum potential productivity. Indeed, the unsustainable elements of agriculture in the United States and other developed regions cast considerable doubt on their capacity to maintain even the present level of production in the long term.

Photosynthetic Limits to Growth

Human beings, like virtually all other organisms on Earth, are dependent on the energy of the sun that is captured by green plants and "fixed" in chemical bonds for their own use and the use of animals and decomposers that feed on them, directly or indirectly. This solar income powers all significant life on Earth and poses the ultimate limit to growth of any one species. It is, of course, absolutely essential to agriculture and a prime limiting factor.

The energy made available each year to biological systems by green plants (above the amount required to maintain their life processes) is known as "net primary production," or NPP. What share of the planet's NPP is used by humanity? How much room remains for further expansion of our species?

Although *Homo sapiens* is only one of possibly 30 million species existing on Earth today, it occupies or exploits at some level roughly 60 percent of the land surface and takes a share of the biological productivity of the oceans as well. Counting just the portion of global annual NPP that human beings and their domestic animals consume directly (as food, feed, and wood products), only about 4 percent of the total estimated NPP produced on land and roughly 2 percent of that in marine and freshwater systems — about 3 percent averaged globally — is used to support humanity (Vitousek et al., 1986).

But human beings co-opt or divert into alternative ecosystems a much larger share of the global NPP than they consume directly. To estimate this indirect impact, the productivity of all croplands and forest plantations, that of all pastureland that has been converted in recent decades from other land uses (usually forest), the biomass lost in human-caused fires in grasslands or forests, the biomass killed but not used in timber harvesting, and the productivity of human-occupied areas (parks, golf courses, lawns, etc.) were calculated. The share of terrestrial NPP co-opted plus that directly used by civilization comes to about 30 percent. Combined with the unchanged share of marine exploitation of about 2 percent, the overall global fraction is nearly 19 percent.

Human impact on the biosphere has not been limited to exploiting an increasing share of the planet's productivity, however. In converting land to other uses, humanity may change its productive capacity—often for the worse. Cropland is generally less productive (except under irrigation) than grassland, which in turn is less productive than forest. Significant losses of productivity have also resulted from desertification, soil erosion, and urban development. Some human activities, such as fertilization by air or water pollutants, may enhance productivity, but the trend has mostly been to reduce it. The net reduction of global productivity because of land conversion and desertification is conservatively estimated at about 13 percent of the potential terrestrial NPP.

Thus not only has humanity co-opted a surprisingly large share of Earth's net primary productivity, but it has appreciably degraded the potential productivity of the biosphere as well. Combining the fractions of global NPP used directly and co-opted with NPP foregone because of human-caused changes, the total human impact on the potential NPP on land is almost 40 percent, and, including the marine component, about 25 percent overall.

The implications of an impact of this magnitude on the planet's total biological productivity for large increases in the human population can hardly be overstated. Even assuming that a doubling of the human population need not cause a doubling of the human share of NPP co-opted, the possibilities are cause for concern. It seems likely that a doubling of human numbers—as is projected in the next century or so by most responsible demographers—would lead to a doubling of direct human consumption (from 4 percent to 8 percent of the terrestrial NPP), unless the fraction of animal products consumed and/or use of wood products per person were considerably reduced. Either, of course, would imply a reduction in average living standards.

It might be easier to control expansion of the fraction of global NPP that is co-opted simply by intensifying use of those areas already being exploited and not opening any new areas. It would be important to prevent further reductions in global NPP as much as possible. To this end, a concerted effort to preserve the remaining undisturbed natural areas on Earth—and especially tropical forest areas—is essential. The simplification and destabilization of ecosystems that follow conversion to less productive human-dominated systems could thereby be avoided, and the flow of essential services from the surviving natural ecosystems could be maintained (Ehrlich et al., 1977; Ehrlich and Ehrlich, 1981).

It should be obvious that maintaining the present inadequate living standards for a human population twice its present size, even for a few decades, without degrading the productive capabilities of Earth and reducing its carrying capacity for human life, would be a monumental, perhaps impossible, task. Yet, though demographic momentum commits the human population to substantial further growth, a doubling in size is not inevitable.

Two models on a smaller scale are available to civilization. Governments could continue to consider population growth of no importance until the environment became so degraded that a natural fluctuation in climatic patterns was enough to plunge vulnerable nations into massive famine—as is happening in over 20 countries in Africa today. Or the world's nations could separately and in concert assess the world's resource base and carrying capacity in relation to available and foreseeable technologies and devise population policies that fit their findings—as China has done for itself. Despite the undeniable political and social difficulties of taking this path, it would seem much easier—and much safer—to halt world population growth as quickly as is humanely possible and begin a slow decline to a permanently sustainable level.

References

Ambroggi, R. P. 1980. Water. *Scientific American* (September).

Birdsall, N. 1980. Population growth and poverty in the developing world. *Population Bulletin* no. 35 (December): 5.

Brady, N. C. 1985. Toward a green revolution for Africa. *Science* 227 (March 8): 741.

Brown, L. R. 1981. *Building a sustainable society.* New York: Norton.

———, and E. C. Wolf. 1984. *Soil erosion: Quiet crisis in the world economy.* Worldwatch Paper no. 60 (September). Washington, D.C.: Worldwatch Institute.

———, et al. 1984. *The state of the world, 1984.* New York: Norton.

———, et al. 1985. *The state of the world, 1985.* New York: Norton.

———, et al. 1986. *The state of the world, 1986.* New York: Norton.

Cross, M. 1985. Waiting for a green revolution. *New Scientist* (April 4).

Cutright, P. 1983. The ingredients of recent fertility decline in developing countries. *International Family Planning Perspectives* 9 (December): 4.

Dregne, H. E. 1982. *Impact of land degradation on future world food supply.* ERS-677. U.S. Dept. of Agriculture, Economic Research Service.

Ehrlich, P. R., L. Bilderback, and A. H. Ehrlich. 1979. *The golden door: International migration, Mexico, and the United States.* New York: Ballantine.

Ehrlich, P., and A. Ehrlich. 1981. *Extinction: The causes and consequences of the disappearance of species.* New York: Random House.

Ehrlich, P. R., A. H. Ehrlich, and J. P. Holdren. 1977. *Ecoscience: Population, resources, environment.* San Francisco: Freeman.

FAO [Food and Agriculture Organization of the United Nations]. 1981. *Agriculture: Toward 2000*. Rome: FAO.

———. 1983. *State of food and agriculture, 1982*. Rome: FAO.

———. 1984. *World food report, 1984*. Rome: FAO.

———. 1985. *1984 Production yearbook*. Vol. 38. Rome: FAO.

———, and IIASA [International Institute for Applied Systems Analysis]. 1982. *Potential population supporting capacities of lands in the developing world*. Rome: FAO.

Frejka, T. 1981. Long-term prospects for world population growth. *Population and Development Review* 7 (September): 3.

Gilland, B. 1983. Considerations on world population and food supply. *Population and Development Review* 9 (June): 2.

Gleissman, S. R., and A. M. Amador. 1980. Ecological aspects of production in traditional agroecosystems in humid lowland tropics of Mexico. *Tropical Ecology and Development,* pp. 601–608.

———, R. Garcia E., and M. Amador A. 1981. The ecological basis for the application of traditional agricultural technology in the management of tropical agro-ecosystems. *Agro-Ecosystems* 7:173–85.

Goliber, T. J. 1985. Sub-Saharan Africa: Population pressures on development. *Pop. Bull.* 40 (February):1.

Harrison, P. 1984. A new framework for the food security equation. *Ceres* 17 (March–April):2.

Johnson, D. G. 1984. World food and agriculture. In J. L. Simon and H. Kahn, eds. *The resourceful earth*. Oxford: Basil Blackwell.

Kerr, R. A. 1985. Fifteen years of African drought. *Science* 227 (March 22):1454–55.

Lappe, F. M., and J. Collins. 1977. *Food first*. Boston: Houghton Mifflin.

Mellor, J. W. 1985. The changing world food situation. Food Policy Statement, International Food Policy Research Institute (January).

Norman, C. 1985. The technological challenge in Africa. *Science* 227 (February 8):616–17.

Population Reference Bureau. 1985. *World Population Data Sheet, 1985*. Washington, D.C.

Postel, S. 1984. *Water: Rethinking management in an age of scarcity*. Worldwatch Paper no. 62 (December). Washington, D.C.: Worldwatch Institute.

Sai, F. T. 1984. The population factor in Africa's development dilemma. *Science* 236 (November 16):801–805.

Simon, J. L., and H. Kahn. 1984. *The resourceful earth*. Oxford: Basil Blackwell.

Spedding, C. R. W., J. M. Walsingham, and A. M. Hoxey. 1981. *Biological efficiency in agriculture*. New York: Academic Press.

UNICEF. 1982. *The state of the world's children, 1982–83*. Oxford: Oxford University Press.

U.S. Bureau of the Census. 1983. *World population, 1983*. ISP WP 83. Washington, D.C.: U.S. Government Printing Office.

———. 1984. *World population, 1984*. ISP WP 84. Washington, D.C.: U.S. Government Printing Office.

USDA [U.S. Department of Agriculture]. 1984a. *World agriculture: Outlook and situation report.* WAS-36 (June).

————. 1984b. *World agriculture: Outlook and situation report.* WAS-38 (December).

————. 1985. *World crop production.* Foreign Agriculture Circular WCP-2-85 (February).

————. 1986. *World agriculture: Situation and outlook report.* WAS-44 (June).

Urban, F., and T. Volrath. 1984. *Patterns and trends in world agricultural land use.* FAER no. 198. Washington, D.C.: U.S. Department of Agriculture.

Vitousek, P. M., P. R. Ehrlich, A. H. Ehrlich, and P. A. Matson. 1986. Human appropriation of the products of photosynthesis. *Bioscience* 36:6, 368–73.

Walsh, J. 1984. Sahel will suffer even if rains come. *Science* 224 (May 4): 461–71.

World Bank. 1982. *World development report, 1982.* Oxford: Oxford University Press.

————. 1984a. *World development report, 1984.* Oxford: Oxford University Press.

————. 1984b. *Toward sustained development in sub-Saharan Africa.* Oxford: Oxford University Press.

————. 1986. *World development report, 1986.* Oxford: Oxford University Press.

Zheng, L., S. Jian, et al. 1981. *China's population: Problems and prospects.* Beijing: New World Press.

5.
Energy and Material Resources

IN THE NAME of this conference, in the Greek mythology whence it comes, in this renaissance so remote from Troy, I see magnificent potential for trenchant symbolism: of prophets, women and men; of Trojan horses; of serpents destroying vision and its sons (truth and innocence?), of fire, pillage, ruin, disaster; of unending search for home; and of rebirth, new golden ages, Rome, and now Texas, following Greece.

A nineteenth-century English poet, known as a pessimist, pleaded (Thomson, 1882):

> O antique fables, beautiful and bright
> O antique fables, for a little light
> Of that which shineth in you evermore
> To cleanse the dimness from our weary eyes
> And bathe our old world in a new surprise
> Of golden dawn entrancing sea and shore.

It was Laocoön, in *The Odyssey,* viewing the great horse left by Odysseus, the wanderer, who said, "I fear the Greeks even when they offer gifts." Laocoön then drove his spear into the horse's flank, and it rumbled.

Homer tells us what the Trojan horse contained. Today, too, we are presented with similar horses brought by those who tell us to have no fear of the future; further, they, the economists, tell us that their knowledge comes straight from the horse's mouth. But the contributors to this book think that the economists have got things turned around.

Before the people of Troy could be persuaded by Laocoön, a Greek appeared. Homer says that his name was Sinon. Could there be a typographical error somewhere? Was his first name (an echo of ages to come on the shore of Latium) Julian?

Then two serpents came over the sea and embraced and destroyed Laocoön and his two sons. I can guess who, in our times, personify the serpents and by whom they were sent, but it seems the better part of discretion to remain silent. Homer does not say explicitly, but the people of Troy took it as omen that the 'great horse was sent by the gods and was to be revered.

That night it was Simon (excuse me, I mean Sinon) who let the Greek warriors out of the belly of the horse to open the gates of Troy to the Greek armies, whence Troy fell.

But, of those who survived, Odysseus, the master plotter, took 20 years to find his way back to Greece; and Aeneas, the Trojan, finally reached the River Tiber to found Rome and the lineage of Caesars, including Julius, which was later to reduce Greece to trivium (although Plato, in contrast to the myths, suggests that it was simply because the Greeks mistreated their natural resources). Do we find evidence here of a cyclic world with renaissance following catastrophe endlessly? Whom are we to believe?

Cassandra, the beautiful daughter of Priam, the king of Troy, was granted by Apollo the gift of prophesying the future. When, later, she displeased him, he could not withdraw the gift but he could and did add to it that her prophecies would not be believed. I find nothing to suggest that Cassandra was a pessimist—only that she could see the future and would not be believed. After the fall of Troy she was claimed by Agamemnon and was slain in jealousy by his adulterous wife, from which deed a long series of murders followed.

Two notes of explanation may be in order. First, the sense of a "prophecy" is that it has divine guidance, that in fact this *is* what will come; in contrast, a forecast, a projection, a prediction, is only a human attempt at prophecy. Second, I am labeling two schools of thought regarding the human prospect as "optimists" and "pessimists," more because they are easy labels and everyone knows whom I mean than because they are entirely appropriate. Others have offered "cornucopians" and "gloom and doom" and so on. These two schools have more trouble communicating with each other than honorable people should have—but perhaps the problem is more complex than it seems. Currently the overt exponent of optimism is Julian Simon (1980, 1981), professor, economist, demographer. He is, I fear, more believed in this decade than are his opponents. Commonly, he is wrong. I must and shall refer to him a few more times in this paper.

I ask you also to forgive me a few more romantic excursions from the dull details of my assigned task: the resource problems of matter and energy.

These two resource areas, matter in its inorganic forms and energy, make a natural pair: dramatically different, dramatically similar, inextricably intertwined. It is inevitable to counterpose them one against the other. Matter is static, stuck to the earth; all that we ever had, excepting perhaps $1/10^9$ (hydrogen, helium, some tektite stuff, minutiae of space trash), is still here. Energy, in contrast, is not material even though associated with matter. And we think of energy more as a flow, admittedly with eddies. What came to us with the earth's primal matter still lingers, dribbling away over billions of years; what comes to us from the sun and the cosmos is here today, gone by tomorrow. Perhaps a year's ration lingers. In the preindustrial age we lived off the short-term flow of energy from the sun; in the industrial age, these few hundred years, this brief interval that M. K. Hubbert (1949, 1969), has termed the "age of fossil fuels," we have been living, in large measure, on that tiny fraction from the sun that has been trapped as coal, oil, and gas. Afterward we will either go back to the flow from the sun or turn to the primal store. And, of course, if we are numerous, technological, and rich, our use will be large; if few, primitive, and poor, it will be small.

While energy manifests itself in diverse ways, we have measures of its use common to all manifestations. The material resource, in contrast, while all of it is matter, manifests itself as the 80-odd durable, earthbound chemical elements, their daughters from radioactive disintegration, their simple chemical compounds (as in sand and gravel), and the more diverse crystalline manifestations of some of these (from diamonds to diatomite). Let us deal with matter first.

Material Resources

A quick glance at the table of contents of a U.S. Bureau of Mines publication, *Mineral Facts and Problems* (1965), would remind us that the Bureau of Mines finds close to 100 different items worth detailing in this resource kingdom. I cannot, of course, even begin to deal with them separately. Most of my information is for the United States—because it is more readily available and comprehensive, and it will usually comprise a large share of the world's activity. Most of my numbers are for 1980. None of what I say has anything to do with national strategic objectives.

By and large these materials are recovered by mining. The earth in its multitude of geochemical processes has been concentrating small portions of its surface according to its chemistry, some here, some there (see, for example, Meyer, 1985; Eaton, 1984). We seek out these ores and mine them. Few of the materials are abundant enough in satisfactory ores that we can say it is hard to imagine exhausting them: perhaps only iron and aluminum, sand and gravel, and rock for crushing. It is hard to realize how puny are our efforts in disturbing the earth's surface, mostly by strip mining, in our searches for the nonfuel minerals. In the United States in 1979 material moved in recovery of such minerals was 5 billion tons, 43 percent of it sand and gravel and rock for crushing, 42 percent of it in the mining of phosphate rock and iron and copper ores (U.S. Bureau of Mines, 1980, pp. 13, 14). All the other nearly 100 items comprised the remaining 15 percent. The total amount can be viewed as moving the top $1/120$ inch of the United States. Such activity was, of course, sharply, very sharply, localized. Most Americans have never seen a mine.

The amounts actually recovered ranged from a billion tons for sand and gravel down to a few hundred ounces (ignoring gemstones); prices (ignoring gemstones and monetary fiction) range from $3 per ton for sand and gravel or crushed rock to $800 per troy ounce for rhodium and $6,000 per pound for lutetium, a rare earth metal. The uses range from the completely obvious to the utterly obscure: 3,500 tons of peat used for "earthworm culture medium."

In trying to bring some order out of such an array, let us first imagine ranking these products according to a number of attributes. Six of these come to mind.

First and most obvious is simply abundance in the earth's crust, thus from iron (50,000 parts per million) to iridium (0.001 ppm).

Next, perhaps, is the amounts used, from sand and gravel to osmium or, again, gemstones (respectively, from the order of 10^{15} grams to the order of 10^5 g).

Third, we might choose the degree to which the item is found concentrated into recoverable ores: thus coal and rock for crushing, close to 100 percent; or, on a different scale, mercury (Hg) more than the 10-times-commoner hafnium (Hf); and yet again copper with a quite different pattern of concentration into ores compared to silver.

Fourth, we might consider price and the elasticity of demand as the sources thin out; are we willing to pay more to seek it out, as it becomes harder to find, or do we abandon its use and turn to something else? Thus, copper gives way to aluminum as an electrical conductor.

Fifth, we can try to rank them by existing patterns of recycling, say, by the fraction lost at each use. Certainly we must guess that the more costly the product the more likely it is to be carefully recycled: diamonds before gravel. But also, suddenly the idea becomes complicated: thus, is a gold coin "recycled" when it changes hands in a transaction or only when it is melted down? Again, some products, in different uses, fall near both ends of this spectrum: thus, the lead burned as tetraethyl lead in gasoline and not recycled at all versus the lead three feet away in the automobile's battery, which is almost completely recycled. If, as a subclassification, we examine things by the way they are used, we find some ways intrinsically less susceptible to recycling: (1) minor components of lubricants (lithium stearate, molybdenum disulfide); (2) surface coatings including paint pigments (e.g., titanium dioxide, a paint pigment, in contrast, as with lead, to titanium metal, which is probably carefully husbanded) and others (e.g., kaolinite on coated papers); (3) materials widely used in minute amounts (as tungsten in light-bulb filaments); (4) small amounts used in admixture with larger, major components (thus minor alloying metals, metallic catalysts in consumer products such as automobiles); and, finally, (5) fertilizer elements, potash, phosphate, and fixed nitrogen applied to cropland (although we do harvest them and consume them, man and livestock, and, in some degree, recycle them as organic manures). I asked my dentist about the fate of gold, silver, and mercury in the crematorium, wondering about atmospheric contamination by the last of these, but he thought the subject too morbid and I have not found the time to ask elsewhere.

Sixth, another consideration in recycling is the permanency of a use: the rock of the pyramids or the Star of India diamond or whatever comes to mind at one extreme, the stone and concrete and steel in durable structures next, the steel in automobiles third, the glass and iron and aluminum in beer cans last. Recycling potential increases with transience of use.

If we were to plot all these six attributes in a suitable fashion, we should have some products standing out as potential problems. Phosphate has been a common choice. I do not think it will turn out that way, because I suspect that a lot of low-grade phosphate is around and that it will command a price sufficient to harvest it. I am not sure of a current best prospect, but helium is worth examination.

This is not at all to say that the problem does not exist. But one must emphasize probabilities, be cautious on certainties. We can point to the progressive decline in richness of ores, beginning with scarcer metals—gold, silver, copper—and now progressing to the commoner iron and aluminum. We can point to new discoveries but must also note the declining rate of discovery as Hubbert (1969) has done especially for petroleum. While we can shrug off the distinction between "proved reserve" and "resource," we can get wide agreement that we have probably found most of the concentrated ores of these materials. A few more spectacular discoveries will turn up, but less and less frequently. It is becoming a tougher ball game by the decade.

New technology does come up—of discovery, of mining, of ore concentration—but most of the great advances are probably behind us: "perhaps" this is so in discovery; "probably" it is so in ore concentration, where the great advance, "froth flotation," is approaching a century in age; "very probably" it is so in mining, where the great advance, "surface mining," began long ago and has now, as Jackim (1974) has shown, come close to the limits imposed by the strength of materials available to us. That is, while we have built dragline shovels for removing overburden that could pick up and move a small house intact, steels do not exist from which to build equipment half an order of magnitude larger.

We cannot, in fact, in concept, continue unendingly to mine ores of decreasing concentration. Winning products from progressively leaner ores involves major costs that increase with the bulk of the ore, independently of the amount of target material within it.

The best I can say for our prospect is that I do not see much potential in this resource kingdom for crisis or panic. It seems likely that these products will steadily and slowly increase in cost, decrease in availability, become more and more of a drag on our level of living. The only concession I can make to the optimists is that the end to such resources ought to come on slowly and usually with warning.

Opinions differ, of course, on such matters. If I were to ask whether science and technology will do as much for human welfare in the next half millennium as it has since Copernicus, the optimists would say yes; at least some of the pessimists would say no. Some would add that the age of science and technology has passed its peak.

Julian Simon (1981) goes further than most other optimists. In *The Ultimate Resource,* with magnificent disregard for the dictionary, by confusing (pp. 51, 52) "finite," "indefinite," "and "infinite," he manages to persuade himself that the world's resources are infinite. He could have supported his position by resort to the best of authorities (Dodgson, 1872), where Humpty Dumpty tells Alice (p. 247); "When *I* use a word, . . . it means just what I choose it to mean—neither more nor less. . . . The question is, which is to be the master [you or the word]." The Queen tells her (p. 226): ". . . jam every other day. . . . The rule is, jam to-morrow and jam yesterday—but never jam today. . . . to-day isn't any *other* day." When Alice says (p. 230), "There's no use trying. . . . one *can't* believe impossible things," the Queen replies (p. 230): "I dare say you haven't had much practice. . . . sometimes I've believed as many as six impossible things before breakfast."

So much for material resources. Simon gives me an easy transition to the subject of energy by saying (1980) that if we run out of copper it will "be made from other metals" (p. 1435). I, despite my pessimistic belief that fusion energy will never be an economic success, am willing to cooperate with Simon and so have calculated the energetics of a process of reacting helium with iron to give copper. To my momentary surprise, it is exothermic, and the energy release, which should be largely convertible to electricity, is 55,000 kwht (kilowatt-hours thermal, that is, of heat, not of electricity or work) per pound of iron converted. At 5¢/kwhe (kilowatt-hours electrical), about what you pay in College Station, this amounts to $2,800 per pound of iron converted and, at the U.S. copper consumption rate of about two million tons a year, it comes to about 750 quads (750 × 10^{12} Btu), or in the neighborhood of 10 times the American energy economy. I herewith abandon all patent rights to Simon and trust that with the enormous financial incentives I have outlined he will not delay in having his technologists come up with the grimy details of a manufacturing process — one that will bankrupt the existing U.S. energy industry and make him wealthy beyond the dreams of Croesus.

Energy

Now to energy. We use it to provide heat or to do work. We use heat either as space or as process heat. Space heat warms our houses, automobiles, stores, factories, offices. We use process heat in the household mostly to cook; in industry we use it to distill petroleum and whiskey, to fire clay into brick, to smelt metals from their ores, to make cement, and to encourage a myriad of other chemical reactions. We use work to lift, to pump, to grind, to transport. We use it in the household mostly by way of electric motors in appliances. In fact, electricity is so easily converted to work that we may as well think of electricity as work. In industry, in addition to pumping and such, we use work to shape, to fabricate materials. We use it, both personally and in industry, to transport people and things. All of the fuel going to automobiles, trucks, trains, ships, airplanes, and pipelines may as well be thought of as providing work.

Primarily, all energy came to us from the cosmos; ultimately to the cosmos it must return, except for the minutiae we have built into pyramids and lesser structures. When we let it go, it will be less useful than when we received it, for we shall have degraded it.

We have learned over human history about certain reservoirs and springs from which energy flows or can be made to flow. And so we harvest it with our chain saws, our oil and gas wells, our coal mines, our geothermal steam wells, our water mills, our windmills, our diverse solar collectors, even our urban refuse collectors. We store it in woodpiles, in oil tanks, in coal heaps, in water reservoirs, in the gasoline tanks of our automobiles, in hot-water tanks. We transport it in pipelines, trains, ships, trucks, transmission lines. We convert it to a form closer to that in which we use it in hydropower plants, steam engines, automobile engines, nuclear piles, electric heaters, and lights. Chlorophyll and some inorganic matter does it to sunlight.

After we have used it, we dispose of it, often simply by neglect, sometimes at considerable expense, as in air conditioning. (Today this room is being cooled by expenditure of perhaps 20 kw simply to get rid of the 100 w that each of us here, after having converted those breakfast-food calories to heat in various metabolic activities, is breathing out as warmer air and evaporated water.)

It, energy, will never run out, but it steadily becomes less accessible and then, by technological jumps, it becomes, at least for a while, more accessible. The great jumps include fire, sailing ships, water mills, steam engines, electric generators, coal mines, oil wells, nuclear piles. One, perhaps in midleap right now, is the photovoltaic cell. One I expect to collapse in midleap is nuclear fusion.

Obviously we have learned an enormous lot about it, and it has eased our lives enormously. Some matters remain obscure: while the sun lives by fusing hydrogen to helium, we have learned to fuse hydrogen only in a warlike manner. Again, while we store and transport small amounts of liquid fuels very neatly in gasoline tanks, we have not learned of a cheap and compact way to store and transport modest batches of electricity, of work. Batteries will not do; they are too heavy and too expensive; we have come to expect more than they can supply.

It should not surprise us, then, that the first places in which a constraint on energy pinches us is in the very use of it that is so new and valued by each of us: individual personal transport, the automobile. After Simon has solved the copper problem, I wish him to arrange for the invention of the cheap, compact storage of work. Then we can load our cars up with work from an electrical outlet and take off on a 500-mile trip.

We have, as I am sure all of us know, been enormously profligate in our use of energy. We have built the leakiest houses imaginable, knowing that to throw heat at them would be cheaper than to keep heat inside them. Some 30 years ago, when my wife and I were building a house, I suggested to the architect that we should insulate it. I had, in fact, already known of Hubbert, and I believed him when he said that things would run out. The architect replied: "I don't advise it. It would cost you two or three hundred dollars, and you'll never get your money back." We have, as we and the rest of the world knows, built the most gas-guzzling automobiles imaginable. Our industry has gauged the cost of energy and concluded that there is no profit in saving it.

But as energy costs creep up, all of this wastrel existence has left us with two great opportunities for reform. First, we are beginning to mend our ways and our equipment to conserve energy, and because we begin so high on the hog, we can conserve an awful lot of it. Second, we can turn to the sources that are more costly than the dirt-cheap energy of coal and oil: to the sun and the wind and the earth's heat and to gasoline from coal for liquid fuel to move our automobiles.

It is too early to say how cheap any of these may become. If they become as cheap as energy is today, we shall be asking ourselves why we dragged our feet. If, more likely, they do not, we will simply sulk and pay more, use less, take some care in use, even think before using. We have, it is true, learned some lessons, but only a trifle of what we will.

We have experienced two short "panics" in gasoline supplies. Our official term is "crisis," but this is a misnomer because *crisis,* from *krinein,* "to decide," suggests a moment from which decisions leading to new courses of action will flow. The gasoline panics have led us as a nation to only minor decisions: thus some directives on automobile gasoline mileage marginally complied with to date; some tax incentives to experiment with alternative energy sources; a program to encourage automobile fuel from biomass that is more misleading than constructive; some deplorable incentives to dam up running water for hydropower; and a corporation to convert other fuels to gasoline and pipeline gas which seems better at tripping over its own feet than at getting the job done.

We are now tending to back away from all these programs as if the energy panic had never happened, as if it were only a bad dream. I cannot tell you whether or when it will happen again, but I can tell you that if we think it will never happen then it certainly will. Contrariwise, if we act as though it might happen, then perhaps it will not. That is really enough to say and all that time permits me to say on energy.

Conclusion

But it brings me back to Cassandra and to Julian Simon. He offers (1981, p. 27) to bet $10,000 even money that the price of minerals will not rise. More precisely, he says that for $10,000 he will contract with you to deliver to you at any future date you specify today the amount of any mineral or grain or fossil fuel or other raw material not under government control that you can buy today for $10,000. But you pay the $10,000 now; presumably he keeps the interest. Perhaps he will actually hedge the bet with his broker (and still collect interest on your money). You cannot win unless prices rise faster than the interest rate. With the current mode in interest rates, this hints at your winning only with prices doubling in 5 years and increasing tenfold in 16 years. You are better off to put your money in your own certificate of deposit. Simon's bet is a sucker bet.

But it also hints at a problem in betting on pessimism. How will you respond if I offer to bet you $10,000 that the world will end tomorrow? It is hard to bet on pessimism and come out a winner. Bet on optimism; you may be wrong (and dead), but if you are dead you do not have to pay, and if you live through whatever it is, you will win. If Cassandra was, in truth, a pessimist, then this is Cassandra's curse.

Finally, if I seem optimistic, it is only because I am persuaded that Herman Daly will tell us tomorrow how to reach a steady-state economy, and Paul Ehrlich how to maintain a less numerous and zero-population-growth society and that they will say it so persuasively that we will heed their advice. If, likewise, I seem to dissent from the conclusions of Meadows and associates in *The Limits to Growth,* my answer is a qualified "Perhaps." If, though, you reject Daly and Ehrlich and we continue to insist on unending exponential growth, then I am completely with Meadows, have said so many times, and see no reason to change. Resource problems are population problems. The highway of growth is the road to disaster; there must be another way.

References

Dodgson, C. L. 1866. *Alice in wonderland.* Reprint. New York: Liveright, 1932.
————. 1872. *Through the looking glass.* Reprint. New York: Liveright, 1932.
Eaton, G. P. 1984. Mineral abundance in the North American cordillera. *American Scientist* 72:368–77.
Hubbert, M. K. 1949. Energy from fossil fuels. *Science* 109:103–109.
————. 1969. Energy resources. In Committee on Resources and Man of National Academy of Sciences. *Resources and man.* San Francisco: Freeman.
Jackim, B. A. 1974. The land movers: Megalomachine excavators. Term paper, University of California, Berkeley.
Meyer, C. 1985. Ore metals through geologic history. *Science* 227:1421–28.
Simon, J. 1980. Resources, population, environment: An oversupply of false bad news. *Science* 208:1431–37.
————. 1981. *The ultimate resource.* Princeton, N.J.: Princeton University Press.
Thomson, J. 1882. Proem. In *The city of dreadful night and other poems.* Reprint. Portland, Me.: Thomas B. Mosher, 1932.
U.S. Bureau of Mines. 1965. *Mineral facts and problems.* Washington, D.C.: U.S. Department of the Interior.
————. 1980. *Minerals yearbook.* Vol. 1. Washington, D.C.: U.S. Department of the Interior.

6.
What the Fate of the Rain Forests Means to Us

ONE MAY WONDER why a subject like the tropical rain forests would be suitable for this symposium. These exotic and picturesque "jungles," covering only about a tenth of the world's surface, are surely far less significant to the future of humankind than such transcendent issues as nuclear war, climatic change, massive environmental pollution, and development for food production—or are they? What are these rain forests like, why are they important to us, and what is happening to them?

Humid tropical forests exist, or have existed, in frost-free tropical areas that have an annual rainfall greater than 1,500 millimeters and no more than two dry months (with less than 100 mm of precipitation) a year. They have an average mean monthly temperature of more than 24° C and are characterized by strong altitudinal zonation (Savage et al., 1982). They are highly productive ecosystems—some of the most productive on earth—a fact that has led many of those concerned with the rapidly growing populations, extreme poverty, and widespread malnutrition that are characteristic of tropical countries to regard them as suitable environments for intensive development over the next few decades.

Within the humid tropics environments are extremely varied. The tropical lowland forests themselves consist of very large numbers of broadleaf evergreen trees, with 100 or more tree species per hectare and a canopy at a height of 30 to 60 meters. Forests at higher elevations are poorer in species, although still incredibly rich, and lower in stature. The soils of the humid tropics are extremely varied. Among them, acid infertile oxisols and ultisols cover about two-thirds of the region; together these are

I am deeply grateful to Bruce Wilcox for his help with estimates of extinction on Barro Colorado Island and elsewhere.

the red soils that are so characteristic of the humid tropics. Relatively fertile high-base soils, on the other hand, cover about one-third of the humid tropics of Asia, but only 12 percent of the African tropics and 7 percent of the American tropics (Savage et al., 1982). These soils are mostly already under cultivation in Asia and are rapidly coming under cultivation in the other two main tropical regions.

How many species of organisms occur in the tropics? We can provide an approximate answer to this question, but only indirectly, as follows (Raven, 1980). There are about 1.5 million named species of organisms. About 1 million of these occur in temperate regions, the remainder in the tropics. When particular groups of invertebrates, fungi, or other relatively poorly known groups of organisms of temperate regions are reviewed and monographed, the numbers of species in these groups usually increase by a substantial fraction, often from one-third more species to twice as many. We may therefore assume conservatively that there are actually 1.5 million species of organisms in the temperate regions of the world, although the actual figure may be substantially higher.

If we then consider the relative numbers of species of well-known groups of organisms, such as birds, mammals, and butterflies, found in temperate and tropical regions, respectively, we find that there are characteristically at least twice as many species in tropical as in temperate regions. Granted that most groups of organisms—particularly the insects, mites, and other arthropods and the nematodes—are very poorly known in tropical regions, and given the ratios of species found in groups that are well known, it can be estimated that there are at least 3 million species of organisms in the tropics. Actually, the number may be much higher than that; for example, Erwin (1982), basing his calculations on extrapolations of numbers of species of beetles found in the canopies of trees in the lowland rain forest of South America, has estimated that there may be as many as 30 million species of insects in the tropics. Even if the more conservative estimate is correct, no more than one out of six of the kinds of organisms found in the tropical forests has even been given a scientific name, much less known in any detailed way, as regards either its biological properties or its possible usefulness for human development. Our state of knowledge about the organisms that make up the tropical forests is abysmal.

This extraordinary richness of biological diversity is not uniformly distributed throughout the world's tropics. Again by using the expedient of considering groups that are relatively well known, like plants, birds, and mammals, we can gain some idea of the patterns of regional diversity. About 90,000 species of plants (vascular plants and bryophytes) occur in temperate regions, about 180,000 species in the tropics. Half of the tropical species occur in tropical Latin America (90,000 species); about 35,000 species occur in tropical Africa (Brenan, 1978); and perhaps 55,000 species occur in tropical Asia. Regionally the highest concentration of species in the world seems to occur in the three countries of northwestern South America, Colombia, Ecuador, and Peru, which together have about 45,000 species of plants in an area of about 2.7 million square kilometers—roughly 30 percent of the size of the United States, which has fewer than half as many species.

Extrapolating from these figures for plants and using the conservative estimate of about 4.5 million species of organisms worldwide, we can estimate that, for example, these three South American countries may be inhabited by at least 750,000 species of organisms, well over 500,000 of which have never even been given a scientific name. By the same token, Madagascar, an island about twice the size of the state of Arizona lying about 400 kilometers off the east coast of Africa, has about 9,000 species of plants and an estimated 150,000 kinds of organisms, more than three-fourths of which occur nowhere else on earth. The significance of these figures will become clear as we proceed, but they certainly serve to establish the extraordinary richness of the tropical biota and our lack of knowledge about it.

We need not dwell here on the potential utility of the plants, animals, and microorganisms of the tropical forests in relation to human welfare. Many of the products used in temperate zones—one thinks of coffee, tea, cocoa, bananas, sugar, pineapples, wood, and many minerals as examples —come to us from the tropics, and we send to the tropics a major proportion of our exports, including half of all the food exported from the United States. Several excellent books, including those of Myers (1983, 1984), Ehrlich and Ehrlich (1981), and Oldfield (1984), have documented in abundant detail the actual and much greater potential importance of tropical organisms as contributors to human welfare. These authors cite the uses of plants, animals, and microorganisms as foods, medicines, and energy sources and for other purposes. Only a microscopic proportion of the available genetic diversity is being utilized, and it would be obvious to any thinking person reading these books that it is very much in our collective interest to explore for economic value among the millions of additional organisms that have never been considered in this context or that are now being utilized on only a local basis.

On these two bases, then—lack of scientific information and potential for benefit—a greatly expanded program of exploration of the tropics and inventory of tropical organisms could easily be justified. Unfortunately, however, time for these important exercises is rapidly running out, and the future possibilities look extremely limited. This prediction can be justified as follows.

Table 6.1. Tropical Closed Forests

Region	Total Area (Million km²)	Undisturbed, 1980 (Million km²)	Annual Deforestation (Thousand km²)
Africa	2.17	1.19 (55%)	13.3
Latin America	6.79	4.55 (67%)	43.4
Asia	3.06	1.01 (33%)	18.3
Total	12.02	6.75 (56%)	75.0

SOURCE: FAO, 1981a–c.

In a study by the Food and Agriculture Organization (FAO) of the United Nations it was estimated that by 1980 about 44 percent of the tropical evergreen forests had already been cut (table 6.1; FAO, 1981a–c). In the same study it was estimated that about 1.1 percent of the remaining forests were being logged each year at that time (1980). In that year the total remaining area of tropical evergreen forest amounted to approximately the size of the United States west of the Mississippi River, with an additional area about half the size of the state of Iowa being logged every year. If clearing were to continue at this rate, all these forests would be gone within 90 years, an alarming enough prediction in itself, but one that certainly constitutes a severe underestimate, as I shall now demonstrate.

The first reason why most tropical forests will be gone long before 90 years have elapsed is that clear-cutting, the only form of forest conversion with which the FAO concerned itself, is only the most direct way in which forests are destroyed. Much more extensive and serious in forest destruction is the role of shifting cultivators and wood gatherers (Myers, 1980, 1984). Because of this factor alone the true rate of forest disturbance is actually two to three times as great as that suggested by the FAO figures, or more than 2 percent a year. At that rate even with no acceleration, all the forests would be converted within less than 50 years, and converted in a way that is almost as serious for the survival of narrowly adapted species of plants, animals, and microorganisms as is clear-cutting itself.

Second, as is documented in other chapters of this book, the population of the tropical countries, already at a level double what it was in 1950, is projected nearly to double again in the next 35 years, to approximately 5 billion. Clearly, for the governments of these countries—already faced with staggering debt, a sluggish world economy, and the rapid loss of the productive capacity of their lands—to be able to expand their economies rapidly enough to continue to care for the needs of their people at 1985 levels would be an unprecedented economic miracle. With about 40 percent of the populations of most tropical countries estimated by the World

Bank to be living in absolute poverty, we can confidently predict that there will be at least twice that many extremely poor people when the population as a whole has doubled and that the pressure they exert on the forests, pressure which is already the major force leading to the forests' destruction, will increase greatly. Under these circumstances there is no doubt that the forests will be destroyed more and more rapidly with each passing year, another indication that they will not last for anything like another 90 years.

The populations of countries that are at least partly tropical or subtropical — most of the developing world — are growing much more rapidly than those of the developed world. Collectively, they now constitute more than half of the world population, China and the developed world each making up about a quarter of the remainder. By the year 2020 the population of the developing world will amount to approximately two-thirds of the world total, that of the developed world only one-sixth. That the populations of the countries of the developed world constituted one-third of the total as recently as 1950 makes clear the speed of the change and its unsettling effect on international relationships. In a period of only 70 years the proportion of the world population living in countries — including the United States — that control about 80 percent of the world's wealth, use about 80 percent of its industrial energy, and consume 80 to 90 percent of its strategic raw materials will have dropped in half.

As other chapters in this book emphasize in different ways, the *tripling* of what was already a record human population in 1950 over a period of only 70 years is an absolutely unprecedented situation. The challenge posed by our sheer numbers to the productive capacity of the global biosphere needs no special emphasis in the context of this symposium. It will, however, be one of the most important factors in determining the shape of our future mode of life and, indeed, the survival of our species; the ways in which these pressures are affecting tropical forests are of general importance and full of meaning for us all.

A third factor of importance in the destruction and deterioration of tropical forests is that the effects of these processes are not distributed uniformly throughout the tropics. Three large forest blocks, those in the western Amazon (mainly in Brazil), in the interior of the Guyanas, and in the Congo Basin of Africa, are larger, are less densely populated, and, therefore, are being exploited more slowly than the other forest regions. Some of the forests in these three regions may actually persist in a relatively undisturbed condition for another 40 years or so, until the surging populations of their respective countries begin to exhaust them. On the other hand, all the remaining forests in other parts of the tropics will surely be gone, or at least profoundly altered in nature and composition, much earlier.

For the most part these forests will not remain undisturbed beyond the end of the present century, just 15 years from now.

To summarize these statistics in another way, about 15 hectares (35 acres) of tropical rain forest are being logged per minute, and at least that much again is being disturbed or degraded in the course of its conversion to other purposes. This process of destruction is apparently irreversible, and it is accelerating rapidly. The tropical forests certainly will never recover from this onslaught, primarily for ecological reasons that we shall now discuss.

Relatively infertile tropical soils are able to support lush forests because most of the limited amounts of nutrients present are actually held within the trees and other vegetation. The roots of these trees spread only through the top few centimeters of soil. The roots recover the nutrients from the leaves that fall to the ground quickly and efficiently, transferring them directly back into the plants from which they have fallen.

Once the trees have been cut, they decay or are burned, releasing relatively large amounts of nutrients into the soil. When this occurs, it is possible to grow crops on the cutover areas successfully for a few years, until the available nutrients are used up. If the cutover areas are then left to recover for many years, and if there is undisturbed forest nearby, the original plant communities may eventually be restored. This process normally takes decades, but it may take centuries, depending on the type of forest involved. It rarely will be allowed to proceed to completion anywhere in the world in the future, however; there are simply too many people and consequently too little time for this to occur in most areas. The relentless search for firewood, the most important source of energy in many parts of the tropics, in the cutover areas is one reason why the forests usually cannot recover.

Shifting cultivation, particularly under circumstances in which the time of rotation must be short, virtually guarantees the continued poverty of the people who practice it. Agricultural development in the tropics without proper management of the soils is no better. Cultivation *can* be sustained on the better tropical soils under ideal conditions, including fertilization, but such conditions lack meaning for the roughly 40 percent of the people in the tropics who make up the rural poor, the people who actually are destroying most of the forests. Trees generally make more productive crops in the humid tropics than do other kinds of plants, and agroforestry, the combining of annual crops and pastures with trees, is probably the most suitable form of agriculture for many of these regions. Unfortunately, very little research is being done in this area, and the practical options are few. Projections for the future world supply that are offered in other chapters of this book make it clear that there has been little progress recently and that the situation for the tropics is particularly grave. Adequate food supplies must, in general, be produced within the countries that need the food, and sub-Saharan Africa merely affords the worst example of our collective failure to achieve this necessary goal.

Consequences of the Destruction of Tropical Forests

Unless we address the problem of how to feed the poor people of Africa and other tropical areas on a sustainable basis, we should expect the instability that has come to be characteristic of many tropical countries to spread and to become increasingly serious as time goes by. If we truly wish to attain our political and economic goals throughout the world, we are going to have to find some way to help alleviate the plight of the billion people living in the tropics who are at the edge of starvation. If we cannot do so, we certainly can expect to fail in our attempts to achieve our political and economic goals in the Third World. Efforts such as the *Kissinger Report* that attempt to outline the conditions for regional stability in the tropics must take into account the ecological realities of the region, which render futile all efforts to achieve stable political and economic systems.

Ultimately because of the endemic, ecologically based poverty that is characteristic of the tropics, the United States and other developed countries are faced with massive immigration from the tropics. In 1982–83 the U.S. Immigration and Naturalization Service apprehended over a million illegal immigrants at the Mexican border alone. The service estimates that 30 to 40 million Latin Americans may enter the country illegally between now and the end of the century, in addition to the numbers who enter legally. The lack of progress in addressing the needs of the rural poor throughout Latin America is responsible for immigration and can be alleviated only when it is viewed in a context that not only addresses the role of rapid population growth in promoting poverty but also takes into account the underlying ecological factors that are involved.

Beyond the social and political consequences of the exhaustion of resources in the tropics exists a problem of still more fundamental importance. I refer to the extinction of a major fraction of the plants, animals, and microorganisms on earth during the lifetimes of most of the people who are living today. The dimensions of this problem can be outlined as follows.

Many tropical organisms are very narrow in their geographical ranges, are highly specific in their ecological requirements, seek out unusual foods, conceal themselves in unique situations, or mate only at highly specific times in particular places. This is the basic reason why the severe disturbance of the forest through shifting cultivation poses such a serious threat to the continued existence of these species. To illustrate the pattern further, allow me to present the following facts. Nearly 20 percent of all kinds of organisms in the world—perhaps a million species—occur only in the forests of Latin America outside the Amazon Basin; another 20 percent occur in the forests of Asia and Africa outside the Congo Basin. All the forests in which these organisms occur will have been destroyed by early in the next century. What would be a reasonable estimate of the loss of species that will accompany such destruction?

The loss of half the species in these forests by, say, 2010 would amount to perhaps a million species, most of them completely unknown. This amounts to the extinction of several species an hour, more than 100 species a day—fewer in the immediate future, more in the early part of the next century, and, because of the subsequent destruction of the remaining large forest blocks, still more in a continuing rate of acceleration. In short, extinction at these rates can be expected to continue for many decades, with the ultimate possibility of reaching stability after the human population does so, but only after many additional organisms have become extinct.

A concrete example of the process of extinction is provided by the birds and plants of Hawaii (see table 6.2). When Europeans first landed in Hawaii about 200 years ago, at least 43 species of land birds occurred there. Since then 15 of these species have become extinct, and 19 are classified as threatened and endangered. Only 9 species—about 21 percent of the total—have relatively flourishing populations. Thanks to elegant research by Storrs Olson, of the U.S. National Museum of National History, Smithsonian Institution, however, we know that the overall picture is actually much worse. Olson has discovered 45 additional species of land birds as fossils. All these birds were present in Hawaii when the Polynesians landed there some 1,500 years ago. In other words, less than a third of the birds that were in Hawaii at that time have survived to the present, and only about 1 in 10 of the original birds still exists at a healthy population level (table 6.3). Undoubtedly additional species of land birds existed in Hawaii 1,500 years ago that have not yet been discovered as fossils; thus these estimates are conservative ones.

For plants the figures are also impressive. The total number of native flowering plant species that existed in Hawaii 200 years ago has been estimated at roughly 1,250. About 10 percent of them have already become extinct, and another 40 percent are threatened or endangered—many of them at the brink of extinction. Therefore, no more than half of the Hawaiian plants that existed 200 years ago remain at reasonably viable population levels at present.

Table 6.2. Number of Native Species in Hawaii

	Land Birds		Plants	
	Number	*Percent*	*Number*	*Percent*
Total, 200 years before present (historical record)	43	100	Ca. 1,250	100
Extinct	13	35	120 +	10
Total, present	28	65	Ca. 1,130	90
Endangered or threatened	19	44	Ca. 500	40
Not endangered or threatened	9	21	Ca. 625	50

SOURCE: For land birds: Olson and James, 1984; for plants: W. L. Wagner, pers. comm., 1984; Federal Register, U.S. Department of the Interior, 1983.

While the situation in Hawaii has been analyzed exceptionally well, it is by no means unique. Large numbers of fossil land vertebrates that have become extinct once their areas were colonized by human beings have been found throughout the West Indies. Another example is provided by the island of Madagascar, which we have already described as being home to at least 150,000 kinds of organisms, most of them found nowhere else. Among these are all the living species of lemurs, one of the major groups of primates, and many other unusual and restricted kinds of organisms. There are 19 living species of lemurs and at least 14 other species that have become extinct since human populations first reached Madagascar. In addition, two species of giant tortoises; up to a dozen species of large, flightless elephant birds; and a hippopotamus have become extinct during the past 1,500 years.

Unfortunately, less than a tenth of the land surface of Madagascar is still covered with natural vegetation (Rauh, 1979), only a fraction of that consisting of tropical forests, the richest kind of vegetation in terms of numbers of species and the home of the most unusual ones. At present these forests grow over only about one-sixth of the lands they once occupied, and their scattered remainders are rapidly being cut over. Occupying an area only about the size of Massachusetts and Connecticut combined, the remnants of natural vegetation in Madagascar are home to one of the richest and most unusual assemblages of organisms found anywhere on earth. Many if not most of these species will almost certainly become extinct during the next two or three decades.

To provide a single example of a mainland area—one of many that might have been selected—let us briefly consider the Atlantic forest region of eastern Brazil. Once extensive, this beautiful forest is home to 20 species and subspecies of primates, two-thirds of which are entirely confined

Table 6.3. Land Birds of Hawaii: 1,500-Year Record
          (Human Settlement)

Total bird species	88
Extinct species	60* (68%)

SOURCE: Olson and James, 1984.
*Fossil evidence, 45; historical collections, 15.

to this region. These include the golden lion tamarin (*Leontopithecus ro-salia*), a species of which fewer than 200 individuals still exist in the wild, and the *muriqui* (*Brachyteles arachnoides*), the largest, most apelike, and most endangered of all New World monkeys. These forests likewise are the only habitat for over half of their plant species, such as the tree legume *Harleyodendron,* discovered for the first time less than a decade ago, and of possible economic importance, like most other legumes. Unfortunately, less than 1 percent of these forests, almost untouched 150 years ago, remain, now only as scattered fragments.

At least three-fourths of the primates of this region are in immediate danger of extinction, this being simply an extreme case of the threat posed to primates, our closest relatives—and therefore a group of great interest to us—worldwide. The remaining forests are simply being cleared, and the demands of São Paulo, probably the world's largest city, are accelerating the process.

Rather than multiplying similar examples from areas such as coastal Ecuador, Central America, tropical Asia, and the West Indies, where the situation is equally grave, we can now place the problem of extinction in the tropics in a more general context. Two decades ago the late Robert MacArthur, of Princeton University, and E. O. Wilson, of Harvard University, pointed out that on islands there is a constant loss of species, apparently random and based on the necessarily small populations that can exist on islands. There is also a gain of species by immigration, so that an island of given characteristics, including size and distance from the source area, will tend to have an *equilibrium* number of species. These concepts have now been applied to the study of the process of extinction in mainland areas.

To understand the processes involved, consider Barro Colorado Island, an island of about 15 square kilometers that was formed between 1911 and 1914 by the damming of the río Chagres to form the Panama Canal. Set aside as a reserve in 1923, Barro Colorado Island was at that time home to 208 species of breeding birds. Over the next 60 years at least 45 of these birds became extinct. At least 6 more species subsequently became extinct. This amounts to the extinction of one-fourth of the total in less than 75 years, with maximum habitat protection provided during the entire period. This substantial extinction has occurred despite the fact that Barro Colorado Island is separated from the source areas on the mainland by a distance of approximately 200 m.

Similarly, the fragmentation of habitats into small patches, a process that is occurring throughout the tropics, has an important effect in accelerating the extinction of the species that may survive temporarily within those patches. In these small populations inbreeding becomes an important factor, just as it is in zoos, and incursions by humans inevitably become more serious and extensive as the size of the patches decreases. The lesson for us is clear: just as species become extinct more rapidly on islands, where their populations are small, than they do elsewhere, so they become extinct more rapidly in isolated patches of forest, and for similar reasons. As more and more of the potential source areas are destroyed, the process is accelerated still more.

The survival of species in isolated patches of tropical forest is being studied experimentally by a group of U.S. and Brazilian scientists headed by Thomas Lovejoy, of the World Wildlife Fund—U.S. and cosponsored by the Instituto Nacional de Pesquisas da Amazonia (INPA), of Brazil. Their project is being carried out in a region near Manaus, in Amazonian Brazil. The ranchers who are clearing the land for cattle production have agreed to leave a series of forest patches, ranging from 1 hectare (2.47 acres) to 1,000 hectares (3.8 square miles), with comparable areas of uncut forest being studied by similar methods. Although the results of the study are still preliminary, they will obviously be valuable in understanding the process of extinction that is characteristic of the tropics worldwide.

Summary

The rapid growth of human populations, extensive poverty, and ignorance of ecological principles that are causing the destruction of tropical forests during our lifetimes promise to drive to extinction something approaching a quarter of the world's biological diversity before our grandchildren have the chance to learn about it. The great majority of the species that will probably become extinct will never have been seen by any scientist and will never have been considered in terms of their potential for the amelioration of the lot of the hungry human beings who are consuming them. The entire basis of our civilization rests on a few hundred species out of the millions that might have been selected, and we have just begun to explore the properties of most of the remaining ones.

The saddest ecological stories are those that involve the permanent destruction of a resource that might have been renewable if we had simply learned to understand it, and that is what is characteristic of our assault on the tropics during the closing years of the twentieth century. The despicable attempts of those unfamiliar with ecology and tropical biology to ignore or attempt to minimize the tragic meaning and lasting importance of these events deserve only our contempt; they are courting disaster for themselves and for all the rest of us as well.

Global stability—in a political or economic sense—can be constructed only on the basis of ecological stability. We must learn about the properties of tropical forests and the organisms that occur in them. If we can utilize them appropriately and in a sustainable way for the benefit of the large majority of our fellow human beings who live in tropical and subtropical countries, we will also be creating the optimal conditions for the survival of the greatest possible number of organisms.

References

Brenan, J. P. M. 1978. Some aspects of the phytogeography of tropical Africa. *Annals of the Missouri Botanical Garden* 65:437–78.

Caulfield, C. 1985. *In the rainforest.* New York: Knopf.

Ehrlich, P., and A. Ehrlich. 1981. *Extinction: The causes and consequences of the disappearance of species.* New York: Random House.

Erwin, T. L. 1982. Tropical forests: Their richness in Coleoptera and other arthropods. *Coleopterists Bulletin* 36:74–75.

FAO [Food and Agriculture Organization of the United Nations]. 1981a. *Forest resources of tropical Africa. Part 1: Regional synthesis. Part 2: Country briefs.* Rome: FAO.

———. 1981b. *Forest resources of tropical Asia.* Rome: FAO.

———. 1981c. Los recursos forestales de la América tropical. Rome: FAO.

Myers, N. 1980. *Conversion of tropical moist forests.* Washington, D.C.: National Academy of Sciences.

———. 1983. *A wealth of wild species: Storehouse for human welfare.* Boulder, Colo.: Westview Press.

———. 1984. *The primary source: Tropical forests and our future.* New York: Norton.

Oldfield, M. L. 1984. *The value of conserving genetic resources.* Washington, D.C.: U.S. Department of the Interior, National Park Service.

Olson, S., and James. 1984. The role of Polynesians in the extinction of the avifauna of the Hawaiian Islands. In P. S. Martin and R. S. Klein, eds. *Quaternary extinction: A prehistoric revolution,* pp. 768–80. Tucson: University of Arizona Press.

Raugh, W. 1979. Problems of biological conservation in Madagascar. In D. Bramwell, ed. *Plants and islands,* pp. 405–21. New York: Academic Press.

Raven, P. H., ed. 1980. *Research priorities in tropical biology.* Washington, D.C.: National Academy of Sciences.

Savage, J. M. 1982. *Ecological aspects of development in the humid tropics.* Washington, D.C.: National Academy Press.

U.S. Fish and Wildlife Service. 1984. *Endangered and threatened wildlife and plants.* 50 CFR 17.11 and 17.12. Washington, D.C.: Department of the Interior.

7.
Acid Rain

ACIDS PRODUCED by the combustion of fossil fuels and the smelting of nonferrous ores can be transported long distances through the atmosphere and deposited on earth on ecosystems that are exceedingly vulnerable to damage from excessive acidity (Oden, 1976; Likens et al., 1979). This is the threat to man and the biosphere discussed here—a threat commonly referred to as the "acid rain" problem. To understand the source of the problem and the extent of damage that has occurred, or is likely to occur, we must explore phenomena on many scales—from the submicroscopic world of molecules and ions to the planet earth and, in between, cells, organisms, lakes, hillside slopes, and forests. Midway between the molecular and the planetary realm is man, the final stop in our journey.

A Molecular Perspective

Chemical processes, acting molecule by molecule, govern the formation of environmental acidity and ultimately shape its fate. The acidity of precipitation, lake water, or a patch of soil is determined by the concentration, $[H^+]$, of hydrogen ions in that medium. The most commonly used unit of acidity is pH, defined as the negative logarithm (to the base 10) of $[H^+]$. A low pH corresponds to high acidity, and a unit decrease in pH corresponds to a tenfold increase in $[H^+]$. A pH of 7 is the neutral point—water with such a pH contains as much acid as it does base. Figure 7.1 shows the pH scale, with some representative values marked on it to provide a reference frame for what follows. Particularly noteworthy is that in large regions of Europe and eastern North America the annual mean pH of rain and snow is below 4.5.

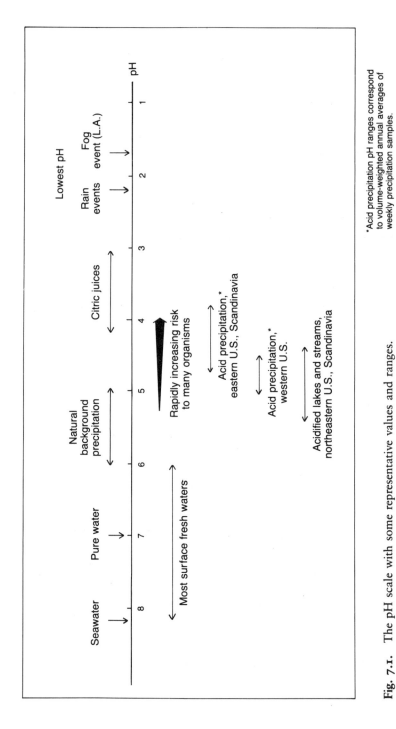

Fig. 7.1. The pH scale with some representative values and ranges.

The two major acids in acid rain are sulfuric acid, H_2SO_4, and nitric acid, HNO_3. These acids are formed in the atmosphere from sulfur dioxide (SO_2) and oxides of nitrogen (NO_x), the gaseous products of fossil-fuel combustion and nonferrous-ore smelting. The hydrogen ions in these acids typically originate from the hydrogen in cloud water or in atmospheric water vapor. The chemistry of the production process is only partly understood at present; it appears that a variety of mechanisms can cause acids to form and that the dominant chemical reactions depend on the location and weather conditions as well as on the chemical composition of the local atmosphere. Since acid formation from the gaseous precursors is an oxidation process, certain oxidants, such as the hydroxyl radical (HO) and hydrogen peroxide (H_2O_2) that occur as trace constituents in the atmosphere, play a major role in the formation process. Sunlight, soot, and trace metals may also expedite the process of acid formation under certain circumstances (NRC, 1981; Novakov et al., 1974). Some of the substances (such as H_2O_2, soot, and trace metals) that convert the precursor gases to acids can result from combustions, just as do the precursor gases themselves.

In chemical reactions where several chemical species combine to form some reaction products, some of the reactants may be so scarce and others so abundant that most of the abundant molecules are unlikely to participate in the reaction. The scarcer reactants are called "limiting" chemicals, and the abundant ones are called "nonlimiting" chemicals. A decrease (brought about by pollution control, for example) in the concentration of a nonlimiting reactant will not have as large an effect on the reaction rate as would a decrease in the concentration of a limiting reactant. This clearly can be an important consideration in the formulation of strategies for acid-rain reduction.

We turn now from sources of acidity in the atmosphere to the fate of acidity when it is deposited in an ecosystem in the form of rain, snow, fog droplets, or even dry particles. Society's main concern is with the biological consequences of acid deposition. But before we can predict the magnitude of the biological damage that acid rain causes, we must first estimate the increase in acidity of a volume of lake water or soil when a specified quantity of acid is added to it. How is this done?

If the substance added to the water or soil were, say, common table salt, then calculation of the increase in salt concentration would be straightforward: the quantity of salt dissolved in the water or added to the soil divided by the volume of water or weight of the soil would give the increase in concentration of the substance. For acidity, however, the situation is more complex. Unlike salt molecules, hydrogen ions can readily be removed or produced in soil and water by internal chemical processes. For example, most natural waters and soils contain alkaline chemicals

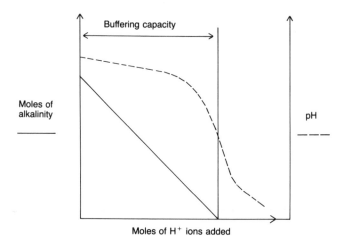

Fig. 7.2. The effect on pH (right axis) and alkalinity (left axis) of adding acid to a closed aqueous system. As more acid is added, the alkalinity steadily declines, whereas pH declines only gradually until the alkalinity is used up: at that point pH dips sharply. Every mole of H^+ added to the system is neutralized by a mole of alkalinity until the alkalinity is used up in the process. The alkalinity present initially is thus a measure of the lake's buffering capacity, or ability to withstand acid input without suffering a large drop in pH.

that annihilate (or neutralize) acidity, removing H^+ ions by chemically converting them into H_2O. Alkalinity is thus one component of an ecosystem's defense against acid precipitation (Stumm and Morgan, 1981). Unfortunately, the neutralizing process is reciprocal: acidity annihilates alkalinity. Because alkalinity is produced through processes (weathering reactions) that proceed at a rate much lower than the rate at which it is used up (through acid precipitation), it is essentially a finite resource and can be exhausted.

Figure 7.2 illustrates graphically what happens when acid is added to a medium containing alkalinity. When the alkalinity of a water volume has been totally exhausted, we say that the water has "acidified." In lake and stream water the most prevalent form of alkalinity is the bicarbonate ion, HCO_3^-, which reacts with H^+ as follows: $H^+ + HCO_3^- \rightarrow H_2O + CO_2$. The evolved CO_2 can escape harmlessly to the atmosphere in this neutralizing process.

Another acid-neutralizing process that takes places in lakes, streams, and soils is the exchange of H^+ ions with nonacidic positive ions, such as Ca^{2+}, K^+, and Na^+, that are found in the solid particles that constitute soils and lake-bottom or stream-bed sediments. This process is called "cation exchange." Yet another set of processes is mineral weathering reactions. Weathering reactions initiated by sulfuric or nitric acid reduce the level of those acids in the environment. Weathering reactions initiated by the natural carbonic acid that results from the dissolution of atmospheric CO_2 in precipitation water can create alkalinity, which subsequently can neutralize acid precipitation.

Another reaction that neutralizes acid precipitation occurs as acidic runoff water percolates through soil containing aluminum, lead, cadmium, mercury, and other metals. In a cation exchange process called "metals mobilization," ionic forms of these metals may be exchanged for hydrogen ions. This leads to a decreased level of acidity and an increased level of dissolved metals in the runoff water. As discussed in more detail below, these toxic metals are more biologically accessible in runoff than when they are soil-bound, and under some cirumstances they pose a threat to life that can exceed that produced by the unneutralized acid runoff (Cronan and Schofield, 1979).

With the fundamental molecular processes relevant to acid deposition described, albeit briefly, we are now ready to journey over 17 orders of magnitude of size to the global realm, where we will examine the impact of anthropogenic acidity on the earth.

Acidification on a Global Scale

In what ways, if any, is acidic deposition changing our planet as a whole? There are two types of planetary changes to consider. First, there are direct chemical changes, which may be of global proportions. In particular, acid deposition may be altering significantly the global H^+ or alkalinity budgets and, in a related fashion, may be accelerating global weathering processes or the rate of mobilization of trace metals. Second, the biological consequences of acid deposition may be of global proportions.

Consider, first, the global anthropogenic rate of emission to the atmosphere of SO_2 and NO_x, the two acid-forming pollutants of concern. In 1980 approximately 85×10^9 kilograms of sulfur in the form of SO_2 and 35×10^9 kg of nitrogen in the form of NO_x were emitted to the atmosphere as a result of fossil-fuel burning and metal smelting. In contrast, the natural background rates of emission to the atmosphere of these gases are about 100×10^9 kg per year of sulfur in the form of SO_2 and a highly uncertain range of between 10 and 100×10^9 kg per year of nitrogen in the form of NO_x (NRC, 1981). (An additional 50×10^9 kg per year of sulfur in the form of hydrogen sulfide and sulfate are emitted to the atmosphere from natural sources as well.) Thus the anthropogenic emissions are a sizable contributor to the total rate at which these gases are loaded into the atmosphere.

Of greater concern to us is knowing (1) what the globally averaged pH of precipitation would be in the absence of the pollutants SO_2 and NO_x and (2) how these pollutants alter that pH value. The background emissions of SO_2 and NO_x have very little influence on the average pH of precipitation because they are very inefficiently converted to sulfuric and nitric acid. Were all the background SO_2 and NO_x emissions converted to these strong acids and the acidifying influence of natural sulfates emitted to the atmosphere was included as well, then the average background pH of rain and snow would be about 4.5. In fact, very small percentages of the background sulfur and nitrogen are converted to strong acids, and the best estimates suggest that the pH of precipitation would be between 5 and 6 in the absence of pollution (Charlson and Rodhe, 1982). The slightly acidic value for this background pH stems largely from the weak carbonic acid, H_2CO_3, which is formed as the carbon dioxide in the atmosphere dissolves in cloud water or falling raindrops, from sulfurous acid (H_2SO_3) formed from background SO_2 dissolved in precipitation water, and from natural background sulfates. In some areas of the world, however, the natural background pH of precipitation can be 6 or even higher because of the presence of alkaline materials, such as limestone dust, in the atmosphere. The Great Basin of the western United States (Harte et al., 1985) and the Tibetan Plateau in central Asia (Harte, 1983) are examples of such regions. In other areas intense volcanic activity or biological processes cause sulfuric acid to form naturally in the atmosphere. Downwind of such sites the natural background pH of precipiatation can be slightly below 5. A value of 5.6 is widely considered to be a good working estimate of the global average background pH of precipitation.

In contrast to the background emissions, anthropogenic emissions of SO_2 and NO_x are rather efficiently converted to sulfuric and nitric acid in the atmosphere. There is now fairly convincing evidence that the conversion process is expedited by the presence of certain oxidizing agents that are found in highest concentration in polluted atmospheres (NRC, 1983). Thus the chemical processes in the atmosphere that are responsible for the conversion of these gases to acidic form take place more rapidly in the polluted air in which anthropogenic emissions are found. Were all the anthropogenic SO_2 and NO_x converted to sulfuric and nitric acid, then the rate of H^+ deposition to the earth's surface would be about 7×10^{12} moles per year of H^+. This can be compared to the background flux of H^+ to earth's surface, which is about 1.5×10^{12} moles per year of H^+. If this anthropogenic flux of H^+ were uniformly mixed in the 5×10^{14}

cubic meters per year of global precipitation, then the average pH of precipitation would be about 4.9. Of course, the anthropogenic acidity is not uniformly dispersed around the earth; indeed, on about 1 percent of the earth's surface annually averaged pH's in the low 4s are observed. Additional acidity can fall to the earth's surface in dry form; subsequent wetting of dry acid particles by rain or snow can acidify surface waters or soils in the same manner that acid precipitation does. All told, at least half of the amount of acid that could potentially be formed from anthropogenic emissions (the 7×10^{12} moles per year of H^+) is actually formed in the atmosphere and descends to the surface in either wet or dry form. The remaining fraction of the sulfur and nitrogen oxides forms nonacidic or only weakly acidic chemical species. The best available evidence is that the fluxes of wet and dry acidity are roughly equal on a globally averaged basis.

We can also compare the global rate of sulfuric and nitric acid formation from pollution with the rate that these acids are produced naturally by various other processes, such as nitrification and photosynthesis. Moreover, we can also compare the rates at which alkalinity is produced globally and trace metals such as aluminum are mobilized with the rate that anthropogenic acidity uses up alkalinity and mobilizes aluminum. Table 7.1 presents a global comparison of natural and anthropogenic global acid-forming and acid-neutralizing processes.

It should be clear from the table that on a global basis anthropogenic acidity dominates precipitation chemistry but that, in turn, the chemical effects of anthropogenic acidity are dominated on a global basis by chemical processes occurring in terrestrial and aquatic habitats. The oceans exemplify this global resilience to acid deposition; the effect of many centuries of anthropogenic acidity deposited in the oceans would have an undetectable influence on seawater pH. By way of contrast, the effect of raising the CO_2 level of the atmosphere from the preindustrial value of about 275 parts per million to a new future equilibrium value of 400 ppm as a result of fossil-fuel burning would be to lower the pH of seawater by about 0.15 pH units, which is a measurable amount.

The purely and directly chemical comparisons expressed in the table should not be construed to mean that anthropogenic acidity will have no global-scale chemical consequences. Widespread chemical changes may arise through the disruption of biological processes, which can act as points of leverage. For example, the process of biological nitrogen fixation is sensitive to the pH of the medium—soil or water—that surrounds the nitrogen-fixing organisms. Conceivably the rate of global nitrogen fixation could be diminished significantly by acidic deposition, and, in turn, this diminution could affect the global nitrogen cycle. Far more likely, however, is the possibility that such damage will occur on a regional scale long before it

Table 7.1. Global Fluxes of H$^+$, Stocks of Alkalinity, and Flows of Alkalinity

Global Fluxes of H$^+$ (10^{12} Equivalents per Year)*	
Precipitation flux from atmosphere to surface in form of carbonic acid, assuming preindustrial value of 275 ppm for atmospheric CO_2 concentration	1.04
Same as above but assuming present CO^2 concentration of 340 ppm	1.16
Precipitation acidity from natural background emissions of sulfur	0.3–1.0
Gross production of H$^+$ in the global nitrification process	400
Gross uptake of H$^+$ in biological nitrogen assimilation	400
Acidity produced from anthropogenic SO_2 and NO_x emissions (approximately half is deposited to earth in wet and half in dry form)	4–5
Global Stocks of Alkalinity (10^{15} Equivalents)	
Cation exchange capacity in top 1 m of soil	30–50
Alkalinity of surface fresh waters	0.05–0.1
Alkalinity of seawater	2,700
Global Flows of Alkalinity (10^{12} Equivalents per Year)	
Production by weathering processes	1–10

*The last four H$^+$ fluxes are associated with alkalinity fluxes. A decrease in alkalinity corresponds to an increase in H$^+$, and vice versa. On an equivalents basis, the magnitudes of these fluxes are equal. The first two processes, involving CO_2 dissolution, do not involve any flow of alkalinity.

shows up on a global one. For instance, in habitats where nitrogen fixation plays a critical role in the nitrogen cycle, acidic deposition may cause major chemical changes.

Widespread forest dieback (discussed in more detail below) caused by acid deposition could have major global climatic repercussions. One reason is that such dieback would increase the concentration of atmospheric CO_2 and thereby contribute to the CO_2 "greenhouse" effect. It would also increase the albedo of the earth's surface, thereby decreasing the amount of solar radiation absorbed at the earth's surface. And it would affect the global transpiration rate, which in turn would alter the amount of water vapor (the major greenhouse gas) and the amount of cloud cover in the atmosphere. The climatic consequences of these changes would undoubtedly be more severe at the regional level, but the possibility of global-scale climate disruption cannot be ruled out.

Having journeyed from the molecular to the global domain and thereby viewed the acid-rain problem from the submicroscopic perspective of sources and sinks and then from a holistic perspective, we now go to where the real action is—in organisms, ecosystems, and finally, society.

Damage to Cells and Organisms

Most organisms live in an environment whose chemical and physical characteristics are conducive to the organisms' well-being. That is not a fortuitous circumstance, of course, for in the course of both evolution and succession organisms adapt to, and to some extent create, their environment. If the chemical properties of their environment are altered too much from those that they are used to, then biological damage is likely to result. For example, typical organisms thrive best at a particular value of the pH of the medium—be it soil or water—in which they live. Many fish, particularly those of the family Salmonidae, which includes trout and salmon, will not reproduce successfully when the pH of their surrounding water drops below approximately 5.5. Most adult salmonids do poorly and eventually succumb to the stress of pH's below approximately 5 (Beamish, 1976; Glass et al., 1982).

Although fish kills resulting from acid rain have seized the headlines, biological damage is by no means limited to these organisms. Salamanders and other amphibia are particularly sensitive to acidic conditions. One of the first victims of lake acidification in the Adirondacks was the spotted salamander, *Ambystoma maculatum* (Pough, 1976). Ironically, in areas of the United States where acid deposition is occurring and surface-water acidification is likely to occur in the future, yet another member of the genus *Ambystoma* may have the honor of presaging more severe damage to come. The area is the western slope of the Colorado Rockies, where very low alkalinity lakes and ponds are found and where precipitation with a mean annually averaged pH of 4.7 to 5 has been observed over the past five years (Harte et al., 1985). During snowmelt in late spring and early summer at a study site in the Rockies, the pH in some of the low-alkalinity surface waters has been observed to drop to values in the neighborhood of 5. This drop in pH occurs during the most acid-sensitive stage (egg development) in the life cycle of the tiger salamander, *A. tigrinum*, which inhabits small subalpine lakes at the site. If acid deposition continues there, these salamander populations could be the sacrificial "canaries in the mine," providing early warning of widespread damage from acid snow and rain that is prevalent throughout the higher-elevation, low-alkalinity regions of the western United States.

Microscopic life is also at risk from acidification. Many species of phytoplankton have a pH optimum in what is called the circumneutral range—6 to 8—and exhibit low reproduction and high mortality at pH's either below or above that range. Both field and laboratory studies confirm that in acidified lakes and streams entire populations of some phytoplankton species have been killed (Marmorek, 1983; Stokes, 1983; Yan and Stokes, 1978; Schindler and Turner, 1982; Tonnessen, 1983). This is not just of esoteric ecological interest, for the phytoplankton are the base of the aquatic food chains. If chemical and physical conditions permit, sunlight and nutrients are captured by phytoplankton, which are then eaten by zooplankton, crustacea, fish, and aquatic birds. In any particular lake or stream some species of phytoplankton may actually thrive under more acidic conditions, but generally such species will not provide a base for the same food chains that the original community of species did. Many species of zooplankton are also adversely affected by acidification. For example, members of the genus *Daphnia* are quite sensitive to water pH, with a tolerance threshold pH of about 5 (Raddum, 1980; Yan and Strus, 1980).

Many nitrogen-fixing organisms (organisms capable of converting molecular nitrogen into ammonia, a nutrient form of nitrogen) are believed to be particularly sensitive to acidification. Although more experimentation is needed here to quantify dose-response relations, it is quite likely that legumes and certain species of blue-green algae and lichen are adversely affected when the pH of their surroundings drops significantly below its accustomed value.

The damages described above are associated directly with low pH values of the media surrounding the organisms. Although the detailed physiological cause of the damage is not known in many cases, limited information available suggests that excessive H^+ concentrations interfere with ion transport, particularly in body organs, such as fish gills, that communicate directly with the surrounding media. Another direct biological effect of acidic deposition is associated with the corrosive action of acid on many substances. Plant leaf surfaces often have a waxy layer that affords the plant protection against fungal and other kinds of invasion and disease. Corrosion of this layer by acid deposition has been suggested as a mechanism to explain at least part of the damage observed on trees growing in regions such as New England and Germany that receive intense acidic deposition. For a review of this and other mechanisms of acid-induced tree damage, see Postel (1984).

Other, more indirect biological effects of acidification have also been identified. As acid runoff flows through soils, the process of metal mobilization reduces the acidity of the water at the same time that it increases the availability to organisms of trace metals such as aluminum, lead, mercury, and cadmium. Unfortunately, for most organisms this trade-off appears to be an unfavorable one—the increase in trace-metal availability at toxic concentrations can do more damage than would the original acidity. When aluminum concentrations in lake and stream waters approach 100 ppb, toxic effects on fish can be detected (Baker and Schofield, 1982). Normally, unacidified waters have aluminum concentrations sufficiently below this value that the metal does not pose a threat to aquatic life. In acidified lakes in many areas of Scandinavia and eastern North America, lake-water concentrations of aluminum exceed 200 ppb; the fish mortalities that have been observed there are now believed to be due to a combination of the direct effects of low pH and the indirect effect of acid-mobilized toxic metals.

Acid runoff in soil can also leach from the root zones of trees such cations as calcium and potassium, which are essential to plant growth. The contrast between this process and toxic metal mobilization is worth highlighting. The toxic metals were formerly bound in soil particles and were biologically unavailable; acidification rendered them soluble and thereby accessible for plant or animal uptake. In contrast, the essential cations were formerly found in bound form from which uptake could proceed at a pace adequate for normal plant needs. When they become soluble as a result of leaching by acidic runoff, they flow out of the root zone (indeed, out of entire watersheds) and are no longer available to meet plant requirements.

Tree damage from acidification illustrates the potential multiple hazards associated with acidic deposition (Johnson and Siccama, 1983). A number of mechanisms by which acidic precipitation could damage trees have been proposed. As mentioned above, one such mechanism is direct damage to the waxy protective layer found on needles and leaves by the corrosive action of acids, which, among other things, may increase the susceptibility of the plant to fungal attack. Acidic precipitation may also interfere with the various mechanisms by which trees obtain essential nutrients such as nitrogen and phosphorus by killing the microorganisms that live in soil or are symbiotically associated with the root structure and that process organic forms of nutrients into inorganic forms that can be used by vegetation. Yet another proposed mechanism is a leaching process in which acid runoff percolating through soil dissolves essential cations and carries them away from the root zone. A fourth possible mechanism involves the toxic metals mobilized by acid runoff; they can damage trees either by direct toxic action or by physical interference with plant functions. As an example of a physical action, it has been suggested by Bernhard Ulrich, a soil scientist in Germany, that aluminum might clog the fine root hairs of trees, thereby interfering with their ability to take in sufficient water; droughtlike symptoms thus might show up even in years with plenty of precipitation. A fifth hypothesis is that the nitrate in nitric acid acts as a growth stimulant, causing trees to extend their growing period into the cold season, which leads to damage to sensitive new growth from freezing. The facts are not yet in place from which to make a convincing assignment of cause to effect. It is possible that some combination of stresses is at work, perhaps different combinations in different forests.

This brief overview of the kinds of biological damage that acid deposition can induce may give the impression that every organism suffers when the surroundings acidify. There is, however, evidence that a number of organisms can tolerate, and indeed thrive in, levels of acidity in their surroundings that exceed those normally encountered. Unfortunately, this prospect should not be greeted with approval or even equanimity, for in many instances these organisms would not be considered desirable, at least by our species. Among fish populations the least interesting from a sports-fishing perspective (for example, suckers as compared with trout) survive the best at low pH. We can even speculate about the possibility of certain disease-associated organisms thriving in acidic waters. Giardia is a protozoan that is associated with a severe gastrointestinal disease that afflicts hikers and mountain climbers. It is contracted by drinking seemingly clean, pure mountain-stream waters in which the microscopic organism lives. This protozoan spends part of its lifetime in the mammalian gut and part free-living in natural waters. Consistent with available information is the possibility that the pH optimum of this organism lies below the normal circumneutral values found in natural waters and that acidified lakes and streams provide a more congenial home for it.

Ecosystems

Over vast regions of Europe and North America precipitation occurs with a pH substantially below the estimated natural background value of 5.6. In the northeastern United States, southeastern Canada, Scandinavia, northern and central Europe, and parts of China the annually averaged pH of precipitation is between 4 and 4.5. In many areas of the western United States, and undoubtedly in areas that have not yet been investigated, precipitation pH averages in the range of 4.5 to 5. Wherever precipitation with a pH significantly below background value occurs on ecosystems with low buffering capacity, chemical and biological impacts are likely to occur eventually.

Freshwater lakes sitting atop granitic bedrock and thus having low buffering capacity provided the first evidence that acidic precipitation could damage whole ecosystems. Such lakes are like the lymph nodes in the human body—they exhibit the first signs of environmental disease and thus serve as early-warning indicators of eventual wider damage. Scandinavian lakes exhibited the first signs of trouble about two decades ago, and in the subsequent years a pattern of wholesale ecological devastation was documented (Almer et al., 1978; Henriksen, 1980). First, the alkalinity of these lakes totally disappeared, and pH values sank below 5 in many of them. As a result the lake-water concentrations of trace toxic metals increased. Trout populations died out, the composition of the planktonic and microbial populations shifted from those formerly habituated to a circumneutral range of pH's to those that could tolerate the increased lake-water acidity. Successful reproductive activity of many amphibia dwelling in the lakes ceased. Although it is not true that *all* life has been extinguished in such lakes, the phrase "dead lakes" has been widely used in the popular media to refer to them. At the present time it is estimated that in Norway and Sweden at least 20,000 lakes of a total of 90,000 investigated exhibit these symptoms and are considered to be "dead" or "dying." Because the organisms that can adapt to acidified lake waters are rarely the sort that are of interest to sports fishers and because the acidified lakes cannot fulfill the ecological role formerly played by the unacidified lakes, these lakes are, indeed, dead functionally, even though not literally.

Stimulated by the early findings in Scandinavia, scientists in eastern North America (where precipitation acidity was similar to that in Scandinavia) began to look systematically at lakes with low buffering capacity to see whether the Scandinavian phenomenon was repeated there. In the Adirondacks and subsequently in parts of Canada compelling evidence for a similar pattern of ecological damage was soon obtained. Presently some 400 lakes in the Adirondacks are considered to be "dead." Good reviews and summaries of these developments are contained in Cowling (1982) and Glass et al. (1982).

The evidence indicating a causal linkage between surface-water acidification and acidic deposition in Scandinavia and eastern North America is of two forms: (1) direct or positive and (2) indirect, resulting from the failure of scientists to develop convincing alternative causal mechanisms to account for the observed patterns of lake acidification. Three pieces of positive evidence stand out. First, a clear correlation exists between geographic areas where precipitation is particularly acidic and areas where low-alkalinity lakes became acidic. Second, elevated sulfate levels are observed in acidified lakes, as expected when the acidifying agent is sulfuric acid in precipitation. Third, an intensive study of lake acidification in the Adirondacks demonstrated that observations of varying degrees of acidification found in lakes in close proximity to one another are consistent with the hypothesis that acid precipitation is the primary cause of lake acidification in that area.

This third argument is worth expansion. Initially, a puzzling feature of the investigations in eastern North America emerged. In the Adirondacks there were situations in which two lakes, which historically were believed to have similar chemical characteristics and were receiving similar amounts of acidic precipitation, exhibited differing responses to that precipitation. One lake might acidify and its pH drop to the mid-4s, while the pH of its neighbor might remain at, say, 6. Such observations were initially interpreted by some scientists to indicate that acidic precipitation could not be the cause of lake acidification. Further research revealed, however, that in such instances soil depth differed in the watersheds surrounding the lakes. Lakes situated in basins with substantial soil accumulation responded more slowly to acidic precipitation (EPRI, 1981). The reason is obvious: the soils surrounding a lake provide buffering agents that offer the lake some protection against acidification—the deeper the soils, the greater the availability of such protection and the longer it takes for the lake to acidify.

While the positive evidence to date that links lake acidification to acidic deposition is compelling, at least two major alternative causative factors have been suggested. First, it has been claimed that acidification could result from altered land-use practices. The absence of correlation between locations of acidified lakes and locations in which land-use alterations has occurred suggests that this explanation does not generally apply. Second, it has been suggested that lakes become acidic naturally because of biological processes and therefore that the role of acidic precipitation is uncertain. It is true that there are naturally occurring acidic lakes, the so-called brown-water lakes, in which organic acids produce low-pH waters. However, the acidified lakes of concern in Scandinavia and eastern North America are clear-water lakes. In contrast to the brown-water lakes, these lakes are biologically very unproductive. Havas et al. (1984) give a particularly insightful critique of these and other proposed alternative causative factors.

In the western United States, where acidic deposition is also occurring but is not as intense as that in Europe and eastern North America, the risk of future lake acidification is a real one (Roth et al., 1985). In that region there are numerous sites, particularly at the higher elevations in the Rocky Mountains, the Sierra Nevada, and the Cascades, where acid deposition is occurring on highly sensitive watersheds. As yet no biological damage from acid deposition has been documented in the West, but evidence for acid-induced chemical change has been reported. In particular, the first stage of acidification—a reduction in surface-water alkalinity—was detected in the West in a survey of stream-water chemistry conducted by the U.S. Geological Survey over a 10- to 15-year period (Smith and Alexander, 1983).

Available data are insufficient to predict the rate at which alkalinity levels will decline in the future in lake and stream waters of the West. But a number of factors suggest that many ecosystems in the high mountains of the western United States may be even more sensitive to acidic precipitation than were those in the northeast. Most noticeably, there is the extremely low alkalinity found in the soils and surface waters of the Sierra Nevada of California, the Cascades of Washington, and parts of the Rocky Mountains (all sites where precipitation is considerably more acidic than background). However, these alkalinity concentrations are probably no lower than those in Scandinavia and the Adirondacks before the onset of acidic deposition there. Five factors distinguish these western sites:

1. A large fraction of precipitation falls as snow, which means that the pulse of acid during spring melt observed in Scandinavia and the Adirondacks may pose a particularly great threat in the western mountains.

2. It is likely that dry deposition of acids contributes relatively more in the West than in Scandinavia or eastern North America (because of the presence of long dry periods in much of the West), which means that a comparison of wet precipitation pH values will give an underestimate of the total acid loading rate in the West.

3. The soils in the western mountains are extremely thin, and the slopes are steep in comparison to those in the East or in Scandinavia, which means that available acid-neutralizing capacity will be exhausted faster for a given pH, or at a comparable rate for a higher pH.

4. High concentrations of potentially toxic acid-mobilizable trace metals occur in the western surface rocks and sols, which pose a biological threat.

5. A short growing season characterizes the high mountains in the West, which means that ecosystem recovery following a late-spring acid pulse will be retarded.

All these factors should dispel any illusions one might harbor that western ecosystems are not at risk simply because precipitation acidity is lower in the West than in areas of the world where severe damage has already occurred.

Acidic precipitation will induce a drop in lake water pH only after the buffering capacities of the lake water, the lake-bottom sediments, and the soils that surround the lake and interact with snowmelt and rain runoff are largely exhausted. With soil-buffering capacity depleted by acidic runoff, one would expect that damage to terrestrial vegetation might also occur, and yet until only a few years ago no evidence for such damage existed. Then in 1982 scientists in West Germany discovered that major damage to trees was occurring in approximately 8 percent of the forested area in that country. A year later the damaged area was up to 34 percent, and in 1984 it was 55 percent (Postel, 1984).

Forest damage has also been documented in the United States in the past few years, particularly but not limited to stands of red spruce in New England (Johnson and Siccama, 1983). Many possible causes of this widespread forest damage have been proposed. Acid precipitation is one; others include oxidative damage induced by ozone (which is produced in the lower atmosphere mainly by chemical reactions that require the presence of NO_x—the same oxides of nitrogen that can also form nitric acid), the direct effects of NO_x and SO_2, and outbreaks of forest pests. While pollutant levels have generally been rising or have remained steadily high in regions with forest damage, the suggestion that drought or pest damage is the underlying cause is weakened by the absence of information correlating the outbreak of recent forest damage with such stresses.

Forest damage may spread to huge regions of the planet in the future, but it is not the only potential regional ecological hazard of acid precipitation. The discussion of other hazards given below is necessarily speculative in view of the sparse information available, but it gives some idea of the potential regional risks of acidic precipitation.

Damage to agricultural crops has been investigated. The evidence at hand, while scanty, suggests that in most regions agriculturally exploited soils are not at great risk. Most such soils are naturally well buffered. In addition, soil amendments used in modern agriculture generally augment natural soil-buffering capacity. Moreover, most crops are annuals, and their growing period is probably too short to allow acid precipitation to cause extensive damage. If damage to crops occurs, it most likely is by direct corrosive action to the plants. For this reason orchard crops may be most at risk, over the long run, but information is lacking here.

In certain habitats slow soil-building and nutrifying processes are vital to long-term ecological integrity. For instance, in subalpine and alpine ecosystems lichens and other organisms play an important role in replacing nutrients lost through leaching processes that wash nutrients downhill and out of the ecosystem. Nitrogen fixation is not the major pathway by which most green plants obtain their nitrgoen, but it is nevertheless a critical process in certain ecosystems. In some nitrogen-limited lakes and coastal waters in the arctic and subarctic, for example, nitrogen fixation carried on by alders and lichens on the surrounding land is an important source of this essential nutrient. In some tropical forests where soil reserves of nitrogen are particularly low, nitrogen-fixing trees constitute a sizable fraction (up to one-half in some areas) of the canopy individuals. Because nitrogen-fixation activity by any organism and by most lichens (whether or not of the nitrogen-fixing kind) is likely to be quite sensitive to acidic deposition, major long-term impacts could occur in such areas. Such damage is likely to be slow in developing and to require a very carefully designed monitoring strategy to detect it in its early stages.

The Human Dimension

Acid deposition can degrade the quality of human life in three ways. First, it can damage ecosystems and thereby deprive us of a priceless source of beauty, joy, and inspiration. Second, it can damage ecosystems and thereby degrade the quality of material benefits that human society derives from healthy ecosystems; these benefits include the maintenance of clean air and water, the moderation of climate, the production of food and fiber, and the maintenance of a genetic "library." Third, it can directly lead to damaging effects on human health.

A nation that poisons its forests and lakes poisons an aesthetic and spiritual well of its people. There is a pathetic sort of positive feedback lurking here, for as children grow up in a world that affords meager opportunity to enjoy wilderness and natural ecosystems, then later, as adults, their incentive to save what little is left for future generations will be less.

The existence of a major confluence of interest between the material well-being of people and the health of ecosystems has been discussed by many authors in a variety of contexts (Harte and Socolow, 1971; Holdren and Ehrlich, 1974). For acid-precipitation damage the examples abound. Recreational opportunities are lost when lakes and streams no longer support viable fish populations; major sources of revenue and jobs dry up when commercial forests and fisheries become less productive; water supplies become more erratic when the integrity of forested watershed slopes is eroded. We cannot now predict the extent to which these linkages between acid deposition and loss of ecosystem services to society will become manifest. Many of the mechanisms by which the damage might occur are identified. It is the inherent unpredictability of ecosystem behavior and uncertainty about the degree to which society will regulate sources of acidity that forces us to view the future with uncertainty in this regard.

Some potential direct effects of acid deposition on human health have likewise been identified, but, again, large uncertainties exist in our ability to predict how severe these will be. Extremely acidic rain and fog have been observed in some heavily polluted urban areas. In a small city on the Tibetan Plateau of China, a rainstorm with a pH of 2.25 was observed (Harte, 1983), while Los Angeles fogs with pH as low as 1.7 have been observed (Munger et al., 1983). Toxic metals mobilized by acidic water can enter human water supplies and produce chronic toxicity. These toxic metals could come from runoff-soil interactions and then enter well water in areas with low carbonate buffering capacity, or they could be mobilized from plumbing pipes, solder joints, and aluminum water containers. Another pathway through which toxic metals can damage our health is food-chain biomagnification. Recently an excess of aluminum has been found in the damaged brain tissue of victims of Alzheimer's disease and of amyotrophic lateral sclerosis. It is too soon to say whether aluminum is a cause of these afflictions and, if so, whether acid deposition is a significant contributing factor (Maugh, 1984).

The works of man are at risk as well. Evidence of pollution damage to buildings, statuary, metals, and paints exposed to urban air abounds. Less clear is the precise role that acid deposition plays in the ensemble of corrosive pollutants found in urban air.

What Should Society Do?

There is compelling evidence in hand that acid deposition has severely altered the chemistry of streams and lakes and destroyed populations in large areas of Europe and eastern North America. Equally compelling evidence exists that the problem is spreading; for instance, there are regions of the western United States that are at risk. And the possibility that acid deposition is partly or entirely responsible for extensive forest dieback in Europe and eastern North America cannot be dismissed. In the face of the scientific uncertainties a number of political postures are possible. We can assume that we have seen the worst and that no new damage will occur; a case could then be made that regulatory action is not needed. Or we can take a worst possible scenario and approach the problem under the assumption that massive forest dieback, devastating human health effects, plummeting productivity of major commercial fisheries, and severe disruption of water supplies will occur in the near future if drastic regulatory action is not taken immediately. The probability that either of these scenarios is correct is small indeed. Much more likely is the possibility that the story of the recent past will continue to unfold, with new forms of damage catching us by surprise and with already identified damage continuing to spread in geographic extent and magnitude. A prudent society should assume no less.

The rapidity with which symptoms of forest damage have come to light is awesome to contemplate. Controlling acidic precipitation, in contrast, is a time-consuming process. Not only does it take time to draft and pass legislation to regulate emissions of acid-precursor gases, but it will take time to implement controls, once enacted. Is it necessary to wait until clear evidence is in hand detailing quantitatively the amounts of acidic deposition in individual sensitive areas that can be attributed to each source of NO_x or SO_2 before seeking regulatory action? It may be argued that it is wasteful of money to regulate a source of acid precursors when compelling data showing the precise degree of culpability of that source are not in hand. However, the symptoms of forest damage develop so rapidly and the magnitude of the damage could be so great that a prudent society ought not make regulatory action contingent on understanding every last nuance of the problem. The risk of underreaction, resulting in massive forest damage as well as continuing aquatic impacts and possible health effects, appears to overwhelm the risk of overreaction and the expense of unnecessary preventive action. To be specific, suppose that legislation is "overreactive" and results in the regulation of individual pollution sources that are not primarily responsible for acid deposition on sensitive sites and that forest damage is not in the least influenced by acid deposition. Has society been more damaged than if no action had been taken and ecosystem damage accelerates? The following consideration suggests that the answer is no.

Acid precipitation is not the only environmental problem caused by the emissions under discussion, and thus there are other reasons to control emissions of NO_x and SO_2 independent of the acid-precipitation phenomenon. SO_2 in combination with other pollutants, such as fine particulates from coal and petroleum combustion, is implicated in human health damage. Tropospheric ozone, which affects adversely both people and vegetation, is created by reactions involving atmospheric nitrogen oxides and hydrocarbons, also produced in fossil-fuel combustion. Therefore, appropriate control strategies that limit the production of the acid precursors would be of benefit, even if it should turn out that the cause of the forest damage is not primarily acidic precipitation or that some of the regulated sources are not responsible for the acid deposition falling at sites where lake acidification is a major problem. Should it turn out that acid deposition does damage forests, however, then the nations that regulate these emissions will have one more reason to be glad they do.

Recent political events in the United States are not encouraging. Legislative attempts to control major sources of acid deposition have been derailed, and so the risks and damages continue. Earl Cook, with his usual insight, perceived the underlying problem ten years ago: "It is a paradox that an affluent society, possessing more resources for study and experimentation than a poor society, appears to be prevented by that very affluence from making decisions that require any sacrifice" (Cook, 1976; p. 379).

References

Almer, B., W. Dickson, C. Ekstrom, E. Hornstrom. 1978. Sulfur pollution and the aquatic environment. In J. O. Nriagu, ed. *Sulfur in the environment,* pp. 271–311. New York: Wiley.

Baker, J. P., and C. L. Schofield. 1982. Aluminum toxicity to fish in acidic waters. *Water, Air, and Soil Pollution* 18:289–309.

Beamish, R. J. 1976. Acidification of lakes in Canada by acid precipitation and the resulting effects on fishes. *Water, Air, and Soil Pollution* 6:501–14.

Charlson, R. J., and H. Rodhe. 1982. Factors controlling the acidity of natural rainwater. *Nature* 295:683–85.

Cook, E. 1976. *Man, energy, society.* San Francisco: Freeman.

Cowling, E. 1982. Acid precipitation in historical context. *Environmental Science and Technology* 16(2): 110A–23A.

Cronan, C. S., and C. L. Schofield. 1979. Aluminum leaching response to acid precipitation: Effects on high-elevation watersheds in the Northeast. *Science* 204(20): 304–306.

Ehrlich, P. R., A. H. Ehrlich, and J. P. Holdren. 1977. *Ecoscience: Population, resources, environment.* San Francisco: Freeman.

EPRI [Electric Power Research Institute]. 1981. *The integrated lake-water acidification study (ILWAS).* Electric Power Research Institute Report no. EA-1825. Palo Alto, Calif.: EPRI.

Glass, N. R., D. E. Arnold, J. N. Galloway, G. R. Hendrey, J. J. Lee, W. W. McFee, S. A. Norton, C. F. Powers, D. L. Rambo, and C. L. Schofield. 1982. Effects of acid precipitation. *Environmental Science and Technology* 16(3): 162A–69A.

Harte, J. 1983. An investigation of acid precipitation in Qinghai Province, China. *Atmospheric Environment* 17:403–408.

———. 1985. *Consider a spherical cow: A course in environmental problem solving.* Los Altos, Calif.: Kaufmann.

Harte, J., and R. H. Socolow. 1971. *Patient earth.* New York: Holt, Rinehart, and Winston.

———, G. Lockett, R. Schneider, C. Blanchard, and H. Michaels. 1985. Acid precipitation and surface water vulnerability on the western slope of the high Colorado Rockies. *Water, Air, and Soil Pollution* 25:313–20.

Havas, M., T. C. Hutchinson, and G. E. Likens. 1984. Red herrings in acid rain research. *Environmental Science and Technology* 18(6): 176A–86A.

Henriksen, A. 1980. Acidification of freshwaters—A large scale titration. In D. Drablos and A. Tollan, eds. *Ecological impact of acid precipitation: Proceedings of an international conference.* Sandefjord, Norway: SNSF Project.

Holdren, J. P., and P. R. Ehrlich. 1974. Human population and the global environment. *American Scientist* 62:282–92.

Johannessen, M., and A. Henriksen. 1978. Chemistry of snow meltwater: Changes in concentration during melting. *Water Resources Research* 14(4): 615–19.

Johnson, A. H., and T. G. Siccama. 1983. Acid deposition and forest decline. *Environmental Science and Technology* 17(7): 294a–305a.

Lawson, D. R., and J. G. Wendt. 1982. *Acid deposition in California.* Society of Automotive Engineers Technical Paper no. 821246.

Likens, G., E. Wright, R. F. Galloway, and T. J. Butler. 1979. Acid rain. *Scientific American* 241:43–51.

Marmorek, D. R. 1983. Changes in the behavior and structure of plankton systems of intermediate pH. In J. Teasley, ed. *Proceedings of a symposium on acid precipitation.* Ann Arbor, Mich.: Ann Arbor Science Publishers.

Maugh, T. H. 1984. Acid rain's effects on people assessed. *Science* 226:1408–10.

Munger, J. W., D. J. Jacob, J. M. Waldman, and M. R. Hoffman. 1983. Fogwater chemistry in an urban environment. *Journal of Geophysical Research* 88: 5109–21.

NRC [National Research Council]. 1981. *Atmosphere-biosphere interactions: Toward a better understanding of the ecological consequences of fossil fuel combustion.* National Research Council, Committee on the Atmosphere and the Biosphere. Washington, D. C.: National Academy Press.

Novakov, T., S. Chang, and A. Harker. 1974. Sulfates as pollution particulates: Catalytic formation on carbon (soot). *Science* 186:259–61.

Oden, S. 1976. The acidity problem—An outline in concepts. *Water, Air, and Soil Pollution* 6:137–66.

Postel, S. 1984. *Air pollution, acid rain, and the future of forests.* Worldwatch Paper no. 58. Washington, D.C.: Worldwatch Institute.

Pough, F. H. 1976. Acid precipitation and the embryonic mortality of spotted salamanders, *Ambystoma maculatum. Science* 192:68–70.

Raddum, G. G. 1980. Comparison of benthic invertebrates in lakes with different acidity. In D. Drablos and A. Tollan, eds. *Ecological impact of acid precipitation: Proceedings of an international conference.* Sandefjord, Norway: SNSF Project.

Roth, P., C. Blanchard, H. Michaels, J. Harte, and M. El-Ashry. 1985. *Acid deposition in the western United States: An assessment.* Washington, D.C.: World Resources Institute.

Schindler, D. W., and M. A. Turner. 1982. Biological, chemical, and physical responses of lakes to experimental acidification. *Water, Air, and Soil Pollution* 18:259–71.

Schofield, C. L. 1980. Processes limiting fish populations in acidified lakes. In D. S. Shriner, C. R. Richmond, and S. E. Lindberg, eds. *Atmospheric sulfur deposition.* Ann Arbor, Mich.: Ann Arbor Science Publishers.

Smith, R. A., and R. B. Alexander. 1983. *Evidence for acid precipitation-induced trends in common ion concentrations at Bench-Mark stations.* USGS Circular no. 910. Denver: U.S. Geological Survey.

Stokes, P. M. 1983. pH related changes in attached algal communities of soft water lakes. In J. Teasley, ed. *Proceedings of a symposium on acid precipitation.* Ann Arbor, Mich.: Ann Arbor Science Publishers.

Stumm, W., and J. Morgan. 1981. *Aquatic chemistry: An introduction emphasizing chemical equilibria in natural waters.* 2d ed. New York: Wiley.

Tonnessen, K. 1983. Aquatic ecosystem acidification in the Sierra Nevada, California: Potential for chemical and biological changes. In G. Hendrey, ed. *Acid precipitation: Aquatic effects.* Ann Arbor, Mich.: Ann Arbor Science Publishers.

Wright, R. F., and A. Henriksen. 1978. Chemistry of small Norwegian lakes, with special reference to acid precipitation. *Limnology and Oceanography* 223: 407–98.

Yan, N. D., and P. M. Stokes. 1978. Phytoplankton of an acidic lake and its responses to experimental alterations of pH. *Environmental Conservation* 5(2): 93–100.

―――, and R. Strus. 1980. Crustacean zooplankton communities of acidic, metal-contaminated lakes near Sudbury, Ontario. *Canadian Journal of Fisheries and Aquatic Science* 37:2282–93.

8.
Toxic Substances: A Cause for Concern?

For the first time in the history of the world, every human being is now subjected to contact with dangerous chemicals, from the moment of conception until death. In the less than two decades of their use, the synthetic pesticides have been so thoroughly distributed throughout the animate and inanimate world that they occur virtually everywhere. They have been recovered from most of the major river systems and even from streams of groundwater flowing unseen through the earth. Residues of these chemicals linger in soil to which they may have been applied a dozen years before. They have entered and lodged in the bodies of fish, birds, reptiles, and domestic and wild animals . . . and in man himself.

So WROTE Rachel Carson in 1962 in *Silent Spring*. Citing an extensive scientific literature, she alerted the public to the potential hazards of widespread, inordinate dependence on chemical panaceas, especially chlorinated hydrocarbons, to control pest species. In particular, she warned that dichloro-diphenyl-trichloro-ethane (DDT) and related compounds were concentrating in the food chain and, consequently, threatening the survival of birds and fish. She believed that the public had a right to know and should have a role in the decision-making process.

After a decade of public debate, scientific argument, government inaction, and false starts, the federal government finally banned domestic use of DDT in 1972. The scientific evidence indicting DDT was overwhelming and dramatic. Who could ignore reports of catastrophic population declines of bald eagles, ospreys, brown pelicans, and peregrine falcons as a result of DDT-thinned eggshells? Less dramatic but equally significant, DDT was being concentrated in freshwater fishes and appeared to affect the behavior and reproduction of adults and the survival of larvae.

The Lake Michigan coho salmon fishing industry was closed because of high levels of DDT in the fish. In the ensuing years the ban was validated by a drop in the level of DDT in the tissues of various vertebrates and, perhaps more significantly, the successful reproduction of affected species of birds.

It has been 23 years since Rachel Carson awakened people to the dangers of excessive reliance on pesticides. Her warnings did not go unheeded. Subsequent scientific findings, reported to the public, stimulated concern, discussion, and, ultimately, legislative action. Moreover the accuracy of Carson's warnings set the stage for continued public concern and involvement.

With only minor modifications Carson's statements apply equally well to a vast array of toxic substances: from elemental metals such as mercury, lead, cadmium, and arsenic, to plasticizers like vinyl chloride and diethylhexyl phthalate; to ubiquitous trace contaminants like dioxin; and to petroleum, which, along with natural gas, is the basis of the organic chemical industry. Yet in his column in the *Christian Science Monitor* of April 16, 1985, Robert Cowen stated:

Excessive fear of toxic chemicals has swept through the news media and into US public thinking since the tragedy at Bhopal, India. That fear needs to be held in check by a realistic appreciation of the public risk, lest overreaction and needlessly punitive regulations stifle an essential basic industry.

Public thinking and concern about toxic substances in the United States have been shaped over the last 20 years by a series of disasters and near disasters, including DDT-thinned eggshells; a several-year, multimilliondollar closure of the fishing industry in the James River following a massive discharge of the pesticide Kepone; the evacuation and "death" of an entire town, Times Beach, Missouri, owing to excessive soil contamination by dioxin; and, most recently, the tragedy alluded to by Cowen, the deaths of more than 2,000 people and the serious injury of many thousands more in Bhopal, India, as a result of an explosion in a chemical plant. The list of incidents is considerably longer; the documented range of adverse effects is growing. Is the public's fear excessive?

Comparison of the current status of both the regulations designed to control toxic substances and the regulatory record with the magnitude of the problem suggests that the answer is no. There is ample cause for concern. In the United States there are some two dozen statutes governing exposure to and the production, use, marketing, transportation, consumption, release, and disposal of toxic and/or hazardous substances. As discussed below, many crucial and far-reaching laws have expired. Congress is sharply divided on reauthorization. One group, reflecting the current administration's avowed policy of less government intervention, is seeking to weaken regulations or, at least, to maintain the status quo by minimizing budget increases, while another, variously endorsed by environmental, health, and labor organizations, is attempting to strengthen restrictions and close loopholes.

The Regulations

The Clean Air Act, the major law intended to protect and enhance the nation's air quality, expired in 1981. It established primary standards to protect human health for seven "conventional" pollutants: sulfur dioxide, carbon monoxide, nitrogen oxides, ozone, hydrocarbons, particulates, and lead. The Environmental Protection Agency (EPA) has listed an additional seven hazardous air pollutants: mercury, beryllium, asbestos, vinyl chloride, benzene, radionuclides, and inorganic arsenic. Air-quality standards have been set for the first four. While the primary air-quality standards are met in most areas of the country, the roughly 20 million metric tons each of SO_2 and NO_2 produced every year are implicated in the problem of acid rain. And it is acid rain that is the most controversial obstacle to passage of a new clean air act. At present there is sufficient scientific debate concerning the causes and effects of and the appropriate solutions to acid deposition that policy decisions are unlikely to be made swiftly.[1] Until the law is renewed, it is unlikely that the EPA will be motivated to identify and set standards for atmosphere-borne toxics, as it was charged to do by the original law.

The primary law protecting the "chemical, physical, and biological integrity of the nation's waters," the Clean Water Act, expired in 1982, except for the sewage treatment grants section, which expired in September, 1985. The original act focused on "point" sources of pollution and thus regulated the discharge operations of some 65,000 direct dischargers (both municipal and industrial) and another 15,000 indirect industrial dischargers. The key issues hindering renewal concerned sewage-plant subsidies, which the White House wanted to eliminate, and the growing recognition that nonpoint-source pollution, such as pesticide-laden agricultural runoff, significantly affects water quality. Passage of a new bill was delayed by continued disagreements about funding of sewer grants. President Reagan threatened to veto it at the funding levels proposed in 1986: $18 billion in the Senate version, $21 billion in the House version.

---

[1] As of mid-September, 1986, acid rain bills were in committee in both the Senate and the House. The administration opposed both versions.

The 1980 Comprehensive Environmental Response, Compensation, and Liability Act, otherwise known as the Superfund, authorized the federal government to respond to spills of hazardous substances and created a $1.6 billion fund for the cleanup of hazardous-waste sites, such as those in Niagara Falls, New York. The fund was generated from taxes on crude oil and 42 petrochemical feedstocks (basic chemical building blocks) plus an additional injection of funds from the government. Although it expired in September, 1985, renewal of the Superfund has been considered a high-priority agenda item; it has had the support of both houses of Congress and the administration. Nevertheless, reauthorization was delayed for a year while the House and Senate wrangled over appropriations—finally agreeing to $9 billion over five years—and the means of generating the funds. While Congress debated, the EPA halted or slowed cleanup work at as many as two hundred hazardous-waste sites.

In 1947, the Federal Insecticide, Fungicide, and Rodenticide Act (FIFRA) was passed. Originally intended to protect farmers from ineffective and dangerous pesticides, it is the nation's primary statute governing pesticide use; but it expired in 1984 and needs comprehensive reworking and strengthening. FIFRA is authorized to ensure that the use of a pesticide will not cause adverse environmental effects, defined as "any unreasonable risk to man or the environment, taking into account the economic, social and environmental costs and benefits of the use of any pesticide" (OTA, 1984). Some of the issues considered in reauthorization efforts were as follows: many state and local governments wanted stricter standards than those set by EPA; older pesticides had to be evaluated with respect to updated safety standards and reregistered if they passed muster (EPA was far behind in this task); and EPA was required to compensate retailers and users if the agency suspended use of a pesticide based on new health-effects data.[2]

Titles 1 and 2 of the Marine Protection, Research, and Sanctuaries Act (Ocean Dumping), which expired in 1982, regulate the municipal, industrial, and radioactive wastes that are dumped in the ocean. (Ocean dumping of high-level radioactive wastes is banned, and there was, until January, 1985, a two-year moratorium on ocean dumping of low-level radioactive wastes—inserted into highway gas tax legislation.) As land-disposal problems and costs increase, there is growing pressure to dispose of wastes in the ocean and to incinerate toxic substances at sea. At issue also is the location of ocean dump sites: no one wants them too close to

---

[2]In early August, 1986, a bill was introduced to a Senate committee which included measures intended to accelerate the review of some six hundred inadequately tested pesticides, facilitate cancellation of dangerous pesticides, and protect groundwater.

home. Hence regional concerns are a major impediment to comprehensive and quick legislation.

Safe for the moment, the Resource Conservation and Recovery Act (RCRA) regulates cradle-to-grave management of hazardous wastes. Enacted in 1976 and reauthorized in 1980 in the wake of the public outcry following disclosures of the toxic-waste problem in Niagara Falls, the law requires the EPA to identify hazardous wastes, establish standards for hazardous-waste facilities, track hazardous materials using a manifest system, and regulate disposal facilities by issuing permits. Unfortunately the scope of the law is limited. The manifests contain no information about the concentration of major constituents in the waste. Only commercial disposal sites are regulated; facilities and practices for waste disposal at the site of manufacture escape close scrutiny. Furthermore, the reauthorized bill was weakened by oil-and-gas-industry insistence that hazardous wastes produced by oil-and-gas drilling be exempted from regulation.

The Safe Drinking Water Act, which expired in 1982, was intended to protect the nation's drinking water, including groundwater, by setting standards of water quality. The law authorized the EPA to set rules for the disposal of hazardous substances by underground injection and to prohibit new injection wells where underground aquifers were threatened (the regulations did not apply to oil-and-gas operations, however). Growing recognition of the scope of groundwater contamination stimulated congressional interest. New regulations under the 1986 reauthorization of the law required EPA to set standards for listed drinking water contaminants and ordered monitoring of public drinking water for unregulated contaminants.

Another major law designed to protect public and environmental health, the Toxic Substances Control Act (TSCA), expired in 1983 and is overdue for reauthorization. The law was established to ensure the safety of new and existing chemicals. Manufacturers were required to submit data on new products to the EPA for safety evaluation. The agency was authorized to prohibit manufacture, limit production, and/or control disposal of unacceptable substances. The EPA, however, has been slow to test and regulate chemicals. According to a National Academy of Sciences Report issued in 1984, there are very few data on the full range of health effects of most chemicals in high-volume commercial use. Efforts to renew the law will involve tightening up the data-collection procedure, expanding and speeding the testing program, and holding the manufacturer liable for damages.

The two-dozen environmental laws were intended to reduce or eliminate exposure to toxic substances during their full life cycles from synthesis or extraction to ultimate disposal. But there are serious holes in the regulatory net. For example, although FIFRA requires that *new* pesticides must be tested for safety and registered for use by the EPA, under TSCA other new chemicals, many of them structurally similar to DDT and related compounds, can be produced with impunity after the manufacturer submits a premanufacture notice (PMN) to the EPA. The agency *requires* information on the chemistry of the substance, the proposed uses, the amounts to be produced or processed, the by-products, the number of workers to be exposed, the duration of exposure, and the method of disposal; the agency *requests* information on environmental and health effects to determine whether the chemical, during its life cycle, will present an unreasonable risk of injury to health or the environment. The agency is authorized to regulate the manufacture, processing, distribution, use, or disposal of the chemical if it is judged to represent an unreasonable risk— *on the basis of what the manufacturer chooses to disclose.* An OTA study (1983) found that only 10 percent of the PMNs submitted to the EPA over a two-year period reported any information from tests used to estimate environmental effects. Although about 50 percent of the PMNs contained toxicity information, only 17 percent provided any data on the likelihood of cancers, birth defects, and/or mutations.

Despite the existence of two major laws concerned with the nation's water, there is no comprehensive, uniformly applicable policy regarding water quality. For instance, the Ambient Water Quality Criteria required under the Clean Water Act are based, in theory, strictly on environmental and health effects, whereas standards set under the Safe Drinking Water Act reflect economic and technological concerns as well as health effects. Moreover, the Ambient Water Quality Criteria are not rules but simply a compilation of data on pollutants on which regulations *may be based.* Only 22 of the more than 60 substances for which federal standards exist are subject to enforcible standards. Because the federal government has been slow to establish standards, many states have promulgated their own, which vary from state to state and differ from federal standards. As a result, people living in different states are not uniformly protected (OTA, 1984). Despite state initiatives, standards or guidelines (either state or federal) have been promulgated for less than half of the potentially toxic substances detected in groundwater (OTA, 1984).

Furthermore, there is no federal legislation specifically designed to ensure the quality of groundwater, although both TSCA and FIFRA regulations apply to potential groundwater contaminants (OTA, 1984). In particular, there are no federal regulations governing surface impoundments (ponds, pits, and lagoons for hazardous wastes) or underground storage tanks (of gasoline, for instance)—major sources of groundwater contamination (Tangley, 1984a). As a result most of the states have begun measures to protect groundwater. Fifty-eight percent of the states have programs designed to detect groundwater contamination, 73 percent have programs to correct or clean up problems, and 14 percent have made efforts to prevent contamination (OTA, 1984).

The EPA assumes the primary burden of regulating toxic chemicals and is empowered to set standards for toxic substances in the air and in surface and underground water (specifically drinking water), monitor air and water quality, test and register new pesticides, test and reregister in-use pesticides, and evaluate data on the roughly 1,000 new chemicals introduced each year. But because many of the laws are vague, the EPA has considerable latitude in interpretation and implementation. At any given time the extent and direction of the agency's activities are a reflection of the current administration's attitudes. Since the Reagan administration began its tenure, the EPA has displayed an increasing tendency to grant exemptions and waivers to polluters, to delay and extend compliance deadlines, to be slow in testing and evaluating chemicals, to be far behind in the task of setting air- and water-quality standards for questionable substances, to relax existing air- and water-quality standards, and to be lax in enforcing regulations (OTA, 1984).

The Records

As a result of expired laws, loopholes and weaknesses in the laws, and the bottleneck effect of the EPA, the regulatory record is one of pluses and minuses. Measured in terms of conventional pollutants, the nation's surface waters have improved considerably since the implementation of water-pollution legislation designed to control point-source discharges; coliform bacteria counts and dissolved solids have been reduced, while oxygen levels have increased sufficiently to permit the reestablishment of biological communities in recently depauperate areas. There is some indication that the quantity of toxic or hazardous substances discharged into surface waters has been reduced (CEQ, 1983). Certainly the amount of municipal and industrial wastes undergoing secondary and tertiary treatment (intended to deal with organic chemicals and heavy metals) has increased. And 21 of the 35 states responding to a survey, the National Water Quality Inventory of 1982, indicated overall positive trends in water quality (CEQ, 1983).

As a result of the Clean Air Act there have been significant reductions in the ambient-air concentrations of carbon monoxide, ozone, sulfur dioxide, particulates, and lead, whereas there has been no overall decrease in the levels of nitrogen dioxide between 1975 and 1983. The lowered ambient-air concentrations correspond to substantial decreases in the emissions of carbon monoxide, sulfur oxides, volatile organics and particulates. Nitrogen oxide emissions, on the other hand, reached peak levels in 1979, seven years after the enactment of the Clean Air Act, chiefly as a result of increases in the transportation sector (U.S. Bureau of the Census, 1985).

Perhaps the most significant and hopeful result of the clean-air legislation has been the dramatic decrease in ambient-air concentrations of lead, from 0.88 $\mu g/m^3$ in 1975 to 0.32 $\mu g/m^3$ in 1982 (U.S. Bureau of the Census, 1985), as a result of reductions in the content of lead in gasoline, mandated in the early to mid-1970s. The reductions were prompted by concern over the estimated 200-fold increase in atmospheric lead concentrations since the pre-Roman era (Settle and Patterson, 1980), attributable chiefly to human activity, and adverse health effects. Lindeberg (1984) reported that, globally, an estimated 250,000 tons of lead were being released into the air each year, 86 percent from automobile emissions (Marshall, 1983).

A dose-response relationship between exposure to lead and neurologic disorders such as mental retardation in children has long been recognized for high blood concentrations of lead (see Landrigan and Houk, 1984). In fact, in 1973 legislation was passed to ban the use of lead in paint following reports showing a strong association between neurologic effects and high blood levels of lead in young children resulting from ingestion of lead-based paint. There has been an increasing number of reports that lead can cause subtle but irreversible reductions in children's intelligence even at lower concentrations (Landrigan and Houk, 1984). Furthermore, lead is a carcinogen in mice and rats, causes decreased fertility and hyperactivity in laboratory animals (Ambio, 1977), and slows the rate of nerve-signal transmissions and heme formation in the blood (Marshall, 1983). In short, while there have been spirited scientific debates about the details of the observed associations between concentrations of lead in the blood or teeth and specific clinical manifestations (see Marshall, 1983; Needleman, 1984; Landrigan and Houk, 1984; and Ernhart, 1984), only the Lead Industries Association has disputed the thrust of the findings.

Until recently, efforts to completely phase-out leaded gasoline have proved unsuccessful. In July, 1984, however, citing studies showing a one-to-one relationship of blood concentrations and lead in gasoline with adverse effects, particularly on inner-city children, EPA head William Ruckleshaus announced that EPA was considering two options to curtail the use of lead in automotive fuel: (1) to impose a 91 percent reduction by January 1, 1986, or (2) to achieve the same goal by 1988. The move would reduce the amount of lead permitted to 0.10 g/gal from the present level of 1.10 g/gal (Marshall, 1984).

On March 4, 1985, after vacillating between the objections of the petroleum and lead industries and the encouragement of environmentalists and health professionals, the EPA ordered refiners to remove 90 percent of the lead currently used as an antiknock additive in gasoline by the end of the year (option 1 above). The agency went further than expected by proposing a total ban on lead by 1988, seven years sooner than previously proposed. The new move was prompted by two studies that link low levels of lead and high blood pressure, particularly in white males. Projections suggested that the reduction might prevent 1.8 million cases of high blood pressure and reduce the number of heart attacks and strokes by 5,000 and 1,000, respectively, in the first year of implementation. Furthermore, the EPA estimates that removal of 90 percent of lead will prevent lead-linked disease in 172,000 children. The action was supported by a cost-benefit analysis indicating that consumers will save $914 million in engine maintenance, $187 million in fuel economy, and $600 million in health costs of toxic effects on children (Sun, 1985).

There have been other successes. For example, between 1973 and 1980 the EPA successfully cut the volume of industrial wastes dumped into the ocean from 5 million tons to just over 2.5 million tons (Lahey and Connor, 1983). Since the hazards of chlorinated hydrocarbons, particularly DDT and polychlorinated biphenyls (PCBs), were recognized and their use restricted or banned, there has been a significant overall decline in concentrations in the tissues of human beings, waterfowl, and species of fish. In the United States, DDT residues in human tissue, for instance, have dropped from 8.07 parts per million in 1970 to 3.64 parts per million in 1979 (U.S. Bureau of the Census, 1985). In 1976 the EPA was considering whether to cancel the registration of the pesticide dibromochloropropane (DBCP), because it had been found to be a carcinogen. In the summer of 1977 an Occupational Health and Safety Administration study revealed that men working in a chemical plant where DBCP was being produced had a reduced sperm count and were sterile. By September, 1977, the EPA had issued a notice to suspend certain uses of DBCP (Voytek, 1981). The response was prompt but perhaps not tough enough.

Alas, the overriding picture of the regulatory record is one of inadequate, slow, or even inappropriate action. For example, the Clean Water Act of 1977 required the EPA to publish Ambient Water Quality Criteria for 65 priority pollutants (those substances that Congress deemed toxic). The *criteria* have been published, but for some substances there are insufficient toxicity data (see Stara et al., 1983). Thus the *standards* for most of the priority pollutants still have not been established. Between 1982 and 1983 the EPA listed more than 75 potentially hazardous substances found in drinking water but has not set standards for those contaminants. Until the standards are established, the law cannot be enforced. Since the enactment of TSCA in 1976, only five chemicals or groups of chemicals have been regulated: fully halogenated fluorocarbons, dioxins, asbestos, polychorinated biphenyls, and vinyl chloride—and those only after extensive debate.

A recent congressional report revealed that tens of thousands of tons of toxic substances are being released into the air by 67 of the 86 large chemical companies surveyed (*New York Times,* 1985). One of these toxics, vinyl chloride, is a known carcinogen in rats, mice, and hamsters and has been associated with liver angiosarcomas in workers exposed to it (Maltoni, 1975). Nevertheless, the EPA has proposed to relax the rules on the emissions of vinyl chloride (*New York Times,* 1985).

In 1979 the Chemical Industry Institute of Toxicology (CIIT) reported that formaldehyde, a ubiquitous chemical used extensively in a number of industries from textile, furniture, and plastic production to mushroom farming, caused cancer in rats. The Federal Panel on Formaldehyde, formed to evaluate the health risks of exposure to formaldehyde, concluded that "formaldehyde should be presumed to pose a carcinogenic risk to humans" (Ashford et al., 1983). A subsequent report by the Consensus Workshop on Formaldehyde (1984) stated that formaldehyde is carcinogenic and mutagenic in laboratory experiments. Nevertheless, although an estimated 1.4 million people are exposed occupationally and another 11 million people may be exposed in the home to vapor from construction materials and insulation, neither the EPA nor the Occupational Safety and Health Administration (OSHA) has taken regulatory action (Perera and Petito, 1982). There are many more examples of questionable regulatory practices.

Some of the regulatory failures are the result of flaws in the original legislation. For instance, the Clean Water Act was specifically concerned with controlling point-source discharges, i.e., municipal and industrial sewage. But the EPA estimates that 30 percent of the lakes and streams in the United States are adversely affected by non-point-source discharges, that is, by agricultural and municipal runoff. Similarly TSCA is not as strong as it might (and should) be because it does not require registration or rigorous testing for registration of new chemicals before manufacture. Too frequently testing is recommended or ordered only after the product has been manufactured—sometimes in vast quantities—and adverse effects have been reported.

The regulations governing pesticide production and use have been loosely interpreted, haphazardly applied, and sometimes not enforced at all, in part no doubt because FIFRA's mandate to prevent unreasonable adverse environmental effects is subject to interpretation. There is recent evidence that, despite its ban in 1972, DDT is being found in increasing amounts in the tissues of some migratory birds in Texas and California (Peterson, 1984). A recent survey of pesticide residues in California fruits and vegetables revealed that DDT was the most common residue (Mott, 1984). In explanation it has been suggested that some farmers may be obtaining DDT from Mexico. The EPA, however, admits that DDT is a contaminant of the insecticide dicofol (trade name Kelthane), which has been registered since 1957. In fact, dicofol is manufactured from DDT. Although studies by the National Cancer Institute suggested in 1978 that dicofol was a carcinogen, EPA did not order definitive tests until 1984 (Mott, 1984). Meanwhile, the pesticide continues to be used and, in the process, releases an unknown amount of DDT.

In a report, "Superfund Strategy," the Office of Technology Assessment (OTA, 1985) assessed the nation's Superfund program and found the following:

1. The EPA has vastly underestimated the magnitude of the problem (see below).

2. Efforts to clean up have been meager. Of the 538 sites originally on the National Priority List, only 30 percent have received remedial attention, and only 6 sites have been completely cleaned up.

3. There has been little or no emphasis on permanent cleanup. The OTA charges that contaminated material has been moved from problem sites and deposited in hazardous-waste landfills that may become tomorrow's Superfund sites, in part because on site containment may be inadequate.

4. Long-term research and development of innovative technologies have received little attention or money. Of the $1 billion spent to date, only $25 million has been spent on technological developments.

Magnitude of the Problem

Ours is a chemically dependent society, not only in the sense of drug abuse but also in the sense that we are "hooked" on a variety of "necessities" that are produced from or with potentially or admittedly toxic substances. What in heaven's name would we do without plastic bags, bottles, wraps, packaging, containers, and so on? And, thanks to computers, some of us have almost completely forgotten how to use pen and paper for either writing or calculating. We are beginning to understand that there are previously unanticipated costs to the "good life." Plastic, in many of its myriad products, is responsible for the nearly ubiquitous distribution of various compounds (e.g., phthalate esters) that, some studies suggest, may cause adverse environmental and health effects. Organic solvents used in the production of components for the electronics industry have heavily contaminated drinking-water wells in California, Texas, Massachusetts, and elsewhere. Many of the solvents, found in exceedingly high concentrations, are thought to cause birth defects, mutations, and cancer, among other things. An extensive toxicological study is being conducted in Santa Clara, California, to determine whether there is link between trichloroethylene (TCE), found in well water, and excessive birth defects in the area.

Is it trivial to be concerned about lacing the environment with plasticizers? Are the contaminated wells just isolated incidents? The more general question is, How big is the problem of toxic substances? The answers to these questions involve an assessment of available data and, ultimately, value judgments. The data to be evaluated include the quantities of chemicals produced, used, and disposed of; the ultimate fate of the chemicals in the environment; and the impact of the substances on human health and environmental integrity. Finally, we must decide whether the data are meaningful.

Between 1965 and 1978 more than 4 million distinct chemical compounds were reported in the scientific literature. Of those compounds 55,000 to 70,000 are produced commercially. About 1,000 new chemicals are introduced to the marketplace each year. More than 400 toxic chemicals, most of which bioaccumulate, have been identified in human tissues (Schnare et al., 1984; Shaikh and Nichols, 1984).

The total world production of six major base organic chemicals (ethylene, propylene, butadiene, benzene, toluene, and xylenes) rose from 2.3 million tons in 1950 to 72.9 million tons in 1982 (*CIH,* 1983–84). It is the synthetic organic-chemical revolution that primarily accounts for the staggering array of compounds on the market and many of the problems associated with toxic substances. In particular, halogenated hydrocarbons—found in pesticides, lubricating fluids, solvents, plastics, refrigerants, flame retardants, and propellants, among other things (OTA, 1984)—have caused documented adverse health and/or environmental effects.

One of the better-known halogenated hydrocarbons is dioxin, or TCDD (of which there are several isomers), a contaminant of trichlorophenol and its products, hexachloraphene (now banned), and the defoliants 2,4-D and 2,4,5-T. Dioxin is noted for its apparently ubiquitous distribution, its tendency to bioaccumulate, and its reputed toxicity. In 1970 some 55 million pounds of 2,4-D and 2,4,5-T were produced in the United States. From 1961 to 1970 the U.S. military sprayed an estimated 43 million liters of the herbicide Agent Orange on 1.7 million hectares of South Vietnamese inland and coastal mangrove forests (Carlson, 1983). Agent Orange, a mixture of 2,4-D and 2,4,5-T, is contaminated with an average of 2 parts per million of dioxins (Fackelman, 1983). Agent Orange or one or the other of its components, 2,4-D and 2,4,5-T, is used routinely by the logging industry and the U.S. Forest Service throughout the Northwest to control unwanted (i.e., broadleaf) perennials in the coniferous forests (Van Strum, 1983). The Hooker Chemical Company admits that some 200 tons of trichlorophenol were dumped at the Love Canal dump site in Niagara Falls, and it has been estimated that the waste contains as much as 130 pounds of dioxin (Brown, 1979; Nader et al., 1981). Dioxin has been found in surface water and groundwater in the Niagara Falls area and elsewhere throughout the country. Fish from Saginaw Bay, Michigan, have TCDD levels as high as 695 parts per trillion (Sylvester, 1982). The U.S. Food and Drug Administration has set 100 parts per trillion as the safe dioxin concentration in edible fish, which is five times higher than Canada's limit of 20 parts per trillion.

Although attention first focused on dioxin as a result of report from Vietnam of increased numbers of spontaneous abortions and birth defects following extensive use of Agent Orange, there is no consensus about the health effects of the substance. It has been compared in toxicity to the botulinus toxin by some (Brown, 1979), called "the most toxic chemical ever made" by others (Sylvester, 1982), and listed as a potent carcinogen by OTA (1984) on the basis of EPA assessments. Studies in Vietnam, which have been criticized by U.S. scientists (Carlson, 1983), report various chromosomal abnormalities, primary liver cancers, and neurasthenic effects in people exposed to the herbicide. There are both a substantial scientific literature showing that TCDD causes cancer in animals and an anecdotal literature indicating that it (or 2,4,5-T or 2,4-D) causes birth defects, spontaneous abortions, and death in birds and mammals (see, e.g., Bonacorsi et al., 1978; Van Strum, 1983), but there remains considerable uncertainty concerning the effects in human beings and on the environment, despite the relatively long history of use and study.

Certain compounds, such as phthalates, have become ubiquitous environmental pollutants because of the volume produced and their ultimate distribution. Phthalates like di(2-ethylhexyl) phthalate (DEHP) impart flexibility to plastics but do not become part of the matrix and can migrate to the environment (Kluwe et al., 1982). The production of some phthalates exceeds 100 million pounds a year. Plasticizers are used so extensively that the potential for exposure to phthalates is quite high. Various studies suggest that phthalate esters may cause leukemia, accumulate in and are toxic to aquatic organisms, are carcinogenic in rats and mice, and show mutagenic activity in *Salmonella* (Hudson, 1982; Kluwe et al., 1982; Tomita et al., 1982). Phthalate esters are included on the 1977 list of priority pollutants, but testing has not been completed. Until conclusive testing is finished, regulation of the production, use, or disposal of questionable phthalates is unlikely.

Some 40,000 pesticides are registered for use by the EPA. The production of synthetic organic pesticides has increased from 648 million pounds in 1960 to 1.1 billion pounds in 1982. About 40 percent of U.S. pesticide production is exported; one-fourth of the exports consist of pesticides that are banned or restricted for use here. It has been estimated that roughly 20 percent of pesticides used in developing countries is for cosmetic purposes on export or luxury crops, such as pineapples and coffee (Dampier, 1983).

While the use of synthetic organic pesticides has increased, there has been a decline in effectiveness. Between 1945 and 1984 the proportion of crops lost to insects actually rose from 7 percent to 13 percent, while there was a 12-fold increase in insecticide application. For corn during the same period pesticide use increased 1,000-fold, and crop losses rose 12 percent (see chapter 3). The change in effectiveness can be attributed, in part at least, to the development of pesticide resistance among some 400 to 500 arthropod pest species, as well as among numerous rodents, nematodes, weeds, and plant pathogens. In addition multiple resistance (resistance to more than one kind of pesticide) is common. In fact, half the resistant arthropods can tolerate two or more classes of compounds, and 17 insect species are resistant to all five classes of insecticides, an indication of the successive deployment of chlorinated hydrocarbons, cyclodienes, organophosphates, carbamates, and pyrethroids (Mlot, 1985).

Changes in agricultural practices based on increased reliance on pesticides have abetted the development of resistance. Many plant varieties developed during the Green Revolution are more vulnerable to insect attack and, therefore, require greater inputs of insecticides. The no-till cropping method, while reducing soil erosion and runoff, requires an increased use of herbicides to control "weeds" that were formerly plowed under. Roughly half the tonnage of pesticides used worldwide is herbicides. Furthermore, chemical manufacturers now market seeds, fertilizer, and pesticides all in one package, which reduces the incentive for the development of resistant strains of plants and increases the likelihood of pest resistance (Dampier, 1983).

Although the quantity of pesticides produced is relatively small compared with the quantity of all synthetic organic chemicals, pesticides are of particular concern because they are intended to kill insects, plants, bacteria, fungi, and mammals, and they are introduced directly into the environment. David Pimentel (personal communication, May, 1985), points out that only 1 percent of the pesticides applied reaches the target organisms; the remaining 99 percent disperse into lakes, rivers, streams, forests, fields, and groundwater. Of the 200 organic chemicals that have been identified as contaminants of groundwater, about 36 percent are pesticides. Some have been found in very high concentrations. Alachlor, for example, has been detected in concentrations ranging from 190 to 1,700 parts per billion (OTA, 1984).

No matter what the use or application of a chemical is, ultimately it ends up in the environment as waste. EPA regulations and the Resource Conservation and Recovery Act (RCRA) define hazardous wastes as those that because of their

quantity, concentration or physical, chemical or infectious characteristics may: (a) cause or significantly contribute to an increase in mortality or an increase in serious irreversible or incapacitating reversible illness; or (b) pose a substantial present or potential hazard to human health or the environment when improperly treated, stored, transported, or disposed of, or otherwise managed.

The EPA has estimated that the United States and its territories generate about 91 billion pounds of industrial hazardous wastes (Epstein et al., 1982). In its report the OTA (1983) estimated that the annual generation of industrial wastes could be as high as 360 billions pounds (four times greater than the EPA's estimate). In 1979 the EPA estimated that between 10 and 15 percent of all industrialized wastes produced in the United States each year should be considered hazardous. Not included are waste oil from service stations, ash from power plants, dredged materials, and contaminated debris, mostly from oil spills (Hill, 1983).

Some 36 million pounds of toxic metals and 130 million pounds of toxic organics are released into lakes, rivers, and streams each year by direct dischargers (Scorecard, 1985). Indirect industrial dischargers release, through municipal treatment plants, another 56 million pounds of toxic metals as well as 190 million pounds of toxic organic chemicals. Pollutants such as chlorinated hydrocarbons and heavy metals persist in sediments and accumulate in tissues. As a result fishing is banned, and warnings are issued against the consumption of fish in many states (CEQ, 1983).

It has been estimated that 96 percent of the total volume of hazardous waste is processed and disposed of at the site of manufacture or at another site owned by the generator. Little information is available about on-site management practices or groundwater monitoring. Similarly, enforcement efforts are limited (Pirages, 1985).

In its assessment of the Superfund program, the OTA (1985) concluded that EPA's estimate of 2,000 to 2,500 sites vastly underestimated the number of sites ultimately to be cleaned up, by ignoring closed industrial landfills and underestimating the number of closed municipal landfills. The

OTA estimated that about 10,000 waste sites would require cleanup on a priority basis, costing perhaps as much as $100 billion. Moreover, the OTA charged that the EPA did not take into account the more stringent requirements for hazardous-waste facilities adopted by Congress in 1984. Similarly the General Accounting Office (GAO) agreed that EPA's number of sites was too low and estimated that there were about 4,170 uncontrolled toxic dump sites—for which the cleanup bill might be as large as $39 billion (The EPA itself identified another 12,000 to 17,000 potential hazardous-waste sites [Salisbury, 1985; Shabecoff, 1985]). Whatever the actual number is, it is clear that the problem of toxic wastes will not be ameliorated quickly or cheaply.

Not only is there uncertainty about the number of waste-disposal sites that will require remedial action, but also there is considerable uncertainty about the composition and the toxicological significance of those identified. At Love Canal, for example, 48 percent of the 400 identifiable chemicals were classified as mutagens, carcinogens, fetal-embryo toxicants, and/or neuro-, hepato-, renal, or pulmonary toxicants (Voytek, 1981). That no toxicological data have been found for the remaining 52 percent of the chemicals is no cause for complacency.

One of the primary reasons for concern about hazardous wastes is that substances leaking from landfills and surface impoundments are contaminating both surface waters and groundwater. In 1975 the EPA estimated that 90 percent of operating landfills were leaking (OTA, 1984). According to the report by the Council on Environmental Quality of 1981, fugitive toxic chemicals have seriously contaminated the groundwater in at least 34 states. The aquifer of the island of Oahu, Hawaii, contains significant concentrations of pesticides. Public and private drinking-water wells from Maine to California have been closed (CEQ, 1981). It has been estimated that 8 million people may be exposed to groundwater contaminated by chemicals from hazardous-waste sites (George Trezek, personal communication, Nov., 1985). About 50 percent of the U.S. population relies on groundwater as its primary source of drinking water. In addition, groundwater use is increasing much faster than the corresponding use of rivers, lakes, and streams (Tangley, 1984a).

The significance of groundwater contamination is just beginning to be understood. According the OTA report of 1984, it is likely that estimates of the extent of contamination of the nation's subsurface water, 1 to 2 percent, do not adequately reflect the level of exposure to contaminants for several reasons. First, groundwater-monitoring operations are far from complete: not all sources, substances, or systems are monitored. For example, the EPA estimates that there are 12 to 14 million private domestic wells that are not monitored. Second, the substances detected to date are widely distributed and abundantly used. For example, dioxins appear to be ubiquitous, and trichloroethylene, which is used in paints, solvents, fumigants, degreasers, and dyestuffs, has been found in wells in Massachusetts, New York, New Jersey, Pennsylvania, Arizona, California, and Texas in concentrations ranging from 210 parts per billion to an incredible 37,000 parts per billion. Third, the industries and activities that produce or release hazardous substances are generally located in areas of high population density, which means that potentially more people are exposed. Fourth, there are serious limitations in existing groundwater-monitoring programs owing primarily to lack of site-specific hydrogeological data. Consequently, the depth or location of a well may be inappropriate, fissures in presumedly impermeable bedrock may go undetected, or a plume of contaminant may travel at unpredictable rates.

Moreover, contamination will continue until adequate measures are taken to prevent further problems. As mentioned earlier, there are serious gaps in federal environmental legislation that undoubtedly have contributed to the groundwater problem. Gasoline is not specifically designated as a hazardous substance under federal regulations, but it may be one of the most common causes of groundwater contamination. The EPA estimates that 75,000 to 100,000 underground storage tanks are leaking about 11 million gallons of gasoline each year. At least two components of gasoline, benzene and ethylene dibromide, are toxic and cause cancer in laboratory animals (Tangley, 1984b).

Assessing the Risks

Clearly there is an enormous problem in terms of the sheer volume of toxic substances that migrate into the environment. But what is the significance? What is the impact on our lives? On other organisms? On future generations?

One of EPA's jobs is to determine whether a substance poses a risk and, if so, how much of a risk. As Wilson and Crouch (1982) point out, a regulator's principal focus is the impact (of a substance) on society, but various groups in the society may face different levels of risk. For example, Burmaster and Harris (1982) estimated the risks associated with drinking water from a well in New Jersey that was contaminated by fairly high concentrations of several organic chemicals. By assuming that the risks were additive, they concluded that about 5,490 additional people would contract cancer in a population of 1 million drinking water for a lifetime. The incremental risks to an individual would be about 1 in 200. As defined by the EPA's water-quality criteria, the "acceptable" level of risk means the induction of 1 extra cancer per 1 million population. It has been conceded that in practice EPA might consider a total risk of 2.44 per 10,000 as acceptable depending on the number of people exposed, the costs of control, and the benefits (Voytek, 1981). By either standard the level of risk incurred by drinking water from the New Jersey well was unacceptably high.

Ideally, risk assessment is based on consideration of a number of factors, such as: (1) both the acute toxicity and chronic effects of a substance on the human population and other species, (2) the exposure route, (3) the probable and observed concentrations, (4) the duration of exposure, (5) the likelihood of exposure, and (6) the extent of contamination and thus the size of the population exposed. But there are a number of problems in assessing the risks of exposure to toxic substances. Complete analysis would involve testing human subjects, which, of course, is not acceptable. Assessment of risks to the human population, therefore, is based on epidemiological data, mutagenicity tests (in which bacteria and mammalian cells are the test organisms), and extrapolation of data from lifetime carcinogenesis tests performed on sensitive strains of rats and mice. Epidemiological data are often difficult to obtain, particularly data on reproductive effects or those relating to cancers. In the first case, records are often incomplete, and, in the second, the time between exposure and the occurrence of the cancer can range from 10 to 40 years.

Because there is a close relationship between potency in mutagenicity tests and carcinogenicity tests for many chemicals, there has been a tendency to assume a one-to-one relationship that may not be valid. For example, it may be decided on the basis of a negative mutagenicity test that a particular substance is of low testing priority, and further tests may be postponed or suspended. There is, however, considerable evidence that different bacterial strains have markedly different sensitivities to various mutagens (Holmberg and Ahlborg, 1983; Marnett et al., 1985). Similarly, there is enormous variation in the susceptibility of test rodents to different carcinogens.

Nevertheless, extrapolation of animal test results to human risk assessment, although controversial (Shaikh and Nichols, 1984) and imperfect, is the best practicable method available. The risk-assessment model on which standards have been set by the EPA and other regulatory agencies has been based on the conservative assumption of a linear dose-response relationship for all carcinogens. No threshold could be presumed because of the limitations of the scientific data and the difficulty in identifying "safe" exposure levels. Recently, however, the EPA has proposed to distinguish between epigenetic carcinogens or promoters, i.e., carcinogens that do not initiate cancers by mutations or damage to the DNA, and genotoxic substances, those that have "the potential to cause a heritable change in the structure or sequence of the genetic material at the level of the nucleic acid, the gene, or the chromosome" (Perera, 1984). Proponents regard epigenetic carcinogens as having a threshold or no effect at low levels of exposure. It is difficult to understand the basis for such a claim. The mechanism(s) of carcinogenesis is (are) imperfectly understood; in fact, there appears to be a variety of possible mechanisms. And recent evidence has appeared that epigenetic carcinogens *can* result in DNA or chromosome damage (Perera, 1984). According to Perera (1984), the overall conclusion of the scientific community is that (1) no rigorous distinction can be made between genotoxic and epigenetic carcinogens at this time and (2) epigenetic carcinogens cannot be assumed to have human population thresholds or to be necessarily "safer" than genotoxic substances.

As currently practiced by regulatory agencies such as the EPA, risk assessment operates to a large extent outside the laboratory. The discussion about whether there are "safe" thresholds for epigenetic carcinogens may be a good example of an argument that is less scientifically than politically or economically motivated (see Marshall, 1982, 1983; Holmberg and Ahlborg, 1983). As Williams and Clark (1983) observe, "The uncertainty in scientific risk assessment continues to be so great that the regulatory process must be considered principally political judgment rather than technical analysis." They cite the example of asbestos, a substance for which the scientific data are conclusive—it is a human carcinogen (it has been estimated that about 2 percent of U.S. cancer mortality is due to asbestos [Weinstein, 1983]). But according to the dichotomous classification scheme, asbestos is an epigenetic carcinogen and has been classified as such on the basis of a negative mutagenicity test (Perera, 1984). Because of political debates comparing its potential social benefit with the degree of hazard, regulation of asbestos has been delayed. As yet it is still uncertain who will pay to remove or seal the asbestos insulation in thousands of schools throughout the country.

While risk assessment has focused principally, albeit imperfectly, on threats to human health, no similar directed effort to ascertain environmental impacts has been made. As Shaikh and Nichols (1984) point out, the tools to evaluate long-term ecotoxicological effects are not sufficiently developed for the task. But the EPA avowed in a recent policy statement that "biological testing of effluents is an important aspect of the water quality-based approach for controlling toxic pollutants" (EPA, 1984). Unfortunately most of the testing programs currently employed lack both "pollutant realism" and "environmental realism" (Cairns, 1981). That is, experimental design frequently ignores consideration of either characteristics of the chemical being tested, such as concentration, that might be realistically found in the receiving ecosystem or physicochemical properties of that ecosystem, such as pH, that can significantly influence the behavior or toxicity of the substance. Too often there is no "biotic realism"; the wrong organism is tested for its response to a chemical under inappropriate biological or physicochemical conditions. Clearly a comprehensive protocol for determining long-term environmental impacts is not just desirable but necessary.

Conclusion

Toxic substances are produced and dispersed in great volume; many are ubiquitous; many accumulate in soils, in aquatic sediments, and in living organisms; and, as the term indicates, they are poisonous. We do not now have, nor can we expect to have soon, complete information on the toxicologicological and ecotoxicological properties of the thousands of chemicals in commercial production. New compounds are introduced daily. The agencies responsible for testing or evaluating and regulating new and in-use substances are far behind in the task. Furthermore, the criteria for determining human health and environmental risks are ill-defined. Lacking an adequate data base on which to make decisions about particular substances, we should adopt a prudent or conservative approach. We need to reduce the sheer load of toxic chemicals released to the environment by reducing the volume of products or wastes. Existing legislation addresses the issue in only piecemeal fashion.

In the United States we have a set of environmental and public health laws intended to prevent the indiscriminate pollution and destruction of the nation's resources. But it is significant that there is no law specifically designed to protect the soil and its biological communities on which our agricultural system depends. Nor is there a law addressed to the maintenance of groundwater quality. And while efforts have been made to save endangered species from extinction, the link between deteriorating environmental quality as a result of pollution by toxic substances and the potential loss of species, communities, and even ecosystems, remains largely unrecognized, despite experiences such as the near death of Lake Erie. In short, we have a patchwork of legislation that focuses on particular aspects of environmental pollution and ignores others. Although our avowed goal is human and environmental protection, we have not developed a conceptual framework, a policy, that would enable us to develop a much-needed comprehensive set of laws.

Given the low probability of developing a comprehensive environmental policy soon, we can encourage Congress to (1) reauthorize expired laws quickly, (2) strengthen extant and reauthorized laws by eliminating exemptions and loopholes, (3) press the EPA and other responsible agencies to speed up and improve their testing programs, and (4) demand stricter enforcement of existing regulations. Public education, concern, and involvement have proved effective in the past and will continue to do so. People have been involved unwittingly in the problems of toxic substances in Times Beach, Missouri; at Love Canal, Niagara Falls; and in numerous other places around the country. As a result legislation has been enacted to ameliorate specific problems. With the realization that toxic substances are everyone's problem, perhaps we can protect environmental and human health.

References

Ambio. 1977. World Health Organization criteria for lead. Vol. 6(4): 240–41.

Ashford, N. A., C. W. Ryan, and C. C. Caldart. 1983. Law and science policy in federal regulation of formaldehyde. *Science* 222(4626): 894–900.

Bonacorsi, A., R. Famelli, and G. Tognoni. 1978. In the wake of Seveso. *Ambio* 7(5–6): 234–39.

Brown, L. R., W. U. Chandler, C. Flavin, C. Pollack, S. Postel, L. Starke, and E. C. Wolf, 1985. *State of the world, 1985.* New York: Norton.

Brown, M. H. 1979. *Laying waste: The poisoning of America by toxic chemicals.* New York: Pantheon Books.

Burmaster, D. E., and R. H. Harris. 1982. Groundwater contamination: An emerging threat. *Technical Review* 85(5): 52–62.

Cairns, J., Jr. 1981. Biological monitoring. Part 6: Future needs. *Water Resources* 15:941–52.

Carlson, E. A. 1983. International symposium on herbicides in the Vietnam war: An appraisal. *Bioscience* 33(8): 507–12.

Carson, R. 1962. *Silent spring.* New York: Houghton Mifflin.

CEQ [Council on Environmental Quality]. 1981. *Contamination of groundwater by toxic organic chemicals.* Washington, D.C.: U.S. Government Printing Office.

———. 1983. *Annual report of the Council on Environmental Quality.* Washington, D.C.: Government Printing Office.

CIH [Chemical information handbook]. 1983–84. London: Shell International Chemical Co.

Consensus Workshop on Formaldehyde. 1984. Report on the Consensus Workshop on Formaldehyde. *Environmental Health Perspectives* 58:322–81.

Cowen, R. C. 1985. Beware the excessive fear of toxic chemicals. *Christian Science Monitor* (April 16).

Dampier, B. 1983. Our widening "circle of poison." *Ambio* 12(2): 88–89.

EPA [Environmental Protection Agency]. 1984. Policy for the development of water quality-based permit limitations for toxic pollutants. *Federal Register* 49(48). (March 9).

Epstein, S. S., L. O. Brown, and C. Pope. 1982. *Hazardous waste in America.* San Francisco: Sierra Club Books.

Ernhart, C. B. 1984. EPA review of lead study [letter to editor]. *Science* 223(4623): 116.

Fackelman, K. 1983. Testing for dioxin exposure. *Bioscience* 33(11): 680–81.

Hill, R. D. 1983. Controlling the epidemic of hazardous chemicals and wastes. *Ambio* 12(2): 86–90.

Holmberg, B., and U. Ahlborg. 1983. Consensus report: Mutagenicity and carcinogenicity of car exhausts and coal combustion products. *Environmental Health Perspectives* 47:1–30.

Hudson, V. W. 1982. TSCA interagency testing committee actions related to phthalates. *Environmental Health Perspectives* 45:135–36.

Kluwe, W. M., E. E. McConnell, J. E. Huff, J. K. Haseman, J. F. Douglas, and W. V. Hartwell. 1982. Carcinogenicity testing of phthalate esters and related compounds by the National Toxicology Program and the National Cancer Institute. *Environmental Health Perspectives* 45:129–33.

Lahey, W., and M. Connor. 1983. The case for ocean waste disposal. *Technology Review* 86(6): 61–68.

Landrigan, P. J., and V. N. Houk. 1984. EPA review of lead study [letter to editor]. *Science* 223(4623): 118.

Lindeberg, P. 1981. Getting the lead out of Swedish petrol: Step by leaden step. *Ambio* 10(6): 351–52.

Maltoni, C. 1975. The value of predictive experimental bioassays in occupational and environmental carcinogenesis. *Ambio* 4(1): 18–23.

Marnett, L. J., H. K. Hurd, M. C. Hollstein, D. E. Levin, H. Esterbauer, and B. N. Ames. 1985. Naturally occurring carbonyl compounds are mutagens in *Salmonella* test strain TA 104. *Mutagen Research* 1482:25–34.

Marshall, E. 1982. EPA's high-risk carcinogen policy. *Science* 218(4576): 975–78.

———. 1983 Revisions in cancer policy. *Science* 220(4592): 36–37.

———. 1984. EPA to repair leaks in leaded gasoline rules. *Science* 225(4662): 605.

Mlot, C. 1985. Managing pest resistance. *Bioscience* 35(4): 216–17.

Mott, L. 1984. Bad apples: Pesticides in food. *Amicus Journal* (Summer).

Nader, R., R. Brownstein, and J. Richard. 1981. *Who's poisoning America: Corporate polluters and their victims in the chemical age.* San Francisco: Sierra Club Books.

Needleman, H. L. 1984. EPA review of lead study [letter to editor]. *Science* 223 (4623): 116.

New York Times. 1985. Toxic waste threat termed far greater than U.S. estimates (March 10).

OTA [Office of Technology Assessment]. 1985. *Superfund strategy.* Washington, D.C.: U.S. Government Printing Office.

———. 1984. *Protecting the nation's groundwater from contamination.* Washington, D.C.: U.S. Government Printing Office.

Perera, F. 1984. The genotoxic/epigenetic distinction: Relevance to cancer policy. *Environmental Research* 34:175–91.

———, and C. Petito. 1982. Formaldehyde: A question of cancer policy? *Science* 216(4552): 1285–91.

Peterson, C. 1984. The return of DDT. *Washington Post National Weekly Edition* (February 13).

Pirages, S. 1985. *Regulating hazardous wastes: Where politics and technology meet.* AESA Issues Brief no. 2. Portland, Oreg.

Purcell, D. 1984. States dispute federal plan to protect workers from chemicals. *Christian Science Monitor* (September 26).

Salisbury, D. F. 1985. Congressional analysts tally up a whopping toxic waste bill. *Christian Science Monitor* (March 11).

Schnare, D. W., M. Ben, and M. G. Shields. 1984. Body burden reductions of PCBs, PBBs, and chlorinated pesticides in human subjects. *Ambio* 13(5–6): 378–80.

Scoreboard [Environment and Energy Study Conference]. 1985. *Environmental, energy, and natural resources status report.* Washington, D.C. (June).

Settle, D. M., and C. C. Patterson. 1980. Lead in albacore: Guide to lead pollution in humans. *Science* 207(4437): 1167–76.

Shabecoff, P. 1985. Toxic waste threat termed far greater than U.S. estimates. *New York Times,* March 10.

Shaikh, R. A., and J. K. Nichols. 1984. The international management of chemicals. *Ambio* 13(2): 88–91.

Stara, J. F., D. Mukerjee, R. McGaughy, P. Durkin, and M. L. Dourson. 1983. The current use of studies on promoters and cocarcinogens in quantitative risk assessment. *Environmental Health Perspectives* 50:359–70.

Sun, M. 1985. EPA accelerates ban on leaded gas. *Science* 227(4693): 1448.

Sylvester, S. L. 1982. Dioxins, discharges, and Dow. *CBE Environment Review.* Chicago: Citizens for a Better Environment.

Tangley, L. 1984a. Contaminated groundwater linked with disease. *Bioscience* 34 (5): 292.

———. 1984b. Groundwater contamination: Local problem becomes national issue. *Bioscience* 34(3): 142–48.

Tomita, I., Y. Nakamura, N. Aoki, and N. Inui. 1982. Mutagenic/carcinogenic potential of DEHP and MEHP. *Environmental Health Perspectives* 45:119–25.

Toxic Substances Strategy Committee. 1980. *Toxic chemicals and public protection: A report to the president.* Washington, D.C.: U.S. Government Printing Office.

U.S. Bureau of the Census. 1985. *Statistical abstract of the United States: 1986.* Washington, D.C.: U.S. Government Printing Office.

Van Strum, C. 1983. *A bitter fog.* San Francisco: Sierra Club Books.

Voytek, P. E. 1981. Aspects of risk assessment strategy. In W. W. Lowrance, ed. *Assessment of health effects at chemical disposal sites: Proceedings of a symposium, Rockefeller University.*

Weinstein, M. C. 1983. Cost-effective priorities for cancer prevention. *Science* 221 (4605): 17–23.

Wilson, R., and E. Crouch. 1982. *Risk/benefit analysis.* Cambridge: Ballinger.

9.
Biotic Services and the Human Estate:
A Scheme to Avoid Hidden Taxes

THERE IS at any time a small number of Great Issues that will affect the course of human events throughout the foreseeable future. Earl Cook, long a student of the great issues, grasped the significance of the inevitable global squeeze on resources brought by the expansion of the human estate into a world of limited resources. Earl wrote and spoke and taught and left an estimable heritage of brilliantly articulated insights that we can but polish. I seek to add to one of these, the threat of progressive biotic impoverishment from the cumulative toxins and toxic effects of the industrialized societies.

The issue is the continued function of the biosphere as a place suitable for the human enterprise. There is a substantial body of observations to confirm that human activities are changing the earth as a whole. We need not look far for evidence. The most powerful evidence is the increase in the carbon dioxide content of the atmosphere, now between 25 and 30 percent above the atmospheric concentration in the latter half of the last century and rising rapidly. Stark local examples of callousness in management of potentially enduring resources are common. Some of the most spectacular exist in the industrialized nations. In the Sudbury region of Ontario, Canada, for example, there is a 100-square-mile area in which the forest has been destroyed by emissions of smelters nearby. The land is barren. I have visited recently the spectacular coastal region of Cubatão, São Paulo, Brazil, where the forests have been destroyed by gaseous toxins, and the slopes, eroding and sliding, now threaten the industries themselves, spread densely over the narrow coastal lowland. A careful local search would reveal small increments of change in the structure of forests in most of the forested regions of the world, increments in a pattern that leads to the extremes seen at Sudbury and Cubatão and a score of other industrial slums

/ 171

around the world. More subtle changes could be found in the chemistry of environment, changes that in many instances involve the release of substances that have profound biotic effects and a very long residence time. Some of these, such as DDT and other poisons used to control pests, have been introduced because they have biotic effects. Others, such as the polychlorinated biphenyls, have been released inadvertently and subsequently found to have effects. Still other chemical changes involve changes in the relative abundance of major nutrient elements.

Such problems have arisen only recently as the human enterprise has increased to become a global force. The threats are many. They range from conventional war with its devastation and misery to the greater misery of nuclear war with its threat of global climatic changes that might last for years, devastate the biota globally, and eliminate large-bodied animals, including human beings. Somewhat more subtle but only slightly less imminent, if measured in the span of a decade or two, is the cumulative effect on the function of the biosphere brought by current patterns of management of the wastes of the human enterprise, industrial, agricultural, municipal, and domestic. There is ample basis for recognition that our systems, even in the most advanced industrial nations, for managing these wastes are flawed in fundamental and highly dangerous ways.

Perspective is important. I approach this issue with the view that, apart from nuclear war, anarchy, an epidemic of AIDS or other parallel catastrophe, the big job for science and government over the next years is the preservation of the human habitat, including especially the normal function of biotic systems in stabilizing the biosphere. I would also advance the proposition that human interests, including economic interests, industrial interests, interests in political stability with human rights protected, and the universal wish for freedom from disease, are all best served by steps that ensure the preservation of biotic diversity globally.

The issue is drawn with those who see human welfare as inevitably, securely, and narrowly tied to the economic system and place all else as secondary. In apposition I would place those who see human welfare as no less dependent on the biotic systems of the earth and set the preservation and management of these systems as paramount. I advance the proposition that we seek a system of living on earth that will work in protecting human interests from erosion over the next decades. Do we have a pattern of use at present that is sustainable?

The world is producing a rapidly increasing volume of wastes that are released into air, onto land, and into lakes, rivers, and oceans. For many persistent wastes the oceans are the ultimate repository, carried there through watercourses and the atmosphere. Any waste with a vapor pressure moves into the atmosphere and, once there, is diffused rapidly throughout the world, to be deposited in rain far from the place of introduction. Because two-thirds of the surface of the earth is water, this process too moves such substances differentially into the sea. The effects are largely irreversible. There is reason to question the circumstances that allow such hazards to accumulate. How have our regulatory systems failed? How might the failure be corrected?

In the industrialized nations, especially the United States, permissive practices that generate the problem have been developed and codified into regulations and law. The rationale has been borrowed from the annals of human toxicology and applied to the environment in general. In the attempt to codify details and exert control over the process, three basic assumptions are made. On the surface these assumptions seem reasonable. It is only on a careful review of their effects that their weaknesses appear.

The first assumption is that there is threshold for effects of any toxin on individuals, on populations, and on ecosystems as a whole. It is reasonable in the eyes of most to assume that there is some low level of exposure to any toxin below which there are no effects or the effects are so small as to be insignificant. The second assumption is that if there are thresholds for effects of any toxin there must also be a general capacity of an ecosystem to render innocuous some quantity of any waste. This capacity, referred to as "assimilative capacity," is assumed to apply to all wastes in some quantity. The third assumption is that the objective is the protection of human health against pestilence or toxic effects. This assumption is in itself permissive in that people are hardy; it is difficult to detect many toxins in food, and it is even more difficult to detect their effects on people because we do not normally allow ourselves to conduct experiments on the effects of toxins on large human populations.

We know much about the world and the position of people in it. We might abstract for the immediate purpose some of the points established through research in ecology over the past few decades, a period of extraordinary advances in knowledge. Several points seem especially important.

First the dominant influence on the human habitat is exerted by the plants and animals of the earth. The carbon cycle provides the most compelling evidence. The annual cycle in the carbon dioxide content of the atmosphere in each hemisphere is correlated with the cycle of metabolism of the forests of the middle latitudes. The carbon dioxide content is drawn down by the excess of photosynthesis over respiration during the summer and increased by the excess of respiration over photosynthesis during the winter. The difference, winter to summer, reaches 15 parts per million (ppm) or more in some places in the Northern Hemisphere.

In addition there has been throughout the past century a progressive, accelerating increase in the carbon dioxide content of the atmosphere caused, first, by deforestation and, more recently, by the combustion of fossil fuels. The accumulation of carbon dioxide is accompanied by an accumulation of methane, carbon monoxide, and nitrous oxide, all of which absorb infrared energy. The effect is expected to be climatic change in the early decades of the next century that will average globally about 1° C per decade and will bring changes in the range of 3° to 6° C per decade in the middle to higher latitudes of both hemispheres. Such rates of change in climate are unprecedented. They are enough to destroy existing forests far more rapidly than forests can be regenerated elsewhere and to produce a large additional release of carbon dioxide into the atmosphere.

The total amount of carbon dioxide released over the past 150 years of the industrial revolution is thought to have been about 160 billion metric tons from fossil fuels; the total from destruction of forests is variously estimated as between about 100 billion metric tons and 250 billion metric tons. Most of the estimates tend toward the middle or lower end of this range. Certainly until about 1960 the release from the biota substantially exceeded the release from fossil fuels. There is no solution to the CO_2 problem without direct attempts to manage the forests of the earth. The power and importance of these influences are difficult to exaggerate.

Second, most of the energy used by people flows from the sun through photosynthesis carried on in the green plants of the earth and transformed into various forms useful to human beings. Those forms include food and fiber, but they also include a wide range of services in stabilizing our habitat. The total amount of carbon fixed and made available to people or other animals plus the organisms of decay is about 75 billion metric tons annually with approximately two-thirds of that produced on land and one-third in the sea. The total seems to be a maximum for current conditions on earth. In fact almost everything human beings do reduces the total. The transformation of forest to agriculture results in a change in the character of the net primary productivity from the leaves, wood, and bark of trees into forms that are edible by man, but the transformation usually reduces the total amount of carbon fixed per unit of land area. There is clear advantage in managing human affairs in such a way as to preserve the net primary production of the earth. Obviously its protection from destruction by the accumulation of wastes in any form is desirable and a major objective in management.

Third, much has been learned about the effects of chronic disturbance on the structure of natural communities. In general the effects follow the principles of biotic impoverishment: larger-bodied rapidly reproducing species are favored under virtually all conditions of chronic disturbance. Forests are more vulnerable than grasslands; grasslands are more vulnerable than lichen mats. As the transition occurs from forest to lesser vegetations, net primary production declines as well. The process includes the loss of species, although the diversity of species may fluctuate along one of these gradients.

Fourth, we have learned much over the past several decades about the circulation of biotically important substances throughout the biosphere. We have learned the following from the circulation of radioactive debris from bomb tests and from the study of the circulation of persistent toxins such as the chlorinated hydrocarbon pesticides, especially DDT:

1. Air is the major route of transport for any particulate matter that becomes airborne. Particles that are small enough to be suspended in the troposphere for days to weeks may move considerable distances. We learned from the transport of radioactive particles during the 1950s and early 1960s that radioactive debris could be moved around the world in the midlatitudes in a few days to three weeks. In a few weeks to months it could be transported across the equator. Particles are removed from the atmosphere in precipitation. The oceans are a major repository simply because of their area, but it is clear that a global contamination occurs easily and rapidly from any substance that can enter the atmosphere and remain suspended for days to weeks.

2. There are many biotic, physical, and chemical factors that lead to potentially very high concentrations of biotically active substances in living systems. Radioactivity and certain pesticides may be concentrated into organisms at levels that are 10^5 or 10^6 times the concentrations present in the immediate environment of those organisms. Although the concentrations of DDT in water usually do not exceed 1 part per billion they may reach tens to hundreds of parts per million on a whole body-burdened basis in certain birds. The transport from the surface into benthic sediments, even the sediments of the abyssal waters of the oceanic basins, occurs in a surprisingly short time. With such transport mechanisms operating and with the potential accumulation to very high concentrations possible, the concepts of thresholds and assimilative capacities are obviously weakened.

3. Another realm of research over the past 20 years has been the role of the behavior-controlling substances, pheromones. These substances occur in nature at concentrations often no higher than $1/10^{11}$ or $1/10^{12}$ and control the behavior of individuals. Anthopleurine, for instance, the alarm pheromone for the sea anemone, has been shown to be effective at a concentration of 1 part in 1.5×10^{11} parts (Howe and Sheikh, 1975). This relationship simply emphasizes the complexity of the chemistry of nature and its vulnerability to change.

4. The contaminations of natural systems with toxins, once they occur, are substantially irreversible. There is no way to remove the PCBs from the striped bass and bluefish and other fish of the East Coast of the United States. Those residues will probably remain a part of the biotic systems of those waters throughout our lives and the lives of our children. With present systems of management of wastes the residues will be joined by several others over the decades of our own lives.

5. There is no way to isolate the human food web from the rest of nature. Just as it is not possible to grow cotton and milk on the same or adjacent farms and preserve the milk from contamination by the pesticides used in controlling the boll weevil, so it is not possible to insulate fish from toxic metals, chlorinated hydrocarbons, or other hydrocarbons included in the wastes of municipalities that are allowed to dump wastes into the coastal waters. Wastes deposited in air enter agricultural fields as easily as they enter the oceans.

These elementary observations, drawn from the progress of the scientific enterprise over the past decades, set forth the context in which we attempt to preserve the physical, chemical, and biotic integrity of the human habitat. That integrity must be preserved over this and ensuing decades in the face of the extraordinary growth of the human enterprise, growth in human population, and growth in the spread of industrialization. Will the present system work for 6 billion people in the year 2000 and for more than 6 billion in ensuing years?

We seem to be extending to municipalities and, ultimately, to nations the license to focus profits narrowly and to disperse costs broadly, the license to compromise the global commons of air, land, and water to avoid addressing, for the moment, the actual costs of dense human habitation. Governments are instituted to avoid such misuse of the common wealth by private interests. One might find it strange to discover scholars and governments allied in such a classic perversion of the public interest.

It is much easier to find the problems than to solve them, but I refuse to accept that these problems will not yield to imagination, research, and inventiveness in science and government. This is the class of problems that Alvin Weinberg referred to several years ago as "trans-scientific," meaning that they are beyond the normal reach of the scientific enterprise. I do not share that view. Just as the scientific enterprise has helped define the problems, so the scientific enterprise can continue to use its analytical capacities, imagination, and inventiveness to discover technical approaches to solutions. While I do not believe that governments should sit idly by expecting a technological cure for the problems, I do believe that the scientific enterprise can aid in the development of cures, helped by government and helping government toward that end. Nor is the private sector immune from criticism here, driven as it so often is by narrow economic interests. Nonetheless there is profit to be made, not only communally but industrially, corporately, and individually, through the discovery and implementation of general solutions to this type of problem.

While we may not have the answers we need, or even a program to produce them, answers can be obtained by following the same rigorous, inventive, demanding course we follow in the pursuit of any other question in science. Some of the requirements for success in the management of toxins and toxic effects might include the following:

1. For the handling of all wastes and toxins (except radioactivity), place the protection and management of the biota first. If that is done, human interests will be broadly protected without resort to precious estimations of risks, estimations that are certain to be controversial and impossible to defend in detail.

2. For radioactivity, place human hazards first, and the biota will be protected. (The reason for separating concerns with radioactivity and other toxins is simply that the effect of ionizing radiation is a genetic effect; the hazard is to the human gene pool. Other gene pools are protected by natural selection. If we protect the human gene pool, then all other other interests of man and the biota will be protected from ionizing radiation. The reverse circumstance is true for other toxins, where the hazard is not simply to the human gene pool but to all life, including human life.)

3. Recognize that there is a need in some circumstances to isolate human influences from the rest of the biosphere and in others to incorporate human influences into the normal structure and function of nature. Is it not reasonable, for instance, for cities as well as industries to be designed in such a way as to have a total influence on the biosphere that approximates the influence of the ecosystems they replaced? And is it not reasonable to expect fragile ecosystems such as tropical forests to be used in such a way that they remain renewable resources, capable of supporting broad human interests indefinitely?

4. Accept and pursue aggressively the inevitable necessity of closing man-dominated ecosystems to the point where they do not leak toxins into the general environment. This will require redesigning industries to be self-contained units. It will also require the redesigning of municipalities to limit their effects on the surrounding air, water, and land.

5. Assign to manufacturing the full costs of products by requiring that the treatment of wastes and the remedy for toxic effects be made part of the cost of business and not diffused broadly into the public realm to ap-

pear as a general, uncontrolled increment of biotic impoverishment imposed on all.

6. Accept the fact that there are some businesses and products that the world cannot accommodate: some technology is simply not useful in a world that is becoming smaller and more closely interconnected within itself.

The objectives sound like dreams. But each has a technical and scholarly component, open to imagination and to research. We can build cities that use a tenth or a hundredth or less water than they use now and a tenth or a hundredth the energy that they use now and discharge proportionately less waste. Why not start the process as part of the general program of reindustrialization? We seek only patterns of use of renewable resources that keep those resources renewable over decades. Will the present system work? I think not. But I can think of how one might start the process of reversing a system that imposes hidden, uncontrolled taxes on its citizens through permissive approaches to pollution couched in superficially reasonable terms.

References

For contemporary discussions of the carbon dioxide problem see:

Howe, N. R., and Y. M. Sheikh. 1975. Anthopleurine: A sea anemone alarm pheromone. *Science* 189:386.
National Academy of Sciences. 1983. *Changing climate: Report of the Carbon Dioxide Assessment Committee, National Academy of Sciences.* Washington, D.C.: NAS Press.
Woodwell, G. M. 1978. The carbon dioxide question. *Scientific American* 238:234.

The literature that challenges the current assumptions governing the management of wastes and the effects of toxins in the context of this discussion is limited, although there have been many studies of the effects of pollutants. One of the most revealing documents is:

E. Goldberg, ed. 1979. *Proceedings of a workshop on assimilative capacity of U.S. coastal waters for pollutants, Crystal Mountain, Washington.* Washington, D.C.: U.S. Department of Commerce.

A second document that is also useful in defining the problem addressed here is:

National Advisory Committee on Oceans and Atmosphere. 1981. *The role of the ocean in a waste management strategy: A special report to the president and the Congress.* Washington, D.C. (January).

The patterns of change in the structure of natural communities under stress are now being defined through contemporary study. One of the most comprehensive summaries of the transitions in structure and function that occur has been drawn from the effects of ionizing radiation, summarized in the context of this discussion in:

Woodwell, G. M. 1970. The effects of pollution on the structure and physiology of ecosystems. *Science* 168:429.

The concepts, however, hark back to the roots of ecology and taxonomy, wherein there was ample basis for recognizing impoverishment in all its forms.

10.
The Ecology of Nuclear War

The use of energy in modern warfare hastens the eventual exhaustion of vital non-renewable resources, produces goods and services that are at best merely unproductive, and has proved strikingly ineffective in reducing gross populations, although it alters demographic structure. . . . Warfare, which more and more depends upon the intensive use of energy, is to many the most worrisome moral arena.

—Earl Cook, *Man, Energy, Society* (1976)

LIKE MANY of the other environmental threats facing humanity, the ecological consequences of nuclear war have only slowly been investigated by qualified scientists and have even more slowly come to the attention of decision makers and the general public. Concern about those consequences — especially the ones that might be mediated by changes in the climate — has grown as nuclear arsenals have increased and as the arms race has become increasingly destabilized (Stonier, 1964; Ehrlich, 1969; Ehrlich et al., 1977; Ehrlich and Ehrlich, 1981). In growing numbers, biologists and physical scientists have ventured into Earl Cook's "worrisome moral arena," convinced that the next world war, unlike the wars of the past, will be strikingly effective at reducing gross populations.

The first quantitative treatment of atmospheric effects was the work of Crutzen and Birks (1982), which dealt with the possible effects of the

I am grateful to Joseph Berry, Anne H. Ehrlich, H. Craig Heller, John P. Holdren, Stephen H. Schneider, and Richard P. Turco for their comments on this manuscript. This work was supported in part by a grant from the Koret Foundation, San Francisco. The manuscript was written in the spring of 1985, and there has been only minor updating since then.

smoke from wildfires ignited in the course of a nuclear war on the amount of sunlight penetrating to the surface of the Earth. This was followed by the pathbreaking work of Richard Turco and his colleagues (Turco et al., 1983; commonly referred to as TTAPS), which for the first time used computer simulation to investigate the possible climate effects of a large-scale nuclear war.

Since the TTAPS work, the results of a number of other computer simulations have been published, including a series by Stephen Schneider's research group (Covey et al., 1984) at the National Center for Atmospheric Research, using a more complex (and more realistic) computer model of the atmosphere. Recently, the Committee on the Atmospheric Effects of Nuclear Explosions of the U.S. National Academy of Sciences (NAS, 1984) examined the entire question in detail, and the academy sponsored a symposium on the subject (Kerr, 1985). All these studies gave the same qualitative kinds of results: that a large-scale nuclear war could produce severe atmospheric-climatic effects. If these should occur, they would provide the dominant ecological impacts, and they are a major focus of this chapter.

The War

It is generally agreed by strategic analysts that a "limited" nuclear war is relatively unlikely (Ball, 1981; Zuckerman, 1982). In fact, it is a stated policy of the Soviet Union to use nuclear weapons if even one such weapon is used against it, and the Single Integrated Operational Plan (SIOP) of the United States government envisions massive use of such weapons against the Soviet Union (Pringle and Arkin, 1983).

This said, however, it is very difficult to estimate the actual scale of a nuclear war. At present, the strategic arsenals of the superpowers contain roughly 10,000 megatons of explosive power carried by roughly 17,000 warheads and bombs. An additional 30,000 warheads or so are available in the so-called theater and tactical arsenals. Future changes in the size of these arsenals are difficult to predict. One possibility is a substantial increase in the megatonnage in the nuclear arsenals because of the deployment of large numbers of cruise missiles. In what follows, I consider a large-scale war, by which I mean one in which a substantial portion of these arsenals is detonated — say 1,000 to 10,000 megatons or more, almost entirely in the midlatitudes of the Northern Hemisphere. The uncertainties in other parameters — such as targeting patterns, degree of accuracy that might be achieved, season of year, and weather conditions during the war — are more likely to govern the actual atmospheric events entrained than the raw megatonnage per se.

Nuclear Winter

Should the war be large enough, and should conditions be appropriate, it appears likely that a complex series of events now known as a "nuclear winter" will ensue. The primary cause would be the ignition of large numbers of extensive fires, some developing into fire storms, by the nuclear detonations. The area ignited by a given weapon depends on, among other things, its size and the altitude of detonation, as well as the weather conditions at the time and the available fuel for the fire (Glasstone and Dolan, 1977). For example, much of the thermal radiation produced by the detonation of a weapon above a cloud layer will be reflected toward space and scattered by the cloud layer, reducing the area ignited. In contrast, if a weapon is detonated under such a layer, some of the upward-directed "bomb light" will be reflected back toward Earth's surface, intensifying the heat effects and perhaps increasing the area ignited.

Under any conditions, thermonuclear weapons are efficient incendiary devices. One has only to realize that the total explosive yield of all the weapons used in World War II was about 6 megatons—less than 0.1 percent of today's strategic arsenal—and that most of the explosions did not start fires. And yet all of the burning that occurred during that war over six years obviously lofted a gigantic amount of material into the atmosphere. After a large-scale nuclear war, the extent of fires would be enormously greater, with perhaps as much as 20 to 200 teragrams (tg)—that is, 20 to 200 million metric tons—of smoke being produced within a few hours or days. In addition, if numerous nuclear weapons are detonated at the surface in attacks on missile silos, large amounts of dust, perhaps as much as 65 tg, could be injected into the stratosphere. The smoke and dust could form a pall of varying transparency over the entire Northern Hemisphere in a matter of a week or so and apparently could then spread to some degree to the Southern Hemisphere.

The overriding climatic effect would be produced by the smoke, which would cause a "reverse greenhouse effect." Normally, a large part of the incoming energy of the sun is absorbed near the Earth's surface because the atmosphere is fairly transparent to incoming visible radiation. On the other hand, water vapor, CO_2, and some other gases are opaque to infrared, and the warmed surface reradiates its energy in the infrared part of the spectrum. The atmosphere thus absorbs most of the infrared and reradiates part of it back toward the surface. Were it not for this greenhouse effect, the average temperature of Earth's surface would be about $-18°$ C ($0°$ F).

A plausible nuclear smoke layer could reverse this pattern, since smoke is mostly opaque to visible light but relatively transparent to infrared. Thus the sunlight could no longer directly warm the surface, while the surface would still radiate away energy. If the smoke is in the middle and upper troposphere (say 10 to 15 km high), and/or in the stratosphere, the result would be a dramatic cooling of the Northern Hemisphere land surface, at least in the mid- to high latitudes. Interior continental temperatures could drop to $-10°$ C or lower even in midsummer. Both cold and darkness (of varying intensity because of patchiness in the clouds) could last for a matter of weeks or even months. The seas, in contrast, would remain relatively warm because of their tremendous thermal inertia.

Indeed, recent work (Covey et al., 1984; MacCracken and Walton, 1984; Thompson, 1985; Thompson and Schneider, 1986) indicates that even a few days of dense smoke cover could reduce land-surface temperatures to below freezing. Furthermore, such transient "quick freezes" could be carried by unpredictable winds to virtually any location in the hemisphere — even if much less smoke were injected into the atmosphere than was hypothesized by TTAPS (1983) or the National Academy study. The possibility of this sort of "weather roulette" is supported by studies at several laboratories (e.g., MacCracken and Walton, 1984; Thompson, 1985; Thompson and Schneider, 1986; SCOPE, 1986, vol. 1).

At least three other major effects would be expected after a large-scale nuclear war. One is hemispheric-scale toxic smog resulting from the wide variety of poisonous compounds produced by incineration of plastic-filled cities, oil wells and refineries, coal stocks, piles of used rubber tires, and so on (e.g., Crutzen et al., 1984). A second effect is greatly elevated levels of radioactivity from prompt and middle-term fallout; in a pessimal case as much as 30 percent of the land surface of the Northern Hemisphere could be subjected to as much as 500 rads over a few days (Ehrlich et al., 1983). A third effect is that, after the atmosphere clears, the returning sunlight would be enriched by UV-B, ultraviolet light of dangerous wavelengths (TTAPS, 1983).

Life in a Nuclear Winter

The key to understanding the impact of a nuclear winter on humanity and other life-forms is simply that all significant ecological systems on Earth are powered by solar energy. The radiant energy from the sun is captured by green plants in the process of photosynthesis and converted into the energy of chemical bonds in carbohydrates — organic molecules such as sugars and starches. The plants can break down those molecules, extract the energy, and use it to drive their life processes — growth, maintenance, and reproduction. In turn, animals can obtain part of this energy by eating plants and extracting it from the chemical bonds of the ingested material. Other animals can obtain it by eating the herbivorous animals. And decomposers gain their share of the energy by breaking down the wastes and dead bodies of other organisms. But the ultimate energy source is the sun, and the key process is photosynthesis; truly "all flesh is grass."

All five of the major impacts involved in the nuclear-winter syndrome amount to assaults on the photosynthetic process. Reduced solar radiation alone will have a dramatic impact on plants. Some plants, such as the tiny phytoplankton that carry on the vast majority of the photosynthesis of the seas, have little in the way of energy reserves. Darkness will kill them or force them into a resting state, and oceanic food chains could be cut off at their bases even though oceanic temperatures would not drop significantly.

Darkness would also have a strong negative impact on terrestrial plants. For example, Alan Longman, of the University of Edinburgh, has done some preliminary, unpublished investigations of the impact of dim light on spring wheat (variety Royal Durum). The plants were grown in a heated greenhouse and given supplementary light except when they were being subjected to periods of one to six weeks of dim-light treatment. Two-week-old plants, when subjected to dim light (1 percent of normal) start to fall over after one to two weeks. A few manage to survive six weeks of dim light, but if restored to full light, they have been set back so far that they are unlikely to yield grain.

Six-week-old plants are much more susceptible to darkness than are younger plants, perhaps because nutrients originally stored in the seeds have been exhausted. Only one week of dim light checks growth, and flowering is delayed. After three weeks of darkness, most of the plants are dying or dead. By the time the plants are nine weeks old and have reached the flowering stage, they have accumulated some energy reserves. Even so, giving them two weeks of dim light at that stage interferes with the flowering process, and there is no yield of grain.

These results indicate that reduction of light alone could, after a war occurring in the spring or early summer, substantially reduce grain production over the entire Northern Hemisphere. Darkness would also have severe effects on natural ecosystems, although these effects are more difficult to predict.

But, of course, the darkness would be accompanied by drops in temperature—perhaps to below freezing even in midsummer. Such chill alone would, during the growing season, kill the above-ground parts of most plants. Some plant species would be exterminated, others would survive only as seeds in the soil, and still others would survive as underground parts that might eventually resprout. Many animals in an area subjected to a nuclear winter would die from the cold and, if the temperature decline were prolonged and severe enough, from a shortage of unfrozen surface water. Most of the remainder would soon starve.

If unusually cold temperatures occurred during the growing season in temperate, subarctic, and arctic regions, organisms that normally endure freezing in the winter would still succumb. Both plants and animals gradually "harden" (increase their tolerance to low temperatures) in response to shortening day length. Many plants appear to disassemble delicate cellular machinery and store it where it will not be susceptible to damage by ice formation. Insects manufacture antifreeze compounds that are deposited in their body fluid. Mammals that hibernate, such as many ground squirrels, build up their reserves of fat during the growing season and go through other physiological preparations for the hibernation season. They will starve before spring if their feeding time is curtailed, or, if nuclear winter occurs in the growing season, they will fail to enter hibernation at all.

If the smoke cloud were patchy, as seems most likely (Covey et al., 1984; MacCracken and Walton, 1984; Thompson, 1985), there could be alternating periods of freezing and relative warmth. This situation would also be the most lethal of all for the biota, since plants and animals would be unable either to harden adequately or to remain active. Moreover, the process of partially hardening and de-hardening repeatedly would quickly exhaust energy reserves of both plants and animals.

Even apparently minor episodes of darkness and cold would suffice to decimate both agricultural and natural ecosystems. But these impacts are reinforced by the other major effects. Pyrotoxins in the air, released by the multitudes of fires in industrial facilities and plastic-loaded cities, would also assault both plants and animals. There is a substantial literature on the impacts of smog on plants (Harward and Treshow, 1975; Marx, 1975). These range from gradually accumulating damage when levels of compounds like sulfur oxides are relatively low, to quite rapid death when concentration of toxins is high. High levels of air pollution can kill most plants exposed to them (Gorham and Gordon, 1960).

The levels of radioactivity experienced by large areas of the land surface of the Northern Hemisphere could be well above the LD_{50} (the dose at which half of exposed healthy individuals die) for human beings, many other warm-blooded vertebrates, some crops, and certain coniferous trees, especially pines (Ehrlich et al., 1983). This means that, in contrast to previous estimates (e.g., NAS, 1975), one would expect serious ecosystem effects from radiation alone. For instance, large stands of coniferous forest might be killed outright and then dry out and present a long-term fire hazard from subsequent ignition by lightning.

Finally, UV-B has a variety of deleterious effects on vertebrates, including human beings. It suppresses the immune system and can cause blindness and skin cancer. It may disorient insect pollinators. And it inhibits photosynthesis, especially in plants that have been growing in the dark (Teramura et al., 1980). The effects of UV-B on any phytoplankton surviving a period of darkness could be especially severe (Calkins, 1982).

All these major effects would, of course, reinforce each other, often acting synergistically (as in the just-mentioned darkness—UV-B effect on plants). In sum they make it clear that a nuclear winter occurring in the growing season would wipe out agricultural ecosystems and decimate natural ecosystems. It seems certain that if a full-scale nuclear winter occurred over the midlatitudes of the Northern Hemisphere in July, civilization there would collapse. It is likely that there would be little significant human survival over much of the hemisphere. Those not killed outright in the war by blast, fire, and prompt radiation would find themselves psychologically shattered, choking and freezing in a smoggy, radioactive darkness. Water supplies would be cut off or contaminated. Once stored food supplies were exhausted, starvation would kill those who survived the other gross insults to their minds and bodies.

Even if a few people in the rich nations survived in deep shelters with self-contained air and water supplies, sanitary facilities, and stores of food, they would face insuperable difficulties. Agriculture would be exceedingly difficult to reestablish. Most seed stocks would have been destroyed, since in modern industrialized agriculture they tend to be stored in centralized facilities, not on farms. Seed stocks not destroyed in the war itself would likely be eaten by starving people. But even if some stocks survived, they would probably not be suitable for planting in the transformed ecological milieu of the postwar world. Moreover, some modern crops do poorly or fail to yield at all without input of fertilizers, pesticides, and, often, irrigation water. These inputs would be largely unavailable. The means of harvesting and distributing any crops grown would be limited or nonexistent. Furthermore, changes in clmate in the first few postwar years might make agriculture very difficult even if all the normal "inputs" were available.

Nuclear Winter—The Uncertainties

There are, of course, many uncertainties connected with the occurrence of a nuclear winter. Some have already been alluded to. A large-scale nuclear exchange in, say, June could have a more catastrophic effect than one occurring in November, after the harvests. Recent studies (e.g., Covey et al., 1984; Thompson, 1985) suggest that temperate-zone temperatures would be much less depressed following a fall or winter war than after a spring or summer war. This makes sense, of course, since there is much less solar radiation for soot and dust to block out at that time of year. Much would depend on whether and how much the climatic effects of a fall or winter war carried over into the following growing season.

A war that occurred when many of the target areas were under cloud, were being wet by rain, or were snow-covered, would certainly ignite fewer and smaller wildfires, since the ignition radii of the weapons would be reduced by clouds or rain, and snow would reflect much of the bomb light. Season would have a much smaller effect on the burning of cities, and probable smaller ignition radii under winter conditions could be compensated by more secondary ignition from heating fires. Another great uncertainty would be the degree of accuracy of the weapons (ICBMs, cruise missiles) used. If, for example, nations planned to strike primarily at less inflammable targets (say, missile fields in plains areas and air bases rather than city centers), much would depend on how many warheads accidentally detonated over urban areas or forests. Current estimates of accuracy are highly suspect; for instance, neither the United States nor the USSR has any experience in firing ICBMs in salvos or over polar routes. Furthermore, accuracy estimates are in terms of circular error probable (CEP), a measure of how big a circle is needed to encompass the fall of half the warheads of missiles fired from the same silo at the same target. It does not speak to where the other half goes or, more important, where the center of the circle would be with respect to the target. CEP is analogous to the "choke" of a shotgun; it will estimate the tightness of the pattern of shot, but not where that pattern will be in relation to the duck.

There is also the unresolved question of what the effects of multiple bursts in small areas over silo fields would be. There is some reason to believe (Turco et al., 1985) that these could result in very large injections of light-absorbing material into the atmosphere.

Furthermore, many questions remain about the behavior of both fires and the atmosphere, questions having to do with the amounts of smoke that would be injected into the upper troposphere and stratosphere, where contaminants are not removed rapidly by natural scavenging processes. Experience with large forest fires (NAS, 1984) and detailed computer modeling of smoke plumes (Cotton, 1984) indicate that much of the smoke would reach at least the upper troposphere, some hand-waving arguments (e.g., Teller, 1984) notwithstanding.

One question of interest relating to fires is how frequently fire storms will be generated, since they clearly have the potential for injecting sooty smoke into the stratosphere. If this should occur on a large scale, it could lead to a great prolongation of nuclear-winter effects, because smoke reaching the stratosphere would have a long residence time.

The fire-storm question is also significant in considering the fate of seeds and other organisms in the soil. In some World War II fire storms, asphalt in streets melted, and deep shelters got very hot. If fire storms can be generated in forest areas, destruction of soil flora and fauna could greatly slow regeneration of a forested ecosystem. The question cannot be answered simply, since behavior of a forest fire started by, say, several successive nuclear bursts—the first splintering and drying wood over an area of perhaps several hundred square kilometers and a second igniting the debris— is difficult to simulate. It is noteworthy that, under the right conditions, a fire in chaparral (a fire-adapted ecosystem) can kill seeds in the soil, alter the soil flora, and volatilize part of the soil's nitrogen supply (Dunn and DeBano, 1977). It must be emphasized, however, that production of the basic nuclear-winter phenomenon does not depend on the generation of fire storms.

Computer modeling has not yet given generally accepted answers to one of the most critical of all questions: How would an atmosphere loaded with soot in the upper troposphere and dust (and perhaps soot) in the stratosphere behave? How would patterns of precipitation change? How patchy would the injected material remain? Could, in fact, the troposphere-stratosphere partition break down? Recent studies suggest that it will.

One should not, however, allow oneself to focus too strongly on these uncertainties. Some are bound to persist indefinitely, and they are not all bad. The persistence of uncertainties is politically beneficial, since it makes war planning by either side much more difficult (Schneider, 1984 and 1986). It is, at any rate, the consensus of atmospheric scientists that very grave climatic effects are possible (NAS, 1984; SCOPE, 1985, vol. 1), especially in the Northern Hemisphere. And it increasingly appears that very nearly a meteorological miracle would be required to avoid all of them after a large-scale war.

The Tropics and the Southern Hemisphere

Perhaps the most important uncertainty about a nuclear winter is the degree to which the effects are likely to spread out of the North Temperate Zone into the Northern Hemisphere tropics and the Southern Hemisphere. A glance at a globe shows that most of Earth's unfrozen land surface (about 80 percent) and most of its people (roughly 4.5 billion, or 90 percent) live in the Northern Hemisphere. Even if no nuclear winter effects crossed the equator, and even if there were no targeting in the Southern Hemisphere (though there almost certainly would be), a nuclear winter in the North would prove a disaster for the South. Many nations of the Southern Hemisphere are heavily dependent on those of the Northern Hemisphere for petroleum (Cook, 1976; Schneider and Mesirow, 1976; Ehrlich et al., 1977) and many other critical resources. In addition, one cannot discount the shattering psychological effects on those of the Southern Hemisphere of the disappearance of most of *Homo sapiens*. Furthermore, the destruction of the tropical regions of the Northern Hemisphere alone would result in species extinctions unprecedented in the last 65 million years. The most recent computer simulations (Thompson and Schneider, 1986) make at least transient cooling to damaging temperatures likely in those regions in wars that are far from "worst cases."

But various climatic models (e.g., Covey et al., 1984; MacCracken and Walton, 1984; Thompson, 1985) confirm the suggestion, based in part on the behavior of Martian dust storms (TTAPS, 1983), that nuclear-winter conditions could propagate in a matter of weeks to the Southern Hemisphere. One would expect them to be less severe there than in the Northern Hemisphere, both because soot and dust would be diluted as they spread farther from the war zone and because of the climate-ameliorating effect of the greater area of ocean in the Southern Hemisphere. Because of this, the conclusion of a large number of biologists (Ehrlich et al., 1983) was that, even in a pessimal case, some groups of human beings would survive in that hemisphere, perhaps in places like the islands in the South Pacific or the Indian Ocean or the fjord lands of southern Chile and New Zealand.

It now seems extremely unlikely, with current arsenals and assumed targeting patterns, that survival would be so limited. If arsenals should increase substantially, however, or targeting patterns change so that considerable megatonnage were assigned to the Southern Hemisphere, the possibility of survival would decrease.

The long-term fate of small surviving groups, however, seems uncertain. The people would presumably be suffering severe psychological shock, and their social, political, and economic systems would be shattered. They would be confronted by an unusual and extremely malign environment, quite likely including relatively high levels of radioactivity and a severely altered flora, fauna, and perhaps climate. If the groups of survivors were very small and scattered, there could also be problems of inbreeding. Whether small groups suffering these handicaps, including an increased load of mutations and cancers, could reorganize, reestablish agriculture, and eventually repopulate the planet is an open question. The biologists who examined the question in the context of the early TTAPS findings

(1983) felt that they could not reject the possibility that *all* surviving groups of people would eventually dwindle away to extinction.

"Minor" Effects

Even if a full-scale nuclear winter did not ensue, the ecological effects of a nuclear war could be catastrophic. An average drop of only 5° to 8° C (from a normal average of, say, 15° to 20° C) would probably be enough to reduce grain production severely in the Northern Hemisphere, which alone might end civilization there. It is crucial to remember that such an *average* drop implies the occurrence of nighttime frosts and a severe shortening of the growing season (one is reminded of the story of the statistician who drowned in a lake that averaged only 2 feet deep). Indeed, it has been estimated that an average drop of only 1° to 2° C would make wheat agriculture uneconomical in Canada (G. Golitsyn, personal communication, November, 1984; SCOPE, 1986, vol. 2). It is clear then, that, even if current estimates of the degree of climatic perturbation are overestimated (remember, they may be *underestimated*), the ecological results of a nuclear war could still be catastrophic.

Potentially serious ecological consequences could follow a nuclear war in addition to the impacts of darkness, cold, smog, radioactivity, and UV-B. For example, large areas might be assaulted with extremely acid rains (Ehrlich, 1983; R. Turco, personal communication, November, 1984). If wildfires destroyed vegetation over large areas, fugitive dust could present major problems, dwarfing those of the American Dust Bowl of the 1930s, when Chicago sometimes had midnight at noon. Not only could blowing dust cause climatic disturbances, but dust can be an effective biocide, killing both plants and animals.

In addition, many of the fluids of civilization that escaped burning — pesticides, PCBs from transformers, industrial solvents, and crankcase oil — would pour from broken bottles, storage tanks, tank cars, engine blocks, and the like and find their ways into sewers, streams, and groundwater. The flush of toxins from cities into streams and rivers would help destroy life there, as well as in estuaries and onshore waters. Furthermore, the flow of rain-flushed silt from denuded land would add to the destruction. And, of course, both wind and water would take their toll of soils wherever anchoring plants did not quickly reestablish themselves.

Ecological Factors Leading to Nuclear War

Ecological factors are also involved in the causation of nuclear war. One of the basic ecological factors, human population growth, has been recognized as such at least since the time of the ancient Greeks. Plato stated that, as its population grows, a nation that

was large enough to support the original inhabitants will now be too small. If we are to have enough pasture and plough land, we shall have to cut off a slice of our neighbors' territory; and if they are not content with necessaries, but give themselves up to getting unlimited wealth, they will want a slice of ours.

Thucydides told how the Greeks conquered nearby islands, "especially when the pressure of population was felt by them" (both quoted in North, 1984).

Modern studies have confirmed the Greeks' intuition. As Nazli Choucri and Robert North, pioneers in the systematic study of the influence of population-resource factors on international conflict, put it (1975, pp. 285–86):

As long as there were ample resources for growth—beyond the horizon if not immediately at hand—and as long as there were outlets for the pressures of growth, human societies could afford to grow and compete, even though the price they paid was sometimes quite high. During the greater part of mankind's history, the planet offered vast, sparsely inhabited territories for exploration and development, and human societies were to some extent buffered from each other.

The interactive processes inherent in population growth, technological advancement, and rapidly increasing demands for resources have always had implications for conflict and violence. . . . People everywhere now confront the enhanced risk that continuing growth and competition, unless channeled in some new ways, may lead to massive self-annihilation.

The conflict-generating effects of increasing population and rising per capita affluence combined with the uneven distribution of petroleum deposits in Earth's surface (e.g., Choucri and North, 1974) have been exacerbated by the wasteful use of these resources. It is not because of its scenic wonders that the Strait of Hormuz is so often featured in the news. Scarcity and maldistribution of other resources, ranging from strategic materials (Ehrlich et al., 1977, pp. 908–10; Ehrlich and Ehrlich, 1985) to rich agricultural soils and water, also help generate international tensions in a growthmanic world. And recently environmental issues have begun to generate serious international friction. Acid rain, for example, has begun to poison relations between the United States and its long-time friend, Canada (Ehrlich and Ehrlich, 1985).

But perhaps the greatest potential source of conflict over the next few generations seems destined to be the relatively great deterioration of the environment in poor nations compared with that in the rich nations. Although deterioration is occurring in all parts of the world, the situation is worsening much more rapidly in the Third than in the First and Second Worlds. The much discussed North-South rift will become a vast chasm.

And the increasingly desperate poor majority in the world will have growing access to nuclear weapons (SIPRI, 1983; Holdren, 1985)—hardly a cheering prospect.

Policy Implications

In what ways should all these ecological factors change the thinking of policymakers on the complex of issues surrounding nuclear war? One must note at the start that, *without any ecological impacts,* a large-scale nuclear war should be unacceptable to any sane policymaker. A recent World Health Organization estimate considered that as many as 1.1 billion human beings could be killed outright in a nuclear war and an additional 1.1 billion so badly injured that they would die without medical aid, which most would not get (Bergstrom et al., 1983). Thus almost half the human population of 5 billion could become casualties in a few hours. This, of course, is a worst-case estimate, but any large-scale war (the only kind considered likely by military planners; see Ball, 1981; Zuckerman, 1982; Holdren, 1985) would result in at least hundreds of millions of deaths.

What could the ecological effects add but more deaths to an already unprecedented catastrophe? One important aspect is the full involvement of nonaligned nations. Some people in those countries have thought that a nuclear war between the United States and the USSR would simply remove those two "imperialist" powers and their satellites. But it is now clear that every nation is potentially at risk. One might hope that this would lead nonaligned countries to exert pressure on the superpowers to live up to their obligations under the Non-Proliferation Treaty, which commits signatory nuclear powers to negotiate seriously to end the nuclear-arms race and achieve nuclear disarmament. Such pressure helped bring about the crucial Partial Test Ban Treaty of 1963, which undoubtedly has prevented countless premature deaths from cancer and birth defects. Before her assassination, India's Prime Minister Indira Gandhi was involved in a "Five Continents" peace initiative appealing to the superpowers to end the arms race. She also lectured on nuclear winter on American television.

A second policy implication of nuclear winter is that it makes even more nonsensical than ever all talk of "winning" nuclear wars, prolonged nuclear-war fighting, and civil defense. That it was already nonsensical can be seen by considering the armament of a single American Trident submarine, of which twenty are planned for deployment by the year 2000. Each carries 24 Trident II D-5 missiles, and each missile can deliver 10 independently targeted 100- to 600-kiloton warheads. One submarine's 240 warheads could demolish all the cities in the Soviet Union and finish that nation as a functional entity. A similar bombardment from a single Soviet missile submarine would destroy the United States. Apart from the direct carnage and destruction, one might note that the food and agriculture systems in both nations are utterly dependent on energy and transport systems that would be destroyed in such an attack.

Under such circumstances, the notion that a nuclear war could be "won" in some meaningful sense is clearly insane. Civil-defense preparation could perhaps, in such a relatively limited (two-submarine) war, save a few lives outside the target cities, at least temporarily. But with such a "tiny" war extremely unlikely, and with a nuclear winter likely to follow a large-scale war, efforts to prepare a civil defense against its effects clearly amount to defrauding the public and a misallocation of public funds (Leaning and Keyes, 1984). At best, even the most elaborate preparations might extend for a short time the lives of a fraction of 1 percent of the population. The motto (ungrammatical) of civil defense should be "Die slow instead of fast."

The prospect of global atmospheric disruption from a nuclear war tends also to make a "counterforce" first strike an unappealing prospect. Even if such a strike did not elicit a retaliatory strike from the nation attacked, it might well cause an effect large enough to destroy agriculture in the attacking nation as well as over most of the rest of the Northern Hemisphere. Much, of course, would depend on the nature and season of the attack, but many airfields, submarine bases, arms-production plants, petroleum refineries, and other "military" targets are in or adjacent to very inflammable cities. And recently the prospect has been raised that multiple detonations over missile silos, even those in prairies, may add more smoke to the upper atmosphere than was previously thought (Turco et al., 1985).

Even a tiny possibility of causing the extinction of *Homo sapiens,* an obliteration of the human past and future, seems to give pause to some people who were able to view a vast (but not complete) slaughter with equanimity. Already it appears to have recruited additional people into the growing numbers committed to doing something.

Of course, on the negative side there are undoubtedly those who will attempt to restructure nuclear forces in such a way as to permit large-scale wars while minimizing the danger of causing a nuclear winter. Already there is talk of using "burrowing" warheads to produce ground bursts that will have minimal incendiary effects from "bomb light" (secondary fires would still be ignited in cities so attacked). In the fevered imagination of the nuclear warriors, I am sure, there are already dreams of control rooms with giant Cray 306 computers analyzing world weather data and weapons deployments, providing a continuing estimate of the probability of a nuclear winter being caused under any attack-response pattern in the MIOP (Multiple Integrated Operating Plan). Indeed such a MIOPic approach seems certain to evolve if the people of East and West permit the insanity to continue — and their leaders to plan on the social equivalent of taping aluminum foil to their temples rather than simply stop playing Russian roulette.

Conclusion

Scientists have been discussing ways to refine estimates of the probability of a nuclear winter following a nuclear war. In my view, the effort would be more than justified because of the degree to which it could enhance knowledge of global ecological pressures. I doubt very much, however, that it will affect the policy implications of the nuclear-winter findings one iota. The reason has to do with the nature of risk. Risk can be viewed as the product of the probability of an event happening and some numerical estimate of the hazard associated with the event. The chance of losing a dollar on the flip of an honest coin is 50 percent. The chance of blowing one's brains out playing one round of Russian roulette with three of six chambers loaded is also 50 percent. The probabilities are the same, but the hazards, and thus the risks, are very different.

In a worst-case nuclear winter, the hazard is as great as one can imagine — the end of one's life, the destruction of civilization, and possibly even the extinction of the human species. Therefore, the second factor in the equation approaches infinity. In such a case, the exact probability (that is, the first factor in the equation) makes little difference — be it 1 percent or 99 percent, the product of the two factors, the risk, is unacceptably large. This is a version of the so-called zero-infinity problem (Holdren, 1976). As long as there is any real chance of a nuclear winter, extreme measures must be taken to avoid nuclear war. Indeed, even if there were *no* chance of a nuclear winter, such measures must be taken — since the "conventional" consequences of a large-scale nuclear conflict are also unacceptably large to any sane human being.

Thus ecological considerations basically reinforce the view that nuclear war must be avoided if the future of civilization is to be secure. But even if it were possible to delete all nuclear weapons from world arsenals, great peril would remain. The potential for chemical and biological warfare technologies to threaten massive destruction of both human beings and ecological systems seems vast — possibly approaching the scale possible with nuclear weapons. And if those "unconventional" weapons are banned, humanity still possesses "conventional" weapons that are much more destructive than those that were employed in World War II. Fuel-air explosives, for example, are now available in the kiloton range; jet attack aircraft can carry more chemical explosive power than the heavy bombers that demolished Germany.

Even if it were possible to move back to the "good old days" of World War II, however, the problem would not be solved. If that war were re-fought today, the cost to humanity would be enormously greater. There are more than twice as many people today as there were then, and they are occupying a planet that is much poorer in resources and more environmentally stressed than the world of 1939. Then only one major region was a net food importer—Europe. Now only one region is a major dependable net food exporter—North America. One would expect that greater population density, the disruption of global trade, and accelerated depletion of resources and degradation of the environment would multiply the casualties of a replay of World War II many times over. And, of course, while nuclear weapons might be banned, the memory of how to make them will inevitably persist. A major feature of any replay of World War II would likely be a rapid race for nuclear rearmament, followed by (as actually happened in World War II) the detonation of every nuclear weapon that could be created.

The bottom line is that large-scale war of any kind is obsolete. The famous dictum of Clausewitz no longer holds; modern war is much more than "the continuation of politics by other means." Ironically, remaining in the realpolitik mind-set that has become increasingly inappropriate since the Congress of Vienna will destroy civilization whether or not there is a thermonuclear holocaust. Without diversion of the resources now squandered on armaments into attempting to resolve the population-resource-environment crisis, *Homo sapiens* will move over decades into the sort of environment that a nuclear winter could create in months.

References

Ashley, R. K. 1980. *The political economy of war and peace.* London: Pinter.

Ayers, R. U. 1965. *Environmental effects of nuclear weapons.* Vols. 1–3. Report no. HI-518-RR. Harmon-on-Hudson, N.Y.: Hudson Institute.

Ball, Desmond. 1981. *Can nuclear war be controlled?* Adelphi Paper no. 169. London: International Institute for Strategic Studies.

Bergstrom, S., et al. 1983. Effects of a nuclear war on health and health services. Geneva: WHO Publ. A36.12.

Brandt, W. 1980. *North-south: A programme for survival.* London: Pan.

Calkins, J. 1982. *The role of solar ultraviolet radiation in marine ecosystems.* New York: Plenum.

Choucri, N. 1984. Perspectives on population and conflict. In N. Choucri, ed. *Multidisciplinary perspectives on population and conflict*, pp. 1–25. Syracuse, N.Y.: Syracuse University Press.

———, and R. C. North. 1974. Dynamics of international conflict: Some policy implications of population, resources, and technology. *World Politics* 29 (special supplement).

———, and ———. 1975. *Nations in conflict: National growth and international violence*. San Francisco: Freeman.

Cook, E. 1976. *Man, energy, society*. San Francisco: Freeman.

Cotton, W. R. 1984. Simulation of cumulonimbus response to a large firestorm — Implication to a nuclear winter. *American Scientist* 73:275–80.

Covey, C., S. H. Schneider, and S. L. Thompson. 1984. Global atmospheric effects of massive smoke injection from a nuclear war: Results from general circulation model simulations. *Nature* 308:21–25.

Crutzen, P. J., and J. W. Birks. 1982. The atmosphere after a nuclear war: Twilight at noon. *Ambio* 11:114–25.

———, I. E. Galbally, and C. Brühl. 1984. Atmospheric effects from post-nuclear fires. *Climatic Change* 6:323–64.

Dunn, P. H., and L. F. DeBano. 1977. Fire's effect on biological and chemical properties of chaparral soils. In H. A. Mooney and C. E. Conrad, eds. *Symposium on the environmental consequences of fire and fuel management in Mediterranean ecosystems*. USDA, Forest Service, General Technical Report no. WO-3. Washington, D.C.

Ehrlich, P. R. 1969. Population control or Hobson's choice. In L. R. Taylor, ed. *The optimum population for Britain*. London: Academic Press.

———. 1984a. North America after the war. *Natural History* 3:84.

———. 1984b. When the light is put away: Ecological effects of nuclear war. In J. Leaning and L. Keyes, eds. *The counterfeit ark: Crisis relocation for nuclear war*. Cambridge: Ballinger.

———, and A. H. Ehrlich. 1981. *Extinction: The causes and consequences of the disappearance of species*. New York: Random House.

———, and ———. 1985. Ecology of nuclear war: Population, resources, environment. In S. Lee and A. Cohen, eds. *Nuclear weapons and the future of humanity*, pp. 93–112. New York: Littlefield, Adams.

———, and H. A. Mooney. 1983. Extinction, substitution, and ecosystem services. *Bioscience* 33:248–54.

———, C. Sagan, D. Kennedy, and W. O. Roberts. 1984. *The cold and the dark: The world after nuclear war*. New York: Norton.

———, A. H. Ehrlich, and J. P. Holdren. 1977. *Ecoscience: Population, resources, environment*. San Francisco: Freeman.

———, J. Harte, M. A. Harwell, P. H. Raven, C. Sagan, G. M. Woodwell, J. Berry, E. S. Ayensu, A. H. Ehrlich, T. Eisner, S. J. Gould, H. D. Grover, R. Herrera, R. M. May, E. Mayr, C. P. McKay, H. A. Mooney, N. Myers, D. Pimentel, and J. M. Teal. 1983. Long-term biological consequences of nuclear war. *Science* 222 (December 23): 1293–1300.

EPA [Environmental Protection Agency]. 1980. *Acid rain.* Washington, D.C.: EPA.

Erwin, T. L. 1982. Tropical forests: Their richness in Coleoptera and other arthropod species. *Coleopterists Bulletin* 36:74–75.

Glasstone, S., and P. J. Dolan, eds. 1972. *The effects of nuclear weapons.* Washington, D.C.: Department of Defense.

Gorham, E., and A. G. Gordon. 1960. Some effects of smelter pollution northeast of Falcon Bridge, Ontario. *Canadian Journal of Botany* 37:2, 327–35.

Harward, M., and M. Treshow. 1975. Impact of ozone on the growth and reproduction of understory plants in the aspen zone of western U.S.A. *Environmental Conservation* 2:17–23.

Holdren, J. P. 1976. Zero-infinity dilemmas in nuclear power. In U.S. Congress, House. *Reactor safety study,* Oversight hearing before the subcommittee on Energy and Power, Committee on Interior and Insular Affairs, Ser. 94-61, pp. 357–64. Washington, D.C.: U.S. Government Printing Office.

———. 1985. The dynamics of the nuclear arms race: History, status, prospects. In Avner Cohen and Stephen Lee, eds. *Nuclear weapons and the future of humanity.* New York: Littlefield, Adams.

Leaning, J., and L. Keyes, eds. 1984. *The counterfeit ark.* Cambridge: Ballinger.

MacCracken, M. C., and J. J. Walton. 1984. The effects of interactive transport and scavenging of smoke on the calculated temperature change resulting from large amounts of smoke. *Proceedings of the international seminar on nuclear war, 4th session: The nuclear winter and the new defense systems: Problems and perspectives.* Erice, Italy, August 19–24, 1984. Also, Lawrence Livermore Laboratory Report UCRL-91446, Livermore, Calif.

Marx, J. L. 1975. Air pollution: Effects on plants. *Science* 187:731–33.

NAS [National Research Council, U.S. National Academy of Sciences]. 1984. *The effects on the atmosphere of a major nuclear exchange.* Washington, D.C.: National Academy Press.

North, 1984. In N. Choucri, ed. *Multidisciplinary perspectives on population and conflict,* pp. 1–25. Syracuse, N.Y.: Syracuse University Press.

Pringle, P. and W. Arkin. 1983. *SIOP.* Norton: New York.

Schneider, S. H., and L. E. Mesirow. 1976. *The genesis strategy: Climate and global survival.* New York: Plenum.

SCOPE 28 [Scientific Committee on Problems of the Environment, International Council of Scientific Unions]. 1986. *Environmental consequences of nuclear war.* (2 vols.) New York: Wiley.

SIPRI [Stockholm International Peace Research Institute]. 1983. *The arms race and arms control.* London: Taylor and Francis.

Stonier, T. 1964. *Nuclear disaster.* Cleveland, Ohio: World.

Teller, E. 1984. Widespread after-effects of nuclear war. *Nature* 310:621–24.

Teramura, A. H., R. H. Biggs, and S. Kussoth. 1980. Effects of ultraviolet-B irradiances on soybean. 2. Interaction between ultraviolet-B and photosynthetically active radiation on net photosynthesis, dark respiration, and transpiration. *Plant Physiology* 65:483–88.

Thompson, S. L. 1985. Global interactive transport simulations of nuclear war smoke. *Nature* 317:35 (September 5).

Thompson, S. L., and S. H. Schneider. 1986. Nuclear winter reappraised. *Foreign Affairs*. Summer.

Turco, R. P., O. B. Toon, T. P. Ackerman, J. B. Pollack, and C. Sagan, [TTAPS]. 1983. Nuclear winter: Global consequences of multiple nuclear weapons explosions. *Science* 222 (December 23): 1283–92.

——, ——, ——, ——, and ——. 1985. On a "nuclear winter." *Science* 227:358–62.

van den Bosch, R. 1978. *The pesticide conspiracy*. New York: Doubleday.

Wijkman, A., and L. Timberlake. 1984. *Natural disasters: Acts of God or acts of man?* Washington, D.C.: Earthscan.

Witchell, S. 1974. Give me that old-time Darwin. *New York Times* (May 3).

Woodwell, G. M. 1978. The carbon dioxide question. *Scientific American* 238(1): 34–43.

Zuckerman, Lord Solly. 1982. *Nuclear illusion and reality*. New York: Viking.

11.
Backing Away from the Brink:
What Could and Should Be Done to Reduce
the Danger of Nuclear War

OF ALL THE problems capable of producing catastrophe for civilization, the possibility of nuclear war is in many ways the most sharply defined and the most widely recognized. The average citizen may be poorly informed about the detailed composition of the world's nuclear arsenals and about nuclear strategy, and specialists may dispute the exact distribution and duration of the climatological consequences of nuclear war, but recognition that such a war is possible and would be a disaster of enormous proportions is nearly universal.

Given this extraordinary degree of awareness of the threat of nuclear war, the degree of public pressure for action to reduce the danger has been surprisingly modest. To be sure, there has been a surge of interest and activism in the past few years that has included the freeze movement, the furor about Euromissiles, the physicians' campaign to remind people of the impact of nuclear war on their own communities, the spread of concern about nuclear winter, and now the "Star Wars" debate. But this relatively lively period in the first half of the eighties represents only the third episode of large-scale public concern since the invention of nuclear weapons 40 years ago.

The previous two episodes of public involvement were the fallout debate of the late fifties and early sixties and the antiballistic missile (ABM) debate of 1969–72. Each of these episodes ended with a government response that addressed the public's specific concerns: the Partial Test Ban Treaty of 1963 put an end to the generation of fallout from testing of U.S., Soviet, and British nuclear weapons in the atmosphere; and the ABM Treaty of 1972 allayed fears of having nuclear-armed interceptor missiles in our backyards with no prospect that they could really protect us.

The surge of concern in the first half of the eighties has been much broader than the first two episodes in the range of substantive issues addressed, and in that sense it is more promising. The current episode has seemed to reflect a deep dissatisfaction with the nuclear peril itself and with the continuation of a nuclear-arms race that grows steadily more expensive even as it grows more dangerous. Concerns this broad and deep probably cannot be put to rest by agreements as narrow as those that ended the earlier atmospheric-testing and ABM episodes. Some sort of more general settlement is widely longed for, and with good reason.

Yet there is a real danger that the anti-arms-race sentiment of the eighties will simply dissipate in disarray and frustration — perhaps with a more or less cosmetic arms-control agreement to its credit, perhaps with nothing at all. This outcome is likely not because the problem of stopping the nuclear-arms race and reducing the nuclear danger is too difficult to solve but rather because we are on our way to letting the nuclear-war issue be recaptured by the "experts." They tell us, "The problem of nuclear strategy is too complex for the public to understand; leave it to the professionals." They tell us, "The problem of arms control is terribly difficult, so don't expect too much from our political leaders." And a particularly pernicious subset of experts — the ever-present peddlers of technological panaceas — tell us to give them a few decades and a trillion dollars or two and they will fix us up with an impenetrable Star Wars defense.

If we let the experts get away with it — the strategists who say it is too complex, the politicians and bureaucrats who say it is too difficult, the weapons builders who say it is just a technical problem and they are working on it — we probably deserve the results. The purpose of this chapter, however, is to argue that there is another possibility: that the issues surrounding nuclear weapons, while complex, are not too complex for most members of the public to understand; that the problem of stopping the arms race, while difficult, is far from impossible; and that the time and circumstances are right for getting on with the job.

The argument is developed here in five steps: (1) a review of the rather easily understood phenomena that have governed the dynamics of the nuclear-arms race from its inception in the 1940s to the present; (2) a description of the status quo at the end of the 1970s (a stalemate, albeit an increasingly precarious one); (3) a discussion of the perverse trends in the nuclear-arms race in the 1980s that are bringing us closer to the nuclear brink; (4) a list of measures that should be taken to back away from the brink; and (5) a brief discussion of the reasons for believing that it could be done.

Dynamics of the Nuclear Arms Race

The Fundamental Confrontation

The roots of the competition between the United States and the Soviet Union are, of course, ideological and political. The two nations are based on profoundly different conceptions of how society should be organized; each sees the other as bent on imposing its form of social organization on as much of the rest of the world as possible; and each believes it essential to prevent its adversary from doing that. This fundamental confrontation, combined with certain elements of what might be called the political psychologies of the two countries, provides the raw material for nearly inexhaustible supplies of mutual mistrust, suspicion, and even paranoia. Each would feel safer, not to mention freer to pursue its own international aims, if it could be militarily stronger than the other; and each believes that, in any case, it cannot afford to be *less* strong than its adversary.

The Technological Imperative

Belief in the desirability of superiority and the necessity of parity has helped elevate to the status of an imperative the ancient tendency to build and deploy whatever weapons the imaginations of scientists and technologists can conceive (Zuckerman, 1982). The technological imperative, in short, is the proposition that whatever weapons *can* be built *should* be built. After all, if we build and our adversaries do not, we may gain the superiority we want; if they build and we do not, we have conceded an intolerable advantage; and if both build, at least we remain even. The answer is obvious: build.

This syndrome is reinforced by certain characteristics common to most scientists and nearly all technologists: they want to see their ideas translated into concrete form and tested, and they want to believe that their contributions are constructive and needed. These characteristics help generate tremendous momentum along the route from research to testing to deployment. Testing validates the scientist's contribution, and production and deployment validate the engineer's. The creators of new technologies naturally—indeed, almost automatically—become advocates of their creations, and their influence in this advocacy is assisted by their obvious claim to special expertise (York, 1970). That most of the nuclear-weapons designers in the Los Alamos and Livermore weapons laboratories have repeatedly and successfully opposed a comprehensive ban on the testing of nuclear explosives is a particularly compelling example of this phenomenon (Greb and Heckrotte, 1983).

The technological imperative is also reinforced by the characteristics of the institutions in which the processes of weapons research, development, production, and deployment are embedded (Barnet, 1972). Of concern are not only the inventors of weapons and the manufacturers, who profit enormously from weapons sales, but also the armed forces, whose branches compete with one another (as well as with their counterparts on the opposing side) in upgrading their arsenals; the government defense bureaucracies, which maintain and expand their influence by guarding jealously the weapons programs under their jurisdiction and by campaigning tirelessly for new ones; and (on the Western side, at least) the defense-oriented legislators who stay in office with the help of the steady flow of money they steer into military facilities and defense industries in their districts (Adams, 1981).

This "military-industrial" complex, as Dwight D. Eisenhower called it in the famous speech at the end of his presidency, is really a military-industrial-scientific-bureaucratic-political complex. It is important to recognize, moreover, that substantially similar forces are at work in the Soviet Union: the motivations of scientists, engineers, generals, and admirals are essentially the same on both sides, and the absence of the profit motive per se in the Soviet Union is compensated for by an even larger role for bureaucratic empire building than that in the United States (Holloway, 1983).

Worst-Case Assessment

Also highly germane to the U.S.-Soviet arms race (and to others throughout history) has been the tendency of each side to assume the worst about the military capabilities and intentions of the other. Each side then tries to design and deploy military forces sufficient to cope with its "worst-case" assessment about the other side, preferably with a further "margin of safety" for prudence's sake. The U.S. government contends that to do any less would be irresponsible, given its obligation to defend not only the nation but its allies and interests abroad. The Soviet government, of course, makes a completely symmetric argument.

Even in theory both sides cannot simultaneously enjoy the "margin of safety" in military capability vis-à-vis the other that each desires. (This impossibility arises from the dual-purpose capabilities—offensive and defensive—of such weapons as tanks, artillery, and fighter aircraft. If it were possible for each side to possess strictly defensive forces in excess of what would be required to neutralize the offensive forces of the other side, the problem of worst-case assessments would be less troublesome.) In practice what happens is that each side exaggerates the military strength of the other side and the deficiencies in its own posture and then uses these exaggerations as the rationale for its own further military buildup.

In the United States this phenomenon tends to be particularly prominent in election years. Eisenhower ran for president in 1952 declaring that a "bomber gap" had developed, the United States allegedly lagging behind the Soviet Union in intercontinental bombers; in reality the United States was far ahead in this category of weapons at the time and has remained so up to the present. In 1960, John F. Kennedy ran for president pointing to a missile gap, which also later proved to have been in favor of the United States. Ronald Reagan's presidential campaign of 1980 was marked by his claims of a "window of vulnerability" and a Soviet "margin of nuclear superiority"; there is reason to think that the accuracy of these claims was similar to that of the 1960 and 1952 versions (Holdren, 1985a).

The Fallacy of the Last Move

Another contributing element in the dynamics of the arms race is the "fallacy of the last move"—the supposition by either side that one more weapons system or other strengthening of its military forces will give it the margin of safety (or superiority) it thinks it needs, as if this move would go unanswered by the adversary. In reality, of course, while each side would *like* to have the advantage of the last move, neither will concede that advantage to the other.

The history of the arms race is punctuated by obvious examples of this phenomenon (York, 1970, 1973). The United States and its European allies tried to compensate for supposed Soviet superiority in conventional forces in the 1950s by introducing "battlefield" nuclear weapons; but once *both* sides possessed thousands of these weapons, it was far from clear what had been gained. In 1970 the United States deployed the first multiple independently targetable reentry vehicles (MIRVs) on ballistic missiles, oblivious to arguments that it would be safer to ban this technology by treaty than to let inevitable Soviet duplication of it diminish our security a few years later. As widely predicted, the Soviets did develop and deploy MIRVs five years behind the United States, leading directly to the "window-of-vulnerability" flap. The Soviets' deployment of highly sophisticated intermediate-range ballistic missiles (the SS-20) in the European region starting in the 1970s (Garthoff, 1983) was another example of "the fallacy of the last move," as they discovered to their consternation when Western European governments agreed to accept U.S. Pershing II and cruise missiles on their territory "in response."

The Action-Reaction Syndrome

So far, of course, there has been no "last move" in the U.S.-Soviet arms race, only action and reaction. Each time one side develops a new weapon or refinement or takes a major geopolitical initiative, the other side feels obliged to emulate or counter it. The reaction may be in kind (for example, one side deploys a particular kind of missile because its adversary is doing so, as seems to be happening with advanced cruise missiles in the 1980s); it may be a specific countermeasure (for example, the buildup of Warsaw Pact air defenses through the 1960s and 1970s to counter formidable NATO advantages in intercontinental and intermediate-range bombers); or it may be a general increase in weapons development in response to a broadly threatening move by the adversary (for example, the U.S. military buildup starting in 1950, in reaction to the Communist invasion of South Korea).

An action-reaction arms race of the sort we have been experiencing for the last 40 years would seem to be almost inevitable given the circumstances: the underlying fundamental confrontation between the two sides; unfettered operation of the technological imperative and worst-case assessment, and the temptations offered by the fallacy of the last move. Avoiding the action-reaction syndrome, then, presumably will require altering some of those circumstances. Before we turn to the question of how that might be done, it is useful to look more closely at the conditions that several decades of action-reaction have created and at the likely consequences of the specific actions and reactions in which the two sides are currently engaged.

The Status Quo in the Seventies

By the mid-1970s the Soviet Union, which had been behind the United States in most measures of strategic nuclear power since the years of U.S. nuclear monopoly in the late forties, had managed to gain a position of practical nuclear equivalence. The arsenals on the two sides were quite different in their detailed composition, but each country unquestionably possessed the capability to retaliate overwhelmingly against even the most devastating "bolt from the blue" attack by the other.

Dimensions of a Nuclear Stalemate

In 1974, for example, before the start of the Soviet Union's MIRVing of its missile force, it possessed nearly 1,600 land-based intercontinental ballistic missiles (ICBMs), some 650 submarine-launched ballistic missiles (SLBMs), and about 150 intercontinental bombers, capable in theory of delivering against the United States some 2,500 nuclear bombs and warheads with a total explosive yield of perhaps 6,000 megatons. The United States possessed about 1,000 ICBMs, 650 SLBMs, and 400 intercontinental bombers, capable in theory of delivering against the Soviet Union some 7,500 nuclear bombs and warheads with a total yield of 4,000 to 5,000 megatons. (The United States was well along in the MIRVing process, but its more numerous warheads were on the average smaller than those of the Soviets.) In addition, the United States had 15,000 to 18,000 "battlefield" and intermediate-range nuclear weapons of various kinds, and the Soviet Union had perhaps 10,000 to 12,000 nuclear weapons in these categories (SIPRI, 1983; Holdren, 1985a).

Given the sizes of the arsenals on the two sides and the invulnerability of substantial parts of these arsenals to destruction in a first strike by the adversary, differences in the details made no practical difference. At the strategic level the circumstance that even a tenth of either arsenal could effectively destroy the other side as a functioning society gave meaning to the concepts of "effective equivalence" and "mutual assured destruction." At the "battlefield" level the existence of thousands of warheads on each side meant that no advantage could be gained from using them. And at the "theater" level (a reference to the possibility of regional nuclear war in such locales as Europe, the Middle East, or Southeast Asia), the huge nuclear forces that could be brought to bear all but guaranteed that any nuclear conflict at this level would destroy the region being contested (Zuckerman, 1982).

The situation was, in short, a stalemate. "Mutual assured destruction," praised by some defense officials as a stabilizing strategic doctrine and maligned by others as MAD, was not in reality a doctrine at all—not a guiding principle, which one might choose to replace, but a technological fact of life (Russett, 1983). And whatever the defects of this situation, including the chances of unleashing these huge arsenals by accident and the moral repugnance of trying to base security on massive hostage holding, it could be said in its favor that at least it provided no incentives for either side to be the first to resort to the use of nuclear weapons. Neither at the battle-field level nor strategically, nor in between, could any military or political gain from such use be anticipated.

Implications of the Stalemate

It might seem to follow logically that the only plausible function for nuclear weapons is to deter the use of such weapons by others who possess them. Certainly that is the considered view of many analysts of the problem (McNamara, 1983; Zuckerman, 1982), including myself. But this conclusion has a troublesome implication, at least for the NATO side of the East-West confrontation: it undermines the doctrine of *extended* deterrence — the explicit threat of resort to nuclear violence in case of conventional attack — that has been a pillar of NATO's posture since that alliance was formed in 1949.

The idea that it is possible and sensible to deter conventional attack by threatening to resort to the use of nuclear weapons originated at the time of the U.S. nuclear monopoly; the rationale was that mustering sufficient conventional military strength to deter a Soviet assault on Western Europe was economically and politically infeasible, while extended deterrence with nuclear weapons offered protection on the cheap. Although the Soviet Union had nuclear weapons after 1949, thermonuclear weapons after 1955, and an intercontinental-delivery capability after 1956, a degree of credibility of NATO's threat to initiate the use of nuclear weapons to defend Western Europe survived through the sixties by virtue of massive U.S. nuclear superiority at the strategic level: the idea that the Soviets would not initiate war in Europe — or if they did would balk at matching NATO use of battlefield and theater nuclear weapons — as long as the possibility of escalation to the strategic level was a greater threat to them than to the United States (Rosenberg, 1983).

Once the Soviets achieved essential equivalence with the United States in strategic weaponry, however, the credibility of "extended deterrence" was severely weakened. Would the United States really be prepared to escalate to total and mutual destruction if the Soviets invaded Western Europe? Soviet deployments of substantial numbers of supersonic Backfire bombers and triple-warhead SS-20 intermediate-range ballistic missiles in the European region starting in the mid- to late seventies, moreover, encouraged the suspicion that the Soviet Union was seeking the capability to fight and win a nuclear war limited to Europe, or at least to deter with regional nuclear superiority any NATO use of nuclear weapons in that theater (see, e.g., Burt, 1983).

The Stalemate under Siege

The resulting uneasiness of European and American adherents of extended deterrence, moreover, was only one of the factors that by the end of the seventies were threatening the stability of the nuclear stalemate of mid-decade (NAS, 1985). Another was the proliferation on both sides of strategic nuclear weapons with much-enhanced utility for preemptive counterforce strikes against the adversary's retaliatory capacity. (Such utility comes from combinations of MIRVing, high accuracy, and short warning that make it possible to destroy more of the adversary's warheads before they can be launched than one uses of one's own to do it. In a crisis where nuclear war becomes a possibility, this capability on one or both sides creates incentives for first strikes where none existed before.) The most dramatic trend of this sort was the Soviets' rapid deployment, starting in 1975–76, of three new types of highly MIRVed ICBMs (4 to 10 warheads per missile). Just as U.S. deployment of MIRVed missiles at the beginning of the decade had fed Soviet fears that the United States was trying to erode Soviet retaliatory capacity, so the Soviet reaction fed American fears of the reverse.

Interacting with and reinforcing these destabilizing factors was a third one. Many military men and strategic analysts had never been happy with the idea of nuclear weapons as pure deterrents, offering no usable military options other than mutual destruction if deterrence failed. From this dissatisfaction arose a pressure to find nuclear technologies and doctrines that would make nuclear weapons usable for military advantage, even after the arrival of essential equivalence made such possibilities difficult to imagine (Freedman, 1981; Russett, 1983). Each side pointed to weapons developments and deployments by the other in the seventies as evidence of an interest in acquiring the capability to fight and win a limited nuclear war; and each side used this "evidence" to justify further modifications of its own nuclear forces in the same direction — all in the name of deterrence, of course.

Action-reaction was alive and well. The SALT II agreements, signed in mid-1979, were withdrawn by President Jimmy Carter from Senate consideration for ratification in early 1980, soon after the Soviet invasion of Afghanistan. (Both sides pledged to adhere for the time being to the unratified agreements, but that is far less binding than a ratified treaty; by mid-1985 even this limited commitment to adhere to a relatively noncon-stricting treaty was in danger of unraveling.) Negotiations to achieve a com-prehensive ban on the testing of nuclear eplosives, which had seemed close to success, also fell apart in 1980. At the end of the year Ronald Reagan was swept into office on a platform promising (among other things) to restore American nuclear superiority over the Soviet Union. What such superiority might mean in a world of some 50,000 nuclear weapons was left unspecified.

Perverse Trends in the Eighties: Edging Up to the Brink

The conditions prevailing at the end of the 1970s put in motion a set of trends that have steadily increased the nuclear danger through the first Reagan term. The Reagan rhetoric on nuclear war has been much more provocative than his predecessor's, and the U.S. military budget has soared (albeit more slowly, owing to moderate restraint by Congress, than the presi-dent has proposed). Negotiations with the Soviets on nuclear-arms con-trol, undertaken in the middle of the first Reagan term seemingly more for public-relations purposes on the U.S. side than in pursuit of a real agree-ment (Talbott, 1984), collapsed at the end of 1983; they were resurrected, without apparent prospect for success in the face of U.S. commitment to Star Wars defense, in early 1985. Notwithstanding the Reagan administra-tion's contributions to the problem, however, it must be said in fairness that some of the most dangerous developments had already been initiated in the Carter years, while others were the doing of the Soviets.

Continuing Counterforce Deployments

Among the developments of the eighties for which the Carter admin-istration must share the blame is the impending deployment of the MX missile, which Carter approved at the height of the SALT II debate in the Senate at the end of 1979. The MX, intended as a response to the theo-retical vulnerability of U.S. Minuteman ICBMs to preemptive attack by the heavily MIRVed Soviet SS-18 and SS-19 ICBMs, was to have two criti-cal characteristics: its basing mode was to make it invulnerable to attack, and it was to restore "parity" by increasing the U.S. counterforce capa-bility against Soviet ICBMs.

Ironically, the Soviets actually were more vulnerable to a U.S. preemp-tive strike than vice versa even before MX deployment (Holdren, 1985a). Years of study of ways to base the MX, moreover, failed to identify any way to make *it* less vulnerable than the Minuteman. President Reagan's Commission on Strategic Forces (the Scowcroft Commission) conceded this point in its April, 1983, report on the matter (Scowcroft, 1983) but declared that this vulnerability was not so important after all because the Soviets lack the capability to attack our ICBMs and our bombers successfully at the same time; since the missile submarines are invulnerable in any event, two out of three legs of the "triad" would survive to retaliate. (Critics of the MX had been saying as much all along; see, e.g., Scoville, 1981.)

The Scowcroft Commission also conceded that highly MIRVed, accurate ICBMs—like the MX and the Soviet SS-18 and SS-19—increase incentives on both sides to strike preemptively in a crisis: they are formidable counterforce weapons if they are fired first and juicy targets if they are not. This means that the Soviets were decreasing their own security as much as ours when they deployed the SS-18 and SS-19 and that we would decrease our security as much as theirs by deploying the MX. Remarkably, the commission went on to endorse the Carter administration's recommendation for MX deployment anyway, proposing to put them in (vulnerable) Minuteman silos! The rationale seems to have been that the Soviet Union must not be permitted to have even the appearance of a capability that the United States lacks (associated, in this case, with land-based ICBMs carrying more than three warheads each) and that the Soviets will not get serious about negotiating limits on such weapons until the United States demonstrates its "resolve" by deploying its own.

Evidently four decades of increasingly dangerous action and reaction in the nuclear-arms race have not taught as much. Unless Congress comes belatedly to its senses, the United States will shortly demonstrate its resolve by deploying a fabulously expensive ($200 million per missile), wholly unnecessary, and extremely dangerous new weapon. The Soviet Union is readying its reaction: a fabulously expensive, wholly unnecessary, and extremely dangerous new 10-warhead ICBM, dubbed the SS-X-24 by Western authorities (DOD, 1985).

Another counterforce weapon in some ways even more pernicious than these new land-based ICBMs has been careening toward deployment on the U.S. side almost unnoticed while MX draws the arms-control critiques. It is the Trident 2 (D-5) SLBM, a 10-warhead missile that for the first time will put on submarines a combination of accuracy and explosive yield sufficient to destroy the most hardened targets (Feivseon et al., 1984). The Soviets will duplicate this capability just as they duplicated every other U.S. innovation, probably within a few years of the D-5's scheduled deployment in 1988. Once both sides have thousands of counterforce warheads on submarines, the resulting combinations of high accuracy and short flight time (from submarines cruising close to the adversary's coastline) will reopen the "window of vulnerability" slammed shut by the Scowcroft Commission: It will then be theoretically possible for either side to mount a successful surprise attack against its adversary's bombers and ICBMs simultaneously, a situation that will further increase first-strike incentives and produce a subsidiary action-reaction arms race in antisubmarine warfare (ASW) and ASW countermeasures.

In parallel with the counterforce trends in intercontinental missiles, counterforce deployments in "theater" (intermediate-range) ballistic missiles are proceeding apace on both sides. This particular action-reaction sequence was started by the Soviets in 1977 with their initiation of SS-20 deployments targeted against Western Europe. Although the Soviet motivation for this move may well have been no more sinister than the same unfocused desire for modernization and upgrading of capabilities that often afflicts their Western counterparts (Garthoff, 1983), the SS-20 deployment aggravated Western European concerns about Soviet nuclear-war-fighting capabilities and intentions in that region and provided an excuse for an upgrading of NATO theater nuclear weaponry that many NATO authorities had wanted anyway. The NATO "response," agreed upon in 1979, was to deploy 108 medium-range (1,800 kilometers) Pershing II ballistic missiles in West Germany and 464 ground-launched cruise missiles (range 2,500 kilometers) in five European countries—West Germany, England, Italy, Belgium, and the Netherlands—starting in late 1983.

Although both the new NATO missiles are said to have extraordinary accuracy (4 to 5 times better than the most accurate ICBMs deployed previously, about 10 times better than that of the SS-20, and more than enough to destroy the most hardened military targets; see IISS, 1984), the Pershing II is the more worrisome of the two with respect to first-strike incentives and contribution to the chances of nuclear war by mistake. The reason is that its accuracy is coupled with a flight time of only 10 to 15 minutes, threatening the Soviets with destruction of missile silos and command centers within its range with such short warning time that they would be unable to react (the cruise missiles, by contrast, have a flight time of two to three hours).

The Soviets have not failed to notice that the Pershing II's capabilities mesh nicely with the "countervailing strategy" for fighting a nuclear war enunciated in Presidential Directive 59 at the end of the Carter years. (That strategy calls for targeting Soviet leaders and command centers, ostensibly to deter them by convincing them that they could not hope to control a nuclear war; see Freedman, 1981; Russett, 1983.) One possible Soviet response to deployment of the Pershing II is to place weapons and command centers within its range on a hair-trigger "launch on warning" posture; the

Soviets have threatened as much explicitly. Such a posture could not fail to increase the chance of nuclear war by mistake.

Another Soviet "response" to the new NATO missiles—this one definite —has been the deployment of additional SS-20s. At the time of the NATO deployment decision in December, 1979, the Soviets had perhaps 200 SS-20s; when NATO deployments began in 1983, they had 378; they figure in April, 1985, was about 415 (DOD, 1985). The final Soviet offer declined by the United States before the Intermediate-Range Nuclear Forces negotiations collapsed in November, 1983, would have reduced the number of SS-20s to 120 in exchange for no deployment of Pershing II and GLCMs (Talbott, 1984).

Complications from Cruise Missiles

The ground-launched cruise missiles being deployed by NATO do not have the crisis-instability characteristics associated with the "prompt counterforce" capabilities of the Pershing IIs and SS-20s, but their deployment may set off an "arms-race instability" by opening up a new arena of competition that will be especially difficult to bring under control. Because cruise missiles are very small, highly mobile, and usable with both conventional and nuclear warheads, each side could find it hard to be sure how many nuclear-armed cruise missiles are in the other side's arsenal. This difficulty will not only complicate future arms-control agreements, but also aggravate the worst-case assessment syndrome that has combined with the action-reaction phenomenon to drive much of the arms race to date.

Sea-launched cruise missiles (SLCMs) for land attack, which the United States began deploying on submarines and surface ships in mid-1984, probably pose even more vexing problems of counting, verification, and worst-case assessment than does the land-based variety. The U.S. Navy says that many of the 4,000 or so SLCMs it plans to deploy will be armed with conventional rather than nuclear warheads (Joint Chiefs of Staff, 1985), but the Soviets will find it difficult to verify that this is so or even to count the total number of missiles deployed. They are busily deploying their own SLCMs, and although these are not yet as advanced technologically as the U.S. models, they will pose problems for us as they are upgraded and multiply.

In still other respects U.S. deployment of SLCMs, instead of pursuing an agreement with the Soviet Union to ban them altogether, has been a particularly egregious example of our shooting ourselves in the foot. In addition to their rapidly growing navy, the Soviets have huge fleets of merchant vessels and fishing trawlers that could be called into service as cruise-missile carriers. Moreover, they already possess a huge air-defense system that has the potential to be upgraded to be able to shoot down U.S. cruise missiles, whereas the U.S. has very little air-defense system at all. (We dismantled most of our air defenses years ago when we saw the Soviets letting their bomber force languish while putting most of their effort into ballistic missiles, against which we were defenseless in any case.) If we wish now to have a defense against Soviet sea-launched cruise missiles, we will have to build a very expensive system nearly from scratch.

Clinging to Extended Deterrence

There is a certain perversity to the idea that deterring conventional war in Europe requires threatening to blow up the world if conventional war does break out there, particularly when the argument offered in support of this posture is that NATO, with 3.5 times the GNP of the Warsaw Pact, is unwilling to pay for an adequate conventional defense. Still, advocates of "extended deterrence" make some arguments that deserve scrutiny —namely that *no* conventional defense could deter conflict in Europe as effectively as does the threat of escalation to global nuclear war and that the consequences of even a conventional war in Europe with modern weapons would be so devastating that this eventuality must be prevented at all costs.

Alas, NATO's extended-deterrence *policy* actually adds little to the deterrence that exists automatically by virtue of the mere existence of nuclear weapons on both sides; and it entails high costs in the form of reduced conventional military preparedness, maintenance of a hair-trigger nuclear posture that increases the chance of nuclear war by mistake or miscalculation, and provision of a perverse example to other countries contemplating how to ensure their own security against potential aggressors. Let us look more closely at why this is so.

In theory the threat to use nuclear weapons against a conventional attack can contribute to deterring such an attack in two ways. First, the potential attacker may fear that the defender's use of nuclear weapons would be a *militarily effective* response to the attack. For this to be so, it must be possible for the defender to use nuclear weapons in ways that deny the attacker his objectives without at the same time destroying what is being defended. This has been the aim of developing nuclear artillery, nuclear land mines, short-range nuclear missiles, and, most recently, the "neutron bomb"; but it has all been in vain. When both sides possess nuclear weapons in superabundance, their use on the battlefield offers no particular advantage to the defending side: a battle being lost with conventional weapons probably will be lost even faster if both sides use nuclear weapons in "limited" ways; and large-scale use of "battlefield nuclear weapons can have no outcome other than the wholesale destruction of the territory being contested (Zuckerman, 1982; Bundy et al., 1982). The idea that NATO's use of nuclear weapons against a conventional attack would be militarily effective is, then, too implausible to have much deterrent value.

The second way the threat to introduce nuclear weapons might deter conventional aggression is through the potential aggressor's fear that *any* use of nuclear forces would escalate to the regional and then to the global scale, thus destroying not just the contested region but the aggressor's homeland as well. Unquestionably, a degree of extended deterrence of this sort exists automatically simply by virtue of the existence of long-range nuclear weapons in the world: no special policy is required to make plain that any large-scale conflict involving the possessors of such weapons conceivably could lead to the weapons being used. But the *policy* of extended deterrence has sought deliberately to make escalation to regional and global use of nuclear weapons seem more likely—more "credible"—than it would otherwise be, and herein lies great danger.

For the first two decades of NATO's extended deterrence policy—from the inception of NATO in 1949 until around 1970—the credibility of the threat to use nuclear weapons against a conventional attack was thought to depend on the superiority of NATO's nuclear forces compared with those of the Soviet Union, not simply in "battlefield" nuclear weapons but also in the longer-range "theater" and intercontinental categories. Such superiority was said to provide "escalation dominance" for NATO: at each possible level of hostilities short of global nuclear war—conventional conflict, "battlefield" use of nuclear weapons, regional nuclear war—NATO would have a credible option to escalate to the next level because its superiority in the corresponding categories of weapons ostensibly gave it the prospect of achieving decisive advantage thereby (Freedman, 1981; Rosenberg, 1983). The prospect of escalation, in other words, would threaten the Soviets more than it threatened NATO.

At least that was the rationale. In reality the concept of escalation dominance was outmoded long before this fact was generally recognized. Given the enormous destructiveness of nuclear weapons, the Soviet Union did not *need* numerical equality with NATO's (mostly U.S.) nuclear forces to be able to inflict intolerable destruction at the regional or intercontinental level. Deliberate escalation had ceased to be a *rational* option for NATO by the early 1960s, perhaps sooner. Escalation might well occur through accidents, mistakes, or irrational decisions—and fear of such possibilities would continue to provide de facto extended deterrence—but surely there was not much *additional* deterrent value in a policy that pretended, against all evidence, that escalation was rational.

Still, NATO clung to its policy of extended deterrence—and clings to it today. By the mid-1970s, Soviet achievement of essential equivalence with NATO in battlefield, theater, *and* strategic nuclear weapons had made the irrationality of an explicit policy of escalation so obvious that prominent political figures began to speak publicly of the need to restore "credibility" to NATO's posture (Olive and Porro, 1983). NATO's response to this predicament, far from changing its declared policy, was to continue to deploy nuclear forces whose characteristics make it plausible that escalation will be *automatic* even if it is irrational (Ball, 1981).

Nuclear artillery, for example, upgraded versions of which are being pursued by the Pentagon even now, promotes automatic escalation from the conventional level because its short range requires it to be deployed near the front; there it is in danger of being overrun by the aggressor's offensive thrusts, producing a "use it or lose it" syndrome that makes its use—indeed its *early* use—almost inevitable. Once the conventional nuclear "firebreak" has been breached at the battlefield level, moreover, the pressures to use the medium-range or "theater" nuclear forces will become intense, largely because the combination of accuracy and vulnerability of the weapons in this category on both sides puts a premium on preemption —trying to destroy your adversary's weapons before he uses them to destroy yours. Finally, the introduction by both sides of formidable long-range "theater" nuclear weapons—the Backfire bomber and SS-20 missile on the Soviet side, the F-111 and Tornado attack aircraft and the ground-launched cruise and Pershing II ballistic missiles on the NATO side—has blurred the distinction between "theater" and "strategic" weapons in ways that increase the likelihood of further escalation. Indeed, in the Pershing II and ground-launched cruise missile deployments, the "coupling" of theater and strategic forces was an explicit part of NATO's rationale; the idea was to help convince the Soviets, for the sake of deterrence, that a nuclear war could not be confined to Europe (Burt, 1983).

The fundamental mistake behind NATO's continuing reliance on an explicit policy of "first use of nuclear weapons if necessary" is the failure to distinguish between two types of threat to peace, one of them quite susceptible to reduction by deterrence and the other hardly susceptible at all. The first type is the threat of premeditated attack by a rational aggressor, who calculates that the expected gain from aggression outweighs the expected costs and risks. The risk that such aggression will lead to the use of nuclear weapons and to escalation toward global nuclear conflict is a powerful deterrent against this type of threat. The second type is the threat of conflict initiated by accident, mistake, or the crazed act of a wholly irrational individual or group. Deterrence by means of increasing the apparent risks of conflict is ineffective against this class of threat.

With respect to the first class of threat as it relates to Europe (and to other arenas where the central interests of the United States and the Soviet Union intersect), the chance of such an attack would be very low even in the absence of nuclear weapons, because the expected costs and risks for the aggressor are formidable in comparison to the possible gains. And the mere existence of nuclear weapons on both sides, carrying an implicit risk that a major conventional conflict would lead to their use, adds a powerful additional deterrent. Accordingly, there is very little threat left to be diminished by the incremental deterrent value of a *policy* of "extended deterrence" and arrangements of nuclear forces intended to back it up.

The threat that conflict will occur as the result of accident, mistake, or wholly irrational act, on the other hand, is more plausible to begin with and is much less susceptible to diminution by deterrence. Quite the contrary, the kinds of nuclear forces engendered by the policy of extended deterrence have increased both the chance that a nuclear conflict will start by accident, mistake, or irrational act and the chance that a conventional conflict started in one of these ways will escalate automatically toward global nuclear war (Zuckerman, 1982; Ball, 1981). NATO's policy, in other words, in the attempt to reduce a threat that already was very small (the threat of rational, premeditated aggression), has been aggravating a much more dangerous class of hazards.

As if that were not enough, NATO's continuing pursuit of a nuclear-force posture that would make deliberate nuclear escalation seem more rational and hence more credible—a fundamentally impossible task—has diverted attention and money from NATO's conventional forces. While these forces are by no means as weak as is often alleged in official analyses (compare DOD, 1985, and IISS, 1984; see also Mako, 1983; Mearsheimer, 1983; and Holdren, 1985a), it is certainly possible to envision improvements that would increase their ability to contain quickly, without escalation to the nuclear level, any conventional conflict that an irrational act or other unforeseeable circumstance might produce (Boston Study Group, 1979; Fallows, 1981). Such improvements are unlikely, however, as long as overreliance on nuclear deterrence of conventional threats continues to distort NATO priorities and procurement.

It should be obvious, finally, that NATO's reserving the right to threaten the use of nuclear weapons to deter conventional aggression cannot fail to increase the legitimacy of such a posture in the eyes of other countries that feel threatened by the conventional forces of a powerful neighbor. If it is legitimate for NATO to rely on nuclear weapons for its security against a Soviet conventional attack, in other words, why is it not legitimate for

Israel, Pakistan, India, Argentina, and others to deter powerful neighbors in the same way? Is this the approach we wish to encourage?

The Prospects for Proliferation

The spread of nuclear weapons to additional nations has so far occurred more slowly than many analysts feared. While it seemed possible that some tens of nations might possess nuclear weapons within a few decades of their invention, as of 1985 only six countries were known to have tested nuclear explosives: the United States, the Soviet Union, England, France, China, and India. In addition, Israel is widely suspected of possessing a modest nuclear arsenal, preparations for nuclear testing have been observed in South Africa and Pakistan, and there is some evidence that a clandestine atmospheric nuclear test was conducted in the South Atlantic in 1979 by parties unknown (Sweet, 1984).

There are two main reasons why the spread of nuclear weapons to additional countries has not been more rapid. First, the complexity and cost of the technology for acquiring significant quantities of nuclear explosive material tended to restrict this capability—for the first few decades of the nuclear era, at least—to major countries with large technical establishments. Second, there have been strong political and military disincentives against acquiring nuclear weapons: the recognition that these weapons have little or no military utility except to deter threats to national survival; awareness that possession of nuclear weapons tends to make one's country a target for nuclear weapons possessed by others; and the international "norm" against proliferation of nuclear weapons, codified in the Non-Proliferation Treaty (NPT).

Signed in July, 1968, and entering into force in March, 1970, the NPT now has 128 parties, including the United States, the Soviet Union, and the United Kingdom but excluding, among others, France, China, Israel, South Africa, Argentina, and Brazil. Parties to the NPT are obliged not to acquire nuclear-weapons technology if they do not already have it; those that have it (the "nuclear-weapons states") are obliged not to transfer it to others. Additionally, nonweapons-state parties must subject their peaceful nuclear-energy facilities to International Atomic Energy Agency (IAEA) safeguards against misuse of these facilities to produce nuclear explosives; and article 6 of the NPT obligates the signers "to pursue negotiations in good faith on effective measures relating to the cessation of the nuclear arms race at an early date and to nuclear disarmament" (NAS, 1985).

By the mid-1980s, unfortunately, the technical barriers to proliferation were crumbling, and the political ones were shaky at best. On the technical side the capability to produce significant quantities of nuclear explosive material has been spreading rapidly, as additional countries acquire uranium-enrichment or plutonium-reprocessing capacity because of (or under cover of) the role of these technologies in commercial nuclear-energy programs (Holdren, 1983). Many of these facilities are not covered by IAEA safeguards because the countries operating them are not parties to the NPT, and it is questionable whether the safeguards are adequate to detect diversion of nuclear explosive materials even from all those facilities that are covered.

On the political side the disincentives against additional countries' acquiring nuclear weapons have been weakened by the behavior of the major nuclear-weapons states as well as by the examples of "minor" or "near" nuclear-weapons states such as Israel, South Africa, Pakistan, Argentina, and Brazil (Sweet, 1984). The major weapons states—especially but not exclusively the United States and the Soviet Union—have continued to test new types of nuclear explosives, to deploy new types of weapons apparently designed to be usable for military advantage, to expand their nuclear arsenals, and in general to ignore their obligations under article 6 of the Non-Proliferation Treaty to try to halt and reverse the nuclear-arms race. NATO, in particular (as noted above, and in contrast to "no first use" declarations by China and the Soviet Union), has provided an especially pernicious example in its continuation of reliance on the threat of first use of nuclear weapons to deter a perceived threat of conventional aggression.

As long as the major nuclear powers continue to behave as though nuclear weapons were the greatest invention since indoor plumbing, they must expect lesser powers (both those that aspire to greatness, such as Brazil and India, and those that especially fear their neighbors, such as Israel and Pakistan) to follow their example in basing their security at least in part on possession of these weapons. With the technical barriers to proliferation no longer effective, moreover, undermining the political obstacles has become much more dangerous: a trickle of proliferants could very quickly become a torrent (Spector, 1985).

The Weaponization of Space

It might be supposed that the history recounted here so far would have convinced decision makers and publics alike that there is no *technical* solution to the problem of security in the nuclear age—that only political restraints on these weapons can protect us. Yet we find ourselves in 1985, at the fortieth anniversary of the invention and first use of nuclear weapons, on the verge of expanding into space the futile and dangerous competition in weapons technology that has misspent our resources, reduced our security, and sapped our morale for four decades.

This new danger has arisen in large part from the resurrection of interest in the possibility of defending cities against nuclear attack. The idea of defense is attractive in theory, of course, but the most perceptive analysts of these matters have understood since 1945 that the power of nuclear weapons is so great and the ways of delivering them are so diverse that effective defense of population centers is impossible in practice. It was for this reason that a surge of interest in defense against ballistic missiles in the late 1960s was terminated by the Anti-Ballistic Missile (ABM) Treaty in 1972: it was recognized both in the United States and in the Soviet Union not only that a sophisticated offense could overwhelm any defense that could be mounted but also that unconstrained pursuit of defensive technologies would provoke unconstrained buildups in offensive weapons—all at great cost but of no net benefit to either side (NAS, 1985).

The ABM Treaty limited the United States and the Soviet Union to two modest operational ABM sites each—each could try to defend its national capital and one ICBM field—and prohibited development, testing, or deployment of "ABM systems or components which are sea-based, air-based, space-based, or mobile land-based" (NAS, 1985). The limitation on fixed ABM sites was later reduced to one each; the Soviet Union has a limited defensive system around Moscow which could be penetrated readily by a U.S. attack; and the United States has chosen to deploy no system at all.

Research (as distinct from development and testing) on ballistic-missile defense was not prohibited by the treaty—such a ban would be almost impossible to define and completely impossible to enforce—and both sides have chosen to pursue such research programs in the intervening years, nominally as insurance against "surprises" that might lead to a strategic disadvantage.

In early 1983, President Reagan became persuaded (apparently by Edward Teller and a few of his younger associates) that progress in such research had brought into view the prospect of defensive weapons so effective that they would render offensive nuclear weapons "impotent and obsolete." In what came to be known as the "Star Wars" speech (delivered on March 23, 1983, and so named by critics because of the central role of space-based weapons in the schemes that caught the president's attention), he committed the United States to renewed pursuit of the chimera of a perfect defense. Now officially called the Strategic Defense Initiative (SDI), this program is projected to spend about $30 billion in its first five-year phase, including the conduct of tests near the end of that period that will clearly violate the ABM Treaty (Longstreth et al., 1985).

In the intensive study and debate that have followed the Star Wars speech, it has become clear that almost no one in the community of technical experts believes that the president's goal of defending the U.S. population against nuclear attack is feasible. The reasons are much the same as they were in 1972, for although technology has advanced in the interim, the changes have benefited the offense no less than the defense (Carter and Schwartz, 1984; Drell et al., 1985). There remain many ways to insinuate at least a few nuclear weapons through even the most elaborate defense, and a few are enough to destroy the main population centers. Unbeknownst to most of the public, therefore, the main goal of the massive SDI program has shifted from defending populations to defending nuclear weapons and the command-and-control centers that would orchestrate their use.

Defense of underground bunkers and ICBMs in hardened silos is technically much easier than defending populations: since it takes nearly a direct hit to destroy such a target, the defense needs only to shoot down those incoming missiles that are approaching a limited number of specific points, rather than trying to protect vast populated areas, and a conceivably achievable success rate of, say, 50 percent is a significant accomplishment when defending a missile field (since half the defended missiles will survive) but a total failure when defending a city (since no one will survive).

The stated purpose of trying to defend U.S. nuclear forces against nuclear attack is to enhance deterrence by reducing the effectiveness of a Soviet counterforce first strike. Alas, there are two gigantic flaws in this proposition. First, absent ironclad ceilings on offensive forces, the chief result of deploying defenses will be to provoke countervailing offensive buildups that will assure each side that it can overwhelm or circumvent the defenses of the other. For this reason pursuit of strategic defense to the point of violating the ABM Treaty undoubtedly will lead to breaching the SALT II limits on offensive forces (unratified but observed until now by both sides)—which, by the way, the Soviets are in an especially good position to do because of the capacity of their existing large ICBMs to carry far more warheads than those permitted under SALT II. An acceleration of the competition in cruise missiles and manned bombers—and countermeasures against these—would be another part of the automatic response to any advances in defenses against ballistic missiles.

Second, defense of nuclear forces along the lines of the SDI will likely include space-based components and long-range "kill mechanisms" that have *some* capacity for area defense (that is, defense of cities) as well as for point defense (that is, defense of nuclear forces). But the result of such capabilities, far from increasing deterrence, will be to *increase* incentives to strike first in time of crisis. One reason is that a partly effective area defense would be more useful against the ragged retaliation of a wounded adversary than against a coordinated and powerful first strike. The side that strikes first, moreover, can use both its offensive and its long-range "defensive" weapons to suppress the defenses of the other side. All of this makes it likely that any preliminary activation of defenses in time of crisis would be interpreted as preparation for a preemptive attack and hence might actually set off nuclear war.

Testing and deploying space-based components of missile defense not only will abrogate the ABM Treaty, provoke offensive countermeasures, and decrease crisis stability but also will stimulate vastly increased efforts in antisatellite (ASAT) weaponry because of the offense's strong interest in the capability to shoot down the space-based components of the defense. This expansion of ASAT technology—and, of course, ASAT countermeasures—will bring the arms race in space into full flower. The resulting competition will be extremely expensive (nothing in space is cheap); it will imperil the stabilizing capabilities of reconnaissance and communications satellites (on which, by the way, the United States is more dependent than is the Soviet Union); and it probably will lead to the demise of the Outer Space Treaty through deployment of nuclear weapons in space (Jasani, 1982).

The Partial Test Ban Treaty of 1963—which prohibits nuclear explosions in the atmosphere, on and under the oceans, and in space—is also unlikely to survive vigorous pursuit of antiballistic-missile technologies. The gamma-ray laser that so attracted Edward Teller (and hence President Reagan) to the possibilities of strategic defense must use a nuclear explosion as its energy source, so any operational test of such a device must violate the Partial Test Ban. The potential of other defensive and antidefensive uses of nuclear weapons, both in the atmosphere and in space, would also generate great pressure for testing.

Backing Away from the Brink

Recognition of the present dimensions of the nuclear danger must not be cause for despair; rather, it should be a stimulus for intensifying the search for remedies—and for political pressure to adopt those partial remedies that are already in view. There follows a description of a set of such steps that, taken together, could halt our approach to the brink and begin the process of backing prudently away.

Preserve the ABM Treaty and the SALT II Agreements

The Anti-Ballistic Missile Treaty of 1972 and the SALT II agreements of 1979 are the twin centerpieces of the web of arms-control agreements that have provided the main restraints on the nuclear arms race to date. The loss of either of these key agreements inevitably would cause the loss of the other, and the loss of both would cause the entire web to unravel — the Partial Test Ban Treaty, the Outer Space Treaty, and the Non-Proliferation Treaty would probably be among the casualties.

Preserving the ABM Treaty will require that both sides recommit themselves to the spirit as well as the letter of that agreement, recognizing that there are no prospects for a perfect defense and that pursuit of imperfect ones in violation of the treaty will only decrease the security and diminish the treasury of both sides. Each side has already accused the other of technical violations of the treaty, and it is essential that the ambiguities in treaty language that have helped give rise to these accusations be clarified through agreed-on statements worked out in the Standing Consultative Commission (which exists to perform just this sort of function). Opening up the treaty for complete renegotiation is not necessary and would pose too great a risk that it would end up weakened rather than strengthened.

Preserving the ABM Treaty and preventing the weaponization of space will also require an early agreement to ban further testing and deployment of antisatellite weapons. Otherwise, testing of weapons with ABM capabilities under the legitimating cover of ASAT activity will be certain to undermine confidence in the ABM Treaty (in addition to the other undesirable consequences of competition in antisatellite weaponry).

Because the sort of component testing and facility construction that necessarily would precede deployment of either ABM or ASAT weapons is easily detectable by the reconnaissance measures at the disposal of both sides, the issue of "verification" should pose no obstacle either to continuation of the ABM Treaty or to conclusion of a ban on further ASAT testing and deployment. The ASAT technologies that have been tested so far by both sides have not yet provided either with enough real ASAT capability to pose an obstacle to stopping now.

The need to preserve the SALT II restraints on offensive nuclear forces, which are important for their own sake, derives also from the circumstance that interest in ABM technologies is driven in part by both sides' pursuit of offensive weapons with characteristics that seem suited for a first strike. Maintaining the limits on such forces is therefore important in maintaining a commitment on both sides to refrain from the pursuit of strategic defense.

Both the United States and the Soviet Union have been pursuing the development of new land-based ICBMs (the Midgetman on the U.S. side, the SS-X-25 on the Soviet side) beyond the "one new type" permitted under the SALT II agreements (DOD, 1985). Neither side needs these weapons to maintain deterrence — and there is no other function they could perform

—so there is no reason to abrogate the SALT II agreements by testing them. Nor is there any reason for the United States to violate the SALT II ceilings on MIRVed launchers, as would happen if it goes forward with Trident submarine deployments scheduled after mid-1985 without dismantling some other MIRVed weapons in compensation.

Prospects for maintaining the SALT II restraints would be much improved by the imposition in addition—either by independent moratoria on each side or by negotiated agreement—of a halt to all flight testing of new ballistic missiles. No new weapon can be deployed without extensive testing, and testing of ballistic missiles is easily detectable by the "national technical means" possessed by both sides. Such a halt would be especially useful in stopping the development of more accurate missiles on both sides, which increasingly have promoted fears of first-strike capabilities and intentions.

Pursue Strategic-Arms Reductions on an Integrated Basis

The SALT II agreements, while far better than no restraints at all, nonetheless permit levels of offensive nuclear forces that are much larger than required for a nuclear deterrent strategy. We should therefore not be satisfied to restrict the arsenals to these levels but seek ways to reduce them. Such reductions, although of symbolic usefulness in themselves as evidence of a commitment by the superpowers to pursue real nuclear disarmament, will be really effective only if they dispose first of the most dangerous weapons—those whose combination of MIRVing, accuracy, flight time, and vulnerability makes them manifestly suited for a first strike. In this connection a further benefit of retaining the SALT II agreements is that the definitions of various categories of weapons agreed to by both sides in the SALT process provide much of the formal framework needed to start on the process of reductions.

It is important that the pursuit of reductions be done in a comprehensive context—that is, without artificial compartmentalization separating "offensive" and "defensive" weaponry, "strategic" and "theater" forces, and so on. The history of attempts at arms control reveals that such compartmentalization is simply a prescription for endless disputes about definitions—that is, about the boundaries of the compartments—and for channeling the arms race into uncontrolled categories (York, 1983a; Holdren, 1985a). A prominent example of the channeling phenomenon is the present development and deployment of cruise missiles by both sides, permitted by gaping loopholes in SALT II.

Negotiate a Comprehensive Ban on Testing Nuclear Explosives

A comprehensive test ban (CTB) applying to nuclear explosives was within reach when the trilateral (United States–USSR–United Kingdom) negotiations on this issue were broken off for extraneous reasons in 1980 (York and Greb, 1979; Greb and Heckrotte, 1983). Such a treaty would stop the underground testing of nuclear weapons by these three countries that has proceeded apace since they signed the Partial Test Ban eliminating atmospheric tests in 1963. There is much reason to think that a CTB could be achieved rather quickly if the negotiations were resumed, and much reason to want one.

The conventional wisdom is that the main reason to seek a CTB is the badly needed demonstration it would provide of the willingness of nuclear-weapons states to do at least this much about their obligations under article 6 of the Non-Proliferation Treaty. This demonstration presumably would provide some reinforcement of the NPT regime against the corrosive tendencies described earlier. But there is actually a more important reason for wanting a CTB: the continuation of nuclear testing is helping sustain the dangerous illusion that there are uses of nuclear weapons, other than deterrence, toward which their design and construction need continuing improvement. This notion of the usability of nuclear weapons is one of the major forces underlying the continuation of the nuclear-arms race, and helping dispose of it with a CTB would therefore be an important contribution toward ending the whole perverse process. One specific result of a CTB, of course, would be to block continued development and testing of gamma-ray lasers for Star Wars applications; this outcome, too, should be welcomed.

Aside from the loss of the opportunity to develop new kinds of nuclear weapons, three arguments are used against agreeing to a CTB: first, that further testing is needed to make nuclear weapons "safer" (less likely to explode accidentally); second, that the reliability of the existing stockpile of nuclear weapons cannot be assured without periodic testing; and, third, that the Russians could cheat (test clandestinely) and thus gain some strategic advantage. None of these arguments is persuasive.

The biggest danger associated with nuclear weapons is that they will be exploded on purpose, not that they will go off by accident; and continued testing is making that main danger even larger. With respect to the reliability of the stockpile, leading weapons experts have testified repeatedly that this can be assured without nuclear explosions (Mark, 1984). Finally, with the sorts of verification measures already agreed on in principle during the negotiations terminated in 1980, no test with a yield much over 1 kiloton would be likely to go undetected (Sykes and Evernden, 1982). Given today's arsenals, it is unlikely that *any* testing program could produce a strategic advantage; certainly a few tests in the kiloton range, which is all that could escape notice, could not do so.

Rethink and Reshape the Defense of Europe

NATO's policy of "first use of nuclear weapons if necessary" poses costs and dangers disproportionate to its modest contribution to an already robust deterrence, and it should be abandoned in favor of a declared posture of "no first use." The new declared policy should be reinforced by corresponding changes in nuclear-force postures, including especially the withdrawal of "battlefield" nuclear weapons from forward positions. This particular step would increase NATO security whether or not it was reciprocated by the Warsaw Pact, because these short-range weapons threaten the territory they are supposed to defend even more than they threaten the potential attacker (York, 1983b).

Because the contribution to deterrence of NATO's present "first use if necessary" policy has been widely overrated, so also has the need to strengthen NATO's conventional forces if that policy is abandoned. The balance of conventional forces in Europe is not easy to evaluate unambiguously, because the answer depends not only on numbers of tanks, artillery pieces, fighter aircraft, and soldiers but also on factors harder to quantify, such as leadership, training, morale, and the cohesion of the respective alliances under stress (Lee, 1983; Steinbruner and Sigal, 1983). In this last respect an enormous problem for Soviet leaders if they contemplated attacking Western Europe would be uncertainty about which way the Polish, Hungarian, Czech, and East German divisions would shoot (see, e.g., Lambeth, 1982–83.) All things considered, NATO's existing conventional strength is probably adequate to deter any rational Soviet leader from ordering an attack (Mearsheimer, 1982), even leaving aside the "existential" deterrent effect associated with the possibility of escalation to use of nuclear weapons despite declared policies of "no first use."

The tendency to propose a NATO buildup of conventional forces to compensate for reduced reliance on nuclear deterrence poses dangers of its own, particularly if the proposed buildup emphasizes "deep-strike" capabilities that appear more offensive than defensive. After all, the "worst-case assessment" and "fallacy of the last move" syndromes that have helped drive the nuclear-arms race operate in the conventional arena as well, and there is no benefit and much danger in an arms race in Europe featuring advanced weapons for conventional attack.

Any "improvements" undertaken in NATO's conventional forces, therefore, ought to emphasize weapons and force postures whose capabilities for defense exceed their capabilities for offense. If each side possesses conventional forces that are stronger in defense than in offense, it becomes possible for both simultaneously to enjoy a margin of safety against attack by the other—a stable situation that *cannot* obtain if the offensive capabilities of each force equal or exceed its defensive capabilities (Nield, 1984).

Upgrade Crisis-Avoidance and Crisis-Control Capabilities

All of the foregoing proposals focus on the characteristics of the weapons and force postures on the two sides, but it should be obvious that the danger of conflict depends not only on the characteristics of military forces but also on the nature of the underlying confrontation and the skills and tools available for preventing confrontation from becoming crisis and crisis from becoming conflict. While deep divisions of viewpoint and interest are sure to characterize U.S.-Soviet relations for decades to come, it is essential that the governments on both sides recognize the need to channel the inevitable competition along lines that do not threaten to destroy the world.

The long-standing tendency of both superpowers to regard the developing countries of the south as simply another arena in which to compete for influence and advantage poses particular dangers (Holdren, 1985b). As countries in the south grow in economic and military power—including, in some cases, the acquisition of nuclear weapons—the local instabilities and conflicts that have been endemic in the Third World threaten to become even more destructive as well as more likely to entangle the superpowers (Macfarlane, 1985). The need for mutual superpower restraint in the south—and even cooperation to defuse dangerous situations—is growing.

With respect to both the "central" confrontation in Europe and north-south issues, there is much to be gained from specific steps to build confidence and reduce the chances of crises growing out of control. Such steps could include regular, private meetings of high military officials of the two superpowers; better emergency communication links; elaboration of an agreed-on "code of conduct" regarding intervention in the Third World; and even jointly staffed crisis-control centers (George, 1983; Ury and Smoke, 1984). Such steps would reduce the chance of war between the superpowers arising from technological or human error, misjudgment, escalation of regional crises, or "third-party" nuclear detonations.

Reasons for Optimism

While the proposals of the preceding section may seem an over-ambitious agenda, the diversity and magnitude of the danger suggest that no less will do. And there are several circumstances that give reason to hope that such a program could be accomplished.

First, notwithstanding widespread hand wringing about the increasing vulnerability of the nuclear forces on both sides to preemptive attack, it remains true today that the margins of invulnerability are high: neither side is in imminent danger of losing the capacity to retaliate overwhelmingly against any attack, and the "margins of safety" in this respect are large. It follows from this circumstance that

1. Unilateral initiatives are possible (either side could give up substantial numbers of weapons without significantly shrinking its margin of safety).

2. Negotiating positions can be flexible (because most details are not really important in the face of these margins).

3. Verification requirements are modest (because it would take a very large, hence easily visible, violation of an agreement to make any significant difference).

Second, *capabilities* for verification are superb. Reconnaissance satellites and electronic intelligence-gathering techniques have reached such a high order of sophistication that both sides can have nearly complete confidence that they know what the other is doing. All the agreements proposed above are verifiable to the extent that the risks associated with the possibility of undetected violations are tiny compared to the risks of leaving these weapons and activities uncontrolled.

Third, there is much reason to think that the Soviets are ready to deal. This does not mean that they have had a sudden attack of altruism or are inclined to compromise their Marxist-Leninist principles. They simply have understood that they cannot achieve their goals through nuclear war or a further nuclear-arms race; they are willing to settle for a nuclear stalemate and to pursue their goals in other ways. I believe that this is the sensible position for the United States and its NATO allies as well; there is nothing to be gained, and much to be lost, by further pursuit of nuclear advantage.

Finally, public support for ending and reversing the nuclear-arms race is strong. Awareness of the nuclear danger is high. People are weary of the social and economic burdens of high military spending and of the psychic burden of an endless competition in weapons of such unimaginable destructive power.

It is essential that this convergence of positive elements—high margins of invulnerability, superb verification capabilities, Soviet willingness to deal, and strong public support—be exploited while it lasts. Now is the time for publics to demand, and for political leaders to deliver, the comprehensive approach that the nuclear danger demands. The window of opportunity may not be open for long.

References

Adams, G. 1981. *The iron triangle.* New York: Council on Economic Priorities.

Ball, D. 1981. *Can nuclear war be controlled?* Adelphi Paper no. 169. London: International Institute for Strategic Studies.

Barnet, R. 1972. *Roots of war.* New York: Atheneum.

Boston Study Group. 1979. *The price of defense: A new strategy for military spending.* New York: Times Books.

Bundy, M., G. F. Kennan, R. S. McNamara, and G. Smith. 1982. Nuclear weapons and the Atlantic alliance. *Foreign Affairs* 60(4): 753–68.

Burt, R. 1983. NATO and nuclear deterrence. In M. Olive and J. Porro, eds. *Nuclear weapons in Europe.* Lexington, Mass.: Lexington Books.

Carter, A. B., and D. N. Schwartz, eds. 1984. *Ballistic missile defense.* Washington, D.C.: Brookings Institution.

DOD [U.S. Department of Defense]. 1985. *Soviet military power, 1985.* Washington, D.C.: U.S. Government Printing Office (April).

Drell, S. D., P. J. Farley, and D. Holloway. 1984. *The Reagan Strategic Defense Initiative: A technical, political, and arms control analysis.* Stanford, Calif.: Stanford University Center for International Security and Arms Control.

Fallows, J. 1981. *National defense.* New York: Random House.

Feiveson, H. A., and J. Duffield. 1984. Stopping the sea-based counterforce threat. *International Security* 9(1): 187–202.

Freedman, L. 1981. *The evolution of nuclear strategy.* New York: St. Martin's Press.

Garthoff, R. L. 1983. The Soviet SS-20 decision. *Survival* 25 (May–June): 110–19.

George, A. 1983. *Managing U.S.-Soviet rivalry: Problems of crisis prevention.* Boulder, Colo.: Westview Press.

Greb, G. A., and W. Heckrotte. 1983. The long history: The test ban debate. *Bulletin of the Atomic Scientists* 39(1): 36–42.

Holdren, J. P. 1983. Nuclear power and nuclear weapons: The connection is dangerous. *Bulletin of the Atomic Scientists* 39(1): 40–45.

———. 1985a. The dynamics of the nuclear arms race: History, status, prospects. In A. Cohen and S. Lee, eds. *Nuclear weapons and the future of humanity.* Totowa, N.J.: Rowman and Allenheld. (Available earlier as ERG Working Paper no. 83-5, Energy and Resources Group, University of California, Berkeley, November, 1983.)

———. 1985b. North-south issues and east-west confrontation. *Bulletin of the Atomic Scientists* 41(7): 97–101.

Holloway, D. 1983. *The Soviet Union and the arms race.* New Haven, Conn.: Yale University Press.

IISS [International Institute for Strategic Studies]. 1984. *The military balance, 1984–85.* London: IISS.

Jasani, B., ed. 1982. *Outer space: A new dimension of the arms race.* London: Taylor and Francis.

Joint Chiefs of Staff. 1985. *Posture statement of the Office of the Joint Chiefs of Staff for fiscal year 1986.* Washington, D.C.: U.S. Government Printing Office.

Lambeth, B. S. 1982–83. Uncertainties for the Soviet war planner. *International Security* 7(3): 139–66.

Lee, Admiral J. M. 1983. *No first use.* Cambridge, Mass.: Union of Concerned Scientists.

Longstreth, T., J. Pike, and J. Rhinelander. 1985 The Impact of US and Soviet ballistic missile defense programs on the ABM Treaty. Washington, D.C.: National Campaign to Save the ABM Treaty.

Macfarlane, N. 1985. *Intervention and regional security.* Adelphi Paper no. 196. London: International Institute for Strategic Studies.

McNamara, R. S. 1983. The military role of nuclear weapons. *Foreign Affairs* 62 (1): 59–80.

Mako, W. P. 1983. *U.S. ground forces and the defense of Western Europe.* Washington, D.C.: Brookings Institution.

Mark, C. 1984. Implications of a comprehensive test ban (CTB) for the stockpile of nuclear weapons. *Pugwash Newsletter* (July).

Mearsheimer, J. J. 1982. Why the Soviets can't win quickly in Central Europe. *International Security* 7(1): 3–39.

———. 1983. *Conventional deterrence.* Ithaca, N.Y.: Cornell University Press.

NAS [National Academy of Sciences]. 1985. *Nuclear arms control: Background and issues.* Washington, D.C.: National Academy Press.

Nield, R. 1984. European security. In Joseph Rotblat, ed. *The arms race at a time of decision: Annals of Pugwash 1983.* London: Macmillan.

Olive, M. M., and J. D. Porro, eds. 1983. *Nuclear weapons in Europe.* Lexington, Mass. Lexington Books.

Rosenberg, D. A. 1983. The origins of overkill. Nuclear weapons and American strategy, 1945–60. *International Security* 7(4): 3–71.

Russett, B. 1983. *The prisoners of insecurity: Nuclear deterrence, the arms race, and arms control.* San Francisco, Calif.: Freeman.

Scoville, H. 1981. *MX: Prescription for disaster.* Cambridge, Mass.: MIT Press.

Scowcroft, General B., Chairman. 1983. *Report of the President's Commission on Strategic Forces.* Washington, D.C.: U.S. Government Printing Office.

SIPRI [Stockholm Internation Peace Research Institute]. 1983. *The arms race and arms control.* London: Taylor and Francis.

Spector, L. S. 1985. Nuclear proliferation: The pace quickens. *Bulletin of the Atomic Scientists* 40(1): 11.

Steinbruner, J. D., and L. V. Sigal, eds. 1983. *Alliance security: NATO and the no-first-use question.* Washington, D.C.: U.S. Government Printing Office.

Sweet, W. 1984. *The nuclear age: Power, proliferation, and the arms race.* Washington, D.C.: Congressional Quarterly.

Sykes, L. R., and J. F. Evernden. 1982. The verification of a comprehensive nuclear test ban. *Scientific American* 247(4): 47–55.

Talbott, S. 1984. *Deadly gambits.* New York: Knopf.

Ury, W. L., and R. Smoke. 1984. *Beyond the hotline: Controlling a nuclear crisis.* Cambridge, Mass.: Nuclear Negotiation Project of the Harvard Law School.

York, H. F. 1970. *Race to oblivion: A participant's view of the arms race.* New York: Simon and Schuster.

————. 1983a. Bilateral negotiations and the arms race. *Scientific American* 249(4): 149–60.

————. 1983b. Beginning nuclear disarmament at the bottom. *Survival* 25 (September–October): 227–31.

————, and G. A. Greb. 1979. The comprehensive nuclear test ban. Discussion Paper no. 84. California Seminar on Arms Control and Foreign Policy, Santa Monica, Calif. (June).

————, ed. 1973. *Arms control: Readings from* Scientific American. San Francisco, Calif.: Freeman.

Zuckerman, Lord S. 1982: *Nuclear illusion and reality.* New York: Viking.

12.
World Economic Modeling

EARL COOK filled a unique and important role in the environmental movement and had a deep impact on the senior author of this chapter through his book *Man, Energy, Society* (1976). Cook was the first writer to integrate completely two separate evolutionary trees of environmental scholarship. The more recent and better known of these trees considered what would happen to this planet if various recent trends were to continue. Scholars expressed concern about the implications of continuously increasing population (Ehrlich, 1968); depleting mineral, fuel, and other resources (Committee on Resources and Man, 1969); and the global effects of environmental pollution (Singer, 1970) and conducted computer simulations to discover the future effects if present trends continued (Forrester, 1968; Meadows et al., 1972).

There had been, however, a much older tradition concerned with the long-run historical effects of environmental-management policies and resource availability on the rise and fall of nations and civilizations. The most profound, interdisciplinary, and wide ranging of all such works was *Decline of the West*, by Oswald Spengler (1926, 1928), which presented a theory explaining why all civilizations decline when the population becomes largely urbanized. At the apex of development most Romans, Mayans, Mesopotamians, or Americans live in great cities, where the principal concern is with money rather than resources, and "world economy is the ac-

Many people have spent a great deal of time helping us with this paper. George David introduced us to the literature on federal-debt management and real estate and spent a great deal of time and effort introducing us to various bodies of theory and data bases. Sherman Stein, David Deamer, Robert May, and Barry Hughes read previous drafts and offered helpful suggestions and opinions. C. S. Holling fostered our interest in this area over many years. John Brewer has been a constant inspiration and source of new modes of thinking for two decades.

/ 233

tualized economy of values that are completely detached in thought from the land, and made fluid." One group of historically oriented environmental scholars was primarily concerned with the long-run destruction of soil by civilizations (Marsh, 1864; Jacks and Whyte, 1939; Hyams, 1952; Dale and Carter, 1955). Braudel (1972, 1973) showed how the nations surrounding the Mediterranean basin gradually lost self-sufficiency in wheat and oak for building ships after about 1560 and consequently lost power to northern Europe, which became dominant thereafter.

Cook's book is imbued with both kinds of environmental analysis. While he was an expert on modern problems, the book is steeped in a historical perspective. It was from his book that I learned about Nef (1932) and the role of the fuel-wood shortage in the rise of the British coal industry and about Albion (1926), who explored the relationship between forests and sea power.

Cook's concern with the historical perspective has been important in shaping our approach to global modeling in the last few years. We store tables of historical data in computers and then attempt to find a set of equations that accounts for the dynamic behavior of the world system during the period for which we have data. This historical perspective has had two major effects on our view of social systems. First, looking at trends in data series over spans of two or more centuries reveals patterns that would otherwise pass unnoticed. Second, one develops a particular view of long-run historical processes. One comes to see the history of nations or civilizations as a recurring sequence of subhistories, all of which have a standard pattern: a process is set in motion which gradually produces some kind of crisis. Then either the nation or the civilization deals with that crisis, and progress continues until some new crisis is confronted, or the crisis is not dealt with appropriately, and the nation or civilization begins a long decline. Two examples illustrate, first, a successful response to a crisis and, second, a lack of appropriate response. In the mid-fifteenth century Britain was a firewood economy. However, a number of developing industries, including glassmaking and metalworking, were very energy-intensive, and gradually, over the period 1450 to 1625, Britain was increasingly troubled by a fuel shortage. Finally, after 1625 there was increasingly rapid replacement of fuel wood first by sea coal, on the surface of the earth, then by coal mined in shallow mines. The crisis was the developing fuel-wood shortage; the solution was the turn to coal. We can express this history quantitatively as in figure 12.1, by plotting the ratio of an index of the average six-day wage to an index of firewood price. This ratio measures consumer purchasing power in terms of the cost of the critical limiting resource for a society. The crisis is expressed by the drop in this ratio after 1535, arriving at a low point around 1630. Solution of the crisis is expressed by the

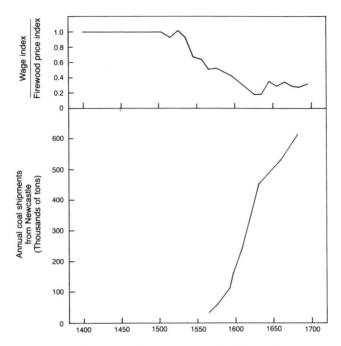

Fig. 12.1. The sixteenth-century British fuel-wood crisis, as reflected in the ratio of average wage index to firewood price index. Top panel: ratio of index for builders' wages to firewood price index for England, 1400–1680. Bottom panel: annual shipments of coal from Newcastle, England, 1565–1685. Data on wages computed from Phelps Brown and Hopkins, 1955; firewood price index from Wilkinson, 1973; coal shipments from Nef, 1932.

rise in the ratio of wages to wood cost after 1630; wood was no longer a critical limiting resource because that role had now passed to coal. An example of a crisis not dealt with was the increasing shortage of oak timbers for shipbuilding and wheat for food in the Mediterranean Basin after about 1580. Imperial Spain did not have a cheap, local substitute for oak or wheat, and the decline of that enormously widespread and powerful empire began then.

The Goals of Our Research

The aim of our global modeling is specifically not to explain short-term business cycles of a few months' or years' duration. Rather, we are

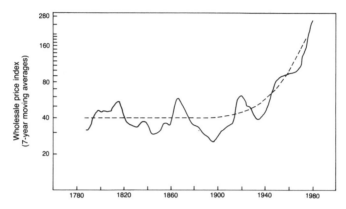

Fig. 12.2. Seven-year moving averages of United States wholesale price index since 1790 (1967 = 100). Points plotted are for the central year of seven. The dashed line was computed from the equation that describes the long-run relation between the index and the year number. Computed from U.S. Department of Commerce, *Historical Statistics of the United States* (1975), series E-23 and E-52.

interested in the root causes of major societal instability of the type illustrated in figure 12.2. The figure is a graph of seven-year moving averages of the U.S. wholesale commodity price index, plotted against year number since 1780. Also plotted on the graph is a dashed line, representing the long-run statistical relationship between this index and year number. Clearly there were major peaks in this index about 1815, 1865, and 1920 and major depressions about 1790, 1843, 1894, and 1933. The recent period also appears as a major decline below the long-run trend line if one examines consumer purchasing power: the trend in the ratio of wages to prices.

Against the background of that figure our research seeks answers to the following questions:

1. Why do depressions occur in the economy generally and specifically in key sectors such as agriculture?

2. Have all depressions occurred for the same reasons?

3. Is the present world economic downturn of the same kind as previous downturns, or does it have some new cause?

4. How do wars affect major instabilities in the economic system?

5. Do major instabilities in the global economic system affect the probability of war? That is, are wars simply terrible accidents, or are they somehow part of the normal dynamic behavior of the global system?

Unusual Features of Our Modeling Approach

In our approach we begin with very simple systems models and add to the complexity of the models only as we find it necessary to improve our ability to explain past behavior of the system. Specifically, we attempt to account for about 99.8 percent of the variance in key systems variables over at least a century, using at most four independent variables. This concern with simplicity is because a growing consensus holds that there is no apparent relation between model complexity and predictive utility in any field of forecasting (e.g., Ascher, 1978; Armstrong, 1978). Indeed, the attack on complex models for policy analysis is becoming quite vigorous. As one reviewer put it, when there is a lack of a theoretical base, or high level of conflict between "experts," "the production of a single, elaborate, untestable, complex dynamic model can be regarded as a . . . waste of scarce research capacity" (McClean, 1977).

Our models use nonlinear equations rather than linear equations because the former more accurately express the dynamic nature of growing systems. Specifically, where stocks of resources can be depleted or markets can be saturated, growth progresses at a declining rate as some limiting value is approached, and the appropriate mathematical description for such situations is nonlinear equations.

We treat war and economic systems as mutually interacting subcomponents of a single system. We find that major economic events, such as depressions, are lagged responses to the economic perturbations associated with war expenditures. Also, causality flows the other direction: economic phenomena affect the likelihood of war.

The key system measures in our models are wages, prices, and the ratio of wages to prices, or consumer purchasing power. These measures seem to us to be more revealing of the status of an average person in a society than such measures as a rate of growth in gross national product, where the economic activity generated by negative effects such as pollution are lumped with the rate of economic activity generated by the construction industry.

Finally, a key characteristic of our models is very long lagged effects, in which an event may be a response to a cause operating as long as 12 years or more previously. Such long time delays seem plausible in light of two examples. About 24 years elapse from the time a person is conceived until the year he or she attempts permanent entry into the labor force. Thus an event whose probability is affected by economic conditions does not have its maximum impact on one aspect of the economy, the unemployment rate, until 24 years later. Second, many years elapse from the time there is an unusual increase in the amount of money entering the economy until the time when supersaturation of housing and capital equipment markets is widely recognized, and employers lay off large numbers of workers, thus contributing to depression-inducing forces.

The Four Key Driving Mechanisms in Our Global Models

We discovered that four causal agents are all that we required to account for the dynamic behavior of the global system. The computer analysis has been conducted with the use of historical statistics of the United States; we have also studied the data from many other countries. There has been a major effort to determine the particular statistical expression which best expresses the impact of each agent, the mathematical expression which most realistically describes the mode of operation of each agent, and the particular parameter values which most accurately describe the relation between causes and effects in the historical record.

The first of the four agents is the supply relative to demand for the resource currently limiting economic activity in society. As demand overwhelms supply, the effects ripple through the social system and ultimately affect wages, the consumer price index, and the ratio of wages to price index: consumer purchasing power. A drop in consumer purchasing power indicates a time of crisis for a society; it must make more efficient use of the critical limiting resource, discover a substitute, or begin an economic decline. The period from 1535 to 1650 in England already mentioned was a clear model for this situation. The corresponding critical limiting resource for the United States today is domestic crude oil.

The situation is expressed by figure 12.3. All four panels of the figure are plotted not against time but against cumulative U.S. oil production in billions of barrels. In the top panel we see how consumer purchasing power first rose and then recently has fallen. The next two panels show why this has happened. Initially wages rose rapidly; more recently, at very high levels of cumulative crude oil production, wages have risen at a decreasing rate. The consumer price index, in contradistinction, rose slowly during the early years of crude-oil exploitation but more recently has risen more rapidly, and more rapidly than wages. The bottom panel offers an explanation, in the change in the constant-dollar cost of the exploratory drilling required to discover a marginal barrel of crude oil in the United States. Since this discovery cost is rising rapidly in inflation-adjusted dollars, it must be a driving force behind inflation. The rising real cost of obtaining oil gradually affects the real cost of everything else in the society. The mechanism by which rising U.S. oil-discovery costs affect inflation is

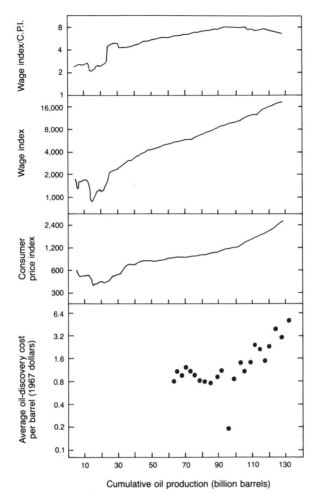

Fig. 12.3. The relation of consumer purchasing power (wage index/consumer price index [CPI]), wage index, consumer price index, and constant-dollar marginal oil-discovery cost for U.S. crude oil to cumulative U.S. oil production. The wage index is based on average annual salaries of contract construction workers. The data are from U.S. Department of Commerce, *Historical Statistics of the United States,* updated with data from *Statistical Abstracts of the United States,* and annual reports of the American Petroleum Institute. These data cover the time span 1910 to the present. The oil-discovery cost per barrel was calculated by dividing the total exploration cost by the number of new barrels discovered in year y. This statistic was computed using the relationship discoveries in year y = reserves at the end of y – reserves at the end of y – 1 + oil production during year y.

complex; however, a key link is probably the shift to dependence on OPEC oil as it becomes more expensive to discover U.S. oil.

The second factor which has an enormous impact on the dynamics of nations is the rate at which federal governments retire the public debt. Few people are aware of the violent fluctuations in this variable; one way they can be expressed is by plotting against year number the size of the public debt 11 years previously divided by the public debt 3 years before. Large values of this variable imply that government has recently been retiring the public debt very rapidly; small values imply recent rapid increase, as occurs during wars. Depressions tend to follow periods of rapid retirement of the public debt. Thus large increases in the ratio of 11-year-old public debt to 3-year-old public debt, as depicted in figure 12.4, are leading indicators of the depressions that occurred in the 1840s, 1890s, and 1930s. Since this topic will appear arcane to most people, we explain where we got the idea for exploring it in the writings of various economists. Overcapacity in basic industries, such as steel, coal, oil, and agriculture, or past over-production of capital items, such as buildings, ships, airplanes, and factories, produces market supersaturation followed by employee layoffs and the beginning of the vicious downward spiral into depression. This idea has been prominent for at least a century among theories proposed to account for depressions (e.g., Burton, 1902; Haberler, 1941; Forrester, 1979). Keynes (1930) noted the excessive construction during the 1920s, which was implicated by Temin (1976) as a possible cause of the subsequent depression, after he had shown that a contraction in the money supply was not the ultimate cause. Wickens (1941) showed that there were only 177,000 vacant housing units in the United States in 1920 but 1.216 million by 1930. Why were so many unnecessary housing units built in the 1920s?

Clearly excessive construction and simultaneous excessive investment in a variety of sectors come about because an unusually large amount of money has been injected into the economy. Several studies have implicated rapid decrease in the federal public debt as an important source for massive new amounts of investment capital in a modern industrial nation. To illustrate, between 1834 and 1837 the U.S. government sold 43 million acres of public land, thus raising enough money to pay off almost all of the public debt (Smith and Cole, 1935). Soon after this massive debt retirement the United States experienced the second-worst depression in its history, that of the 1840s. Gaines (1962) pointed out the great significance of massive fluctuations in the public debt. Federal public debt increases rapidly during wartime and then decreases rapidly during the postwar years, when war debts are being repaid to the public. During the Civil War the public debt increased by a factor of 30, and during World War I it increased by $23 billion. Between 1919 and 1930, $9.3 billion of this debt was paid back

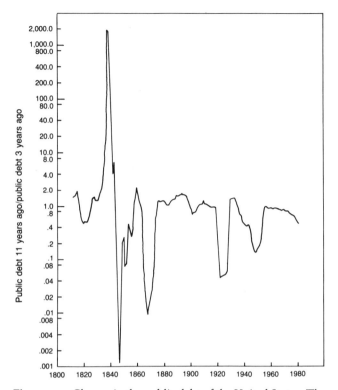

Fig. 12.4. Change in the public debt of the United States. The statistic plotted is the ratio of the debt 11 years previously to the debt 3 years previously; high numbers indicate that the debt has recently been retired very rapidly (that is, a lot of money has been injected into the economy). The raw data are from U.S. Department of Commerce, *Historical Statistics of the United States,* time series Y-493, updated with the same time series from *Statistical Abstracts of the United States.*

to the public, thus introducing a vast amount of money into the economy. The remarks by Clark (1931) are typical of those by economists who have speculated about the significance of rapid public-debt retirement: ". . . the runaway stock market of 1929 might logically be taken as a symptom (among other things) of a supply of investable funds larger than we well knew what to do with. Thus the retirement of the war debt may have had some connection with the stock market crash which ushered in the present depression."

We can postulate a mechanism for producing major economic fluctuations. When a nation rapidly increases its public debt for a few years,

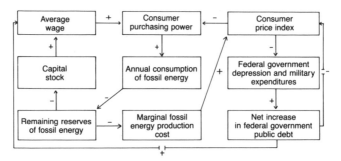

Fig. 12.5. Flow chart depicting hypothesized causal relationships among nine important variables describing the status of a society.

it draws money out of the domestic economy, creates a high level of pent-up demand relative to supply for a variety of goods and capital-stock items, and sets the stage for a few years of vigorous growth when the debt is subsequently retired. After a war the huge surge of money into the economy resulting from the redemption of government war bonds and other federal paper finally, after several years, creates overinvestment and excessive inventories and eventually sets the stage for a subsequent collapse. In this view the Great Depression of 1933 was in part simply a lagged response to the Great War of 1914–18.

Further, fluctuations in national debt also reallocate national wealth over different categories of investment. War expenditures remove resources from consumer goods and put people to work making things that eventually will be destroyed or scrapped. Paying off war debts probably takes money away from investment in infrastructure investment and moves it toward investment in consumer goods and housing.

Putting together the ideas expressed to this point, we have the flow chart in figure 12.5, which, we will show, accounts for almost all the long-run variation in wages and prices. This flow chart expresses the notion that, as the remaining reserves of the currently limiting resource decline (crude oil in the United States in this century), not only do all prices increase, but also the capital stock increases, and this is the factor that drives up wages. This theory is illustrated by what happens when, for example, a lawyer increases income startlingly by moving from a town of 50,000 population to a city of 10 million. The lawyer did not suddenly become more intelligent or get more training; rather, there was a sharp increase in the capital stock with which he worked.

The third factor that introduces great instability into modern societies is the interaction between fluctuations in the birthrate and the impact

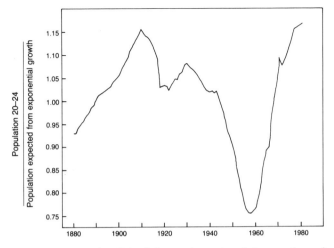

Fig. 12.6. For the United States the ratio of the number of people 20 to 24 years of age each year to the number expected from an exponential growth curve fitted to the data. Raw data from U.S. Bureau of the Census, *Current Population Reports,* series P-25, nos. 310, 311, 519, and 929. The exponential equation used was $N = \exp(7.635 + .01219y)$, where N represents the total U.S. population 20 to 24 years old, in thousands, and y represents the year number less 1,800. This equation accounted for all but 12.8 percent of the variance in population number over the period 1880 to 1981, inclusive.

on the labor force about 24 years later. Figure 12.6 illustrates this phenomenon. In this figure the size of the population 20 to 24 years of age in the United States each year since 1880 as a proportion of the size expected under constant exponential growth is plotted against year number. This trend expresses two things: the age-specific birthrate about 23 years earlier and the current supply of new prospective labor-force entrants relative to the demand. The shallow notch in this trend around 1920 reflects the shallow depression around 1896, and the deep notch around 1957 reflects the deep depression around 1933. Clearly here is a mechanism that has the potential for economic events in one year to have a large impact on the economy 24 years later.

Finally, the effects of events in any nation impact other nations through a number of causal pathways that cross international boundaries: wars and international gradients (or differentials) with respect to supplies, demands, prices, or differences in interest rate. We have a remarkable example at present when a vast amount of capital is entering the United States in response to high interest rates and, in effect, is important in financing both a federal budget deficit and a huge deficit in our international balance of trade. In the 1970s excessive monetary growth in the United States transmitted inflation worldwide (Darby et al., 1983).

This fourth factor is required to account for the amazing degree of synchronization that shows up in time series in different nations. Thus the downturn in 1843 shows up in statistics on immigration into the United States, indices of building starts in the United States, United Kingdom and United States railroad construction, and brick production in and timber imports into the United Kingdom (Rostow, 1978). The nadir between 1894 and 1896 showed up in 15 countries as far apart as Australia and Sweden (Rostow, 1978). The downturn of 1932 to 1934 was remarkably in phase among countries. The nadir month was April, 1932, in Germany, July in France, August in the United Kingdom, and March, 1933, in the United States.

Our Approach to Modeling

Our approach to developing a mathematical model to describe long-run trends in wages and prices has been to consider the wage index or the price index for any year as the product of four terms corresponding to the four factors previously enumerated. The first of these terms expresses the impact of cumulative crude-oil use on the value taken by wages, or prices in each year. The other three terms account for deviations about this trend line produced by the other three factors (change in the federal government public debt, the population of 20- to 24-year-olds relative to the number expected from an exponential trend, and international capital transfers). To illustrate our method in detail, we give a condensed version of our procedures and results using only the first three of the four factors.

Wages (or prices) can be considered as the product of three terms, A, B, and C. A expresses the impact of cumulative crude-oil use on the trend line for wages (or prices). B expresses the impact of changes in the federal public debt in producing deviations above or below that trend line. C expresses the effect of deviations about the long-run exponential growth trend in the number of 20- to 24-year-olds in producing deviations about the trend in wages (or prices). Thus we have the simple equation

$$Y = ABC. \tag{12.1}$$

There are two equations of this form in our model. In one equation Y represents W, the average annual wage, in current dollars, for a precisely defined category of worker, a contract construction worker. In the other equation Y represents P, the consumer price index in current dollars (1967 = 1,000).

In figure 12.3 these indices were plotted against cumulative U.S. crude-oil production on semilogarithmic graph paper. The trend line for the wage index bent downward slightly, and the trend line for the price index bent upward sharply. Therefore, we know that the equation which describes the effect of cumulative crude-oil production on the trends in wages and prices is not the well-known exponential growth curve but rather a growth curve in which the exponent itself is a function of cumulative crude-oil production. To discover the most appropriate mathematical expression to describe the long-run relationship between cumulative crude-oil use and wages or prices, we used nonlinear least-squares regression analysis of data from different time periods. From this work we found that the impact of crude oil on wages or prices was a function of a term that was itself an exponential function of cumulative crude oil use, as in the expression

$$A = p1 \{\exp [p2 \ O \ \exp(p3 + p4 \ O)]\}, \qquad (12.2)$$

in which O represents cumulative U.S. crude oil production up to and including the last day of the year, and the four parameters are calculated using nonlinear least-squares estimation.

We also discovered, through trial and error, that a useful equation to describe the effect on wages and prices of change in the federal public debt was

$$B = p5 + p6 \ G + p7 \ G^3, \qquad (12.3)$$

in which G represents a variable we call the federal government "payout," and there are three parameters to be estimated by nonlinear estimation.

"Payout," in turn, was defined as

$$G = \frac{D(y - 13) - D(y - 3)}{[GNP(y - 13) + GNP(y - 3)]/2} + 1.2, \qquad (12.4)$$

where $D(y - 13)$ represents the public debt of the U.S. federal government in year $y - 13$, and GNP $(y - 13)$ represents the U.S. gross national produce in year $y - 13$. The quantity 1.2 is added so that values of G will be positive for all years. Equation 12.4 is an expression for the amount by which the U.S. federal public debt declined over the period 13 years ago to 3 years ago, relative to the average value of the GNP in that interval. Thus it is a measure of the amount of money being injected into the economy over a 10-year span, starting 13 years ago, owing to the retirement of public debt. The reasoning behind the choice of the quantities 10, 13, and 3 is as follows. First, supersaturated markets for houses and other major investments are produced not by excessive construction in a small number of particular years but rather by the sum of excessive construction over an extended series of years. We know from observation that people who engage in speculative construction are eternally optimistic and very resistant to information suggesting that future sales may weaken. After all, they improve their financial situation relative to that of other people by being high-stakes gamblers. This is why we assume that there will be a 3-year lag from the end of the decade when the market is supersaturated to the first year at which construction is decreased sharply enough to have an impact on wages and prices. We knew that these numbers would be approximately 13, 10, and 3 from study of historical data series; the choice was finalized by statistical analysis to determine which lags and lag lengths accounted for most of the variance in the dependent variables (the deviations of wages and prices about their trend lines as computed from cumulative crude-oil use).

Finally we discovered that, after accounting for the impact of cumulative crude-oil use and payout on wages and prices, there was a residual variance that could be accounted for by population. This effect could be best expressed using the linear equation

$$C = p8 + p9\ x, \tag{12.5}$$

where x represents the number of 20- to 24-year-olds each year as a proportion or multiple of the number expected from an exponential growth trend.

We can demonstrate the existence of this population effect by showing the results obtained when only the equation $Y = AB$ is fitted. For this part of the analysis figures 12.7 and 12.8 compare actual and calculated wages and actual and calculated prices. In each figure we have separated the postulated effects of cumulative oil production and "payout" so that one can see for each year how much of the observed value we attribute to each variable. The component of the variation that our interpretation suggests is due to cumulative crude-oil production alone is indicated by the dotted lines; the additional effect owing to "payout" is indicated by a solid line.

Our analysis to this point did not, however, account for 100 percent of the year-to-year variation in either wages or prices over the century. To explain why, we can use two different lines of argument. Note that in both figures 12.7 and 12.8 the solid line in the top panel (actual wages or prices) is too high relative to the solid line in the bottom panel (calculated wages

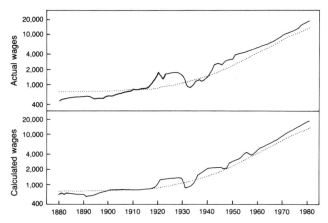

Fig. 12.7. Top panel: solid line is actual average annual wage of U.S. contract construction workers. Dotted line is wage calculated from equation (12.3) (assuming wage determined by cumulative crude-oil use alone). Bottom panel: solid line is average wage of contract construction workers calculated from equations (12.3) and (12.4) combined (assuming wage determined by cumulative crude-oil use and payout jointly). Dotted line assumes wage determined only by cumulative crude-oil use.

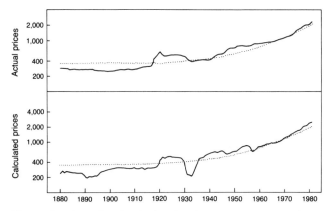

Fig. 12.8. Actual and calculated U.S. consumer price indexes (solid lines in top and bottom panels, respectively). In both panels the dotted lines indicate the trend in the component of consumer price indexes calculated from cumulative crude-oil use alone (i.e., equation [12.3]).

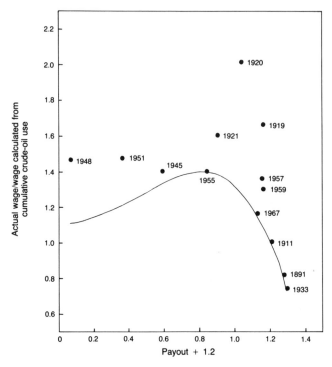

Fig. 12.9. Actual annual average wages of contract construction workers in the United States relative to wages calculated
from cumulative crude-oil use alone. The solid line is calculated
from payout as well as cumulative crude-oil use.

or prices) around 1919 to 1921 and again around 1957 to 1962. Referring
back to figure 12.6, we see that unusually high wages and prices coincided
with shortfalls in the number of 20- to 24-year-olds (around 1919 and 1958)
resulting from the depressions about 24 years before. Or, consider figure
12.9. This figure depicts the equation we calculated from the data to describe
the impact of "payout" on wages. Many of the data points were well described by this equation, such as those for 1891, 1911, 1933, 1945, 1955,
and 1967, as indicated by the points for those years. Some, however, are
outliers. At least two kinds of phenomena account for the discrepancy.
One of these is our third factor: the number of 20- to 24-year-olds each
year relative to the number expected from a long-run exponential-growth
pattern, with year number as the independent variable. Thus about 24 years
after the nadir of the depression of the 1890s and the nadir of the depression of the 1930s, that is, in the periods 1919 to 1921, and 1957 to 1958,

Table 12.1. Estimates of Parameters in Equations for Computation of Wages and Prices

Parameter or Statistic	Equation for Wages	Equation for Prices
$p1$	759	109
$p2$	0.0315	0.00922
$p3$	− 0.000376	− 0.00718
$p4$	− 0.00227	0.00362
$p5$	1.61	2.22
$p6$	0.628	− 0.154
$p7$	− 0.593	− 0.341
$p8$	1.017	2.41
$p9$	− 0.282	− 0.357
Residual sum of squares as proportion of total sum of squares	0.00327	0.0155
Sample	99 years, 1880 to 1981, excluding 1918–20	

new entrants into the labor force were in short supply relative to demand, the shortage thus driving up wages. We found that in these same years prices were also unusually high. Thus the effect of this factor must be expressed by equation (12.5).

The statistics on the final fits to the data are assembled in table 12.1. We discovered that in the period 1880 to 1981 three years stood out as being statistical outliers: 1918, 1919, and 1920. This was due in part to wartime shortages of labor and consumer goods; therefore, we eliminated them in our curve-fitting experiments. The final fits we obtained were far better than those indicated in figures 12.7 and 12.8; the residual variance was half that associated with the solid lines in those two figures.

This sketch of our approach may be adequate to convince some people that it holds promise for understanding the global economy. The approach can be extended by developing similar equations for all countries and then developing another set of equations to express the impact of various factors, such as interest-rate differentials, on capital transfers between nations.

The results to this point are adequate to suggest answers to some of the questions we posed at the outset. Clearly, not all depressions occur for the same reason. Our analysis (only part of which has been described here) suggests that the U.S. economic downturn of the 1840s came about because of vast quantities of new money being generated by land sales by the federal government and a resulting rapid decrease in the public debt. The depressions of the 1890s and the 1930s were due to the retirement of the war debt from the Civil War and World War I, respectively. The present worldwide economic downturn has been caused by an increase in the rate of growth in consumer prices relative to wages, as world stocks of crude oil are depleted, the market prices at the margin being set by U.S. oil-exploration costs.

The War Connection

What remains to be discussed is the connections of the economic system to war.

The results presented suggest the existence of a causal pathway from war to the economy. Wars lead to rapid increase in the federal public debt. Rapid repayment of this debt after the war injects an ultimately excessive amount of investment capital into a nation. This in turn leads to simultaneous supersaturation of several important markets, such as housing and agriculture, and this leads to layoffs and depression. If this causal pathway in fact operates, a depression may be viewed as a lagged response to a previous war.

We now explore the possibility that the causality also flows in the other direction, that is, from the preconditions for depression to war.

A curious feature of figure 12.3, in which rates of change in federal public debt were plotted, is that large reductions in this debt serve as leading indicators for either depression or war. This leads to the curious notion that wars and depressions are alternate system responses to the preconditions for depressions. To put it differently, a war may be an accidental or planned event to avoid the occurrence of depression. The accident could come about because a nation took steps to avoid a depression, such as using military-hardware manufacturing to alleviate high unemployment, which were interpreted by another nation as ominously threatening. Three examples illustrate how wars may be caused by economic stress. The Civil War period would probably have been a serious recession or depression if there had been no war. From 1857 to the beginning of the war the value of U.S. building permits dropped 45 percent, wages for carpenters on the Erie Canal dropped 14 percent, and the wholesale price index for all commodities dropped 20 percent.

In the period 1905 to 1914 preceding World War I, an extraordinary number of days were lost to industrial disputes in France, Germany, and the United Kingdom (Mitchell, 1975). The critical event in converting a local conflict between Austria-Hungary and Serbia into a world war was general mobilization in Russia in late July, 1914. An "apparently well-informed Russian . . . asserts that . . . general mobilization was strongly urged as a salutary measure against . . . internal industrial and revolutionary danger, rather than as a necessary military precaution against German attack" (Fay, 1948). Saint Petersburg and all the other larger cities in Russia were in the throes of an extensive workingmen's strike at the time of the mobilization. In this instance war may have been seen as a means of directing outward hostility that otherwise would have been directed against the present government because of a depressed economy. Another mechanism by which depressed economies can lead to war is the use of armaments-production programs to deal with high unemployment rates. Such programs can be rationalized to the domestic population by overestimating the armaments buildup in other countries. To illustrate, Francis Neilson, a member of the British Parliament from 1910 to 1915, showed how British politicians consistently misrepresented to the British electorate German plans for building naval vessels to rationalize a rapid increase in construction expenditures for naval vesels (Neilson, 1916). From 1909 to 1914 some British politicians were arguing for rapid buildup in the British navy to meet the threat posed by a rapid buildup in the German navy. In fact, during this period new construction expenditures for warships increased by 68 percent in Great Britain, but by only 1.3 percent in Germany (Neilson, 1916). There is ample evidence that the nations that became principal parties in World War I had economic problems for which military preparations would have appeared as a short-term solution. To illustrate, there was "the poverty and misery of certain classes of society in the British Isles, part of which was due to the collapse of business enterprises owing to the superior efficiency of the competing Germans" (Bakeless, 1972). In Germany, 1914 was a year of economic difficulty. Various products "which had been going to the British market were supplanted by British manufactures. The unemployment problem was beginning to show itself at the same time that the cost of living rose" (Bakeless, 1972). There seems little doubt that World War I was an accidental by-product of the use of military preparations as a tool for solving domestic economic problems.

We are not arguing that the precise nature of the causal pathway from economic crisis to war is constant from war to war. Also, we are not arguing that there is only one such pathway for each war; there are likely several. Further, we are not arguing that wars necessarily come about because each of the nations which becomes involved in a war was an instigator. In World War II, Hitler used rapid militarization and rapid industrialization jointly during the 1930s to produce a spectacular decline in the German unemployment rate and improvement in the economy. World War II was not, however, an accidental by-product of his economic plans; it was a central goal. Thus a war need not be a systemic result of simultaneous economic difficulties in several nations. All it takes is the use of militarization by one of them as a means of solving economic difficulties, and many other nations may be sucked into a vortex.

There is a provocative and speculative argument suggesting that wars and depressions or serious recessions are alternate global system responses to economic stress resulting from supersaturated markets. There is apparently a strong tendency toward an 18-year rhythm in global affairs, and the affairs of all developed nations, in which nadirs are either economic downturns or wars. To illustrate, the second-worst depression in U.S. history occurred in 1843. Adding 18 to that year number repeatedly, we get 1861 (the Civil War), 1879 (a serious recession), 1897 (a depression), 1915 (a world war), 1933 (a depression), 1951 (the Korean War), 1969 (a serious recession), and 1987. We are arguing not for some type of mystical cycle-producing mechanism but rather for a dynamic process associated with a cycle of under- and overinvestment. The pacemaker in this cycle may be the length of a human generation. Each generation believes that it can get rich quick with minimum effort through speculative investment and is incapable of communicating the full significance of its findings to its children's generation. Most parents will understand what we are saying.

Our research suggests that wars are not phenomena for which blame can be readily assigned but rather systemic phenomena arising out of economic stress. This notion of wars as systemic phenomena is held by many scholars (e.g., Barnes, 1952; Schmitt, 1966). Indeed, the notion that wars and depressions are two different responses to stress was advanced by Boulding (1962). The multination responsibility for World War II is far back in time and resulted from punitive settlement of World War I, as it was so identified by the brilliant English economist Keynes at the time (1920).

The underlying cycle-producing mechanism in society is not rigid but rather creates a strong tendency toward periodicity. We believe, however, that this periodicity is vulnerable to modification by government action. This notion conforms with the finding that a good predictor is government debt policy—a variable under control by society. We interpret our findings to mean that a prior sequence of events is a far more reliable predictor of the next event than is a periodicity argument.

In short, we view economic fluctuations and wars as constituting a closed, circular causal feedback system which operates at a global level. Wars are important determinants of economic fluctuations, but nadirs in economic fluctuations increase the probability that at least one nation will initiate the sequence of events that increases the probability of war for all.

What Would Cassandra Have Said?

We have shown that the long-run changes in wages and prices can be explained as responses to the supply-demand situation for the currently critical limiting resource, changes in government expenditures, typically primarily the result of military expenditures, and depression of prices and wages by excessive population. It seems unlikely that many people in this civilization would have predicted this finding or that, having seen it, would be prepared to take it seriously.

In Greek mythology Apollo ordained that the prophecies of Cassandra should never be believed. Aware of her fate, we make two predictions. Either the United States will make a major effort to increase the efficiency of energy use, increase dependence on renewable-energy sources, and institute a vigorous policy of discouraging population growth, as in China and Singapore, or there will be a significant decline in the standard of living, clearly detectable within 20 years.

Second, either the United States or the Soviet Union will make an effective, joint effort to end the cold war and reduce military spending significantly, or both will be reduced to second-power status by the economic consequences. Also, our work suggests that such changes must be made very gradually, rather than suddenly and violently. If the reduction in military expenditures is not undertaken, the dominant nations on earth will become Japan and China, both of which have decided that the nuclear-weapons contest makes no economic sense, even if one survives it.

References

Albion, R. G. 1926. *Forests and sea power*. Cambridge, Mass.: Harvard University Press.

Armstrong, J. S. 1978. *Long range forecasting: From crystal ball to computer*. New York: Wiley Interscience.

Ascher, W. 1978. *Forecasting: An appraisal for policy-makers and planners*. Baltimore, Md.: Johns Hopkins University Press.

Bakeless, J. 1972. *The economic causes of modern war: A study of the period 1878–1918*. New York: Garland.

Barnes, H. E. 1928. *In quest of truth and justice*. Chicago: National Historical Society.

Boulding, K. E. 1962. *Conflict and defense: A general theory*. New York: Harper.

Braudel, F. 1972, 1973. *The Mediterranean and the Mediterranean world in the age of Philip II*. Vols. 1 and 2. New York: Harper and Row.

Burton, T. E. 1902. *Financial crises and periods of industrial and commercial depression*. New York: D. Appleton.

Clark, J. M. 1931. *The costs of the World War to the American people.* New Haven, Conn.: Yale University Press.

Committee on Resources and Man. 1969. *Resources and man: A study and recommendations.* San Francisco: Freeman.

Cook, E. 1976. *Man, energy, society.* San Francisco: Freeman.

Dale, T., and V. G. Carter. 1955. *Topsoil and civilization.* Norman: University of Oklahoma Press.

Darby, M. R., J. R. Lothian, A. E. Gandolfi, A. J. Schwartz, and A. C. Stockman. 1983. *The international transmission of inflation.* Chicago: University of Chicago Press.

Ehrlich, P. R. 1968. *The population bomb.* New York: Sierra Club/Ballantine Books.

Forrester, J. W. 1968. *World dynamics.* Cambridge, Mass.: Wright Allen.

————. 1979. Innovation and the economic long wave. *Management Review* (June 16–24).

Gaines, T. C. 1962. *Techniques of Treasury debt management.* Glencoe, N.Y.: Free Press of Glencoe.

Haberler, G. 1941. *Prosperity and depression.* Geneva: League of Nations.

Hyams, E. 1952. *Soil and civilization.* London: Thames and Hudson.

Jacks, G. V., and R. O. Whyte. 1939. *Vanishing lands: A world survey of soil erosion.* New York: Doubleday, Doran.

Keynes, J. M. 1920. *The economic consequences of the peace.* New York: Harcourt, Brace and Howe.

————. 1930. *A treatise on money.* Vol. 2. *The applied theory of money.* New York: Harcourt, Brace.

McClean, M. 1977. Getting the problem right—a role for structural modeling. In H. A. Linstone and W. H. Clive Simmonds, eds. *Futures research—New directions,* pp. 144–57. London: Addison-Wesley.

Marsh, G. P. 1864. *Man and nature.* Cambridge, Mass.: Harvard University Press.

Meadows, D. H., D. L. Meadows, J. Randers, and W. W. Behrens, III. 1972. *The limits to growth.* New York: Universe Books.

Mitchell, B. R. 1975. *European historical statistics, 1750–1970.* New York: Columbia University Press.

Nef, J. U. 1932. *The rise of the British coal industry.* Vols. 1 and 2. London: George Routledge.

Neilson, F. 1916. *How diplomats make war.* New York: B. W. Huebsch.

Phelps Brown, E. H., and S. V. Hopkins. 1955. Seven centuries of building wages. *Economica* 22:195–206.

Rostow, W. W. 1978. *The world economy—history and prospect.* Austin: University of Texas Press.

Schmitt, B. E. 1966. *The coming of the war, 1914.* New York: Howard Fertig.

Singer, S. F. 1970. *Global effects of environmental pollution.* Dordrecht: Reidel.

Smith, W. B., and A. H. Cole. 1935. *Fluctuations in American Business, 1790–1860.* Cambridge, Mass.: Harvard University Press.

Spengler, O. 1926, 1928. *The decline of the West.* Vol. 1. *Form and actuality.* Vol. 2. *Perspective of world history.* New York: Knopf.

Temin, P. 1976. *Did monetary forces cause the Great Depression?* New York: Norton.

U.S. Department of Commerce. 1975. *Historical statistics of the United States.* Washington, D.C.: Government Printing Office.

Wickens, D. L. 1941. *Residential real estate.* New York: National Bureau of Economic Research.

Wilkinson, R. G. 1973. *Poverty and progress! An ecological model of economic development.* London: Methuen.

13.
The Limits to Growth Revisited

The Limits to Growth is but one in a long series of books that have disturbed industrial society by pointing out the long-term and total-system implications of short-term, narrowly focused decisions. Others in this tradition, both before and after *Limits,* include *A Sand County Almanac,* by Aldo Leopold; *The Challenge of Man's Future,* by Harrison Brown; *Silent Spring,* by Rachel Carson; *The Population Bomb,* by Paul R. Ehrlich; *Resources and Man,* by the National Academy of Sciences; *Small Is Beautiful,* by E. F. Schumacher; *Man, Energy, Society,* by Earl Cook; and *The Global 2000 Report to the President,* edited by Gerald O. Barney. Each of these books has had its own particular approach and message. But all of them arose from a common philosophy, one that is very distinct from the one embedded in the modern world's institutions and culture.

No matter how well they are aimed, literary grenades tossed from the sidelines at the assumptions of an entrenched establishment can cause only temporary local disturbances. Each of these books was discussed widely until society found one reason or another to dismiss it, and eventually the discussion faded away. It would be easy to be cynical about the whole process and to label it futile—to feel like one in a succession of Cassandras.

But none of these books has really disappeared. Those of us on the sidelines treasure and are sustained by all of them, quote from them, assign them to students. Each book in some way engenders another. The view they put forth—that all species on earth are precious; that the ecosystem is to be harmonized with, not dominated; that society has purposes beyond production and consumption; that greed, waste, and inequity are unnecessary and immoral—is still alive and healthy although far from politically dominant today.

There are lessons to be learned from these books: lessons about the larger society and its ways of handling unorthodox ideas, and lessons about how all of us can be more effective in expressing and in living our ideas and ultimately in making them prevail. In this chapter I draw some of those lessons from the only one of those books I have any right to discuss, *The Limits to Growth*. My purpose in doing so is to encourage future Cassandras, and perhaps to help them know in advance some things I had to learn the hard way.

A Brief History

In 1970 the Club of Rome went to MIT to ask Jay Forrester's System Dynamics Group to construct a computer model of the world. The members of the club, all distinguished men of commerce, science, or government, had made a list of 66 "continuous critical problems" troubling the global society. The problems on the list are still with us, though some have risen and some have fallen in public attention. They include hunger, pollution, terrorism, the arms race, resource depletion, urban slums, economic instability, racism, and juvenile delinquency.

The club wanted to know how these problems are interlinked, what causes them, and, most important, what could be done to solve them. The System Dynamics Group, including Dennis Meadows and me, took on at least part of the job and ended up linking five sectors—population, industry, food production, natural resources, and the environment. Four books were produced from the study (Forrester, 1971; Meadows, Meadows, Randers, and Behrens, 1972; Meadows and Meadows, 1973; Meadows et al., 1974); one of them, *The Limits to Growth*, became world famous, or, depending on your point of view, world infamous.

Since then I have learned that the most important question to ask about any human work, whether a poem, a painting, a scientific discovery, or a computer model, is who was behind it. As I look back now on the group that produced *The Limits to Growth*, I see us as astonishingly young (the oldest was 30), touchingly idealistic, very eager, naive, and bright. We were all educated in the sciences, and we certainly had a strong technocratic streak. We thought that rationality should rule the world, but we would have been appalled at the idea that our particular group or computer model should do so.

Dennis and I were just back from a year in Asia. We were very much in touch with our planet in all its variety and quite upset at what we saw happening to its people and its ecosystems. We were righteous and impatient, as young people so often are, and fundamentally hopeless. We did not think that anyone would listen or change. Soon after *The Limits to Growth* came out, we moved to a farm in New Hampshire to learn about homesteading and wait for the coming collapse. We definitely felt like Cassandras, especially as we watched the world react to our work.

The Message of *The Limits to Growth*

The Limits to Growth put forth three conclusions, which seemed to us remarkably simple and straightforward, and still seem so 15 years later:

1. If the present growth trends in world population, industrialization, pollution, food production, and resource depletion continue unchanged, the limits to growth on this planet will be reached sometime within the next 100 years. The most probable result will be a rather sudden and uncontrollable decline in both population and industrial capacity.

2. It is possible to alter these growth trends and to establish a condition of ecological and economic stability that is sustainable far into the future. The state of global equilibrium could be designed so that the basic material needs of each person on earth are satisfied and each person has an equal opportunity to realize his individual human potential.

3. If the world's people decide to strive for this second outcome rather than the first, the sooner they begin working to attain it, the greater will be their chances of success.

The first of these statements may be one of the most pessimistic forecasts made in this century—it certainly was received that way. The second, I think, is one of the most optimistic—and I do not believe that it was heard at all.

The computer model that spelled out these conclusions in some detail was publicly available and quite transparent as computer models go. It is still used as a teaching model in many universities. The assumptions within it that lead to its conclusions are simple and yet sophisticated in that they recognize the dynamic interplay between a growing population and its environment. Those assumptions are as follows:

1. Any entity that creates itself out of itself will, unless interrupted, grow faster and faster—that is, grow exponentially. Human population and capital plant (factories, machines) are such entities. It takes people to make people, and the more people there are, the more people can be made. In the same way it takes factories to make more factories. Therefore, the

world's population and capital will grow, if they grow at all, exponentially. (And that is exactly what they have been doing, vigorously, for the past century.)

2. No quantity can grow exponentially for very long in a finite environment. Some sort of signal or pressure must arise from the finite and increasingly stressed environment to suppress the growth.

3. An exponentially growing entity in a finite environment will come to a smooth accommodation with its limits (a sigmoid growth curve) *if and only if* it receives some sort of accurate, prompt signal at all times telling it where it is with respect to its limits, and only if its growth is controlled instantly and accurately in response to that signal. If your car is accelerating and you see a stoplight ahead, you need continuous, accurate visual signals and quickly responding muscles and brakes to alter that acceleration into a smooth stop exactly at the light. Imagine what would happen if your brakes responded with a three-minute delay.

4. If the signal to the growing entity about its relationship to its limits is delayed or inaccurate, or if its response is delayed, and *if the environment is not erodable when overstressed,* then the entity will overshoot its limits for a while, make a correction and undershoot, and then overshoot again in a series of oscillations which usually damp down to an equilibrium with the environmental limits.

5. If the signal or response is delayed *and the environment is eroded when overstressed,* then the growing entity will overshoot, erode its carrying capacity, and create a collapse in the carrying capacity and eventually in itself. The result will be a new low-level equilibrium, with a permanently degraded environment and population.

This chain of logic is straightforward and indisputable as a set of abstract systems principles. The only question is which set of conditions applies to the human race. *The Limits to Growth* says that the human population–capital system is structured for an overshoot and collapse. The earth's resource base is erodable, the industrial ethic is one of continuous growth, social decision-making processes are interminable, and leaders ignore, distort, and deny any signals that growth is creating problems. Furthermore, the numbers, admittedly uncertain, indicate that a collapse can happen within a time period interesting to present society. The computer model is simply an elaborate working-out of the numbers.

By the same chain of logic the way to avoid the collapse is, above all, to interrupt the exponential growth deliberately, to decide on a level of population and industrial output that is desirable and sustainable and stop there — in other words, to define social goals around some idea of "enough" rather than "more." It would also help to improve (and pay attention to) the signals that indicate when the environment is stressed, to shift away from the use of nonrenewable resources, and to prevent the erosion of renewable resources.

Just to be sure the record is clear, I want to emphasize that we had complete confidence in our reasoning and our message 15 years ago, and we still have it now. Though I and other people have made many other models since, though the data base is much better now than it was then, though I have listened to and thought about the hundreds of criticisms leveled at *Limits,* I have learned nothing in the past 15 years to cause me to change the *Limits* model or its conclusions.

But if you happen to want to dispute seriously the basic message of *Limits,* you would simply have to demonstrate at least one of the following propositions:

1. That population and capital growth are not inherently exponential, or that there are social forces already in place that will control and finally stop the exponential growth in time to avoid any limits.

2. That the human race knows exactly where the planet's physical limits are at all times and has in place the mechanisms to adjust population and capital growth rapidly whenever or wherever the limits are approached.

3. That the earth's resources are not erodable when overstressed.

4. That the earth is infinite, or that its physical limits are many orders of magnitude larger than our present stresses on them; or, alternatively, that the human race can access resources from somewhere else in space at a rate sufficient to compensate for resource destruction on earth.

The Reaction

Many ecologists and anthropologists who already think in systems terms and understand population-resource interactions wondered why we bothered to publish such obvious stuff. Many environmental activists who had their own reasons for wanting growth to stop welcomed the book as further ammunition for their cause. Some careful readers who had never thought about such issues before were deeply moved by the book and said so, in speeches, broadcasts, and newspaper columns.

The message was taken especially seriously in Europe and in Japan, where the media featured it and parliaments debated it. *Limits* won a German peace prize. It was translated into dozens of languages and sold millions of copies—no one has kept track of how many. It was adopted as a textbook in hundreds of universities. I still meet, nearly everywhere I go, people who tell me that the book changed their lives, gave them a good idea, gave them a career direction. I bother to say all this to encourage future Cassandras to put out their own messages. There are always individuals who are ready to hear, think, and act in a responsible way—and you can support or inspire them.

But while the message of *Limits* was already obvious to some and obvious when they thought about it to others, it was not one bit obvious to many. It was infuriating.

We were attacked with equal energy from the right and the left and from the solid middle of academic economics. Mobil Oil mounted an advertising campaign to say "Growth Is Not a Four-Letter Word." President Richard M. Nixon asked for a thorough investigation of our group and put our publisher on his enemies list. The National Labor Caucus showed up regularly to disrupt our speeches. The book was derided in the Soviet Union. Above all, the country's leading economists outdid each other in writing scathing reviews. The hostility to the book was astounding to us, and it went on for years.

Among the most responsible of our critics were other computer modelers around the world who thought the model was too simple or too biased or too technically unsophisticated. They proceeded to make their own world models to show us how it should have been done. Over the past decade at least 20 such models have been made in many countries of the world and many parts of the United Nations system. The resulting discussion has been a careful, rational comparison of assumptions and conclusions.

The computer forces one's assumptions out in the open where others can examine them, and it also forces a basic rigor—everything sold must be bought; everyone born must die; an electric generating plant, once in place, must remain an electric generating plant and cannot transform itself into a tractor factory. It also cannot run without fuel, labor, and maintenance. This insistence on simpleminded accounting eliminates much irresponsible rhetoric. Therefore, the conversation among the global modelers, while not always friendly, was at least informative, and in the end it produced some valuable insights about the linkages in the world socioeconomic system (Meadows, Richardson, and Bruckmann, 1982).

Incidentally, none of the subsequent models has disproved the basic conclusions of *Limits*. Some have spelled out those conclusions in considerably more detail. Others have addressed other issues entirely, such as distribution between the rich and the poor of the earth, and have not investigated the question of environmental limits.

But most of the reactions to *Limits* were not careful or rational; they were emotional. As we watched the storm rage, we were amazed at its intensity. It was then that we began to learn the lessons that all Cassandras learn sooner or later.

Lesson 1: Expect a Reaction

We actually did not expect much of a reaction, and I remember feeling the earth shake under me when the publisher called to tell me that copies of the book were being sent to all world leaders and to all members of Congress and that *Time* magazine wanted an advance copy. Because we had not prepared or even thought about the possibility that the world might take an interest in a computer model about the world, the subsequent events controlled us more than we controlled them.

If you have written clearly and well, and if your message is not just more of what everyone else is saying, and if your publisher is doing the job of bringing the work to people's attention, you will get a reaction. Welcome it, and, as far as possible, prepare for it.

Lesson 2: Do Not Take It Personally

Any message sent into the world is a Rorschach test. The responses it generates reveal more about the receivers than about the message itself. It took far too long for me to realize that, to stop being hurt, and to lean back and enjoy the show. It was at that point, when I stopped feeling defensive, that I really began to learn.

Any society *is* a society because of deep, usually unexamined, shared beliefs. These beliefs are rarely stated aloud—they do not need to be. They are the internal chatter that each person involuntarily and constantly repeats. They are exhibited continuously in statements and actions that affirm and ratify the beliefs and that, therefore, are socially acceptable.

When you yourself are a member of the society, you are essentially blind to the shared beliefs, because they are all you see or know—like water to the fish. A fine way of beginning to see them is to say or do something that lies outside the beliefs. To say that economic growth has limits and is not all that desirable anyway is an excellent way to probe some of the deepest unconscious beliefs of industrial society—as long as you do not take the ensuing outrage personally.

Lesson 3: Watch Your Labels and Symbols

None of us involved in *Limits* foresaw the symbolic power of MIT, the computer, and the mystical cabalistic connotations of a group called the Club of Rome. That combination alone was sufficient to guarantee the world's attention, no matter what we ultimately said. The world's attention is not easy to get, and it is useful to employ powerful symbols to get it. The problem is that a large fraction of the audience never goes beyond the symbols.

Some people still think that, whatever we said, it must have been technocratic, or intrinsically right, or intrinsically inhuman, because it came from MIT. Others are still under the impression that we are under the influence of the Catholic church, because of the Club of Rome (which has absolutely no relation to the Catholic Church). Others know for sure that, because a computer was involved, whatever we said is to be believed, or disbelieved, without question. All these people reacted to the symbols and never got the message at all.

The title of the book had the same effect. A book called *The Limits to Growth* could have been filled with nothing but blank pages, and some people would still have thought it was an anticapitalist plot or an anti-Communist or an anti-Keynesian or an anti-Third World one. They never saw the book for its cover.

After about two months of oscillation, the press finally found the label they wanted to apply to us. It was "doomsday predictors"—not at all what we would have chosen, and not an accurate representation of what we said. That label was perhaps the ultimate thought stopper in the discussion.

There are several lessons here. There is a fine line between symbols that attract attention and symbols that derail the conversation. It is probably necessary to use powerful labels and symbols, but not as unconsciously as we did. There is no point in getting a lot of publicity for a message you do not intend. Be sure that the trappings around you, including tools, sponsors, spokespersons, and titles, communicate the actual message you want to communicate. And apply your own label to yourself before others do. One of the primary powers you have in a public discussion is to control the language of the argument.

Lesson 4: People Expect Oracles, Not Choices

We had thought that our message about the future was about as unremarkable as the old Chinese saying, "If we don't change our direction, we will end up where we are heading." The obvious response to such a statement, we thought, was to discover that we do not like where we are heading and therefore to change direction.

But there is something deep within our culture that insists on hearing statements about the future as absolute predictions, not conditional ones. We still have the Greek oracle in our societal subconscious. We think that the future happens to us instead of being created by us, that it is to be predicted, not chosen. That kind of thinking automatically twists a simple warning about how to avoid trouble into a "doomsaying," an unconditional prediction of trouble. And no one wants to listen to prophets of doom.

There are 17 different computer projections in *Limits* showing 17 different futures, each resulting from a different option open to society. One of them shows a future in which 6 billion people have a European standard of living that is sustainable indefinitely into the future. We honestly think that is possible. And we are called prophets of doom.

It is difficult to speak about the future to a society that has such a simpleminded and fatalistic way of listening. And it is terribly sad to realize that, because of that way of listening, one is speaking to a basically unempowered audience. "If the future just happens, then no one can do anything that counts. There is no point in getting up and doing anything. Please do not ask what we really want in life, how we would like the future to be. It is too painful to answer such questions; our hopes can never be realized. Just tell us what is going to happen, so that we can prepare ourselves as best we can."

That is the filter screening our messages. The only thing I know to do about it is to point constantly to the filter itself, to make it visible, and to debunk it emphatically. People need to confront the unstated assumption that they are powerless and to see that there is no basis for that assumption. One tactic here is to present plenty of evidence to the contrary. I now store up and constantly share stories of individuals and groups who have really made a difference, who have consciously and deliberately chosen a future and brought it into being.

Lesson 5: The Power of a Paradigm

I remember thinking, as I listened to various critics of *Limits* assert that technology will solve all our problems or that prices will rise and create new resources: "Are these people living in the same world I am? How can we be reading the same newspapers, looking at the same data, traveling in the same places, and be seeing such different things?"

Fortunately, about that time I discovered Thomas Kuhn's book, which explained to my satisfaction what was going on. We are not living in the same world, he said. We see only the evidence that our very deep subconscious assumptions about the world—which he called paradigms—allow us to see. We actively create our perceived worlds, according to the way we already think the world is (Kuhn, 1969).

It is possible for a technological optimist to read the *New York Times* and conclude that technologies are indeed working to make the world a better place, and for a technological pessimist to read the same issue and conclude that technology leads to nothing but spills, explosions, vile new toxins, and general mess-ups. The two readers would notice, and fail to notice, different sets of articles. Even if they read the same article, about the Three Mile Island incident, for instance, one would say, "I always knew one of those plants would blow up some day," while the other would conclude, "See, it did not blow up; the system worked."

Once one catches on to the presence and power of paradigms, including one's own, it is great fun to watch people snap up and treasure the evidence that confirms what they already thought, and to discount, disbelieve, not notice, and lie about the evidence that does not. It is somewhat less fun to encounter the irrational, hostile, almost inarticulate reaction that is produced when someone feels that his or her paradigm is being seriously threatened.

That, I think, is the primary explanation for much of the response to *Limits* and to the other books in the Cassandra series. They manage to threaten some of the most deeply ingrained social assumptions. They say that man is not the center and purpose of the universe (centuries after Galileo that one still dies hard). That quality is at least as important as quantity. That what serves the short-term greed of individuals does not serve the long-term need of nations. That there are other goals for humankind besides material accumulation. That some of our most socially vaunted activities are unjust and unsustainable.

And with *Limits* we assaulted the paradigm of economic growth without fully appreciating the degree to which we were calling into question whole personal, corporate, and national identities. Those who penetrated the symbols surrounding the book, those who understood the concept of conditional forecasts, those who really got the message—some of them had to strike out more strongly than anyone else, because they recognized how deeply they were threatened. Their reaction will lead us in a minute to another lesson, about often-repeated lies.

But first, is there a lesson in the recognition of the presence and power of paradigms? Certainly it is necessary to know that they exist and that no one is free from them. It is useful to understand that we are in fact involved in a paradigm battle; we are seeking to redefine whole social identities and purposes. It is not a trivial task. We cannot expect one study, one book, or one person to accomplish it. And we cannot expect people to give up ideas they treasure, except in exchange for even more appealing and affirming ideas, ideas that assure them that they still have a place and a purpose in the universe.

I think that the lesson is to be very aboveboard about the paradigm clashes we generate. Again, we need to point to the conceptual filters, our own as well as those of others, and to carry the whole conversation onto a higher level. It is not a discussion about who is right and who is wrong. Paradigms are by their nature never right: they are only assumptions. But they have different kinds of handiness—they allow different concrete results to be manifested in the world. If you think that the earth is at the center of the universe and that everything else circles around it, you can predict eclipses quite well and even do accurate earthly navigation. But out of those assumptions you could never plan the trajectory of a space vehicle.

What can be accomplished and what not even imagined with the present societal paradigm? What does a different set of filters let us see and do? Paradigms, like the future, can be chosen deliberately, to make something desirable happen. What paradigm do we need to create the future we want?

In these discussions we also need to be compassionate. Our ideas literally tear other people's worlds apart. We are already at home in the new world we have created for ourselves, but others are not. We have to make them feel welcome.

Lesson 6: The Often-Repeated Lie

The media, after making much of the symbols around *Limits* and then declaring it a piece of doomsaying, finally understood it as a threat to a dominant societal paradigm. They then utilized a tool that is especially handy to the media, the often-repeated lie. *Time* magazine in particular excelled in never allowing itself to refer to *The Limits to Growth* in any context without putting the word "discredited" in front of it. Who discredited the study, when, and on what grounds is never mentioned.

In fact *Time* did the discrediting all by itself, because its paradigm had been confronted, and it needed to have *Limits* discredited. And in general the ploy worked. Most people, especially in the media, consider *Limits* discredited, although they could not begin to tell you why.

That example of the often-repeated lie is trivial compared with what we hear regularly on the nightly news.

What is the lesson here? Not to be surprised when it happens. And

I think that another lesson is not to be tempted into the same tactic. Often-repeating is something we will have to do, and that is a hard lesson for academic types, who get bored easily. But please let us often-repeat not lies but the truth, as far as we know it. Which actually is the last lesson.

Lesson 7: The Often-Repeated Truth

There need to be more Cassandras. Each of us needs to speak out more. As long as the internal conversation of society is repeating ceaselessly that more is better, that nature is separate from and subordinate to man, that the poor are somewhat less than human, that individuals do not make any difference, that hunger and war and scarcity are inevitable, we need to be repeating the contrary aloud. We need to go on doing it until the internal conversation begins to echo us, and then our job is done.

Most of the books in the series I mentioned at the beginning of this paper recognize three major changes that will be necessary before there is a satisfactory and sustainable world society. One is the stabilization of the human population. The second is the stabilization of the annual flow of energy and materials through the economy. The third is the just distribution of both material and nonmaterial goods so that every member of the human race is included, supported, acknowledged, and enabled to contribute fully to the joint enterprise.

In the fifteen years since *Limits* was published, there has actually been amazing progress on the first of these agenda items. In 1972 the word "population" could not be said aloud in the United Nations. The suggestion that populations should not grow so fast was heard as genocide.

Now, although populations are not yet stabilized and there is plenty of work to do, the point has been repeated often enough that it has been made. Virtually every woman in the world has heard that it could actually be possible for her to choose the number of children she will have, instead of passively accepting whatever comes—a revolutionary and tremendously empowering idea. Nearly every government is at least aware of the size and rate of growth of its own population and of the implications of that growth on requirements for jobs, schools, and resources.

One government, which encompasses one-fifth of the earth's people, has actually done a simple calculation of available resources, determined how many people can be supported, and implemented a plan to bring the population to that level. The most amazing part of China's plan is that it aims for a population *decrease*. The plan says that the present 1 billion people will, because of age structure, have to expand to 1.2 billion but then will be brought down over a 100-year period to the government's target of 700 to 800 million. Whether or not it succeeds, the very presence of a plan like that signifies a tremendous shift in ways of thinking.

The second and third items, to stabilize economic activity and create a just distribution, still require repeating and still more repeating. When a government or corporation crows about a 5.4 percent growth rate, voices need to be raised everywhere asking: "Growth of what? For whom? At what cost? Who paid that cost? Toward what end? How will we know when we get there? How much is enough? What is all this growth for, anyway?"

A guru of my acquaintance says that people will give up anything for enlightenment. They will leave family and job, give away their wealth, sit in uncomfortable positions meditating for hours each day. They will give up anything *except the idea that they are not already enlightened.*

Similarly, societies will do anything to be materially secure — destroy the earth, enslave their people, make war on other people — anything except give up their ideas, the very ideas that are in the way of their own security. Fortunately, the truth that we must often repeat, the idea that we must substitute for the crippling ideas that are now ruling society, is a delightful one, once you see it. It is the second of the three conclusions of *The Limits to Growth.* The earth is a fruitful, beautiful, and resilient planet. *Homo sapiens* is a strong and ingenious species. If the global society just decided to do it, it would be simple to create a secure, equitable, sustainable, and sufficient life for everyone — much simpler than trying to maintain continuous physical growth on a finite planet.

References

Barney, G. O., ed. 1981. *The global 2000 report to the president of the U.S.— entering the 21st century.* New York: Pergamon.

Brown, H. 1956. *The challenge of man's future.* New York: Viking.

Carson, R. 1962. *Silent spring.* Boston: Houghton Mifflin.

Cook, E. 1976. *Man, energy, society.* San Francisco: Freeman.

Ehrlich, P. R., 1968. *The population bomb.* New York: Ballantine.

Forrester, J. W. 1971. *World dynamics.* Cambridge, Mass.: MIT Press.

Kuhn, T. S. 1969. *The structure of scientific revolutions.* Chicago: University of Chicago Press.

Leopold, A. 1949. *A Sand County almanac.* New York: Oxford University Press.

Meadows, D. H., and D. L. Meadows. 1973. *Toward global equilibrium.* Cambridge, Mass.: MIT Press.

———, ———, J. Randers, and W. W. Behrens. 1972. *The limits to growth.* New York: Universe Books.

———, J. Richardson, and G. Bruckmann. 1982. *Groping in the dark: The first decade of global modeling.* New York: Wiley.

Meadows, D. L., et al. 1974. *The dynamics of growth in a finite world.* Cambridge, Mass.: MIT Press.

NAS [National Academy of Sciences]. 1967. *Resources and man: A study and recommendations by the Committee on Resources and Man.* San Francisco: Freeman.

Schumacher, E. F. 1975. *Small is beautiful: Economics as if people mattered.* New York: Harper & Row.

14.
Moving to a Steady-State Economy

TWO ASPECTS of moving to a steady-state economy will be considered. The first is movement from growthmania toward the steady-state paradigm in our thinking: What are the main theoretical and moral anomalies of the growth economy, and how are they resolved by the steady state? The second aspect is the movement from growth toward the steady state in actual practice—a look at some practical failures of the growth economy, viewed as forced first steps toward a steady state.

Before we consider these two topics, it is necessary to define what is meant by a "steady-state economy" (SSE) and by a "growth economy." Growth, as here used, refers to an increase in the physical scale of the matter-energy throughput that sustains the economic activities of production and consumption of commodities. In an SSE the aggregate throughput is constant, though its allocation among competing uses is free to vary in response to the market. Since there is no production and consumption of matter-energy in a physical sense, the throughput is really a process in which low-entropy raw materials are transformed into commodities and then, eventually, into high-entropy wastes. Throughput begins with depletion and ends with pollution. Growth is quantitative increase in the physical scale of throughput. Qualitative improvement in the use made of a given scale of throughput, resulting either from improved technical knowledge or from a deeper understanding of purpose, is called "development." An SSE therefore can develop, but cannot grow, just as the planet earth, of which it is a subsystem, can develop without growing.

The steady state is by no means static. There is continuous renewal by death and birth, depreciation and production, as well as qualitative improvement in the stocks of both people and artifacts. By this definition, strictly speaking, even the stocks of artifacts or people may occasionally grow temporarily as a result of technical progress that increases the durability and repairability (longevity) of artifacts. The same maintenance flow can support a larger stock if the stock becomes longer-lived. The stock may also decrease, however, if resource quality declines at a faster rate than increases in durability-enhancing technology.

The other crucial feature in the definition of an SSE is that the constant level of throughput must be ecologically sustainable for a long future for a population living at a standard or per capita resource use that is sufficient for a good life. Note that an SSE is not defined in terms of gross national product (GNP). It is not to be thought of as "zero growth in GNP."

Ecological sustainability of the throughput is not guaranteed by market forces. The market cannot by itself register the cost of its own increasing scale relative to the ecosystem. Market prices measure the scarcity of individual resources relative to each other. Prices do not measure the absolute scarcity of resources in general, of environmental low entropy. The best we can hope for from a perfect market is a Pareto-optimal allocation of resources (i.e., a situation in which no one can be made better off without making someone else worse off). Such an allocation can be achieved at any scale of resource throughput, including unsustainable scales, just as it can be achieved with any distribution of income, including unjust ones. The latter proposition is well known, the former less so, but equally true. Ecological criteria of sustainability, like ethical criteria of justice, are not served by markets. Markets singlemindedly aim to serve allocative efficiency. Optimal *allocation* is one thing; optimal *scale* is something else.

Economists are always preoccupied with maximizing something: profits, rent, present value, consumers' surplus, etc. What is maximized in the SSE? Basically the maximand is life, measured in cumulative person-years ever to be lived at a standard of resource use sufficient for a good life. This certainly does not imply maximizing population growth, as advocated by Julian Simon (1981), because too many people simultaneously alive, especially high-consuming people, will be forced to consume ecological "capital" and thereby lower carrying capacity and the cumulative total of future lives. Although the maximand is human lives, the SSE would go a long way toward maximizing cumulative life for all species by imposing the constraint of a constant throughput at a sustainable level, thereby halting the growing takeover of habitats of other species, as well as slowing the rate of drawdown of geological capital otherwise available to future generations.

I do not wish to put too fine a point on the notion that the steady state maximizes cumulative life over time for all species, but it certainly would do better in this regard than the present-value maximizing growth economy, which drives to extinction any valuable species whose biological growth rate is less than the expected rate of interest, as long as capture costs are not too high (Clark, 1976).

Of course many deep issues are raised in this definition of the SSE that, in the interests of brevity, are only touched on here. The meanings of "sufficient for a good life" and "sustainable for a long future" have to be left vague. But any economic system must give implicit answers to these dialectical questions, even when it refuses to face them explicitly. For example, the growth economy implicitly says that there is no such thing as sufficiency because more is always better, and that a 20-year future is quite long enough if the discount rate is 10 percent. Many would prefer explicit vagueness to such implicit precision.

Moving from Growthmania to the Steady State in Thought: Theoretical and Moral Anomalies of the Growth Paradigm That Are Resolved by the Steady State

The growth economy runs into two kinds of fundamental limits: the biophysical and the ethicosocial. Although they are by no means totally independent, it is worthwhile to distinguish them.

Biophysical Limits to Growth

The biophysical limits to growth arise from three interrelated conditions: finitude, entropy, and ecological interdependence. The economy, in its physical dimensions, is an open subsystem of our finite and closed ecosystem, which is both the supplier of its low-entropy raw materials and the recipient of its high-entropy wastes. The growth of the economic subsystem is limited by the fixed size of the host ecosystem, by its dependence on the ecosystem as a source of low-entropy inputs and as a sink for high-entropy wastes, and by the complex ecological connections that are more easily disrupted as the scale of the economic subsystem (the throughput) grows relative to the total ecosystem. Moreover, these three basic limits interact. Finitude would not be so limiting if everything could be recycled, but entropy prevents complete recycling. Entropy would not be so limiting if environmental sources and sinks were infinite, but both are finite. That both are finite, plus the entropy law, means that the ordered structures of the economic subsystem are maintained at the expense of creating a more than offsetting amount of disorder in the rest of the system. If it is largely the sun that pays the disorder costs, as it is with traditional peasant economies, then we need not worry. But if these entropic costs (depletion and pollution) are mainly inflicted on the terrestrial environment, as in a modern industrial economy, then they interfere with complex ecological life-support services rendered to the economy by nature. The loss of these services should surely be counted as a cost of growth, to be weighed against benefits at the margin. But our national accounts emphatically do not do this.

Standard growth economics ignores finitude, entropy, and ecological interdependence because the concept of throughput is absent from its pre-analytic vision, which is that of an isolated circular flow of exchange value, as can be verified by examining the first few chapters of any basic textbook (Daly, 1985; Georgescu-Roegen, 1971). The physical dimension of commodities and factors is at best totally abstracted from and at worst assumed to flow in a circle, just like exchange value. It is as if one were to study physiology solely in terms of the circulatory system without ever mentioning the digestive tract. The dependence of the organism on its environment would not be evident. The absence of the concept of throughput in the economists' vision means that the economy carries on no exchange with its environment. It is, by implication, a self-sustaining isolated system, a giant perpetual-motion machine. The focus on exchange value in the macroeconomic circular flow also abstracts from use value and any idea of purpose other than maximization of the circular flow of exchange value.

But everyone, including economists, knows perfectly well that the economy takes in raw material from the environment and gives back waste. So why is this undisputed fact ignored in the circular-flow paradigm? Economists are interested in scarcity. What is not scarce is abstracted from. Environmental sources and sinks were considered infinite relative to the demands of the economy, which was more or less the case during the formative years of economic theory. Therefore, it was not an unreasonable abstraction. But it is highly unreasonable to continue omitting the concept of throughput after the scale of the economy has grown to the point where it is obviously scarce, even if this new absolute scarcity does not register in relative prices. The current practice of ad hoc introduction of "externalities" to take account of the effects of the growing scale of throughput that do not fit the circular-flow model is akin to the use of "epicycles" to explain the departures of astronomical observations from the theoretical circular motion of heavenly bodies.

Nevertheless, many economists hang on to the infinite-resources assumption in one way or another, because otherwise they would have to admit that economic growth faces limits, and that is "unthinkable." The usual ploy is to appeal to the infinite possibilities of technology and resource substitution (ingenuity) as a dynamic force that can continuously outrun depletion and pollution. This counterargument is flawed in many respects. First, technology and infinite substitution mean only that one form of low-entropy matter-energy is substituted for another, within a finite and diminishing set of low-entropy sources. Such substitution is often very advantageous, but we never substitute high-entropy wastes for low-entropy resources in net terms. Second, the claim is frequently made that reproducible capital is a near-perfect substitute for resources. But this assumes that capital can be produced independently of resources, which is absurd. Furthermore, it flies in the teeth of the obvious complementarity of capital and resources in production. The capital stock is an agent for transforming the resource flow from raw material into a product (Georgescu-Roegen, 1971). More capital does not substitute for less resources, except on a very restricted margin. You cannot make the same house by substituting more saws for less wood.

The growth men are left with one basic argument: resource and environmental limits have not halted growth in the past and therefore will not do so in the future. But such logic proves too much, namely, that nothing new can ever happen. A famous general survived a hundred battles without a scratch, and that was still true when he was blown up.

Earl Cook offered some insightful criticism of this faith in limitless ingenuity in one of his last articles (Cook, 1982). The appeal of the limitless-ingenuity argument, he contended, lies not in the scientific grounding of its premises nor in the cogency of its logic but rather in the fact that

the concept of limits to growth threatens vested interests and power structures; even worse, it threatens value structures in which lives have been invested. . . . Abandonment of belief in perpetual motion was a major step toward recognition of the true human condition. It is significant that "mainstream" economists never abandoned that belief and do not accept the relevance to the economic process of the Second Law of Thermodynamics; their position as high priests of the market economy would become untenable did they do so. [Cook 1982, p. 198]

Indeed it would. Therefore, much ingenuity is devoted to "proving" that ingenuity is unlimited. Julian Simon, George Gilder, Herman Kahn, and most of all Ronald Reagan trumpet this theme above all others. Every technical accomplishment, no matter how ultimately insignificant, is celebrated as one more victory in an infinite series of future victories of technology over nature. The Greeks called this hubris. The Hebrews were warned to "beware of saying in your heart, 'My own strength and the might of my own hand won this power for me" (Deut. 8:17). But such wisdom is drowned out in the drumbeat of the see-no-evil "optimism" of growthmania. All the more necessary is it then to repeat Earl Cook's trenchant remark that "without the enormous amount of work done by nature in concentrating flows of energy and stocks of resources, human ingenuity would be onanistic. What does it matter that human ingenuity may be limitless, when matter and energy are governed by other rules than is information?" (Cook, 1982, p. 194).

Ethicosocial Limits

Even when growth is, with enough ingenuity, still possible, ethicosocial limits may render it undesirable. Four ethicosocial propositions limiting the desirability of growth are briefly considered below.

1. *The desirability of growth financed by the drawdown of geological capital is limited by the cost imposed on future generations.* In standard economics the balancing of future against present costs and benefits is done by discounting. A time discount rate is a numerical way of expressing the value judgment that beyond a certain point the future is not worth anything to presently living people. The higher the discount rate, the sooner that point is reached. The value of the future to future people does not count in the standard approach.

Perhaps a more discriminating, though less numerical, principle for balancing the present and the future would be that the basic needs of the present should always take precedence over the basic needs of the future but that the basic needs of the future should take precedence over the extravagant luxury of the present.

2. *The desirability of growth financed by takeover of habitat is limited by the extinction or reduction in number of sentient subhuman species whose habitat disappears.* Economic growth requires space for growing stocks of artifacts and people and for expanding sources of raw material and sinks for waste material. Other species also require space, their "place in the sun." The instrumental value of other species to us, the life-support services they provide, was touched on in the discussion of biophysical limits above. Another limit derives from the intrinsic value of other species, i.e., counting them as sentient, though probably not self-conscious, beings which experience pleasure and pain and whose experienced "utility" should be counted positively in welfare economics, even though it does not give rise to maximizing market behavior.

The intrinsic value of subhuman species should exert some limit on takeover in addition to the limit arising from instrumental value. But it is extrememly difficult to say how much (Birch and Cobb, 1981). Clarification of this limit is a major philosophical task, but if we wait for a definitive answer before imposing any limits on takeover, then the question will be rendered moot by extinctions which are now occurring at an extremely rapid rate relative to past ages (Ehrlich and Ehrlich, 1981).

3. *The desirability of aggregate growth is limited by its self-canceling effects on welfare.* Keynes (1930) argued that absolute wants (those we feel independently of the condition of others) are not insatiable. Relative wants (those we feel only because their satisfaction makes us feel superior to others) are indeed insatiable, for, as Keynes put it, "The higher the general level, the higher still are they." Or, as J. S. Mill expressed it, "Men do not desire to be rich, but to be richer than other men." At the current margin of production in rich countries it is very likely that welfare increments are largely a function of changes in relative income (insofar as they depend on income at all). Since the struggle for relative shares is a zero-sum game, it is clear that aggregate growth cannot increase aggregate welfare. To the extent that welfare depends on relative position, growth is unable to increase welfare in the aggregate. It is subject to the same kind of self-canceling trap that we find in the arms race.

Because of this self-canceling effect of relative position, aggregate growth is less productive of human welfare than we heretofore thought. Consequently, other competing goals should rise relative to growth in the scale of social priorities (Abramowitz, 1979). Future generations, subhuman species, community, and whatever else has been sacrificed in the name of growth should henceforth be sacrificed less simply because growth is less productive of general happiness than used to be the case when marginal income was dedicated mainly to the satisfaction of absolute rather than relative wants.

4. *The desirability of aggregate growth is limited by the corrosive effects on moral standards resulting from the very attitudes that foster growth, such as glorification of self-interest and a scientistic-technocratic world view.* On the demand side of commodity markets growth is stimulated by greed and acquisitiveness, intensified beyond the "natural" endowment from Original Sin by the multibillion-dollar advertising industry. On the supply side technocratic scientism proclaims the possibility of limitless expansion and preaches a reductionistic, mechanistic philosophy which, in spite of its success as a research program, has serious shortcomings as a world view. As a research program it very effectively furthers power and control, but as a world view it leaves no room for purpose, much less for any distinction between good and bad purposes. "Anything goes" is a convenient moral slogan for the growth economy because it implies that anything also sells. To the extent that growth has a well-defined purpose, then it is limited by the satisfaction of that purpose. Expanding power and shrinking purpose lead to uncontrolled growth for its own sake, which is wreck-

ing the moral and social order just as surely as it is wrecking the ecological order (Hirsch, 1976).

The situation of economic thought today can be summarized by a somewhat farfetched but apt analogy. Neoclassical economics, like classical physics, is relevant to a special case that assumes that we are far from limits—far from the limiting speed of light or the limiting smallness of an elementary particle in physics—and far from the biophysical limits of carrying capacity and the ethicosocial limits of satiety in economics. Just as in physics, so in economics: the classical theories do not work well in regions close to limits. A more general theory is needed to embrace both normal and limiting cases. In economics this need becomes greater with time because the ethic of growth itself guarantees that the close-to-the-limits case becomes more and more the norm. The nearer the economy is to limits, the less can we accept the practical judgment most economists make, namely, that "a change in economic welfare implies a change in total welfare in the same direction if not in the same degree" (Abramowitz, 1979). Rather, we must learn to define and explicitly count the other component of total welfare that growth inhibits and erodes when it presses against limits.

Moving from Growthmania to the Steady State in Practice: Failures of Growth as Forced First Steps Toward a Steady-State Economy

This section might well consist only of a series of references to other chapters in this book. No doubt the biggest growth failure is the arms race, where growth has led to less security rather than more and has raised the stakes from loss of individual lives to loss of life itself in wholesale ecocide. Excessive population growth, toxic wastes, acid rain, climate modification, devastation of rain forests, and the loss of ecosystem services resulting from these aggressions against the environment represent case studies in growth failure. Seeing them as first steps toward an SSE requires the conscious willing of a hopeful attitude.

All the growth failures mentioned above are failures of the growth economy to respect the biophysical limits of its host. Rather than repeat what has been so well discussed elsewhere in this book, I would like to consider some symptoms of growthmania within the economy itself, rather than in the environment. Three examples will be considered: money fetishism and the paper economy, faulty national accounts and the treachery of quantified success indexes, and the ambivalent "information economy."

Money Fetishism and the Paper Economy

Money fetishism is a particular case of what Alfred North Whitehead called the "fallacy of misplaced concreteness," which consists in reasoning at one level of abstraction but applying the conclusions of that reasoning to a different level of abstraction. It is to argue that, since abstract exchange value flows in a circle, so do the physical commodities constituting real GNP. Or, since money in the bank can grow forever at compound interest, so can real wealth, and so can welfare. Whatever is true for the abstract symbol of wealth is assumed to hold for concrete wealth itself.

Money fetishism is alive and well in a world in which banks in wealthy countries make loans to poor countries, and when the debtor countries cannot make the repayment, the banks simply make new loans to enable the payment of interest on old loans, thereby avoiding taking a loss on a bad debt. Using new loans to pay interest on old loans is worse than a Ponzi scheme, but the exponential snowballing of debt is expected to be offset by snowballing real growth in debtor countries. The international-debt impasse is a clear symptom of the basic disease of growthmania. Too many accumulations of money are seeking ways to grow exponentially in a world in which the physical scale of the economy is already so large relative to the ecosystem that there is not much room left for growth of anything that has a physical dimension.

Marx, and Aristotle before him, pointed out that the danger of money fetishism arises as a society progressively shifts its focus from use value to exchange value, under the pressure of increasingly complex division of labor and exchange. The sequence is sketched below in four steps, using Marx's shorthand notation for labels.

1. *C-C'*. One commodity (C) is directly traded for a different commodity (C'). The exchange values of the two commodities are by definition equal, but each trader gains an increased use value. This is simple *barter*. No money exists, so there can be no money fetishism.

2. *C-M-C'*. *Simple commodity circulation* begins and ends with a use value embodied in a commodity. Money (M) is merely a convenient medium of exchange. The object of exchange remains the acquisition of an increased use value. C' represents a greater use value to the trader, but C' is still a use value, limited by its specific use or purpose. One has, say, a greater need for a hammer than a knife but has no need for 2 hammers, much less for 50. The incentive to accumulate use values is very limited.

3. *M-C-M'*. As simple commodity circulation gave way to *capitalist circulation,* the sequence shifted. It now begins with money capital and

ends with money capital. The commodity or use value is now an intermediary step in bringing about the expansion of exchange value by some amount of profit, $\Delta M = M'-M$. Exchange value has no specific use or physical dimension to impose concrete limits. One dollar of exchange value is not as good as 2, and 50 dollars is better yet, and a million is much better, etc. Unlike concrete use values, which spoil or deteriorate when hoarded, abstract exchange value can accumulate indefinitely without spoilage or storage costs. In fact, exchange value can grow by itself at compound interest. But as Frederick Soddy (Daly, 1980) pointed out, "You cannot permanently pit an absurd human convention [compound interest] against a law of nature [entropic decay]." "Permanently," however, is not the same as "in the meantime," during which we have, at the micro level, bypassed the absurdity of accumulating use values by accumulating exchange value and holding it as a lien against future use values. But unless future use value, or real wealth, has grown as fast as accumulations of exchange value have grown, then at the end of some time period there will be a devaluation of exchange value by inflation or some other form of debt repudiation. At the macro level limits will reassert themselves, even when ignored at the micro level, where the quest for exchange value accumulation has become the driving force.

4. M-M'. We can extend Marx's stages one more step to the *paper economy,* in which, for many transactions, concrete commodities "disappear" even as an intermediary step in the expansion of exchange value. Manipulations of symbols according to arbitrary and changing tax rules, accounting conventions, depreciation, mergers, public relations imagery, advertising, litigation, etc., all result in a positive ΔM for some, but no increase in social wealth, and hence an equal negative ΔM for others. Such "paper entrepreneurialism" and "rent-seeking" activities seem to be absorbing more and more business talent. Echoes of Frederick Soddy are audible in the statement of Robert Reich (1983, p. 153) that "the set of symbols developed to represent real assets has lost the link with any actual productive activity. Finance has progressively evolved into a sector all its own, only loosely connected to industry." Unlike Soddy, however, Reich does not appreciate the role played by biophysical limits in redirecting efforts from manipulating resistant matter and energy toward manipulating pliant symbols. He thinks that, as more flexible and information-intensive production processes replace traditional mass production, somehow financial symbols and physical realities will again become congruent. But it may be that as physical resources become harder to acquire, as evidenced by falling energy rates of return on investment (Cleveland, et al., 1984), the incentive to bypass the physical world by moving from M-C-M' to M-M' becomes ever greater. We may then keep growing on paper, but not in real-

ity. This illustration is fostered by our national accounting conventions. It could be that we are moving toward a nongrowing economy a bit faster than we think. If the cost of toxic waste dumps were subtracted from the value product of the chemical industry, we might discover that we have already attained zero growth in value from that sector of the economy.

Faulty National Accounting and the Treachery of Quantified Success Indicators

Our national accounts are designed in such a way that they cannot reflect the costs of growth, except by perversely counting the resulting defensive expenditures as further growth. It is by now a commonplace to point out that GNP does not reveal whether we are living off income or capital, off interest or principal. Depletion of fossil fuels, minerals, forests, soils, etc., is capital consumption, yet such unsustainable consumption is treated no differently from sustainable yield production (true income) in GNP. But not only do we decumulate positive capital (wealth), we also accumulate negative capital (illth) in the form of toxic-waste deposits and nuclear dumps. To speak so insouciantly of "economic growth" whenever produced goods accumulate, when at the same time natural wealth is decumulating and man-made illth is accumulating represents, to say the least, an enormous prejudgment about the relative size of these changes (Hueting, 1980). Only on the assumption that environmental sources and sinks are infinite does such a procedure make sense.

Another problem with national accounts is that they do not reflect the "informal" or "underground" economy. Estimates of the size of the underground economy in the United States range from around 4 percent to around 30 percent of GNP, depending on the technique of estimation (Tanzi, 1983). The underground economy has apparently grown in recent times, probably as a result of higher taxes, growing unemployment, and frustration with the increasing complexity and arbitrariness of the paper economy. In terms of our previous discussion it is as if the excesses of the paper economy cause a reversion all the way to the barter economy. Some of the inefficiency of barter is overcome by setting up networks of traders with a multilateral clearing system of credit units, usually kept on someone's home computer. Like household production, of which it is an extension, none of these informal productive activities are registered in GNP. Their growth represents an adaptation to the failure of traditional economic growth to provide employment and security. As an adaptation to growth failure in the GNP sector the underground economy may represent a forced first step toward an SSE. But not everything about the underground economy is good. Many of its activities (drugs, prostitution) are illegal, and much of its basic motivation is tax evasion, although in today's world there may be some noble reasons for not paying taxes.

The act of measurement always involves some interaction and interference with the reality being measured. This generalized Heisenberg Principle is especially relevant in economics, where the measurement of a success index on which rewards are based, or taxes calculated, nearly always has perverse repercussions on the reality being measured. Consider, for example, the case of management by quantified objectives applied to a tuberculosis hospital, as related to me by a physician. It is well known that TB patients cough less as they get better. So number of coughs per day was taken as a quantitative measure of the patient's improvement. Small microphones were attached to the patients' beds, and their coughs were duly recorded and tabulated. The staff quickly perceived that they were being evaluated in inverse proportion to the number of times their patients coughed. Coughing steadily declined as doses of codeine were more frequently prescribed. Relaxed patients cough less. Unfortunately the patients got worse, precisely because they were not coughing up and spitting out the congestion. The cough index was abandoned.

The cough index totally subverted the activity it was designed to measure and reward because people served the abstract quantitative index instead of the concrete qualitative goal of health. Perversities induced by quantitative goal setting are pervasive in the literature on Soviet planning: set the production quota for cloth in linear feet, and the bolt gets narrower; set it in square feet, and the cloth gets thinner, set it by weight, and it gets too thick. But one need not go as far away as the Soviet Union to find examples. The phenomenon is ubiquitous. In universities a professor is rewarded according to number of publications. Consequently the length of articles is becoming shorter as we approach the minimum publishable unit of research. At the same time the frequency of coauthors has increased. More and more people are collaborating on shorter and shorter papers. What is being maximized is not discovery and dissemination of coherent knowledge but number of publications on which one's name appears.

The purpose of these examples of the treachery of quantified success indexes is to suggest that, like them, GNP is not only a passive mismeasure but also an actively distorting influence on the very reality that it aims only to reflect. GNP is an index of throughput, not welfare. Throughput is positively correlated with welfare in a world of infinite sources and sinks. But in a finite world with fully employed carrying capacity, throughput is a *cost.* To design national policies to maximize GNP is just not smart. It is practically equivalent to maximizing depletion and pollution.

The usual reply to these well known criticisms of GNP is: "So it is not perfect, but it is all we have. What would you put in its place?" It is assumed that we *must* have some numerical index. But why? Might we not be better off without the GNP statistic, even with nothing to "put in its place"? Were not the TB patients better off without the cough index, when physicians and administrators had to rely on "soft" qualitative judgment? The world before 1940 got along well enough without calculating GNP. Perhaps we could come up with a better system of national accounts, but abandoning GNP need not be postponed until then. Politically we are not likely to abandon the GNP statistic any time soon. But in the meantime we can start thinking of it as Gross National Cost.

The Ambivalent "Information" Economy

The much-touted "information economy" is often presented as a strategy for escaping biophysical limits. Its modern devotees proclaim that "whereas matter and energy decay according to the laws of entropy . . . information is . . . immortal." And, further, "The universe itself is made of information—matter and energy are only simple forms of it" (Turner, 1984). Such half-truths forget that information does not exist apart from physical brains, books, and computers and, further, that brains require the support of bodies, books require library buildings, computers run on electricity, etc. At worst the information economy is seen as a computer-based explosion of the symbol manipulations of the paper economy. McDonald's will feed us the high-tech burger, consisting of a thick patty of information between thin silicon wafers. More occult powers are attributed to information and its handler, the computer, by the silicon gnostics of today than any primitive shaman ever dared claim for his favorite talisman. And this in spite of the enormous legitimate importance of the computer, which needs no exaggeration.

But other notions of the information economy are by no means nonsensical. When the term refers to qualitative improvements in products to make them more serviceable, longer-lasting, more repairable, and better-looking (Hawken, 1983), then we have what was earlier referred to as "development." To think of qualitative improvement as the embodiment of more information in a product is not unreasonable.

But the best question to ask about the information economy is that posed by T. S. Eliot in "Choruses from 'The Rock'":

> Where is the wisdom we have lost in knowledge?
> Where is the knowledge we have lost in information?

Why stop with an information economy? Why not a knowledge economy? Why not a wisdom economy?

Knowledge is structured, organized information rendered intelligible and understandable. It is hard to imagine embodying a bit of isolated information (in the sense of communications theory) in a product. What is required for qualitative improvement of products is knowledge — an understanding of the purpose of the item, the nature of the materials, and the alternative designs that are permitted within the restrictions of purpose and nature of the materials. Probably many writers on the subject use the term "information" synonymously with "knowledge," and what they have in mind is really already a "knowledge economy." The important step is to go to a "wisdom economy."

Wisdom involves a knowledge of techniques plus an understanding of purposes and their relative importance, along with an appreciation of the limits to which technique and purpose are subject. To distinguish a real limit from a temporary bottleneck, and a fundamental purpose from a velleity, requires wise judgment. Growthmania cannot be checked without wise judgment. Since events are forcing us to think in terms of an information economy, it is perhaps not too much to hope that we will follow that thrust all the way to a "wisdom economy," one design feature of which, I submit, will be that of a dynamic steady state.

The main characteristics of such a wisdom economy were adumbrated by Earl Cook (1982) in his list of nine "Beliefs of a Neomalthusian," and I will conclude by listing them:

1. "Materials and energy balances constrain production."

2. "Affluence has been a much more fecund mother of invention than has necessity" — i.e., science and technology require an economic surplus to support them, and a few extra but poor geniuses provided by rapid population growth will not help.

3. "Real wealth is by technology out of nature"; or, as William Petty would have said, technology may be the father of wealth, but nature is the mother.

4. "The appropriate human objective is the maximization of psychic income by conversion of natural resources to useful commodities and by the use of those commodities as efficiently as possible"; and "The appropriate measure of efficiency in the conversion of resources to psychic income is the human life-hour, with the calculus extended to the yet unborn."

5. "Physical laws are not subject to repeal by men," and of all the laws of economics the law of diminishing returns is closest to a physical law.

6. "The industrial revolution can be defined as that period of human history when basic resources, especially nonhuman energy, grew cheaper and more abundant."

7. "The industrial revolution so defined is ending."

8. "There are compelling reasons to expect natural resources to become more expensive."

9. "Resource problems vary so much from country to country that careless geographic and commodity aggregation may confuse rather than clarify";—i.e., "It serves no useful purpose to combine the biomass of Amazonia with that of the Sahel to calculate a per capita availability of firewood."

Earl would have been the last person to offer these nine points as a complete blueprint for a wisdom economy. But I think we will all recognize that he got us off to a very good start.

References

Abramowitz, M. 1979. Economic growth and its discontents. In M. Boskin, ed. *Economics and human welfare.* New York: Academic Press.

Birch, C., and J. Cobb. 1981. *The liberation of life.* Cambridge: Cambridge University Press.

Clark, C. W. 1976. *Mathematical bioeconomics.* New York: Wiley.

Cleveland, C. J., et al. 1984. Energy and the U.S. economy: A biophysical perspective. *Science* 225.

Cook, E. 1982. The consumer as creator: A criticism of faith in limitless ingenuity. *Energy Exploration and Exploitation* 1(3).

Daly, H. E. 1980. The economic thought of Frederick Soddy. *History of political economy* 12(4).

————. 1985. The circular flow of exchange value and the linear throughput of matter-energy: A case of misplaced concreteness. *Review of Social Economy* (December).

Ehrlich, P., and A. Ehrlich. 1981. *Extinction.* New York: Random House.

Georgescu-Roegen, N. 1971. *The entropy law and the economic process.* Cambridge, Mass.: Harvard University Press.

Hawken, P. 1983. *The next economy.* New York: Ballantine.

Hirsh, F. 1976. *Social limits to growth.* Cambridge, Mass.: Harvard University Press.

Hueting, R. 1980. *New scarcity and economic growth.* Amsterdam: North-Holland Publishing Co.

Keynes, J. M. 1930. The economic possibilities for our grandchildren. In *Essays in persuasion.* New York: Norton.

Reich, R. B. 1983. *The next American frontier.* New York: Penguin.

Simon, J. 1981. *The ultimate resource.* Princeton, N.J.: Princeton University Press.

Tanzi, V., ed. 1983. *The underground economy in the United States and abroad.* Lexington, Ky.: Heath.

Turner, F. 1984. Escape from modernism. *Harper's* (November).

15.
How Can We Improve Our Chances?

A List of Suggestions

I was asked to make a summary of the conference, an assembly of all the good ideas that were put forth by all the Cassandras, under the title "How Can We Improve Our Chances?" I have to admit puzzling over the words "we" and "chances." Who is meant by the "we"? Improve our "chances" for what?

To enlighten myself, I asked people at the conference exactly that question, "How can we improve our chances?" with no further elaboration. The people I asked were not bothered at all by what I had found ambiguous; they just went right ahead and told me how we can improve our chances.

They produced a rich list. Here are some of the things they said:

1. As a number-one priority we can stabilize the human population.

2. We can try to bring the concept of sustainability into all decision making.

3. We can create a political organization, like the Green parties in Europe.

4. We need to add something to the price signal so that it will be a better indication of real scarcity and will therefore stimulate more sensible allocations and decisions.

5. We can help other people ask and answer the questions we are addressing, share our data and methods, get people in each part of the world to be measuring and defining their own carrying capacity for themselves and thereby informing their own decisions.

6. We should help the large environmental organizations to organize their public education efforts so that they are concerted and therefore more powerful; we should do it by concentrating on the big common messages, on colorful stories that illustrate our points, and on humor, cartoons, and a light approach.

7. We should have a Cassandra Hot Line, an 800 number people could call. (I am not sure who is to answer the phone or whether they are to dispense data, solace, or predictions.)

8. We can provide more information on the richness of the tropical forest as a resource — and get that information from the indigenous peoples, who know it better than we do.

9. We can find a way of informing leaders and the public about the insidious, almost invisible loss of essential resources like topsoil so that they can put protective regulations in place in time, instead of too late.

10. We can speak up for the most neglected parts of the biota, the soil microorganisms, which link together all food chains and to which we never pay sufficient attention.

11. We can conduct environmental briefings for viable presidential candidates two years before the campaign begins, so that they will have time to listen.

12. We can focus on human resource development as well as on natural resources — especially in the Third World, people are a neglected resource.

13. We can do much more with school curricula. Kids in school are a captive audience. We need to work not only with the science curriculum, teaching how the world works, but also with general decision-making skills.

14. We can have more such conferences, with other kinds of people in attendance, especially educators and politicians.

Most of these suggestions imply that the "we" in question is all humanity, or at least all environmental activists and other right-thinking people. The "chances" seem to refer to the chances for avoiding catastrophe, or perhaps the chances to make a better world.

I would like to add to the list of suggestions here by interpreting the "we" very narrowly, to refer to myself, the other speakers at the conference, and others who think of themselves as Cassandras. And I would like "chances" to mean chances to stop being Cassandras, in the sense that we retain and improve our ability to see the future consequences of present actions, but that we free ourselves of the curse of not being listened to. Rather than focus on things to *do* and the kinds of power and organizations we need to *have,* I would like to ask how we need to *be.* We need to do the things that need to be done in a certain way, with an inner strength and an outward compassion. Otherwise, no matter what we do, it will not suffice.

In my exploration of how we need to be in order not to be Cassandras, I will be making three highly debatable assumptions. I assume that if our viewpoint has not prevailed it is primarily because of some way that we *are* that contradicts or weakens the strength of what we say and do. I also assume that we can change, or a better word would be "rediscover," who we are. And finally, I assume that the redefinition of who we are not only is the key to releasing our own credibility and power but also is somehow at the very foundation of what our industrial society is and why it does not want to listen to what we say.

I have no intention of defending these assumptions. I think that they belong not in the domain of truth but in the domain of belief, as do the opposite assumptions—that our failures arise not from us but from our adversaries, that we cannot change who we are, and that who we are, our character, philosophy, and morality, has nothing to do with our effectiveness. In the domain of belief the question is not what is true but what set of beliefs produces the results you want.

So let us see what kinds of results we can produce by believing that who we are is the central question.

Who Are the Cassandras?

When I look at the people who call themselves Cassandras, including the speakers at this conference, I see a lot of good, and a lot to work with. I see people who are extremely well informed, who go out of their way to keep themselves plugged into the world's information currents—people I know I can go to for the most recent data, or for a succinct summary of the latest hypotheses about acid rain or nuclear winter. Most of us are at home with numbers, equations, and theories and are clear thinkers. Most have as deep an understanding of the way the planet works as any other human beings have.

There is a moral side to this understanding. Not only do we study the workings of the planet, but we have some sort of personal identity with them. I do not know which comes first; we loved the earth, so we chose to study it, or we studied the earth and thereby fell in love with it. In any case I know that I feel real pain when I see a bulldozer scooping up topsoil or a forest being clear-cut. Something of me has been hurt. I think that most of us "environmentalists" feel that way. We are motivated to our work by an extended identity, one that goes beyond our own skins and our own comforts. I would call any such extended identity, whether it extends to persons or things or ecosystems, love. We are motivated not by greed but by love.

The "Cassandras" I know are amazingly courageous. It takes courage as well as endurance to go out again and again to say things people do not want to hear, to listen to the names people call us as they ignore our warnings and go on with their depredations. It especially takes courage because most of us do not really think we will prevail. We are often frustrated, angry, sad, and lonely. We feel that we are voices crying in the wilderness *for* the wilderness. It would be so much simpler to be in some other business. But we keep at it, day after day, year after year.

Because of our deep concern we have gone beyond our scientific training to be communicators, often at the expense of our credibility in our own scientific fields. We are popularizers, outreachers. As a group we are unusually articulate and, for academicians, fairly canny about the way information works on political decisions.

We work rather effectively, although not very deliberately, as a community. We stay informed about and constantly use each other's work. We pass around powerful information. We respect, defend, and support each other in hundreds of ways, although we rarely have much time to spend together. I think we could be more effective as a community with a little thought and organization, but informally we already hold together well.

Above all, *we are not really Cassandras.* We have had too much influence to deserve that label. As a group we have shaped the thinking and the policies of our society, certainly not as much as we would have liked to, and not yet enough to turn around the trends that most worry us. But we have added whole concepts to the culture — the tragedy of the commons, the population bomb, limits to growth, lifeboat ethics, Spaceship Earth. We have shaped the environmental legislation of the industrial nations. We are recognized and have access to the media far beyond that of most other members of our professions.

In short, we are part of, though by no means all of, that elect set of people in any society who are its idea generators — the people who interpret society to itself, set up its arguments, frame its issues, define its categories, coin its phrases. We are at the primary social leverage point, the source of ideas. As John Maynard Keynes (1936, pp. 383–84) said:

The ideas of economists and political philosophers, both when they are right and when they are wrong, are more powerful than is commonly understood. Indeed the world is ruled by little else. Practical men, who believe themselves to be quite exempt from any intellectual influence, are usually the slaves of some defunct economist. Madmen in authority, who hear voices in the air, are distilling their frenzy from some academic scribbler of a few years back. I am sure that the power of vested interests is vastly exaggerated compared with the gradual encroachment of ideas.

Changing the System—Physical Change versus Information Change

Of course, we are not the only people shaping the ideas of society. There are plenty of voices, stronger at the moment than ours, saying that the environment is a luxury not worth the cost, that there are no limits to exploitation, and that virtually all other human values must be subordinated to the values of material accumulation and military power. To prevail, we are going to have to use the power of ideas more skillfully than they do. That means, I think, understanding fully and profoundly, first, how ideas create societies and, second, how they create our own selves and our effectiveness.

I study the structure of systems; that is my profession. Economic systems, biological systems, geophysical systems, all have interconnections— the flow of materials, energy, and information through them—that we call their structure and that dominate their behavior. If a system is behaving perversely, its structure must be changed before any other behavior is possible.

In some sense we all know that, and many of us, when we see a world in which hunger and poverty are endemic, ecosystems are being degraded, and weapons are growing irrationally, call for a change of the system. When we do that, however, we have little real sense of what a change in the system means, or where systems come from in the first place.

I submit that our terribly complex socioeconomic systems are shaped by two basic forces. The first is the physical operation of the universe, which we human beings like to think we understand. When I model a system, my belief in physical laws causes me to be sure that material quantities are conserved; they do not unaccountably appear into or disappear out of the system. Perpetual-motion machines are not allowed. Work is not done without expenditure of energy. Human beings are born, age, and die. Factories and machines stay where they are put, and they slowly wear out. Products are made out of materials, not just money or labor or capital.

These physical characteristics of systems follow what Garrett Hardin has called class I truth—what we say or believe about them has absolutely no influence on how they behave. They are the least changeable parts of a system's structure. They are the *constraints* within which a system has to operate; they are not the ultimate source or guiding force.

The *source* of system structure, the real leverage point for change, is its information—the shared, slowly changing, often unspoken set of social beliefs, and the locally available, always changing streams of specific information, which together influence all human decisions, actions, technologies, and organizations. The human information system works on the physical universe, constrained by its laws, but within those laws there is scope for all the varied inventions, organizations, and cultures that human beings have produced over the ages.

The information sphere operates almost entirely as Hardin's class II and class III truths. In this arena things are very much influenced by what is wished, believed, and said. Class II truths have the slippery tendency to be made true by the very act of saying them: "Reagan cannot lose the election." "Every child must have a Cabbage Patch doll." "The Russians are out to destroy us." Class III truths can be made untrue or destroyed in the saying: "There will be a secret attack on Tehran next week." "I think I'm about to sneeze." "I am not an alcoholic."

Simply making the distinction between the physical part of systems and the information part already goes a long way toward untangling snarled thinking. Economics, for example, keeps slipping into the belief that prices can create physical resources, forgetting that prices are information and resources are matter and energy. Though prices and resources are indeed interrelated in economic systems, one is not a substitute for or guarantee of the other. Many of us make a similar mistake about technology. Technology is information, independent of the constraints of space and time. Information can indeed solve problems, but only as it is embedded in physical capital fueled by physical materials, labor, and energy, which have real costs and take real time to put into place.

But the worst confusion between the physical and information parts of systems comes when we think of changing a system. We tend to picture system change in physical terms—building or tearing down something, forcing or restraining something, investing or moving or taking or subsidizing, hiring or firing or organizing or pushing around. It always seems like a lot of physical effort and sacrifice. No wonder talk of changing a system makes people cringe.

Over the very short term social systems are indeed dominated by their physical setups—how many people there are and where, what kinds of buildings and roads and factories there are, what kinds of channels the money flows in, what materials and genes have accumulated where in the ecosystem. If a system is to be changed very thoroughly and quickly, bombs and bulldozers are indeed the best agents. But over the long term *social systems are shaped almost entirely by the information-sphere,* within the constraints of physical laws.

E. F. Schumacher illustrated this point when he noted that repeated inputs of physical capital have not turned India into a prosperous industrial society, whereas Europe after World War II, about as devoid of physical capital as India, rebuilt with amazing speed. The information-spheres of the two places were entirely different, and so physical capital produced different results.

Here is another example, one of my favorite systems stories. A suburb was built in Holland with many houses, identical in every way, except that in some of the houses the electric meter happened to be put in the basement, where no one ever saw it, and in other houses the meter was in the hall by the front door. Though there were no other differences, electricity consumption was one-third lower in the houses with the meter in the hall. The difference was only in the availability of information. Do you begin to see how easy changing a system can be, if the right information is just put into the right place?

Systems arise, in the long term, from information and ideas. They can be changed most easily through information and ideas. Like the atmosphere, the information-sphere flows through us, through our minds, so thoroughly and constantly that we are hardly aware of it. We take information in and put it out. Every word we speak, every action and gesture either reinforces and endorses the socially shared information-sphere or challenges and changes it.

That is our work, to shape the information-sphere of society so that it supports systems of sufficiency, sustainability, and justice, instead of scarcity and waste, degradation and oppression. As Thoreau said in *Walden,* "It is something to be able to paint a picture—it is far more to carve and paint the very atmosphere and medium through which we look."

Doing that work effectively requires excruciatingly thoughtful and precise speaking and acting. With every word we are literally shaping reality, for ourselves and others. We have got to be more careful, and more powerful, in what we say, beginning with what we say about ourselves.

Down with Cassandra, Up with Socrates

First and foremost and immediately, let us drop the label "Cassandra." It reinforces the idea that we are predicting instead of offering choices and therefore affirms one of the information sphere's most damaging assumptions: that people are helpless about the future. Even worse, it reveals a deep assumption that we are making about ourselves—that we are ineffective, that we will not be listened to.

That is a class II truth. It is self-fulfilling. It arises either from a deep assumption about our own personal inadequacies or from an equally deep assumption about the basic contrariness of the whole human race (or both).

In either case, I submit that the evidence, if it were possible for us to see it without bias, does not support the assumption. If we stop selectively treasuring up the observations that support the Cassandra point of view, we can see that, along with the people not listening to us, there are plenty of people who are. For every truly greedy and hateful member of the human race there are thousands who care, who are willing to contribute, who are already consciously doing something to make the world a better place.

Since, deep inside, many of us truly believe ourselves to be Cassandras —I certainly have spent considerable time believing that—I submit that that belief itself has undercut our effectiveness in ways more subtle and more powerful than we can understand.

The best way I know to convey that assertion is to try to describe the total shift that occurred within me when I suddenly knew that in fact millions of people were going to read *The Limits to Growth*. The shift was profound but wordless; it is almost impossible to describe. It was one of those moments when the whole world suddenly looks different—a lightning strike, a light bulb coming on, an "aha" experience. Only in the light of the new and contrary way of looking could I see how deeply and unconsciously I had been living in the assumption that my work would make no difference. When that unseen class II truth disappeared, not only I but the whole team behind the book completed the writing differently and acted differently. On the surface we were doing the same things, but we were doing them with incredible energy, concentration, focus, ease, and grace, because, for the first time, we were telling ourselves that we would indeed make a difference.

If you have ever done any real work on yourself—trained for a marathon or given up smoking or drinking, for instance—you know what I am talking about. The toughest work of all is to make the incessant chatter inside you start saying, "I can run 26 miles," rather than, "I can't run 26 miles." The running is totally different when you know you can do it.

By labeling ourselves Cassandras, but, more important, by thinking of ourselves as Cassandras, we are sapping our own internal energy and creating not-being-listened-to as a reality. Please, let us adopt another label. There must be someone of Greek legend who lovingly drew out of people the wisdom that was already in them, someone who assumed and thereby created nobility in his fellows, someone who led the way toward a better world, not by exerting physical might and bashing around systems but by clearing up the information-sphere. Someone who was listened to, not only then but still, centuries later.

The name that comes to me is Socrates. I would rather be a Socrates than a Cassandra.

What Does It Mean to Be a Socrates?

Since I am using both Cassandra and Socrates here as symbols, I am free to define them to serve my purpose. No matter what the Greeks thought about those two characters, here is how I would describe their modern descendants.

Cassandras have a lot of knowledge, a mine of information, which is not really carefully sorted, fact from opinion, assumption from value. Although the Cassandras of my acquaintance are far more intellectually honest than most of their opponents, still they intermix their biases with their knowledge and sort the evidence to suit their preconceptions.

A *Socrates* would be relentless in the pursuit of intellectual integrity. He or she would screen every word spoken or written, to be sure that facts, assumptions, and values were sorted out and labeled correctly. There would be an unceasing effort to make all inputs to the information-sphere concise, clear, compelling, and as truthful as possible, in order to empower others to act on the best possible information.

A *Cassandra* unconsciously tinges all information with hopelessness. He or she communicates grimness, struggle, sacrifice, and impossibility; is quick to present the obstacles and problems in a situation; remembers and relates stories primarily about mistakes and failures.

A *Socrates* communicates hope, potential, and possibility and presents opportunities as well as obstacles. He or she is honest and accurate in describing difficulties but portrays them as challenges and learning experiences, not as proof of basic unworkability. The stories told are of good news, of what is working, of real successes that others can copy. The underlying belief of a Socrates is that success is possible, maybe even easy.

The *Cassandras* of the world assume that their audience is hostile or lethargic or selfish or weak or simply not listening. Although they interact with individual people in an open, loving, and empowering way, their impression of the mass of humanity is hopelessly negative. They speak of and to people condescendingly. They do not believe that anyone really cares. They feel and act as though they are carrying the burden for humanity all alone.

Those who aspire to be *Socrates* assume that the people they address are willing, open, able, caring, and noble. They view their job not as kicking recalcitrant humanity into action but as releasing in humanity that sense of community and contribution that is yearning to be expressed. They speak to people on the level. They feel no lonely burden, because they include everyone as potential partners.

The *Cassandras* create terrible pictures in people's minds. They are eloquent in sharing their fears and in describing what will happen if the world does not shape up. They are clear about what is to be avoided. But they have not really defined or shared the world of sufficiency and sustainability they are working toward. They are more comfortable describing disasters than visions.

A *Socrates,* while acknowledging the potential for disaster, is above all a person of vision, who gives people a clear image of a world to move toward, as well as a world to move away from. Like Martin Luther King, a Socrates has a Dream and is able to articulate it as if it were real and present so that others can identify in it their own dream and experience it concretely enough to start building it.

No one can be classified as pure Cassandra or pure Socrates. I certainly see each of them within myself. But the environmental movement has largely been perceived as Cassandra, doomsaying, people- and progress-hating, destructive rather than constructive. I believe that is an exaggerated but not entirely false perception of how many of us have *been* in public.

Our strong point is our perception of nature, in all its complexity and richness and awesomeness. We acknowledge and treasure all that is here; we celebrate and defend wholeness. Our ethic is that of Aldo Leopold (1949, p. 262). "A thing is right when it tends to preserve the integrity, stability, and beauty of the biotic community. It is wrong when it tends otherwise." About nature we are visionary. That is something new and vital that we are adding to the information-sphere.

Our weak point is our perception of humanity, including ourselves. We absorbed a demeaning concept of humankind from the information-sphere without questioning it, and we got an especially strong dose of it with our scientific training. Joseph Wood Krutch (1959) says:

Though man has never before been so complacent about what he *has,* or so confident of his ability to *do* whatever he sets his mind upon, it is at the same time true that he never before accepted so low an estimate of what *he is.* That same scientific method which enabled him to create his wealth and to unleash the power he wields, has, he believes, enabled biology and psychology to explain him away — or at least to explain away whatever used to seem unique or even in any way mysterious. . . . Truly he is, for all his wealth and power, poor in spirit.

We do not see human beings in their full complexity and richness and awesomeness. We do not acknowledge or treasure all that is there, celebrate and defend the wholeness of people, which is a part of, inseparable from, the wholeness of nature. We have not been trained, or even permitted, by the information-sphere of industrialism to understand sufficiently either other people or ourselves.

E. F. Schumacher (1977, pp. 133–34, 139–40) says:

The quality of our understanding depends decisively on the detachment, objectivity, and care with which we learn to study ourselves. . . . Instruction on cultivating self-knowledge . . . is the main content of all traditional religious teachings but has been almost entirely lacking in the West for the last hundred years. That is why we cannot trust one another, why most people live in a state of continuous anxiety, why despite all our technologies communication becomes ever more difficult, and why we need ever more organized *welfare* to plaster over the gaping holes torn by the progressive disappearance of spontaneous social cohesion. . . .

The world . . . is a place where the things modern man continuously talks about and always fails to accomplish *can actually be done.* The generosity of the Earth allows us to feed all mankind; we know enough about ecology to keep the Earth a healthy place; there is enough room on the Earth, and there are enough materials so that everybody can have adequate shelter; we are quite competent enough to produce sufficient supplies of necessities so that no one need live in misery. Above all, we shall then see that the economic problem is a convergent problem *which has been solved already:* we know how to provide *enough* and do not require any violent, inhuman, aggressive technologies to do so. There *is* no economic problem and, in a sense, there never has been. But there is a moral problem, and moral problems are not convergent, capable of being solved so that future generations can live without effort. No, they are divergent problems, which have to be understood and transcended.

The real public discussion we are engaged in is only apparently about the Clean Air Act or toxic wastes or a nuclear freeze. Those issues are the surface manifestation of the essential argument, which is about Who We Are—that is, who we *all* are, the whole human race in its place in the universe. Our opponents are saying that we are, and ought to be, Hector, or Prometheus, or Croesus, or maybe Attila. We, the environmentalists, are affirming their basic point, viewing man as a warrior, transformer, materialist, and destroyer but asserting that he ought not to be. Meanwhile, we view ourselves as Cassandras, admitting that we do not really believe in any alternative. It is not a very powerful position from which to argue.

We need to engage the issue at its foundation and reshape the most basic assumption of the information-sphere. We need to assert that human beings also have within them a Socrates, a Christ, a Buddha, a Gandhi. We need to point out that truth, wisdom, self-insight, and compassion are also human qualities and that they can be found and developed in anyone. To do that successfully, we need to find, express, and become comfortable with the Socrates within ourselves.

References

Keynes, J. M. 1936. *The general theory of employment, interest, and money.* Reprint; New York: Harcourt, 1964.
Krutch, J. W. 1959. *Human nature and the human condition.* New York: Random.
Leopold, A. 1949. *Sand County almanac.* New York: Sierra Club/Ballantine, 1970.
Schumacher, E. F. 1977. *A guide for the perplexed.* New York: Harper & Row.

16.
Romance and Resources

MOST OF US, no matter what our social origin, wish that our condition were in some way better than it is, that we were richer, more talented, younger, more attractive, healthier, more respected than we are. While the world around us may force unpalatable truths upon us, our minds, responding wondrously to our desires, create romantic worlds of illusion and hope, illusion for the here-now, hope for the here-after. In the Western world, a world of resource frontiers, romance is a positive externality of the economic process known as "resource development." Even the word "development" is a romantic euphemism for efficient exploitation and exhaustion of resources.

The Meaning of Resource Romance

Romance is a luxury available to the beneficiaries of the profitable exploitation of natural resources, to those who have made economic life a positive-sum game by unlocking nature's stores and flows of energy. Those fortunates have here-now romance; the unfortunates of this world, for whom economic life remains a zero-sum, or even a negative-sum, game have only here-after romance, commonly called "religion" or "faith." The almost incredible success of Western man in creating and sustaining an economy based on natural-resource bonanzas for more than 450 years has for many turned the romance of discovery and economic advance into a here-now religion called "progress."

Here-now romance is seeing things, including yourself, as you would like them to be, rather than as you fear they are. It is a belief system that we use to determine such things as what is right and proper, what we expect to happen, or, better yet, what we want to happen in certain situations rather than descriptions of what is actually happening. This romantic system of beliefs serves as a moral and intellectual screen through which we filter information, thereby structuring our perception of reality. In philosophy it is the noble savage rather than the hairless ape. In economics it is the "invisible hand" of social welfare rather than income distribution by force. In demographic theory it is the demographic transition, as opposed to Malthusian controls on population. In engineering or physics it is perpetual motion rather than time's arrow of entropy. In Las Vegas or Monte Carlo it is the feeling that we are going to beat the house odds. In marketing it is the idea that a certain brand of automobile, deodorant, or toothpaste will make us irresistible. In resources it is striking it rich and never running out, whether it is oil, arable land, or water, the romance of an endless frontier.

Because Western man has been for centuries a miner, of soil nutrients and groundwater as well as of iron ore and gold, it seems appropriate to note that a famous mining engineer, T. A. Rickard, started his book *The Romance of Mining* by noting that "the god of prospecting is Billiken, the imp of good luck," and he closed the book with a toast to the prospector, whom he called "the herald of empire and the pioneer of industry." In other words, Rickard's prospector filled the same role in the progress religion as did the Pathfinder of James Fenimore Cooper and the Daniel Boone of manifest destiny. This role, depending as it does on the luck of discovery, is fully as romantic as that of the noble Indian of Francis Parkman, the virtuous farmer of Thomas Jefferson, or the nature worshiper of John Muir and Liberty Hyde Bailey.

Whenever romance has become institutionalized, it has drawn attackers. Almost 400 years ago Cervantes tilted at the windmills of institutionalized chivalry. During the Enlightenment, Voltaire slashed at the Panglosses of the universal-beneficence establishment who condoned cruelty and slavery in the name of religion. Still later Malthus, himself a curate, gently pricked the hot-air balloons of the institutionalized exponents of perpetual economic progress. But romance is sturdy, and its prophets have continued to prosper.

Mainstream thought of the late eighteenth and early nineteenth centuries had its prophets expounding romantic notions with regard to natural resources. Montesquieu (1748) said ". . . flocks increase with the people to take of them." In other words, food production increases as population increases. A few years later Count Buffon said, "The power of nature is inexhaustible." Consequently, there is no need to worry about resource scarcity. About the same time Adam Smith (1776) proclaimed his "invisible hand," which could, under the proper economic system, turn a myriad of selfish acts into a social good. Toward the close of the eighteenth century Condorcet (1795) came with his long prose hymn to the attainable ideal of human perfection linked with material abundance. In the early nineteenth century most readers probably agreed with William Godwin, who wrote (1831) that "the productivity of the earth can be endlessly improved," a Baconian variant of Montesquieu's dictum. It is interesting to note that Godwin thought Malthus immoral rather than simply incorrect, a point of view that persists to this day as neo-Malthusians often are described as "doomsayers." This suggests that the cultists of provident·progress are expressing religious conviction as well as romantic outrage.

Still, English skeptics dared to be heard. The self-serving rationalizations of early beneficiaries of the industrial revolution were criticized by persons as diverse as John Stuart Mill and Karl Marx, when the revolution, in the mid-nineteenth century, was only beginning to trickle some of its benefits down to the lower three-fourths of the British working classes. Toward the close of that century, as unrepaired defects in the industrial enterprise became perceived more widely, there arose in England a new kind of romance, the romance of socialism—a romantic way to solve resource problems while righting the maldistribution of income and wealth.

However interesting the nineteenth-century skirmishes between romance and reason in debates about resources and social justice, the most effective foe of romance in that century was neither philosopher nor political economist but a would-be minister turned scientist, Charles Darwin. The triumph among intelligent Englishmen of Darwin's view of evolution forced new attention to the Malthusian thesis that population tends to outgrow the resources on which it depends for support. Together Malthus and Darwin knocked *Homo* into the pitiless light of the ecological ring. Romantic man, his designed universe in shambles, his immortality shaky, and his material progress threatened, was on the ropes. But like all other believers, he fought back. He rebuilt the ramparts of his faith with such success, and saw so many justifications of it in his reading of subsequent economic history, that today what Malcolm Muggeridge once called the Church of Christ Economist is rich and flourishing, especially in America, where its establishments are warmed by the fires of economic creationism led by articulate and dynamic evangelists such as Julian Simon and the late Herman Kahn.

The Limitless Frontier: American Romance

The land frontier closed in the United States about 1900, but the resource frontier did not. For all the 80-plus years since the turn of the century, agricultural production in the United States has kept rising, producing more food than is consumed. The greatest increases have come in the past 30 years. This surplus-producing capacity has, in some ways, been politically embarrassing, requiring price supports, export stimulation, subsidized storage, and production disincentives. Crude oil and natural gas, the energy basis of our highly developed and affluent economy until the last decade, kept flowing from the ground. So great was our supply that crude oil and natural gas were wasted until the 1930s, when demand finally caught up with the supply. Reserves and production of the major industrial metals are in better shape now than they were 70 years ago. Timber, rapidly being depleted in the early years of this century, is now more than holding its own. Our resource frontier has been abundant, and as a result we have adopted a frontier economic philosophy. This philosophy is especially strong in Texas, where the frontier has been exceptionally prolific.

People on a resource frontier tend to be strong "supply-siders." On a resource frontier the supply of necessities is there for the work of taking and converting raw materials into food, shelter, and clothing. By definition the potential supply on a frontier exceeds that needed for subsistence; consequently, the next step in frontier development is the harvesting, digging, cutting, and pumping of excess supply for export and sale to more developed communities. Thus the frontiersman becomes a supplier.

Because he has demonstrated his ability to convert natural raw material into useful goods, the frontiersman looks upon himself, with considerable justification, as a creator of resources, often forgetting the scale of nature's efforts in providing him his materials and energy. He does not say that he exploits nature but says that he develops resources—as well as cities and nations. He is Rickard's "herald of empire and pioneer of industry," for he makes empire and industry possible. In the history of mining the rich prospector is exceedingly rare; it is the developer who follows the prospector and reaps the large rewards from the discovery of nature's storehouses. Likewise, it is the developer who follows the farmer, converting agriculturally productive land to its "highest and best use," which, for the developer, is residential or commercial property with concrete as its cash crop.

From the successful frontier communities of Western man comes his belief in his continuing ability to create fertile fields from barren wastes, to overcome the increasing leanness and depth of ores, to discover new and abundant sources of energy, to replace wasting coal measure and faltering oil fields, and, finally, if need be, to mine the moon and colonize space.

It is no accident that the frontier has been romanticized by the descendants of those who, while conquering it, probably cursed it heartily. The frontier vision is both escape and promise. For example, the principal escape features in the frontiers of Fenimore Cooper, of Francis Parkman, of Zane Grey, of Frederick Jackson Turner, and of John Wayne are nobility of character, brought forth by the harsh conditions of life at the cutting edge of civilization and triumphs over evil — the evil associated with older, declining, unhealthy, and unjust communities. Escape merges into promise when we note that in the romantic frontier there is no inescapable poverty, and a person's worth depends on individual merit and not on accidents of birth. D. W. Meinig (1969) captures the spirit of the frontiersman as he describes the Texan:

. . . individualistic and egalitarian, optimistic and utilitarian, volatile and chauvinistic, ethnocentric and provincial . . . under the influence of older rural and moral traditions . . . regards government as no more than a necessary evil, distrusts even informal social action as a threat to his independence, and accepts violence as an appropriate solution to certain kinds of personal and group problems. Material wealth is much admired for its own sake, but industriousness has no particular virtue; land has prestige, but especially in the form of the ranch or plantation. . . . There is an acceptance of equality among one's own kind, but a rigid sense of superiority over other local peoples, and a deep suspicion of outsiders as threats to the social order.

The frontier is regarded as the hearth of democracy, where the six-gun may temporarily be the great equalizer, but property rights form a much more secure basis for upward mobility independent of inherited wealth, family status, or culture. The great promise of the frontier lies in its being seen as a positive-sum game in which the few may attain great wealth without taking anything away from the many who may advance more modestly. Accordingly, the frontier has always beckoned the masses and the disadvantaged, not the aristocrats and the wealthy. The frontier philosophy, strongly undergirded by frontier history, leads naturally to the belief that man as a species is exempt from ecological constraints such as carrying capacity, which is why some sociologists speak to the exemptionalist paradigm, for what others call the growth or cornucopian model (Dunlap and Catton, 1980; Dunlap, 1980).

The Exemptionalist: An Economic Creationist

Contemporary exemptionalists are legion. In his book *The Ultimate Resource* (1981), Julian Simon maintains that natural resources are in essence infinite and that the growth of human populations, contrary to much popular opinion and substantial documentation, is a social good. Simon's book, which received a standing ovation from his congregation, represents the most nearly complete statement of the romantic views of the economic creationist. With an appealing here-now romance Simon and the late Herman Kahn presented an all-day session at the American Association for the Advancement of Science meetings in 1983 in Detroit, Michigan, where fellow exemptionalists gathered to attack the conclusions of the *Global 2000 Report,* a report that was less than optimistic about the world's resource future. So popular is this contemporary romanticism with the present administration that Simon was invited to join the American delegation attending the second United Nations conference on population in Mexico City, where they presented the free-market romantic persuasion on world population.

Simon sees man, the consumer of resources, as also the creator of resources, possessing a capacity to create more than he needs for subsistence. Thereby this frontiersman of unlimited supply is able to improve his level of living even while his numbers increase. Accordingly, man is Simon's "ultimate resource."

Simon's faith is expressed in certain propositions: (1) basic resources are getting more abundant and cheaper, not scarcer and more costly, and will continue to do so; (2) food production is growing faster than population; and (3) human population growth is good because the more people there are, the more genius and talent there will be to extend the human ability to "create" new resources.

According to Simon and his many followers, "Price is the appropriate measure of raw material scarcity," and "Both the cost and scarcity of materials continuously decline with the growth of income and technology." Inherent in this statement is the economist's substitution model of the production function, which implies substitution of nonphysical inputs for physical ones. Simon believes that, in the long run, energy as well as minerals will become more available and less costly:

We must constantly struggle against the illusion that each time we take a pound of copper from the earth there is less left to be used in the future. Too often we view natural resources as we view the inventory of the paper-clips warehouse; ship some of the paper clips, and fewer are left to ship. We must constantly remember that we *create* new paper clips and replenish the warehouse's inventory. . . . In exactly the same way, we *create* new supplies of copper and oil. That is, we expend time, capital, and raw materials to supply the service that an expensive product (or resource) renders. [Simon, 1981a, p. 32; emphasis added]

Time and capital are the major ingredients needed to draw raw material from the ground, and technology (a product of time and capital) will solve the problem in an innovative and cost-saving manner. There are no limits to ingenuity of man and assistance from technology:

The school of thought I represent . . . is not cornucopian. I believe that human ingenuity, rather than nature, is limitlessly bountiful. . . . I believe that with knowledge, imagination, and enterprise, we can muster from the earth all the mineral raw materials that we need and desire, at prices that grow smaller relative to other prices and to our total income. In short, our cornucopia is in the human mind and heart. [Simon, 1981b, p. 41]

Market economists like Simon believe that nonphysical factors such as capital (money) and technology can be substituted for physical resources. If we are to accept this assumption, production can increase as material input decreases. With the continuation of this process indefinitely, there will be material output without material input—the creationist's version of perpetual motion. As the creationist's perpetual-motion machine produces more captial than is consumed, old resources can be stretched and new ones created. To this way of thinking, the world can get along nicely without the need of natural resources (Solow, 1974, p. 11).

Simon's creationist beliefs extend to land resources as well. The frontier-development philosophy of the market economist views land as indestructible and as a commodity—a commodity of limitless supply for private exploitation. Simon does not believe that there is a limited amount of arable land that can be used for production of food supplies: ". . . the total stock of agricultural land is increasing. . . . new agricultural land is being made as some older land goes out of cultivation, leaving a very satisfactory net result for our agricultural future" (Simon, 1981a, p. 239). That growing populations need additional land for purposes other than food production, thus converting more and more croplands into nonagricultural uses such as energy production, transportation, and sprawling urban centers, seems of little consequence to Simon and his followers: "Many acts that we tend to think of despoiling the land actually leave increased wealth for subsquent generations. . . . ask yourself which areas in central Illinois will seem more valuable to subsequent generations—the places where cities now are, or the places where farmlands are? I think the former" (Simon, 1981a, p. 238).

If one is to believe that future generations will benefit from capital formation and the building of cities and that they will both be richer and have more knowledge than we, why should the present generation try to conserve and use our physical resources wisely? The immediate goal then would be to endorse increasing capital through aggressive exploitation of resources, enabling future generations to create whatever they may need. In this view resource exploitation is a perpetual positive-sum game.

The romantic belief that the market allocates resources efficiently is the basis for the conviction that the unplanned, or at least undirected, market economy provides for the best of all possible worlds, as well for the suspicion that Simon and his followers may be modern-day Panglosses.

The Neo-Malthusians: Simon's "Doomsayers"

Neo-Malthusians hold that the increasing cost of resources eventually will overcome the ingenuity of man and limit human population and living levels. Neo-Malthusians are also called ecologists, implying that the human species is subject to, not exempted from, ecological constraints. Whatever the choice of sobriquet, they argue:

(1) from the sharp restrictions in space and time on the conditions of the origin of the energy and mineral resources on which industrialized society depends, restrictions which mean that the best and biggest probably already have been discovered;

(2) from evidence that the volumes of useful materials in low-grade deposits and small oil fields do not increase commensurately with the increased work required to find and exploit such deposits;

(3) from the fact that energy alternatives, including fusion power, do not appear to offer the continuing decrease in energy costs required to maintain production at constant costs from leaner ores and smaller oil and gas fields;

(4) from the fact that arable land is limited and being depleted, and that the inputs needed to maintain crop production are already too expensive for many people of this world;

(5) from a conviction that diminishing returns from resource investment reflect physical rather than economic laws. [Cook, 1983, p. 192]

Economic creationists like Simon are expressing beliefs. In a contest for the mind of the perplexed, beliefs have a great advantage over reasoned conclusions; the latter usually involve a degree of uncertainty, and thus cannot be stated as firmly, simply, and reassuringly as can beliefs. The neo-Malthusian is unaccustomed to admitting that any of his conclusions have the character of belief, but some of them surely do. The foremost of the neo-Malthusian–ecologist beliefs are that *reason leads to truth* and that *truth is an ultimate good*. These beliefs set apart all true scholars from most of the rest of mankind, break up many marriages, and cause much unhappiness. In 1969, in his remarks in the *Annual Review of Plant Physiology* entitled "Resistance to Knowledge," Hans Gaffron pointed out that "we, 'the intellectuals,' are talking mainly to one another. Judging from what happens in the real world, very little of what is called common, or even obvious, knowledge among this small group seems to influence the behavior of the people and their chosen leaders who together constitute the living power of the species" (Gaffron, 1969, p. 1). The scholars and the conclusions that flow from them make certain that they will be alternately praised and reviled, as their conclusions alternately support or contradict the yearnings of the body social.

Earl Cook, a physical scientist and mining engineer, and I, a social scientist, found subjects of mutual interest bringing us into the ecological ring—he arriving much earlier than I and with a more solid understanding and respect of the physical environment. We spent many hours over the few years we had together looking at the interrelatedness of the systems most familiar to each of us. From our thoughts came the following neo-Malthusian beliefs on which we would carry forth our efforts:

1. We believe that materials and energy balance constrain production. A physical output cannot occur without a physical input. Materials and energy (physical), including arable land, differ fundamentally from information and capital, which are nonphysical. Nonphysical inputs are not subject to conservation laws or the entropy law—the law which recognizes that even the material universe is subject to an irreversible qualitative change. Accordingly, nonphysical information can increase without end, but materials and energy cannot.

2. We believe that affluence has been a much more productive mother of invention than has necessity, or any law of averages that produces a certain ratio of geniuses in every population. The discoveries and inventions that propelled a small fraction of mankind to levels of living undreamed by medieval monarchs, and allowed some of that minority to romanticize nature while exploiting her, came from the ingenious and aggressive use of resource surplus to meet the basic needs of human beings. Science and technology advance only in societies that can afford them and that value them; they do not mature in societies that are forced to devote all human effort to mere survival, such as in our developing nations of today. Therefore, we cannot agree with the romantic notion supported by Simon and other economic creationists that technology and human welfare are automatically advanced by population growth.

3. We believe that real wealth is by technology out of nature but that nature furnished a large portion of that wealth. Without the tremendous amount of work done in nature in concentrating flows of energy and stocks of resources, human ingenuity would be onanistic. When matter and energy are governed by other rules than those governing information, what does it matter that ingenuity may be limitless, that there may be a cornucopia "in the human mind and heart"?

4. We believe that physical laws are not subject to repeal by men and

that they transcend the laws of men. Of all the "laws" of economics, the "law" of diminishing returns comes closest to a physical law. In many cases it reflects physical laws. To maintain present levels of environmental quality, speed of transport, and resource productivity will require continued large amounts of nonrenewable energy resources as well as higher costs of renewable ones. As the work costs of obtaining many resources, including food, reflect increasing use of marginal land and leaner deposits, energy costs would need to decrease to keep product costs from rising. To increase present levels will almost surely require more than a commensurate increase in energy inputs.

5. We believe that the industrial revolution can be defined as that period of human history when basic resources, especially inanimate energy, grew cheaper and more abundantly available (production and consumption rose while prices declined) through geographic and geologic discoveries and by increasingly efficient conversion of discovered resources into goods and services. The most significant discoveries were underground energy stocks.

6. We believe that the industrial revolution so defined is ending and that the human cost of basic resources, especially of food and fuel, is rising. Studies by economic geologists have demonstrated a reversal of the secular declines in the prices of fuels and most metals within the last few decades. Although some economists, notably Harold Barnett, dispute this reversal, there is no doubt that the replacement costs (marginal-supply costs of crude oil and natural gas) have been rising steeply. Should a temporary slackening of demand create a so-called glut of either oil or gas, as we see today, the market price falls below the finding and development cost for "new" oil and gas, and is in no way a guide to future scarcity as Simon would claim it is. Prices reflect very short-term considerations, especially during periods of high interest and inflation rates, which are commonly changes in actual or perceived demand.

7. We believe that there are compelling reasons to expect natural resources to become more expensive, reasons that are geochemical, geophysical, and energetic. Rising cost is the other face of the warning stage of the depletion history of an earth resource, including mined soil, after technology and the economies of scale start to lose the battle against greater depth and decreasing natural concentrations of useful materials.

This neo-Malthusian or ecological view of resources is not romantic, but it is not gloomy either, except for those to whom work is tragedy and thought is pain. But most people want to believe Simon, who is astonishingly frank about his theoretical method. In one interview Simon admitted that he had to show that more people need not cause scarcities or environmental decay in the long run — to show that population growth is not a terrible evil. This argument suggests a reason why persons whose faith is in reason have shown such unseemly emotion toward Simon and "called me names," as he has complained. Simon acknowledges that his "increasing optimism" (romantic views) about the world's future pulled him out of a period of severe depression. He now offers the romance of resource creationism as an escape for others similarly afflicted.

The Debate

Simon's message soothes the rich and brings hope to the poor. To those who want to believe that the problems of hunger and poverty that afflict much of the world can be solved short of mass starvation and political repression, to those worried by inflation and unemployment in the industrialized nations, this voice of faith is seductive. Simon even claims that famine is difficult to define and would attribute the African plight to poor nutrition and disease, not necessarily starvation stemming from inadequate food production and distribution. None of us want our future foreclosed, nor that of our children and grandchildren. We in the developed nations are addicted to the freedoms of affluence, products of an expanding resource frontier. We value upward mobility in an expanding economy. People in poor societies passionately want a better life for their children, and political leaders in those countries maintain control as much through stimulation of that hope as through police power. The concept of limits to growth threatens vested interests and power structures; even worse, it threatens value structures in which many lives have been invested.

The economic creationist's romance is faith implying help from somewhere up above either in the form of Adam Smith's invisible hand, invoked to produce a global demographic transition to a stable population sometime in a distant prosperous future, or in the form of providential repeal of the Second Law of Thermodynamics, so that adequate energy will always be available for the work needed to support large, highly consumptive populations. The truth of geophysicists, geochemists, thermodynamicists, and agronomists seems to be no longer the truth that will set us free but the truth that will enslave us. Simon's argument appeals also to those who reject the concept of population control on religious, ethical, or political grounds, including some of the world's largest religious groups as well as doctrinaire Marxists. Clearly, the majority is on the side of the exemptionalists, those who promise a better life with no significant transfer of wealth from rich to poor.

Contrary to Simon's romantic beliefs, the growing population of the world, assisted by advances in modern medicine and better nutrition, lengthening life spans as well as reducing infant mortality, is straining the ability of our global resources to feed its numbers. Garrett Hardin wrote: "The basic conservative concept of ecologists is the idea of carrying capacity, which defines the population of the propositus species that can be supported by a given territory year after year without degrading the environment — that is without lowering its carrying capacity subsequently" (Daly, 1980, p. 119). A given fact is that the increased number of people on this planet will coexist in an environment where resources are limited. There are no new land frontiers to convert miraculously into croplands with large producing capacities. Orville Freeman (1982) pointed out that the grain-producing countries have come close to their production potential. With an increase of 70 million people annually to the 4.6 billion already here, world demand for food will continue to increase. Although industrialized nations, with assistance from mechanized agriculture and increased yields (energy-intensive inputs) have increased food supplies in both absolute and per capita terms, a similar case does not exist for the developing nations of the world, where population growth is greatest and both natural resource and food-producing capacity are most limited. Many nations, primarily in Africa and South Asia, areas of greatest need, have experienced a decrease in food production in both absolute and per capita terms. A grim reality and no romantic solutions exist to accommodate uncontrolled growing populations with sufficient food supplies in the time necessary to avert disaster.

Creationist followers tend to ignore or minimize the importance of certain facts that have a direct impact on food-production capability, such as: (1) climatic limitations that produce floods as well as droughts, thereby reducing crop yields; (2) soil degradation in the form of soil erosion, salinization, alkalinization, and chemical losses which contribute negatively to efforts to increase food production in the available croplands of the world; (3) desertification caused by drought as well as human exploitation; (4) an inadequate water supply in the form of either rainfall or irrigation; (5) insect infestation requiring use of costly pesticides that may not be affordable in countries in greatest need; and (6) inadequate energy supplies necessary to introduce cost-effective mechanized agriculture, including fuel for machinery and irrigation pumps. With limited physical inputs and limited capital few will be able to afford the technological inputs needed for miracles — miracles associated with frontiers richly endowed with natural resources.

Resource Policy: Romance or Reason

James Hutton (1726–97), founder of scientific geology, noted that all past changes in the earth's surface are the results of the same physical laws that operate today, an observation often quoted as, "The present is the key to the past." In a speech before the U.S. Senate in 1890, John Sherman stated, ". . . the best prophet of the future is the past." Too often, however, here-now romanticists fail to acknowledge an appreciation or awareness of resource history and physical laws, both of which have an impact on the present as well as the future. The romantic notion of frontiers awaiting exploitation by the "ingenuity of man" seems to be a law of reality accepted by exemptionalist policymakers. Perhaps they should consider the following:

1. The control of energy resources and other industrial raw materials has been the basis of national power since the start of the decline of gold and silver as empire makers. This decline started in July, 1588, with the defeat of the Spanish Armada with the assistance of English natural resources.

2. National power has never rested entirely on the development of internal markets; control of external supplies and markets is required, which usually implies command of trade routes. Sir Walter Raleigh said it very well: "Whoever commands the sea commands the trade: whoever commands the trade of the world commands the riches of the world, and consequently, the world itself"—a good description of the philosophy behind the British Empire. Since the decline of Spain and Portugal as world powers, the most powerful nations of the world have been those which in their early years enjoyed a surplus of arable land and coal: Great Britain, Germany, France, the United States, and, belatedly, the Soviet Union.

3. The natural resources that count, including arable land and coal, are unevenly distributed through the world. Not only are there resource have and have-nots, but the fact of difference in industrial development and economic power among nations means that there are resource-rich but poorly developed countries which must sell their resources to developed countries to have any hope of becoming industrialized themselves, or even, in some instances, to feed themselves.

4. Some resources are more important than others. Food, water, and energy are the most important. Without energy the resource environment is limited. Even food supply is a function of energy availability in the form of fuel and fertilizer.

5. The political fragmentation of the world into some 150 nations of widely differing resource endowments, capital accumulations, religions, and forms of government means that the geopolitics of resources has over-

riding importance in world affairs and that each nation will have its own view of the resource policy best suited to its aspirations.

6. A starving man will barter almost anything for food; consequently, food-production capacity is the world's most valuable resource.

7. Aquifer depletion, oil depletion, and soil erosion act as constraints on the world's most valuable resource, food production.

8. Egypt is today designated a "developing" nation; Greece was once the center of Western civilization; Rome fell in A.D. 476; Spain and Portugal were once world powers; Great Britain, France, Germany, and other smaller nations colonized the world; and the Ottoman Empire belonged to the Turks.

Resource policy has varied from nation to nation throughout history depending on availability and nationally perceived needs. With respect to use of our nonrenewable resources, modern policies have encouraged the following: (1) unrestricted exploitation for the benefit of the exploiters; (2) controlled exploitation with government ownership or taxation as a means to spread the benefits; (3) modest attempts to prevent or reduce exploitation that would diminish a renewable resource such as clean air, potable water, or wildlife; and (4) rare attempts to save something for future generations. At present the exemptionalists, controlling the major markets as well as the main planned national economies, are triumphant, pointing to the industrial-technological revolution as their vindication. The ecologists, for whom resource depletion and pollution are worldwide threats to human progress, have had some small successes in the area of pollution and endangered species but have been able to slow the exploitation of nonrenewable resources only where it manifestly conflicts with environmental preservation.

With the disintegration of the colonial system the global political environment now includes many more sovereign nations pursuing national policies independent of but within a globally interdependent society. Many of the problems of the global environment today can be traced to political roots deeply embedded in the past. The entry of many new nations into the world community followed the industrialization of the established nations of the world, which used the resources of their former colonies to attain world power. Newly acquired nationhood in an already technologically advanced era is likely to exacerbate instability as well as uncertainty. Yet even in those developed nations where political changes are institutionalized by means of constitutions which provide for the orderly change of political leaders, there exists a level of uncertainty as well as instability inherent in changes of leadership.

However persuasive the argument, it may not be possible for any government, stable or unstable, old or new, to plan and carry out policies that promote the intergenerational transfer of nonrenewable resources or the preservation and wise use of renewable resources. Prevailing beliefs dictate policies, and the policies favored today promote exploitation for the following reasons: (1) the desire of the exploiters, who often call themselves developers, for power; (2) increased consumer demand in developed and developing nations for the products and services that flow from exploitation; and (3) the demands of others than the exploiters to be included in the benefit flows. These others can effect their demands through expropriation and cartel control of production when the original exploiters are foreigners (a prime example is OPEC), or by means of taxation or nationalization when the exploiters are citizens. Those who have no means of coercion, such as the lesser-developed or oil-importing nations, or unborn generations in any nation, have little hope of diverting such benefits toward themselves.

Resource policy is an extremely complex subject. Policies advocated reflect both interests and philosophies. In the United States the interest of Texas, Oklahoma, Louisiana, and Kansas in oil and gas differs from that of the New England states. The same holds true for the interests of the farm belt, the interests of the food-producing areas differing from those of the food-consuming areas. Oil-importing countries have a different view of OPEC from that of oil-exporting countries. If we seriously consider the welfare of future generations instead of just the interests of our own generation, our view of resource policy may change. "But who is really interested in the survival of the species, in contrast to that of his family, his own culture, and the few people who represent the latter most brilliantly?" (Gaffron, 1969).

Time may change an exporting country into an importing country for both food and energy; since we all want to sell high and buy low, our policy will change. No resource policy designed to protect the interests of future generations, except through the accumulation of profits, has ever claimed more than lip service, either in the United States or in other countries, developed or developing.

In the United States the physical part of our resource frontier is aging while the cultural part remains vigorous. Oil-and-gas reserves are declining; we are already importing fossil fuels from other nations; groundwater supplies are being depleted, and the combination of available surface and groundwater is clearly insufficient for the needs of the coming century; our soil-conservation measures may turn out to be pitifully inadequate when we can no longer afford expensive replacements for natural soil fertility. However, the dynamics and mystique of the economic frontier remain the

Table 16.1. Intellectual Traditions of Growth Criticism

Biophysical or Means-based		Ethical or Ends-based	
Physical econo- mists and bio- economists	Frederick Soddy Kenneth Boulding N. Georgescus- Roegen John Ise A. J. Lotka J. Culbertson R. Wilkinson	Early critics of industrialism	John Ruskin Thomas Carlyle Henry Thoreau William Morris
		Distribution	G. K. Chesterton H. Belloc
Ecologists	Rachel Carson Paul Ehrlich Garrett Hardin Barry Commoner Eugene Odum	Rural agrarian critics of industrialism	Narodniki P. A. Kropotkin L. Tolstoy M. Gandhi
Systems ecologists	Howard Odum Kenneth Watt	Humanist economists	J. S. Mill E. F. Schumacher E. J. Mishan D. Goulet
Geologists	M. K. Hubbert Earl Cook Harrison Brown Preston Cloud		H. Daly
		Critics of technological society	Lewis Mumford Ivan Illich Jacques Ellul Theodore Roszak
Systems engineers	Jay Forrester Dennis Meadows Bruce Hannon Mihajlo Mesarovic and Edward Pestal	Emerging theology of ecology	Thomas Derr John Cobb Frederick Elder
Conservationists	G. P. Marsh William Vogt David Brower Denis Hayes	Political science of survival	William Ophuls Richard Falk L. K. Caldwell
Demographers	K. Davis N. Keyfitz		
Physicists	A. Lovins D. Abrahamson J. Holdren H. Bent		

SOURCE: Daly, 1979.

conceptual basis of our dominant cultural institutions, including the university. The physical deterioration of the frontier is expanding the arena of confrontation for the resource paradigm—the exemptionalist and the ecological.

The frontier or growth model is romantic, inspires hope, and requires belief that man, alone among living creatures, can bend the logic of the universe. The ecological or neo-Malthusian model is rational, creates concern, and calls for faith in the proposition that human reason, unaided by Providence, can create a comfortable earthly abode within the constraints imposed by universal logic and the constitution of this planet—a sustainable society. The greatest problem for the ecologists from Charles Darwin to Garrett Hardin and Paul Ehrlich, from Thomas Malthus to Dennis Meadows, King Hubbert, and Earl Cook (see table 16.1), is that they ruin romance. It is no wonder that they are called "doomsayers" and "spoilers" and that a commercial advertisement recently pleaded to put the "magic" back into the marketplace.

Faced with the evidence of possible severe future shortages of resources and of environmental degradation, together with uncontrolled population increases, we would like to believe that John Wayne and his technological cavalry will come riding over the hill in time. Others may prefer to rely on the "magic" of the marketplace. Both views are romantic, which means in conflict with reason. But, then, when did we allow reason to stand in the way of what we want to believe?

The world will not run out of resources, but they will grow more scarce and more costly. As they grow more costly, more and more people will not be able to afford them. . . . struggles for control of the world's remaining rich stores of energy will intensify. These stores are arable land (and surplus food), crude oil, coal, and nuclear fuels. . . . What I see is neither ecocatastrophe nor global warfare (although both remain possible), but the slow strangulation of economic hope and political freedom due to population growth finally overcoming the ability of battered nature to support the human horde. [Cook, 1982, p. 200]

References

Brown, L. R. 1978. *The worldwide loss of cropland.* Worldwatch Paper no. 24. Washington, D.C.: Worldwatch Institute.

———, and W. U. Chandler. 1985. *State of the world.* New York: Norton.

Cook, E. 1976. *Man, energy, society.* San Francisco: Freeman.

———. 1981. Tragedy of turfdom. *Social Science Quarterly* 63 (March): 23–29.

———. 1982. The consumer as creator. *Energy Exploration and Exploitation* 1:189–201.

Daly, H. E. 1977. *Steady-state economics.* San Francisco: Freeman.

————. 1979. Entropy, growth, and the political economy. In V. Kerry Smith, ed. *Scarcity and growth reconsidered.* Baltimore, Md.: Johns Hopkins University Press.

————, ed. 1980. *Economics, ecology, ethics.* San Francisco: Freeman.

Dunlap, R. E. 1980. Paradigmatic change in social science. *American Behavioral Scientist* 24:5–14.

————, and W. R. Catton. 1980. A new ecological paradigm for post-exuberant sociology. *American Behavioral Scientist* 24:15–47.

Ehrlich, P. R. 1981. An economist in wonderland. *Social Science Quarterly* 63 (March): 44–49.

Freeman, O., and R. Karen. 1982. Farmers and the money economy. *Technology Forecasting and Social Change* 22:183–200.

Gaffron, Hans. 1969. Resistance to knowledge. *Annual Review of Plant Physiology* 20:1–40.

Georgescu-Roegen, N. 1975. Energy and economic myths. *Southern Economic Journal* 41 (January): 347–81.

————. 1971. *The entropy law and the economic process.* Cambridge, Mass.: Harvard University Press.

Hardin, Garrett. 1968. Tragedy of the commons. *Science* 16 (December 13): 1243–48.

————. 1980. Second thoughts on "The Tragedy of the Commons." In H. Daly, ed. *Economics, ecology, ethics,* pp. 115–20. San Francisco: Freeman.

Meinig, D. W. 1969. *Imperial Texas: An interpretive essay in cultural geography.* Austin: University of Texas Press.

Simon, J. L. 1981a. *The ultimate resource.* Princeton, N.J.: Princeton University Press.

————. 1981b. The scarcity of raw materials. *Atlantic Monthly* 247 (June): 33–41.

Solow, R. 1974. The economics of resources or the resources of economics. *American Economic Review* (May): 1–14.

Webb, W. P. 1952. *The great frontier.* Boston: Houghton Mifflin.

Wortman, S., and R. W. Cummings, Jr. 1978. *To feed this world.* Baltimore, Md.: Johns Hopkins University Press.

Editors' Epilogue

As THE analyses assembled here make clear, the concerns of contemporary Cassandras about the future are diverse and unsettling: the growing pressures of overpopulation, the spreading perils of toxic substances, the increasing threat of thermonuclear war, and more. Irrespective of the individual focuses of their particular concerns, however, the Cassandras share a belief in the interrelatedness of the subproblems that in the aggregate constitute the "human predicament"—in the importance of the interactions between them and in the need to attack them with solutions that respect their interconnectedness.

Overpopulation contributes to poverty, and poverty breeds overpopulation. Reckless depletion of resource "capital" often damages the environmental machinery that provides humankind with resource "income." The planet's forests—crucial mediators of the hydrologic cycle, protectors of soil, and custodians of species diversity—are threatened simultaneously by overharvesting for fuel wood and lumber, the encroachment of agricultural lands and settlements, air pollution, and acid rain; and their diminution adds to the climate-threatening burden of atmospheric carbon dioxide already swollen by the last century's binge of combustion of fossil fuels. Human poverty and environmental impoverishment compound one another, and together they compound the chances of international conflict and nuclear war. And resources spent on tanks, fighter planes, and "Star Wars" will not be available to reforest denuded hillsides, scrub the acid-producing sulfur from the smokestacks of smelters and power plants, or build up food production in sub-Saharan Africa.

Also evident in the analyses assembled here is a shared optimism that a dismal future is *not* preordained. Our Cassandras clearly believe that now, more than ever, human beings have the power to make choices that can improve their prospects for a prosperous and secure world, as well as the prospects of their descendants for many generations to come. In this respect the Cassandras are far from the hopeless "doomsayers" that their critics often call them. They see hope in the future, ways out of the predicament, a pleasant and sustainable habitat for all of Spaceship Earth's human and nonhuman passengers—if only the choices that only human beings can make are made sensibly.

The Cassandras, then, have not been saying simply "doom"; they have been saying "doom, *if* . . . ," and offering alternative courses of action that can prevent the "if" from coming true. They would hardly have devoted so much time and energy to a cause they considered already lost.

In any case, we like to think that Earl Cook would have enjoyed himself at the Cassandra Conference. Both his friends and his ideas were much in evidence there.

About the Contributors

JILL SHORE AUBURN completed her Ph.D. in Zoology at the University of California, Davis. She also holds a master's degree in biology and psychology from Miami University, Oxford, Ohio. Her research interests center on the application of computers to systems-analysis problems.

VIOLETTA BURKE COOK is a staff assistant to the Dean of the College of Agriculture at Texas A&M University, serving in the International Agriculture Programs Office as a coordinator of international development projects. Her research interests focus on resource decision-making in developing nations and global energy policies. She has served on numerous interdisciplinary committees, including the board of the Association of University Directors of International Agriculture Programs and its Legislative Committee. She has also held positions as a legislative assistant to the late Senator Patrick V. Namara of Michigan, and a lecturer in political science, Texas A&M.

PAUL CRAIG is Professor in the Department of Applied Science at the University of California, Davis, and a Faculty Affiliate of the Energy and Resources Group at the University of California, Berkeley. After obtaining his Ph.D. in physics from the California Institute of Technology, Pasadena, he did physics research at the Los Alamos and Brookhaven national laboratories and energy-policy analysis at the National Science Foundation. He has recently published a textbook, *Nuclear Arms Race: Technology and Society* (with J. A. Jungerman).

HERMAN E. DALY is Alumni Professor of Economics at Louisiana State University, Baton Rouge. His interests in economic development, resources, environment, and population have resulted in some 50 articles in professional journals and anthologies as well as four books, including *Steady-*

State Economics and *Economics, Ecology, and Ethics*. He has been Ford Foundation Visiting Professor at the University of Ceará, Brazil; Visiting Fellow at the Australian National University; and Senior Fulbright Lecturer in Brazil; and he has been an advisor to many national and international organizations.

ANNE H. EHRLICH is Senior Research Associate in the Department of Biological Sciences at Stanford University. She is the coauthor of eight books — among them *Population, Resources, Environment, Ecoscience,* and *Extinction* — and of over 100 technical papers and popular articles on topics ranging from population genetics to nuclear winter. She served on the Executive Committee of the Board of Directors of Friends of the Earth from 1976 to 1985 and has held many other national and international advisory posts.

PAUL R. EHRLICH is Bing Professor of Population Studies and Professor of Biological Sciences at Stanford University. He is the author of some 20 books and several hundred scientific papers and popular articles on biological science and on various dimensions of the human predicament. He is a Fellow of the National Academy of Sciences, the American Academy of Arts and Sciences, and the American Association for the Advancement of Science and a recipient of the John Muir Award of the Sierra Club.

GARRETT HARDIN is Professor Emeritus of Human Ecology at the University of California, Santa Barbara. Of his more than 200 scholarly publications the best known is his classic of 1968, "The Tragedy of the Commons." His dozen books include *Nature and Man's Fate, Exploring New Ethics for Survival, Mandatory Motherhood: The True Meaning of "Right to Life,"* and *Stalking the Wild Taboo.*

JOHN HARTE is Professor of Energy and Resources and of Plant and Soil Biology at the University of California, Berkeley, and Faculty Senior Scientist at the university's Lawrence Berkeley Laboratory. His three books and some 60 published articles and reports have focused mainly on such regional and global environmental problems as acid precipitation, human impacts on climate, impact of energy technologies on water resources, and nuclear winter. He is a member of the Board of Trustees of the Rocky Mountain Biological Laboratory and of the National Council of the Federation of American Scientists.

CHERYL E. HOLDREN is Research Assistant to the Director of the California Academy of Sciences, Senior Investigator at the Rocky Mountain Biological Laboratory, and a consultant with Future Resources Associates, Berkeley. She has published on the population genetics of butterflies, insect-plant interactions, coral-reef ecology, toxic substances, and endangered species. From 1982 to 1985 she served on the Executive Committee of the Board of Directors of Friends of the Earth.

JOHN P. HOLDREN is Professor of Energy and Resources at the University of California, Berkeley. His publications span energy technology, global environmental problems, development issues, and nuclear-weapons and arms control. He is a recent Chairman of the Federation of American Scientists, a member of the Executive Committee of the Pugwash Conferences on Science and World Affairs, a Fellow of the American Academy of Arts and Sciences, and a MacArthur Foundation Prize Fellow.

DANIEL LUTEN is Senior Lecturer in Geography, Emeritus, at the University of California, Berkeley. After receiving his Ph.D. in chemistry from that university, he held positions as a research chemist in the petroleum industry, technical advisor in the natural resources section of the civil administration of occupied Japan (1948–50), and visiting professor at eight colleges and universities around the United States. He has published extensively on population, environment, energy, and other natural resources and is a former President of Friends of the Earth.

DONELLA H. MEADOWS is Adjunct Professor of Environmental Studies and Policy Studies at Dartmouth College, Hanover, New Hampshire. She has been a senior scientist at the International Institute for Applied Systems Analysis, Vienna; at the East-West Population Institute, Honolulu; and the Resource Policy Group, Oslo, Norway. Her research interests have focused on the application of systems analysis to problems of global development, U.S. energy and agricultural policy, and regional sustainable resource use. Her books include *The Limits to Growth* and *The Electronic Oracle: Computer Models and Social Decisions*.

DAVID PIMENTEL is Professor of Insect Ecology and Agricultural Sciences in the Department of Entomology and the Section of Ecology and Systematics at Cornell University, Ithaca, New York. He has published extensively on insect biology, pesticides and herbicides, agricultural practices and their energy use, biomass energy, public health, economic development, and environmental education, and he has chaired many national and international committees and panels on these topics. He is a Fellow of the American Association for the Advancement of Science.

PETER H. RAVEN is Director of the Missouri Botanical Garden, Engelmann Professor of Botany at Washington University, and Adjunct Professor of Biology at Saint Louis University and the University of Missouri, all in Saint Louis. He has published eight books and about 300 scientific papers on his specialties, plant classification and distribution, tropical botany, and preservation of tropical forests. He is a member of the Council of the National Academy of Sciences, a Fellow of the American Academy of Arts and Sciences, and a MacArthur Foundation Prize Fellow.

STEPHEN H. SCHNEIDER is Head of the Natural Systems Group and Deputy Director of the Advanced Study Program at the National Center for Atmospheric Research, Boulder, Colorado. In addition to some 65 scholarly papers and book chapters on all aspects of climatology, he has written three books and edited two others on the interaction of climate with food production and other human problems. He is the founder and editor of the interdisciplinary journal *Climatic Change.*

KENNETH E. F. WATT is Professor of Zoology and Environmental Studies at the University of California, Davis. He is the author of several books — including *Ecology and Resource Management, Principles of Environmental Science,* and *The Unsteady State* — and about 100 other publications. Since 1968 he has been building computer simulation models of the interactions of population, land, energy, transportation, the economy, and international trade, aimed at improving policymaking. He has been a consultant to a wide variety of government and nongovernment organizations in the United States and abroad.

GEORGE M. WOODWELL is Director of the Ecosystems Center at the Marine Biological Laboratory, Woods Hole, Massachusetts; past President of the Ecological Society of America; and recent Chairman of the Board of the World Wildlife Fund. He is the author of more than 200 scientific papers, articles, and books on ecology and on science and public affairs. He participated in the founding of both the Environmental Defense Fund and the Natural Resources Defense Council. He is a Fellow of the American Academy of Arts and Sciences.

Index

The Cassandra Conference was composed into type on a Compugraphic phototypesetter in ten point Sabon with two points of spacing between the lines. Sabon was also selected for display. The book was designed by Arlene Sheer, composed by Metricomp, Inc., printed offset by Thomson-Shore, Inc., and bound by John H. Dekker & Sons, Inc. The paper on which this book is printed bears acid-free characteristics for an effective life of at least three hundred years.

TEXAS A&M UNIVERSITY PRESS : COLLEGE STATION